THE ART OF
EDITING

FIFTH EDITION

THE ART OF
EDITING

Floyd K. Baskette
Late, University of Colorado

Jack Z. Sissors
Medill School of Journalism, Northwestern University

Brian S. Brooks
University of Missouri School of Journalism

Macmillan Publishing Company
New York
Maxwell Macmillan Canada
Toronto

Editor: David Chodoff
Assistant Editor: Patrick Shriner
Production Supervisor: Publication Services, Inc.
Production Manager: Aliza Greenblatt
Text Designer: Aliza Greenblatt/Publication Services, Inc.
Cover Designer: Natasha Sylvester

This book was set in Bembo by Publication Services, Inc., and printed and bound by Hamilton
Printing Co. The cover was printed by Lehigh Press.

Macmillan Publishing Company
866 Third Avenue, New York, New York 10022

Macmillan Publishing Company is part of the Maxwell Communication Group of Companies.

Maxwell Macmillan Canada, Inc.
1200 Eglinton Avenue East
Suite 200
Don Mills, Ontario M3C 3N1

Library of Congress Cataloging-in-Publication Data
Baskette, Floyd K.
    The art of editing / Floyd K. Baskette, Jack Z. Sissors, Brian S. Brooks. —5th ed.
      p. cm.
    Includes index.
    ISBN 0-02-306295-9
    1. Journalism–Editing. 2. Copy-reading. I. Sissors, Jack Zanville, 1919- . II. Brooks, Brian
S. III. Title.
PN4778.B3 1992   91-12606
808'.06607–dc20   CIP

PREFACE

We are delighted to present the Fifth Edition of *The Art of Editing,* a text that in its first four editions met with widespread acceptance and approval. We believe there is good reason for that success: *The Art of Editing* remains the most comprehensive and up-to-date text in its field.

In this edition, as in the earlier ones, we have attempted to explain how editors do their jobs. Because no two editors work alike, generalizing about the editing process in a textbook is a difficult chore. In all cases, we have tried to explain how we believe most editors would approach a task or problem. In doing so, we have supplied numerous examples of editors' successes and failures as displayed in the pages of U.S. and Canadian newspapers. It is important to remember that these examples offer merely *one* approach to editing a story. There may be many other ways. In editing, there is often no absolute, no right and wrong. We believe, as the title of this book suggests, that editing is an art, not a science. For examples of how it should be done, we have gone to the artists.

The editors who have helped us with these examples are too numerous to mention. We have taken examples, both good and bad, from newspapers from coast to coast. Through these examples, we learn how to edit and how not to edit. We learn how to write headlines and how not to write headlines. We learn how to design pages and how not to design pages. But through it all, we learn. There is no end to the process of education in daily journalism.

Journalism is an interesting, exciting and stimulating profession. Editing is a vital and important part of journalism, both print and broadcast. Newspapers, magazines, radio and television would not be nearly as good without editors as they are with editors. They can be superb with top-flight editors. We hope this book inspires some to consider editing as a career.

Much of the text is intended as preparation for the prospective newspaper copy editor, the pathway into editing chosen by most students. But the basics of editing apply to magazine and broadcast editors as well. Most of the techniques are the same, and the excitement is universal.

Still, it is difficult for any book to capture the excitement of the copy desk because the beginner must first master the intricacies of the editor's art. Attention to detail is of primary importance to the editor, and we believe this book attends to that detail more thoroughly than any other. We hope we have done so as interestingly as possible.

This edition features some important updates in the use of technology at newspapers. The era of digital photography is upon us, and traditional editing methods continue to give way to the proliferation of the computer. Furthermore, database technology is becoming increasingly important as a source of news and fact verification. We cover all these developments throughout the text thoroughly and have made numerous other improvements.

We are indebted to our colleagues, students and editors who read chapters and offered many helpful suggestions. Special gratitude is extended to Sandra Scott, an attorney and teacher whose advice was invaluable in updating the chapter on press law, and to Barbara Luebke, who wrote the section on stereotyping in Chapter 7.

Additionally we would like to thank the following reviewers whose comments have helped greatly in the improvement of this fifth edition: Deborah M. Geisler, Suffolk University; Stephen Greene, San Jose State University; Harry Marsh, Kansas State University; Cleve Mathews, Syracuse University; John Soloski, University of Iowa.

We hope this edition has been prepared with the same high standards set by our colleague, Floyd K. Baskette, who died in 1979. His name remains on the title page of this edition because his work is of enduring quality, and much of it remains from the first two editions.

We have changed and updated, but one old axiom holds true: Editing is an art no matter where or by whom it is practiced. To those who will accept the challenge of careful editing, this volume is dedicated.

Columbia, Missouri   B.S.B.
Evanston, Illinois   J.Z.S.

CONTENTS

PART I

THE COPY EDITOR
IN PERSPECTIVE

CHAPTER 1

THE EDITOR

THE STATE OF EDITING

Columnist James J. Kilpatrick, one of the great newspaper writers of our time, laments the demise of editing quality in newspapers. He writes:

> To read almost any American daily today is to conclude that copy editors have vanished as completely from our city rooms as the ivory-billed woodpecker has vanished from the southern woodlands. We appear to have reared a generation of young reporters whose mastery of spelling, to put the matter mildly, is something less than nil. . . . Once there was a white-haired geezer in an eye shade to intercept a reporter's copy, and to explain gently but firmly to the author that *phase* and *faze* are different words, and that *affect* and *effect* ought not to be confused. The old geezer has gone, and literacy with him.[1]

Kilpatrick's fond memories of the good old days probably are enhanced by the passage of time. The fact is that newspapers always have made errors, and the newspapers edited by crotchety old copy editors wearing green eye shades were no exception. Still, few would disagree with Kilpatrick that language skills in general have deteriorated. Newspapers, without a doubt, have been affected.

Too many reporters and editors at today's newspapers are products of an educational system with misguided priorities. There was a time not so long ago when it was fashionable to consider phonetic spelling adequate. Rote memorization of spelling words was a waste of time, educational trendsetters told us. Grammar was viewed as an exercise in nit-picking. That abandonment of the basics is commonly acknowledged today as one of the great tragedies of modern education. Now, a back-to-basics movement has swept the country, and there is evidence that teachers in today's elementary and secondary schools—some of whom were victims of the errors of the past—are at least attempting to emphasize language skills. Unfortunately, that won't help those who failed to learn, including many reporters and editors now on the job.

Kilpatrick writes:

---

[1] James J. Kilpatrick, "Doesn't Anyone Edit Copy Anymore?" *Washington Journalism Review*, October 1984, p. 44.

Figure 1-1.   Columnist James J. Kilpatrick is convinced that the copy editors of today are not as good as those of earlier generations.

Let us contend, in sweet charity and self-defense, that virtually all of [the mistakes in newspapers are] a consequence not of ignorance but of the carelessness that walks with a wandering mind. If that is the best we can say, what have we said? Not much. I know that newspapers operate under the terrible pressure of deadlines. That fact . . . may help to explain, but it provides a feeble excuse.[2]

Another feeble excuse for mistakes is offered by broadcasters who say, "Grammar isn't important in radio or television. Spoken English and written English are different." That may be true, but should it be? Clearly, the answer is no. The generations that have grown up with television unfortunately don't even blink when broadcasters read on the air, "The City Council voted today to raise *their* salaries to $15,000 a year." Such mistakes in the use of pronouns are so common that many people don't even notice. Nor do they notice when a newspaper advertisement reads, "This group of pearls *are* specially selected by our buyers." Nor when words are misspelled as in *occassions, accidently, wintery* and *accomodate*. Fortunately, many people *do* notice, so perhaps there is hope.

Journalism, whether print or broadcast, is a profession that demands a mastery of language skills. Words, not cameras or microphones or video display terminals, are the primary tools of the trade. As in any craft, mastering the use of those tools is essential to success. Good editors know that, and they value highly those who possess those skills. This book is designed to help.

THE EDITOR'S DUTIES

Every editor edits. That is, every editor determines to some extent what will and will not be published or broadcast. Usually, those decisions are based on

[2] Ibid., p. 47.

that editor's perception of the mission and philosophy of the publication or broadcast station.

This book emphasizes the skills of editing, but learning those skills without a thorough understanding of the philosophy of editing would be like learning to hit a baseball without knowing why hitting is important. Why bother to hit if you don't know to run to first base? In editing, it is important to know not only *when* a change in copy should be made but also *why* that change should be made.

Good editing depends on the exercise of good judgment. For that reason it is an art, not a science. To be sure, in some aspects of editing—accuracy, grammar and spelling, for example—there are only right and wrong answers, as often is the case in science. But editing also involves discretion: knowing when to use which word, when to change a word or two for clarity and when to leave a passage as the writer has written it. Often, the best editing decisions are those in which no change is made. Making the right decisions in such cases is clearly an art.

The editing skills taught herein will be those used at newspapers in general and at newspaper copy desks in particular. Those same skills, however, apply directly to magazine and broadcast editing. Editing for those media differs slightly from newspaper editing because of special requirements, so separate chapters to highlight those differences are included in this book. Still, the skills required of all editors are much the same as those required of newspaper copy editors, the valuable members of a newspaper's staff who have the final crack at copy before it appears in print. Copy editors, it has been said, are the last line of defense before a newspaper goes to press. As such, they are considered indispensable by top editors but remain anonymous to the public. Unlike the names of reporters, who frequently receive bylines, copy editors' names seldom appear in print.

Some believe that absence of recognition accounts for the scarcity of journalism graduates who profess interest in copy desk work. Editing, it is said, isn't as glamorous or as exciting as reporting. But those who view desk work as boring clearly have never experienced it. To the desk come the major news stories of the day—the space walk, the eruption of a volcano, the election of a president, the rescue of a lost child. The desk is the heart of the newspaper, and it throbs with all the news from near and far. Someone must shape that news, size it, display it and send it to the reader.

The copy editor is a diamond cutter who refines and polishes, removes the flaws and shapes the stone into a gem. The editor searches for errors and inaccuracies, and prunes the useless, the unnecessary qualifiers and the redundancies. The editor adds movement to the story by substituting active verbs for passive ones, specifics for generalities. The editor keeps sentences short so that readers can grasp one idea at a time and still not suffer from writing that reads like a first-grade text.

Editing is creative work, too. Editors at many newspapers have opportunities to do page layout, and few newspaper jobs require more creativity than that.

Ah, but editing isn't as much fun as writing, some say. Why learn editing skills if you want to write? Columnist Kilpatrick knows. Although considered one of the great writers of our time, he bemoans the demise of *editing* skills.

Good writers know that good editing can make their prose even better. Good writers know that good editors can save them great embarrassment. They also know that editing skills complement writing skills. Editing the work of others helps you learn to avoid their mistakes when you write. Editing also helps you learn the importance of clarity. Often, what is clear to the writer isn't clear at all to the editor—or to the reader. There also is this reality: Almost everyone who enters newspaper, magazine or broadcast work eventually will do some editing.

So there is general agreement among the enlightened that editing is important. But there is less agreement about just what an editor is supposed to do. Kenn Finkel of the *Dallas Times Herald* tried to outline the duties of an editor at a workshop on editing skills:

> The editor is the conscience of the writer and the newspaper. He does his job when he challenges. He should approach every story with a challenge to see if it meets the newspaper's standards. It is his duty to help every story he edits.
>
> The editor should, when time allows, read a story from top to bottom before making changes. It is important to understand all of what the writer is trying to say.
>
> Having read the story through, the editor can remove words, correct grammar, smooth sentence flow and do other things that make a story more pleasing to the reader.
>
> The editor must make sure that all questions are answered. If he has questions, then the reader will. The editor can attempt to find the answers and work them into the story. Or he can return the story to the writer (call the wire service if it's a wire story) to get the answers.
>
> There is more to editing than making a story read smoothly. The editor must satisfy himself that the story is fair; that both sides of an issue are presented; that, if a person accuses another in a quote, the accused gets a chance to reply; that topics mentioned in the abstract are brought to specifics; and that there are no unanswered questions.
>
> The editor need not be a great writer to work efficiently. But he should be able to recognize good writing when he sees it. He should know when an adjective is performing an important job and when it is clutter.
>
> A good editor has a love for the language. He is tuned to subtle rhythms or the awesome power of combinations of words. He should edit by sound, *listen* for good writing.[3]

The *Bulletin* of the American Society of Newspaper Editors asked some of the nation's top editors what they look for when hiring copy editors. Replied David Lipman, managing editor of the *St. Louis Post-Dispatch:* "A commitment to accuracy. An inner ear for English that lives and breathes. The knack of grasping not only what a story says but also what it fails to say. The good sense to leave well enough alone. Finally, a sense of humor."[4]

---

[3] Kenn Finkel, speech to Penney-Missouri Newspaper Workshop, Columbia, Mo., March 8, 1983.

[4] "10 Editors Tell What They Look for in a Copy Editor," *ASNE Bulletin,* February 1984, p. 30.

Marjorie Paxson, publisher of the *Muskogee* (Okla.) *Phoenix & Times Democrat,* offered this. "A person who knows grammar, spelling and pays attention to detail. A perfectionist. One who can handle routine without having a fidget fit; who will use creativity and imagination to offset the routine; who is well-informed on a variety of subjects. A quick thinker with initiative, alertness, intelligence and awareness."[5]

It's little wonder that editors have trouble finding people who meet all those criteria. Much is demanded of the copy editor.

THE VALUE OF THE COPY EDITOR

No position on the newspaper offers greater opportunity for growth than that of copy editor. Work as a copy editor provides the chance to continue an education and an incentive to climb to the top of the newspaper's hierarchy. Copy editors must of necessity accumulate a warehouse full of facts they have gleaned from the thousands of stories they have been compelled to read and edit or from the references they have had to consult to verify information.

Copy editors are super detectives who incessantly search stories for clues about how to transform mediocre articles into epics. The legendary Carr Van Anda of *The New York Times* studied ocean charts and astronomical formulas to find missing links in a story. Few editors today would correct an Einstein formula, as Van Anda did, but if they are willing, they can probe, question, authenticate and exercise their powers of deduction.

Historically, a stint on the copy desk has been considered important to professional advancement at newspapers. The desk serves as an important spawning ground for administrative editors because those who serve there have a more complete picture of how the newspaper operates than those who do not. The reporter has little feel for copy flow and production requirements; copy editors develop that in the normal course of their duties. Thus, if two equally talented individuals are contending for promotion, the one with copy desk experience probably will have the inside track.

There are encouraging signs that the lot of the copy editor is improving. Many newspapers pay copy editors more than reporters as an incentive for the best and brightest to work at the desk. Journalism schools and departments have awakened to the reality that copy editors are more difficult to find than reporters and have responded by improving course offerings in editing. This, in turn, encourages more good students to pursue careers in editing. No longer do editors require that newcomers work as reporters before becoming copy editors; many now realize that wanting to be a copy editor is more important than having experience as a reporter. Many of the best newspapers in the United States and Canada now have editors who never worked as reporters.

Furthermore, the artificial barriers that once prevented women from becoming copy editors have been torn down. No longer is the copy desk a

---

[5] Ibid, p. 31.

man's domain. Women with editing skills have risen to important positions at many newspapers, large and small.

All this indicates that new life may yet be breathed into the profession of copy editing. If, as Kilpatrick and others suggest, there is a serious problem with the quality of editing, many journalists have hope that things will improve. They have hope that the art of editing is not a lost art.

CHAPTER 2

THE EDITOR
AND THE READER

THE READERSHIP PROBLEM

One of the keys to being a good editor is understanding the audience you are serving. Yet in the view of James K. Batten, chief executive officer of Knight-Ridder Inc., too many young journalists are "disconnected."

In Batten's opinion, too many newsrooms "are overstocked with journalistic transients. . . . Their eyes are on the next and bigger town, the next rung up the ladder. . . . There is always the temptation to make their byline files a little more glittering at the expense of people and institutions they will never see again."[1]

Batten's view is reinforced by the occasional polls that show the public holds journalists in low esteem. In such polls, journalists usually rank with used-car salesmen and politicians, high on the ladder of disapproval. Accurate or not, the public perception is that journalists will do anything for a good story and don't care whom they trample to get it. While such an uncaring attitude may well be a reason that newspapers and their readers seem to have drifted apart, it is merely one of many. The hard facts show that:

- In 1970, 98 percent of U.S. households subscribed to a daily newspaper, but by 1989 that number had dropped to 67 percent.
- Total daily circulation of U.S. newspapers has remained flat, increasing only from 62,108,000 in 1970 to 62,695,000 in 1988. The American Newspaper Publishers Association reports that in the same period, the number of adults in the United States grew by 36 percent, and the number of households rose 44 percent.

Those statistics and similar ones set off alarm bells in the 1980s as publishers and editors began to ask: "What are we doing wrong?" While it may seem simple to answer such a question, in reality it is not easy at all. There may be as many plausible reasons for the decline as there are newspapers.

THE THEORIES OF DECLINE

One of the main theories of this decline is that television news is drawing away readers. At first glance, that would seem to be true. In 1982, only 30 percent

---

[1] Eleanor Randolph, "Extra! Extra! Who Cares? Newspapers Face the Incredible Shrinking Reader," *The Washington Post*, April 1, 1990.

of those surveyed thought that television provided all the information they need about a big story. By 1987, that figure had increased to 42 percent. Yet during the same period, television viewing began to decrease, and the trend is continuing. February 1990 ratings showed viewership down 6 percent in prime time, 15 percent in daytime and 11 percent for the nightly news from the same period a year earlier. And survey after survey has revealed that television news viewing and newspaper readership are complementary, not competitive. That is, people who watch television news also are likely to be newspaper readers.

Another theory is that newspapers have been hurt by the changes in lifestyles of young women, the people who historically did most of the household shopping. In past decades, women stayed home, raised children, clipped coupons from the newspaper and went out to do the shopping. Because of that, the young woman was a natural target for advertisers. Now, according to Lou Heldman of Knight-Ridder Newspapers, more than 70 percent of women aged 25 to 46 are working outside the home, and the percentage is rising. Predictably, readership surveys of people in this category indicate that they have quit reading newspapers or reduced readership dramatically. The reason? There is less time for such activity.

Yet another theory holds that newspapers don't appeal to younger readers in general and that they are edited by people out of touch with the younger generation. In 1970, surveys showed that 73 percent of the 18- to 24-year-old age group read a newspaper on an average weekday. By 1989, that figure was down to 57 percent. Concludes Albert Gollin, vice president of the Newspaper Advertising Bureau, "With each generation, the habit of newspaper readership has weakened."[2]

Most editors agree that this alarming trend must be reversed. Says Gregory Fauve, executive editor of the *Sacramento Bee,* "I think we have to stop putting out newspapers for 54-year-old editors like me." Some newspapers have pursued that tack with more fervor than others. The *Syracuse* (N.Y.) *Herald-Journal* tried youth-page articles that addressed the readers as, "Hey you. Yeah, you." Or, on occasion, "You knuckleheads" or even "Yo, buttheads." Explains youth page editor Larry Richardson, "We decided we would give [our readers] things that they wanted to read, not only things we think they should read."[3]

Critics of that approach argue that newspapers should avoid pandering to the marketing concept of simply giving people what they want. Newspapers, they argue, are a public trust and should be above such things. Yet the reality is that newspapers are manufactured products that must be marketed and sold if they are to survive.

That reality led to the formation in the late 1980s of a journalistic think tank called New Directions for News. The organization, based at the University of Missouri School of Journalism, is funded by almost all the major newspaper groups in the United States. NDN has been a leading force in convincing editors to rethink the way they edit newspapers. A hallmark of its efforts has been the organization of brainstorming sessions at which ed-

---

[2] Ibid., p. C-1.
[3] Ibid.

itors have come up with suggestions as diverse as printing newspapers that smell like baked bread to wrapping a news digest around the outside of the regular newspaper (Figure 2-1). While not all the ideas are good, or even plausible, such sessions force editors to contemplate change, something that all newspapers need to consider.

NDN also has helped to spark the creation of prototype sections for newspapers. Many of these have attempted to appeal to those disappearing younger readers.

The consensus among editors is that newspapers must change if they are to survive. Unfortunately, there is no consensus at all about what that change must encompass.

THE CONTRARY VIEW

Despite the consensus that newspapers must change, some argue that concerns about the industry's health are overstated. They point to some powerfully persuasive statistics to support their view:

• Newspapers still get the biggest slice of the advertising pie (Figure 2.2). According to McCann Erickson, newspapers get 26.4 percent of the ad dollars spent each year while television gets 21.8 percent, direct mail 17.9 percent, radio 6.6 percent and magazines 5.1 percent.[4]
• Competitors are in no better shape. Television's impact is increasingly fragmented by the proliferation of cable television, and overall viewership seems

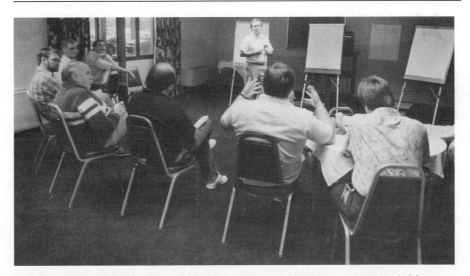

Figure 2-1.   Editors of Hearst Newspapers participate in a brainstorming session led by executives of New Directions for News. [Photo courtesy of New Directions for News]

---

[4] Ibid.

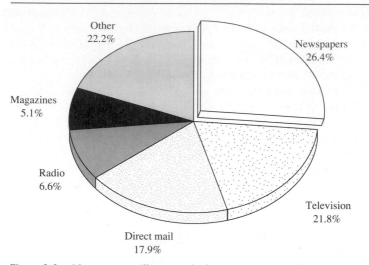

Figure 2-2.   Newspapers still receive the largest percentage of advertising dollars.

to be declining. Similarly, magazines are hurt by the burgeoning number of special-interest titles that merely confuses the public. Direct mail is threatened by its reliance on low postal rates.

One who thinks newspapers are relatively healthy is Benjamin Bradlee, executive editor of the *Washington Post*. "I don't see any point in shutting down now and saying it's too hard," Bradlee says. "If we could lick the ink [ruboff] problem, I think we could do very well."

Indeed, the newspaper industry continues to be one of the most profitable in all U.S. industry, a fact that sometimes is lost among all the talk about declining readership, flat circulation, the disappearance of afternoon dailies and the decline in the number of daily newspapers overall. According to industry analysts, during the 1980s newspapers turned an extraordinarily high operating profit of almost 25 cents on every dollar. Even if that estimate is a bit high and the profit margins are shrinking, the fact remains that newspapers are extremely profitable. That, some say, is hardly the sign of an industry in serious trouble.

EVALUATING THE MEDIA MIX

No one suggests that in an age widely heralded as the Information Age, the desire for information will wane. Instead, the main question is how that information will be consumed. One can make a persuasive argument that no medium is doing a good job of satisfying the public's thirst for information. Perhaps that's because no one medium has all the technological advantages. Radio has immediacy of delivery on its side. But so does television, which adds the appeal of color and moving pictures. Conversely, newspapers are far better suited than either of the broadcast media to carry large amounts of information and to provide the space necessary for analysis. Newspapers also have the advantage of portability and selective consumption—you choose what you want to read when you want to read it. With radio and television, you take what you are given when it is being offered.

Those realities may help explain why the arrival of television did not spell doom for newspapers, as many predicted in the 1950s. They also may explain the overall confusion in the information marketplace. It may well be that technology has not yet delivered the so-called "killer medium," the one that is destined to put the others out of business.

It's not too difficult to envision what kind of medium that might be. Imagine a television set (or home computer) that allowed subscribers not only to watch the evening news but to call up *The New York Times* text version of stories that piqued their interest. Such a device also would allow subscribers to print out the classified ads or grocery coupons and consume the news in the form they wanted, when they wanted.

Even better, such a "newspaper" might be programmed especially for the individual. While giving the latest world news, it also might inform a subscriber that a doctor had canceled a medical appointment. Or it might help that subscriber balance a checkbook or order groceries for home delivery. It might even alert the stamp collector to the latest news in the world of philately.

One who envisions such a system is Nicholas Negroponte, director of the Media Lab at the Massachusetts Institute of Technology. "I would pay $10 a day for that newspaper," he says. "That would be a really important newspaper for me to read every morning." Negroponte's goal is to design just such a device at an affordable price. The key, of course, is making such a device affordable. The quality of screen images also must improve; it's clear that reading text on current screens is not something many consumers choose to do in their spare time. Various experiments with video delivery of written information have proven that.

As the technology to develop the ultimate information medium evolves, editors are experimenting with pieces of that technology to bring new delivery mechanisms to consumers. Starting in the 1970s, editors began experimenting with videotex and teletext, means of delivering information electronically to computer or television screens in the home. More recently, newspapers have been marketing fax newspapers, summaries of the news delivered to businesses or individuals; or audio newspapers (also known as audiotext), recorded up-to-the-minute news offered on dial-in telephone lines.

LESSONS TO BE LEARNED

From this discussion evolves an increasing awareness that the media industry, of which newspapers are a part, is in a state of change. This change is brought about largely by changing lifestyles:

- Both spouses are working in more and more families, and there are more and more single-parent households. The number of people choosing to remain single also is increasing, contributing to the growth in the total number of households. (Newspaper readership often is measured in market *penetration,* number of households divided by circulation.)
- As a result, leisure time is shrinking, and newspaper reading is a leisure-time activity.
- More and more competitors—direct mail, special-interest publications and an increasing number of television channels—are competing for that decreasing amount of time.

If indeed such trends are occurring, they would be persuasive arguments for shorter, easier-to-read newspaper articles with eye-catching color and graphics. That's exactly the formula used by the Gannett Company to create *USA Today,* which came from nowhere in the 1980s to become one of the nation's top-circulation newspapers.

Many newspaper editors, while emulating the best of *USA Today* (its colorful and informative graphics, in particular) are hesitant to turn their publications into localized clones of that newspaper. Some deride *USA Today* as an appeal to the lowest common denominator—giving people only the news they want, not what they need. Still, it's difficult to ignore the lesson of success that *USA Today* has provided. Clearly, the newspaper has set new standards for color and for innovative uses of charts and graphs in newspapers. Its colorful weather map has been copied by many of the nation's large dailies, and information graphics are the latest rage.

Editors who pay attention to such developments are able to respond more quickly to changes in the marketplace than those who don't. That is not meant to suggest that editors should rush out and change their papers to emulate *USA Today.* For many that would be a serious mistake. But Gannett's editors were innovative in their approach to this newspaper, and to ignore the lessons of their success would be foolish.

THE INFOMEDIUM

If Nicholas Negroponte's view of the future is close at all to what we can expect, a process of evolution will bring the various media closer together. What is a medium that has moving pictures as well as text? Is it a newspaper, a television or neither? Is it merely a news medium or an information medium, complete with a wealth of information about how we can improve our lives? How such a medium evolves will be determined as much in the laboratories of engineers as in the corporate boardrooms of the media industry. Driving it all will be the desires of the public, which will discover what it wants only when it knows what is possible and how much it will cost.

Ultimately, newspapers, television and perhaps the other media are likely to evolve into a new infomedium that combines the best attributes of them

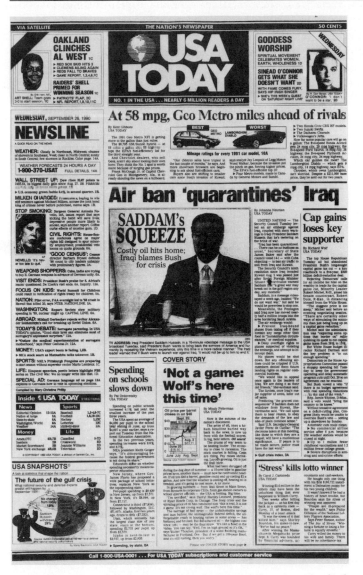

Figure 2-3.   USA Today's splashy use of color and extensive use of information graphics made it an American trendsetter. [Courtesy of USA Today]

all. The wise young journalist of today should therefore view himself or herself not as a print journalist or a broadcaster but as an information provider. After all, what is more important, the message or the way it is delivered? Says Susan Miller, director of editorial development for Scripps Howard Newspapers, "[Newspapers] aren't dying, but I think we have to change." She told executives of her group that for the year 2000 "we have to stop worrying about whether it will be a fax newspaper or computers. If we get the topics right . . . then we'll survive. If we get the topics wrong, nobody's going to want us in any form."[5]

Clearly, the selection of the proper marketing approach is critical to the future of all media, not just newspapers.

THE NEWSPAPER AS A COMMODITY

As newspapers increasingly moved to a marketing approach in the 1980s, newsrooms were forced to change their relationships with other departments. There was a time not so long ago when newspaper editors had the luxury of working almost independently of the other managers of their newspapers. Newsrooms were sacred, and no one in advertising or circulation departments presumed to tell editors how to edit their newspapers.

Now, editors meet regularly with top management executives and the heads of other departments to develop marketing strategies. There is a realization that news departments must work with other departments to develop marketing plans for their products. Sometimes that results in decisions to change the content of newspapers. Usually the final decisions about such changes are left to editors, but today the heads of other departments are more likely to make suggestions. Most editors are inclined to listen. Advertising and circulation people have extensive contact with the public, and often they hear compliments and complaints about their newspapers that editors never hear. Good editors appreciate hearing those things.

The danger, of course, is that the editor may go too far in an attempt to accommodate others. A newspaper full of nothing but what the public *wants* to read would be a poor one in most editors' judgment. Editors must balance what the public *wants* to read with what it *needs* to read. Only then will the newspaper fulfill its role as guardian of the public's welfare. Today's editors know that the key to a newspaper's integrity—not to mention its existence— lies in its ability to remain financially sound. A marginally solvent newspaper may be more susceptible to advertiser influence on editorial decisions. So attention to the demands of the marketplace is important. But it also is important to remember that the press is the only private institution mentioned in the U.S. Constitution. That is tacit recognition that newspapers, while competing in the marketplace, also have a special mission in our society.

The fact that editors are now active participants in marketing the newspaper should not be viewed negatively. The fact is that a newspaper is a manufactured product, a commodity, and like other products it must be marketed aggressively. A newspaper's marketing strategy probably will work best if all departments—including the news department—are working to accomplish the same goals.

Editors of the 1990s know that successful market strategies are a plus: Their newspapers will be stronger, and more people will read the work of their staffs. Only then will the full potential of a free press be unleashed.

[5] Ibid.

SOME GENERALIZATIONS
ABOUT U.S. AUDIENCES

Each newspaper should conduct its own market research to determine what readers like and dislike about the product. What works in New York City may not work at all in Fort Scott, Kansas. Extensive research has been conducted at the national level, however, and these studies give us some important clues about how newspapers are perceived.

Probably the most important study of this type was conducted by Ruth Clark, president of Clark, Martire & Bartolomeo Inc., a market research firm, for the American Society of Newspaper Editors.[6] The study, funded by United Press International as a service to the industry, revealed these major findings:

1. Readers expect *news* in their newspapers, whether it's national, state, regional or local. What editors call *hard news,* or late-breaking developments, is most important.
2. Readers want information about health, science, technology, diet, nutrition and similar subjects but will figure out for themselves how to cope with these problems. Newspapers don't need to tell them.
3. Overall, readers like their newspapers. Most think they are indispensable, although younger readers aren't so sure. Most agree that newspapers are here to stay, regardless of the potential that television and computer screens may have for disseminating information.
4. On the negative side, readers sometimes feel manipulated by editors and question whether they are fair and unbiased in covering and allocating space to various constituencies.[7]

People believe their own newspaper tends to be better than most, and that should be encouraging to editors. A minority of readers, although a substantial one at 39 percent, believes the local newspaper is biased. Most (57 percent) believe that newspaper stories in general are usually unfair. More than half (53 percent) believe that newspaper stories are usually accurate, but 84 percent describe their own paper as accurate.[8] Editors need to deal with the issue of bias, whether real or perceived, because it has enormous implications. They need to find ways to make their newspapers more believable. The problem is greater at the national level, however. While most people believe that newspapers are unfair, 88 percent believe their local paper really cares about the community. Translating that feeling of concern to the national level would lead to major improvement in the public's perception of newspapers.

[6] Ruth Clark, Clark, Martire & Bartolomeo Inc., "Relating to Readers in the '80s," American Society of Newspaper Editors, May 1984.
[7] Ibid, p. 9.
[8] Ibid., p. 10.

Clark's study found that readers want complete newspapers, even in small communities. Readers of smaller newspapers (under 75,000 circulation) place more emphasis on local and regional news, while readers of larger newspapers tilt toward national and international news. But when it comes to performance, readers of smaller papers give them poorer marks on national and international news, while readers of larger papers are not satisfied with the local coverage they receive.

If newspapers are to win the battle for the reader's time, Clark believes they should follow these suggestions from readers:

1. Give us a complete, balanced paper with solid reporting of national and international news but equal quality in coverage of local news.
2. Strike a balance between bad news and other important news we need to know. Don't sensationalize or attempt to manipulate public opinion.
3. Give us the important details we don't get from television news, but remember we're short of time.
4. Do a better job of covering the new subjects of major interest—business news, health, consumerism, science, technology, schools and education, family, children and religion.
5. Realize that women today are interested in the sports and business pages you used to put out for your male readers. Of course, women are still interested in food, fashion and other traditional subjects, and you should keep those features going. But recognize they are not the attractions they once were.
6. Make us feel we belong. You need to widen your focus if you are to win more regular readers among young people, working women and members of minority groups. We look at your newspaper to see if we belong, and too often we feel we do not. It's a sore point and a source of grievance.
7. Tell us more about yourselves—your editors and reporters.
8. Count us in on the fight to preserve the First Amendment. We're ready to support *our* right to know.
9. Get to know us better. We are a far more serious, concerned, interested and demanding audience than you have served in the past.[9]

The editor who pays attention to those findings and edits a newspaper accordingly should have little trouble achieving acceptance of the product in the marketplace.

CREDIBILITY AND THE MEDIA

A major factor in the newspaper-reader relationship is credibility. If readers believe that newspapers are biased and unfair, as Ruth Clark found, it is only reasonable to assume that they will read them with skepticism.

[9] Ibid., p. 17.

Newspapers reinforce such doubts about their credibility when they obstinately refuse to admit their errors, when the names of people and places are consistently misspelled or inaccurate, and when hoaxes of one sort or another are uncovered. One such event that shocked newspaper editors occurred in 1981 when the Janet Cooke affair was revealed. Cooke, a reporter for the *Washington Post,* won a Pulitzer Prize for a story about a child named Jimmy who became a heroin addict. Subsequently, it was learned that Jimmy didn't exist and that Cooke had invented the fictional youngster as a composite of situations involving children she had learned about while doing research for her story. The resulting publicity damaged the credibility of the press nationwide.

The *Washington Post* also was involved in another of the most celebrated scandals in American history, the Watergate affair, which eventually led to the resignation of President Richard Nixon. Through a series of stories featuring anonymous sources, the *Post* and reporters Carl Bernstein and Bob Woodward unraveled the involvement of Nixon and his aides in the burglary of the Democratic Party headquarters in the Watergate apartment complex in Washington, D.C. The service the newspaper performed in that investigation probably is unparalleled in U.S. newspaper history, but along the way the many stories with anonymous sources raised serious questions about the credibility of the media. Editors today are reluctant to use anonymous sources without compelling reasons to do so.

Editors concerned about their credibility have tried to find ways to convince the public that newspapers are in fact reliable. These range from simple steps such as the attempt to reduce annoying typographical errors to elaborate schemes designed to check the accuracy of reporters' work.

To enhance the newspaper's image, today's editors readily admit errors. Some papers run a daily notice, prominently displayed, inviting and encouraging readers to call attention to errors in the paper. Another editor regularly conducts an accuracy check of his newspaper's locally written news stories. A clipping of the story is mailed to the source along with a brief query on the accuracy of facts in the story and headline. Another editor invites persons involved in controversy to present amplifying statements when they feel their positions have not been fully or fairly represented.

More corrections are being printed, even though this practice is distasteful to editors. When the old *Minneapolis Star* had to print four corrections on one day, the editor warned the staff, "Let's hope it is a record that is never equaled—or something besides the sky will fall." The *Boca Raton* (Fla.) *News* candidly tells its readers of its corrections under the heading, "Dumb Things We Did."

More balance in opinion is evident in the use of syndicated columnists whose opinions differ from those of the newspaper and in expanded letters-to-the-editor columns.

Some newspapers are using ombudsmen to hear readers' complaints. More are providing reader-service columns to identify newspapers with readers' personal concerns. More attention is being given to internal criticism in employee publications or at staff conferences.

A newspaper's credibility depends essentially on its accuracy and balance. In the endeavor to ensure accuracy both in fact and in language, the copy editor's role is paramount.

READABILITY MEASUREMENTS

Readership measurements reveal the extent to which an item is read. Readability measurements reveal the ease with which an item can be read, or, more accurately, they try to gauge some of the factors that make reading difficult.

A readability measurement is no formula for writing, nor was it ever intended to be. Rather, it is a tool that may be used in rewriting or editing to improve the writing or to check the writing style from various departments of a paper or from the wire services.

Most readability formulas are based on concepts long familiar to newspaper editors. Short sentences generally are easier to read than long ones, and short words generally are more comprehensible than long ones. Two of the better-known formulas developed by readability experts use sentence and word lengths as key ingredients. The Flesch formula, devised by Rudolph Flesch, uses 100-word samples to measure average sentence length and number of syllables. The formula multiplies the average number of words in the sentence by 1.015 and the total syllable count by 0.846. The two factors are added, then subtracted from 206.835 to arrive at a readability score.[10] Some newspapers periodically use computers to test the readability of news stories.

Robert Gunning uses a similar procedure to determine the *fog index*. He adds the average sentence length in words and the number of words of three syllables or more (omitting capitalized words; combinations of short, easy words like *butterfly;* and verb forms made into three syllables by adding -ed, -es or -ing). The sum is multiplied by 0.4 to get the *fog index*.[11]

Suppose the sample contains an average of 16 words to the sentence and a total of 150 syllables. By the Flesch formula, the sample would have a readability score of 64, which Flesch rates as standard or fitting the style of the *Reader's Digest*. In the same sample, assuming hard words make up 10 percent of the text, the *fog index* of the Gunning scale would be 10, or at the reading level of high school sophomores and fitting *Time* magazine style.

The wire services thought enough of both formulas to get an evaluation of their news reports. Gunning conducted the evaluation for United Press (now United Press International), and Flesch did two measurements for the Associated Press.

Neither Flesch nor Gunning tests content or word familiarity. All they suggest is that if passages from a story or the whole story average more than 20 words to the sentence and the number of hard words in a sample of 100 words exceeds 10 percent, a majority of readers will find the passages difficult to understand.

[10] Rudolph Flesch, *The Art of Readable Writing* (New York: Harper & Row, 1949), p. 197.
[11] Robert Gunning, *The Technique of Clear Writing* (New York: McGraw-Hill, 1952), pp. 36–37.

The formula designers would not recommend that copy editors pare all long sentences to 20 words or fewer and all long words to monosyllables. Long sentences, if they are graceful and meaningful, should be kept intact. Mixed with shorter sentences, they give variety to style and provide the pacing necessary in good writing. A long word may still be a plain word.

An editorial executive of *The New York Times* preferred to measure density of ideas in sentences rather than sentence length itself and came up with a pattern of "one idea, one sentence." A special issue of the newsroom publication *Winners & Sinners* was devoted to this pattern and reports of reading tests on two versions of the same articles. One tested the comprehensibility of the articles as written originally. Another tested the articles when rewritten to lower the density of ideas in the sentence. The "one-idea, one-sentence" dictum is not taken literally even at the *Times,* but the editors insist, "Generally it speeds reading if there is only one idea to a sentence."

The number of unfamiliar words in passages also has been found to affect readability. Edgar Dale and Jeanne S. Chall at The Ohio State University prepared a list of 3,000 words known to 80 percent of fourth-graders. The word-load factor in the Dale-Chall formula consists of a count of words outside the list. Only 4 percent of the words on the Dale-Chall list have three or more syllables.[12]

Editing stories to reduce the number of words outside the word-familiarity list would be time-consuming and impractical. The lists would have to be revised periodically to take out words that no longer are familiar and to add new words that have become part of everyday language—even to fourth-graders.

Most readability formulas use a few fundamental elements but neglect context or story structure. Thus, a passage in gibberish could rate as highly readable on the Flesch, Gunning and Dale-Chall scales. This was demonstrated by Wilson L. Taylor at the University of Illinois Institute of Communications Research. Taylor developed the *cloze* procedure (from "close" or "closure" in Gestalt psychology) to test context. In this procedure he omitted certain words—usually every fifth word—and asked respondents to fill in the missing words. He then graded them on the number of correct words they could fill in. Of passages from eight writers, the Taylor method ranked samples of Gertrude Stein's semi-intelligible prose as the second most difficult. The most difficult was a passage from James Joyce.[13] Both the Dale-Chall and the Flesch scales rated the Stein passage as the easiest to read and the Joyce passage in a tie for fourth with a passage from Erskine Caldwell. To test for human interest, Flesch measures personal words and sentences. Sentences that mention persons and have them saying and doing things increase readability.

The *cloze* procedure suggests that unfamiliar words may be used and understood if they are placed in a context in which the reader can guess their meaning.

[12] Edgar Dale and Jeanne S. Chall, "A Formula for Predicting Readability," *Education Research Bulletin,* **27**:45–55 (February 18, 1948).

[13] Wilson L. Taylor, "Cloze Procedure: A New Tool for Measuring Readability," *Journalism Quarterly,* **30**:415–33 (Fall 1953).

NEWS JUDGMENT

Once editors have learned as much as they can about their audiences through readership research, and once they have learned as much as they can about readability from Flesch, Gunning and others, they must apply their knowledge the best way they can. They have no time to conduct research to determine whether a story will be widely read, nor do they have time to apply readability formulas. Typically, they apply the same criteria used for decades to determine whether a story is to be used at all, whether it is to be used in full or in part, and where it is to be placed within the newspaper. These criteria are

1. *Audience.* No two audiences are alike, so it is reasonable to assume that readers' tastes differ from city to city. Audiences may differ even within a city. Readers of *The New York Times,* for example, may have tastes that differ significantly from those of readers of the *New York Daily News.* Good editors have a feel for the interests of their audiences, and in many cases readership research has helped to clarify those interests.
2. *Impact.* The number of people affected by an event is often critical in determining how extensively an account of it will be read. If garbage rates are to increase throughout the city, the story has more impact than it would if the garbage rates of only 15 families were affected.
3. *Proximity.* If the event happened nearby, it may be more interesting to a newspaper's readers than it would be if it happened in another country.
4. *Timeliness.* News is important when it happens, and old news is of little value to readers.
5. *Prominence.* Prominent people are of more interest than those who are not. If the president changes his hairstyle, that may be news. If the local butcher does so, chances are that few people care.
6. *Oddity.* A 30-pound tomato may be interesting, and therefore newsworthy, because such a tomato is unusual. Events that are firsts or lasts, and therefore historic, also may be unusual enough to merit attention in the news.
7. *Conflict.* Sports events, crime, political races and disputes often are newsworthy because conflict unfortunately plays such an important role in modern society.

Seldom does a news event qualify for inclusion in the newspaper on all these counts. The editor weighs each story to determine if it has one or more of these values. If the story does, there is a good chance it will be printed. If it includes most or all of these criteria, it may well be worthy of Page One. Judging the news, then, is at best an inexact science, despite the wealth of readership research available.

UNDERSTANDING YOUR READERS

Readers' needs and wants are in transition because of changing lifestyles. It is therefore important for the editor to keep in touch by reading everything about a community that time permits. It also helps to keep an open ear to topics of discussion at the local health club, at parties and anywhere else that people gather. An editor who knows what people are talking about has a good idea of what newspaper articles would interest them.

Some editors have tried other means of taking the pulse of the community. Some have tried open forums; others have tried so-called focus groups, representative samples of readers assembled into small discussion groups. Such sessions often are recorded for the benefit of editors. Whatever the technique employed, there is no substitute for learning your community, even if that is an inexact science.

CHAPTER 3

THE EDITOR AND THE NEWSPAPER

THE CHANGING NEWSPAPER

In the first half of this century, the entertainment industry was fond of glamorizing newspapers in stage plays such as *The Front Page,* which later was made into a movie. Superman's alter ego, Clark Kent, was a reporter for the *Daily Planet* in the 1950s television series, then was revived in a series of Superman movies in the 1980s. Ed Asner starred as "Lou Grant" in a popular television series featuring a grumpy old city editor at a Los Angeles newspaper. But perhaps no movie has ever raised the image of newspapering as much as *All the President's Men,* the engaging story of how *Washington Post* reporters Robert Woodward and Carl Bernstein uncovered the Watergate scandal that led to the resignation of President Richard Nixon.

Much of the glamor that surrounded newspapers in the early part of the century revolved around their competitive nature and the colorful characters who worked at them. Stories of editors and reporters consuming a pint of gin between editions are legendary in the newspaper business, which seems to have attracted more than its share of strange characters in that era.

Times have changed, and newspapers have changed with them. Today's newsroom may lack the hustle and bustle depicted in the movie classics. Indeed, with bank after bank of computer terminals, newsrooms of today resemble the quiet offices of insurance companies more than the newsrooms of the past with their clattering Teletype machines and typewriters. Editors no longer ship copy from desk to desk by shouting for copy boys; today, such movement is accomplished quietly with the stroke of a key on a computer keyboard.

To longtime observers of the industry, many of the strange characters have disappeared, too, as newsrooms have become more highly professionalized. For many years, reporting staffs were dominated by high school graduates who wrote well but had little or no formal training in their profession. Today's news departments, in contrast, are dominated by graduates of schools of journalism or liberal arts colleges. It is unusual today to find a reporter who does not have a college degree.

The changes don't stop there. Newspapers experienced little technological advancement from the mid-1880s, when Ottmar Mergenthaler invented the Linotype machine, until the early 1970s, when computer terminals were introduced into newsrooms. During the past two decades, newspapers have become one of the most highly computerized industries. Predictably, that automation has had a major impact on newspapers and the people who staff them.

And, as we already have seen, technology promises to change the way we do things even more in the years to come. In this changing environment, the reporters and editors of today must bridge the gap between the techniques and technologies of the past and the future. For example, while most newspapers now do all their editing on computer terminals, it still is important to learn the traditional copy-processing techniques carried over from the days of paper-and-pencil editing. At some point in each editor's career, that knowledge will be invaluable.

Learning about the newspaper environment of today starts with an understanding of the way newspapers, both large and small, are organized. But it also involves learning about the techniques and tools used to produce the newspaper. This chapter is designed to help.

STAFF ORGANIZATION

More than any other factor, the size of a newspaper determines the extent of an editor's duties. Editors of some weekly newspapers take and process pictures, write and edit stories, lay out pages, write headlines, set type and paste up pages. A few may even operate the printing press. Most dailies, on the other hand, have specialists for each of those duties.

Large dailies, known as metros, sometimes have beat reporters who write only about government, sports, entertainment or other types of news, photographers who take only certain types of pictures and copy editors who handle only certain types of stories. The *Louisville Courier-Journal,* for example, once had a copy editor–lawyer who specialized in crime and court stories and other items with legal implications. That same newspaper had another copy editor who was completing his work on a doctoral degree in education. Predictably, he handled all the newspaper's education stories.

The size of a newspaper also determines how the copy desk is organized. Many small newspapers have universal desks (Figure 3-1) charged with processing copy from all departments.

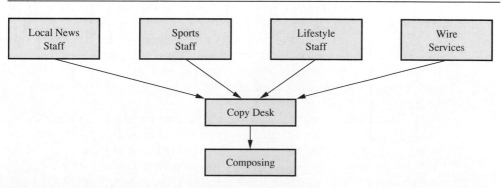

Figure 3-1.   Universal copy desk system.

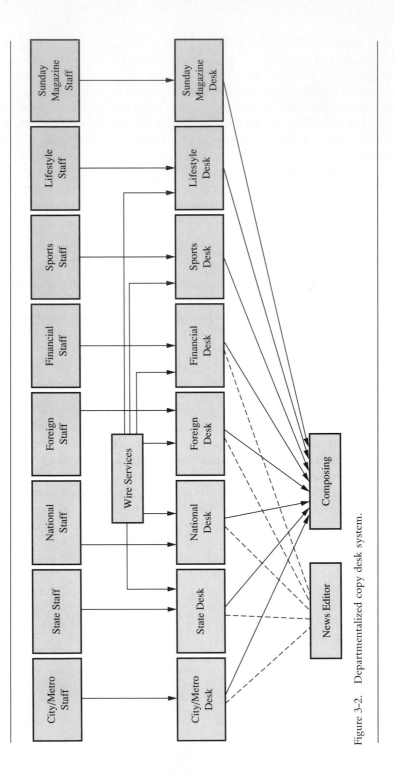

Figure 3-2. Departmentalized copy desk system.

Most metros have departmentalized copy desks (Figure 3-2). In this system separate desks handle local, national, international, sports, business, lifestyle and possibly other categories of news. Editors of those desks supervise the reporters who gather the news as well as the copy editors who process the reporters' work. Wire and local news are grouped by category, and each desk edits and designs its own pages. The news editor or an assistant managing editor coordinates the activities of those desks. That editor decides which stories are to be held for the front page and other key pages, where major stories contributed by the various desks are mixed. A separate staff, supervised by the coordinating editor, edits those pages.

Many newspapers use a semidepartmentalized system (Figure 3-3) in which one desk handles all but sports, lifestyle and Sunday magazine copy. Staffs of those desks do their own editing and page layout.

There are, of course, almost as many variations on these organizational forms as there are newspapers in the United States. It is possible, however, to make some generalizations about the titles and job descriptions of those who write and edit newspapers (Figure 3-4).

At the top of the organizational ladder is the *editor,* or *editor-in-chief,* who is responsible for the editorial content of the newspaper. This includes everything from local to international news in categories ranging from sports to business to entertainment. The editor's responsibilities even include the comics and the editorial page.

The editor's top assistants are the *editorial page editor* and the *managing editor.* Both report directly to the editor, so the news and opinion functions of the newspaper are distinctly separate. The editorial page editor deals with opinion; the managing editor, who may have one or more assistant managing editors, is responsible for all news-gathering operations.

Typically, the *city editor, news editor* and *photo editor* report directly to the managing editor, but at larger newspapers that may not be the case. The city editor supervises local news gathering, the news editor directs the copy

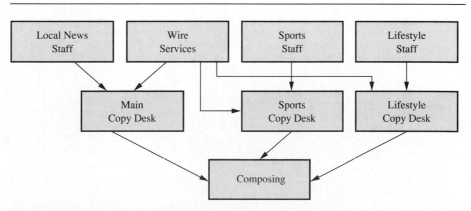

Figure 3-3.   Semidepartmentalized copy desk system.

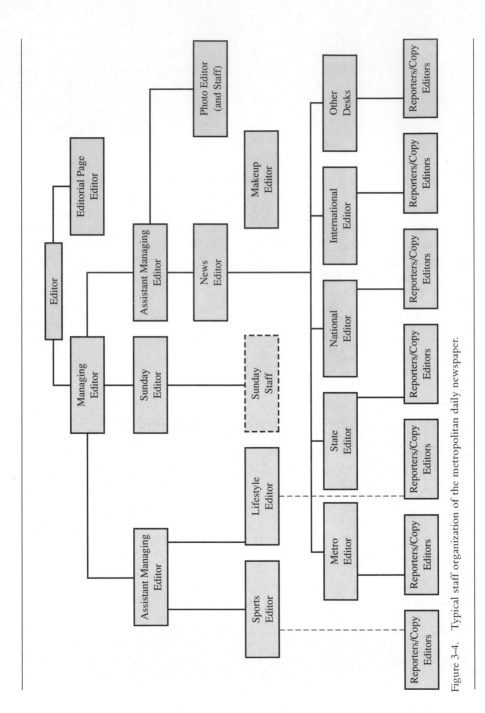

Figure 3–4. Typical staff organization of the metropolitan daily newspaper.

desk, and the photo editor, as the title implies, supervises the photography department and helps to determine how pictures are used.

The sports, lifestyle and financial editors, and editors of other specialized desks, may report directly to the managing editor, or, particularly at large newspapers, to an assistant managing editor.

Reporters, copy editors and *photographers* report to the desk editors to whom they are assigned, regardless of the system. Editorial assistants known as copy clerks run errands for the editors. Modern electronic newsrooms have technicians who keep electronic terminals and other equipment operating properly.

Internal organization of the copy desk is structured according to the needs of the newspaper. Typically, a universal or semidepartmentalized desk is headed by the *news editor,* who may double as *copy desk chief* or *slot editor.* The *slot editor,* a term derived from the structure of the traditional U- or H-shaped copy desk (Figure 3-5), sits in the middle of the U or H—the slot—and is charged with layout of the newspaper. The term *slot* persists, although most newspapers have abandoned the traditional copy desk in favor of a series of clustered office desks to accommodate electronic editing terminals more easily (Figure 3-6).

Copy editors, once known as *rim men* or *rim women* because they sat on the outside, or rim, of the U- or H-shaped desk, also may be assigned specific duties and perhaps other titles. The *wire editor* sifts through the thousands of

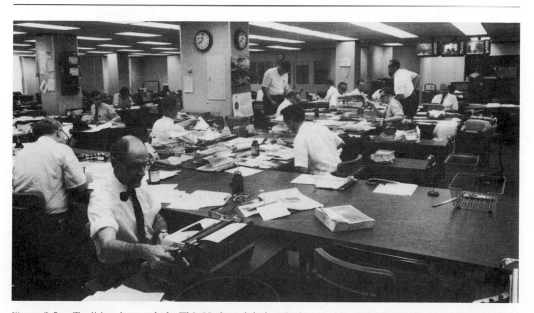

Figure 3-5.   Traditional copy desk. This H-shaped desk, which served both the *Louisville* (Ky.) *Courier-Journal* and the *Louisville Times,* provided working space for more than 20 copy editors. The center arm of the H was occupied by the news or slot editor, assistant news editor, managing editor and assistant managing editor. The newsroom has since been redesigned to accommodate the hardware of the new technology. [*Photo courtesy of the* Courier-Journal *and the* Louisvile Times.]

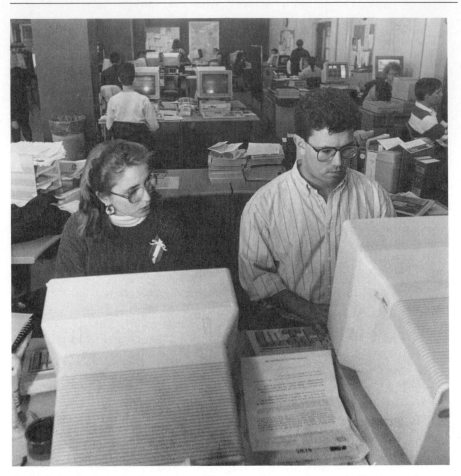

Figure 3-6.   Computerized newsroom. All news stories are written and edited on modern computer terminals at today's newspapers. [Photo by Jeff Adams.]

words of material sent to the newspaper from one or more wire services. The *state editor* processes a page or two of news from throughout the state, and yet another editor may be assigned nothing but the front page. This system allows one individual to concentrate on the content and appearance of that key page.

Although the range of duties tends to increase as the size of the newspaper decreases, the goal of the editor—to produce the best possible newspaper—remains the same.

COPY FLOW PATTERNS

Just as the size of the newspaper determines the extent of an editor's duties, the production system in use determines the tools with which he or she works.

As recently as 1970 almost every newspaper in the United States employed the traditional copy-processing system. Reporters wrote their stories on typewriters, and editors penciled in corrections until finally the paper copy was sent to the composing room to be converted into type. The emergence of electronic editing in the early 1970s changed that pattern radically. Most newspapers now use video display terminals (VDTs), keyboards with attached television-like screens similar to those used for years by airline reservations agents.

In less than 10 years VDT technology transformed the typical newsroom from a bastion of 19th-century methods into a showcase of contemporary computer technique. Nothing quite like it had occurred in the newspaper industry since the introduction of Mergenthaler's Linotype machine.

The technology used affects the way reporters and editors go about their jobs, but copy flow patterns are similar in all systems. When VDTs were introduced, manufacturers tried to duplicate existing copy flow patterns to minimize changes in entrenched newsroom procedures.

The process begins with the reporter, who writes the story and submits it to the editor who assigned it, usually the city editor or metro editor. That editor reads the story, makes the corrections in the process, and either approves the story for publication or returns it to the reporter for revision. When the story is ready, it is sent to the news editor or copy desk chief. That editor determines the length of the story, decides where it should be placed in the newspaper and assigns a headline based upon its position on the page layout.

The editor then passes the story to a copy editor, who carries out the editor's instructions. The copy editor trims the story to fit the space reserved, does the final editing and writes the headline. The story then is returned to the news editor, who approves the headline and scans the copy before sending both to the composing room for typesetting.

That, in simplified form, is the basic copy flow pattern. The exact procedure, however, is determined by staff organization and the technology in use at the newspaper. Because computerized and traditional technologies are distinctly different, it is necessary to describe these systems separately.

THE TRADITIONAL PROCESS

Reporters working at newspapers that use traditional copy-processing techniques write their stories on manual or electric typewriters. An original and two or three copies, constituting a "book," are prepared. Inexpensive paper, often newsprint cut to $8\frac{1}{2}$-by-11 inches, is used. Stories are double- or triple-spaced, depending on the newspaper's custom, to allow the reporter and editors to make handwritten corrections using established copyediting symbols (see Figure 3-7). A perfect manuscript is not expected, nor is it necessary, but relatively "clean" copy helps to minimize errors of misinterpretation later in the production process.

The reporter saves one carbon copy of the story for future reference and submits the original and other carbons to the city editor. The original is used

Take out word and ~~and~~ close up space

Add word

Retain ~~crossed-out~~ portion (stet)

Transpose letters or words or

capitalize word: lower-case letter

Indent for paragraph

(No ¶) Don't indent

Insert period: ...John said

Insert comma: John who...

Insert apostrophe: Johns other wife

Insert quotation marks: John said, I'll go.

Insert hyphens: Jack and Jill School

Insert parentheses: (John is his last name.)

Use a circle to indicate:

   Abbreviation: (Colonel) Smith

   No abbreviation: the (col.) said

   Use figure: (six hundred)

   Spell out figure: He had (5) boys

   Directions to compositors:

(bf)   Set boldface. Wavy line also denotes boldface: At the Alladin

(lf)   Set lightface

(bc)   Set boldface capitals

(bflc)   Set boldface capital and lower-case

(sc)   Set small capitals. Two lines under letters denote small capitals: Macky

(sh)   Subhead. Write the subhead between lines of copy

(ital.)   Set in italic type. Underscore denotes italic: fog index

(Rom.) Set in Roman type

(dc)
(15-pica) Set type in double-column measure or in measure indicated

Figure 3-7.   Copy editing symbols.

for copy processing, and the carbons are filed for future reference or used as substitutes for misplaced originals. Editors use the same copy editing symbols as the reporter to make changes as the story makes its way through the editing process (Figure 3-8).

Either the slot editor or the copy editor marks typesetting instructions on the copy. When the story reaches the composing room, the compositor must know which typeface to use, what size of type is needed, the width (or measure) of the column, and whether special handling is desired. Special settings are required for inset pictures (called half-column cuts or thumbnails), initial letters (large capital letters at the beginning of the text) and other special treatments for typographical impact.

Headlines are written either at the top of the story, the method often used for headlining brief articles, or on separate half sheets of standard-size copy paper. They, too, must be marked for typesetting.

Finally, the story and headline are sent to the composing room, where compositors set the type. After the type is set, proofs are made and a proof-reader compares the typeset version with the edited copy. The proofreader uses proofreading symbols (see Appendix II) to mark corrections, which are set and placed in position in the typeset copy. Editors also use proofreading symbols, which differ slightly from copy editing symbols, when reading proofs of typeset copy or when making changes in text from one edition to the next.

The whole process of editing and typesetting with traditional methods is riddled with redundancy. Editors consider redundancy in the newsroom a desirable trait because the more times a story is read, the more errors are detected and deleted. They object, however, to redundant keyboarding in the composing room, where errors easily can be introduced.

Figure 3-8.   An example of edited copy.

THE COMPUTERIZED PROCESS

Editors and reporters at most newspapers in the United States and Canada have video display terminals or networked personal computers on which to work. Editors consider computer terminals the best tools available for writing and editing copy (Figure 3-9).

Video terminals give editors final control over what is set in type, and, consequently, what appears in the newspaper. Compositors are not necessary because the work of reporters and editors is stored in computer memory and subsequently used to drive high-speed phototypesetting machines. Proofreaders also are unnecessary because phototypesetters are extremely accurate; machine errors, common with old, hot-metal linecasters, are almost nonexistent. This means that at most newspapers an editor is the last to read a story before it appears in the newspaper. Control of the newspaper's content is placed where it belongs—in the hands of the editors.

As a result, editors place a premium on talented copy editors who refuse to accept what is merely adequate and instead strive for perfection. No longer can editors tolerate the copy editor who believes, "That's good enough. The composing room will straighten it out." Unfortunately, too many of those people were tolerated in the past.

Editors who employ talented copy editors like the computerized editing process. Their papers are more accurate and contain fewer typographical

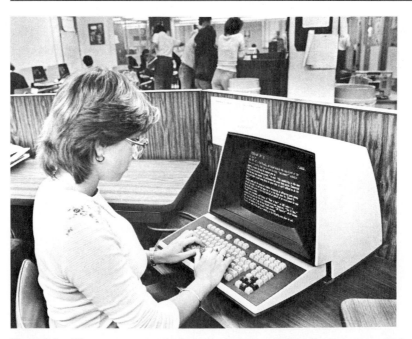

Figure 3-9.   The reporter at work. Reporters at U.S. and Canadian newspapers today use computer terminals as a writing tool.

errors than in the past. No longer is there the danger that a compositor will misinterpret an editor's hand-scrawled instructions.

Reporters and editors using computer terminals write and edit on the keyboards attached to their video terminals. More than 20 manufacturers sell computers for newspaper use, so there is little standardization. Almost all use a standard typewriter keyboard layout for alphanumeric functions, but there the similarity ends. Most terminals have keys for text editing and manipulation, but the manufacturer decides where those keys are placed. This proves to be a disadvantage for the newcomer to a newspaper, who may have learned to use editing keys placed to the left of the alphanumeric portion of the keyboard rather than to the right. Increasingly, that problem is being solved as newspapers begin using personal computers with standardized keyboards.

A lighted rectangle, called a cursor, indicates the position in the text where the next character will be placed. A bank of cursor control keys or a mouse allows the user to move the cursor forward, backward, up or down. Errors are corrected by inserting characters, overstriking or moving blocks of text from one position to another until perfect copy is produced. Another bank of keys permits text manipulation. With these keys, stories are filed in computer memory, recalled for editing, and routed from editor to editor and finally to the phototypesetter through a series of queues, the electronic equivalents of in-baskets.

At some point, an editor must place a computer-coded instruction, called a format, at the top of the story to instruct the phototypesetter to set the type as the editor wants. Other codes may be inserted to produce initial letters, insets for half-column pictures or other special treatments.

When computer terminals were first introduced, some argued that editors had become compositors because they had taken on duties formerly handled in the composing room. Newsroom employees with union representation made this contention in labor negotiations, and in some cases the issue was taken to arbitration. Almost without exception, arbitrators ruled that the technology employed had not substantially changed the duties and functions of copy editors.[1] Their reasoning was that editors had been required to mark copy for typesetting, insets and other special handling even when traditional copy-processing procedures were employed. Formats used in the best computer systems allow markup similar to that always used; there is no need for the editor to learn complicated typesetting codes.

Similarly, contentions that editors now have more responsibility because of the absence of compositors and proofreaders fell on deaf ears. Editors always had been responsible for the content of the newspaper; now they had been given tools to do that job more effectively.

---

[1] Significant decisions in this area were made in arbitrations between the Newspaper Guild of Pittsburgh, Local 61, and Post-Gazette Publishing Co., and between the Vancouver-New Westminster Newspaper Guild, Local 115, and Pacific Press Limited, publisher of the *Vancouver* (B.C.) *Province* and *Sun*. In the Vancouver decision, the arbitrator found that duties of some key personnel and some clerks had been changed as a result of the introduction of VDTs, but no substantial change was found in the duties and functions of copy editors.

Such disputes tend to distort the fact that computers have won widespread acceptance. In one nationwide survey of copy editors, 89 percent said they preferred working with computers to working with pencil and paper.[2] That same survey showed that editors believe computer editing allows them to be more accurate and that with computers they are more likely to make the extensive revisions necessary to produce a truly exceptional newspaper. An impressive 46 percent indicated that computers had helped them become more accurate editors. Only 10 percent thought that computers had affected editorial accuracy adversely.

EMERGING TECHNOLOGIES

Some newspapers have started designing pages on computer terminals as a means of eliminating the labor-intensive composing room makeup process. In this system, known as pagination, full-page phototypesetters produce completed pages or laser technology creates printing plates, and the composing process is eliminated altogether. Pagination creates additional work for the copy desk, which must make precise decisions about where stories are to be trimmed and how to avoid widows (short lines at the tops of columns), and similar decisions that printers once made. Most newspapers that have switched to pagination have been able to eliminate jobs in the composing room but have found it necessary to add to the copy desk staff.

A few newspapers also have started programming for cable television, videotex and teletext, all of which are forms of electronic home delivery of news in text format (see Chapter 19). Often, the copy desk is responsible for such programming, and copy editors take turns preparing text for such cablecasts. A couple of newspapers, including Long Island's *Newsday,* have tried to market television-like newscasts produced by newsroom personnel.

Still other newspapers have started publishing fax newspapers, which transmit late-breaking news to subscribers' facsimile machines. In some ways, fax newspapers replace afternoon dailies, many of which have disappeared. This development allows coverage of the latest stock market trends, perhaps even closing averages, and late-breaking news that is likely to affect businesses. Most often the subscribers to such services are businesses, which have permission to make an unlimited number of copies for distribution. The newspaper charges a fee for the service and thus creates another source of revenue for the expenses it incurs in covering the news.

Other newspapers are experimenting with audio news delivery. This often involves digitized recordings of news with computer-controlled playback. Unlike tape-recorded messages, digitized messages can be played on more than one line simultaneously.

In each case, the copy desk, as the clearinghouse for news, is likely to be involved. A person who goes to work at a newspaper copy desk may well be involved in editing one of these products.

[2] Linda J. Shipley, James K. Gentry and John W. Clarke, *VDT vs. Pencil: A Comparison of Speed and Accuracy,* University of Missouri School of Journalism (1979).

OTHER TOOLS OF THE EDITOR

The computer terminal probably is the most important tool used by today's editor, but there are many others. A well-equipped copy desk will have lots of other sources, primarily to help editors check facts.

The Associated Press publishes the *Associated Press Stylebook and Libel Manual,* used as the style guide by most U.S. newspapers. Many newspapers, both large and small, publish supplements to the AP book to establish local style rules. A few newspapers, mostly metros, publish their own stylebooks that differ from AP's (for details, see Chapter 6).

The *AP Stylebook* is a useful reference tool as well as a complete guide to resolving conflicts in spelling, grammar and similar areas of concern to the editor.

AP establishes as its official dictionary *Webster's New World Dictionary,* and *Webster's Third New International* is the supplemental dictionary of choice when an unabridged dictionary is needed. Most newspapers follow suit, and reporters and editors can expect to find these at almost any newspaper.

Beyond that, each newspaper will have a reference library, or morgue, that contains back stories from the newspaper and its nearby competitors. Increasingly, these libraries are being computerized, and access to them is available from any computer terminal in the newsroom.

Each newspaper also will have a collection of reference books for the editor's convenience. Among the many books included in such libraries are thesauruses, almanacs, city directories, telephone books, encyclopedias, and state and federal manuals. These, too, are increasingly being placed on computer disks or CD-ROMs so they can be accessed from any terminal.

External databases also can be of immense help to reporters and editors. If an editor needs to check a fact, hundreds of newspapers' libraries are available on services such as VuText, DataTimes and Dow Jones News Retrieval. Federal, state and local governments also have on-line databases, or electronic bulletin boards, designed to permit easy access to government information.

Each year, more and more newspapers subscribe to such services to broaden the resources available to staff members. Reporters make ample use of such services when doing background checks to see what other newspapers have written on a subject. The importance of such services to editors, however, should not be dismissed. Facts can be checked here as easily as in the *World Almanac.*

THE EMERGENCE OF INNOVATIVE DATABASES

Editors who are aware of the latest in newspaper technology realize that database technology is merely beginning to evolve. Increasingly, reporters and editors are being made aware of the importance of putting this technology to work in innovative ways.

For example, a reporter doing an investigative report might create a special database just to keep up with all the bits of information he or she has collected. Or a reporter might create a database to keep up with hundreds of news sources.

At the moment, much work of this type is being done on personal computers located alongside the reporter's word-processing terminal. The problem with most newsroom computer systems of today is that they allow the reporter and editor to do little besides word processing. Newsroom workstations of the future will have to include spreadsheet and database programs. Clearly, word processing is but one of the many functions reporters and editors will have to perform.

Editors aware of these needs increasingly are turning to networked personal computers and in the process are dumping older systems with limited functions. Personal computers work well as word processors but also allow reporters and editors to run the many other excellent programs available for PCs.

A great example of how technology can be used to improve the quality of journalism can be found in the burgeoning number of prize-winning articles that have resulted from computer-assisted reporting.

For many years, much information has been available from U.S., state and local agencies on nine-track mainframe computer tapes. The problem was that most reporters had no idea how to access that information. Elliot Jaspin, a Pulitzer Prize–winning journalist, changed all that when he perfected

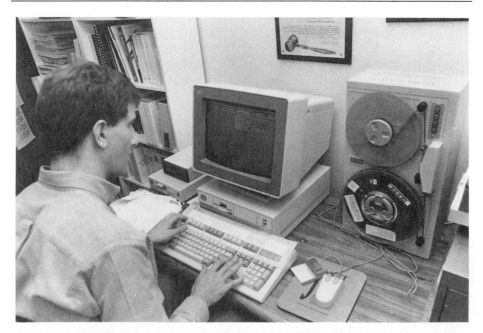

Figure 3-10.   Data from nine-track mainframe tapes, obtained from government agencies, increasingly is a source of information for reporting. [Photo by Jeff Adams.]

a computer program that allowed journalists to extract data from those tapes and transfer those data to a relational database on a PC. Once that was done, it became possible, for example, to compare a computerized statewide list of school bus drivers to the state's drunk-driving convictions to see how many school bus drivers had DWI convictions. It also became possible to make sense of the thousands of campaign finance reports filed by congressional representatives, as this *Los Angeles Times* article shows:

House Members Spend Freely to Bolster Roles

On a warm Sunday afternoon last September, more than 400 Democrats gathered on a small Brooklyn beach for a party to celebrate the 50th birthday of a well-known local celebrity: Rep. Stephen J. Solarz, D-N.Y.

The party cost thousands of dollars, but neither the congressman nor his well-wishers were asked to contribute a dime. All the catering and entertainment bills were paid out of Solarz's $1.6-million campaign treasury.

While Solarz, like most of his colleagues in the House, faces only token opposition Nov. 6, he considered the party a good investment anyway.

Social events such as this are the glue that holds together Solarz's local political organization, the grassroots machinery that maintains his influence in his district and discourages others from running against him.

"It generates the kind of goodwill that can be helpful at election time," Solarz says.

Solarz is by no means unusual. A comprehensive computer-assisted study by *The Times* of campaign spending patterns among members of the U.S. House of Representatives found that incumbent congressmen routinely spend tens of thousands of dollars on things that have little to do with direct appeals for votes but much to do with sustaining personal political machines and for bolstering lawmakers' own influence inside Congress itself.

The Times found that more than 20 percent of the more than $145 million spent by incumbents in the current two-year election cycle has gone for such purposes.

To accomplish these objectives, House members use a wide variety of techniques—throwing big parties, mounting expensive direct-mail campaigns that not only raise money but polish the congressman's image among crucial constituencies and making sizable contributions from their campaign coffers to charities and other candidates.

Not surprisingly, the congressmen who spend the most money on these activities are very senior members who have little or no opposition in the Nov. 6 election but do have access to large volumes of money from political action committees. . . . [3]

THE LOS ANGELES TIMES
©Copyright Times Mirror Company, 1990

The *Times* article continued with rich detail about specific uses of campaign money, all extracted from federal computer records. A sidebar explained how the story was done:

[3] "House Members Spend Freely to Bolster Roles," Los Angeles Times, October 29, 1990, p. A-1.

The *Los Angeles Times* computer-assisted study of campaign spending is based on an analysis of 229,169 separate expenditures reported to the Federal Election Commission (FEC) by the 798 candidates currently seeking seats in the U.S. House of Representatives. The data includes all money spent by these candidates from Jan. 1, 1989, through Sept. 30, 1990.

Copies of each report were obtained by *The Times,* and every expenditure was entered into the database under one of 273 different categories.

For purposes of analysis, candidates were divided into three major groups—incumbents, challengers or candidates for open seats. They also were classified according to the intensity of their races—unopposed, contested or involved in a close race.

Candidates such as John P. Murtha, D-Pa., who won his primary by less than a 55 percent majority, were included in the "close race" category. Uncontested races included both those without general election opposition and those where opponents have raised less than $5,000. All other candidates were classified as "other contested."

By and large, *The Times* relied upon the candidates' descriptions of each expenditure to classify the outlay. In some cases where the purpose of an expenditure was not clear on the report, candidates were asked for an explanation.[4]

THE LOS ANGELES TIMES
©Copyright Times Mirror Company, 1990

The manual preparation of such a report without the help of computers would have taken months, perhaps years. The ability to do such reporting should greatly enhance the quality of journalism.

Editors involved in producing such articles will have to learn how to present massive amounts of statistical data in charts as well as in text. To help accomplish that, the University of Missouri and Indiana University–Purdue University at Indianapolis have established institutes to teach students and working journalists how to employ such techniques. Missouri, through its Missouri Institute for Computer-Assisted Reporting, also is creating a mainframe-based repository of computerized information of use to all newspapers. Such a repository might include federal census records, environmental safety records, airliner maintenance records and similar items. All this would be accessible nationwide.

Once such a repository is in place, editors who want to trace the maintenance history of an airliner that has crashed need only tap into the database. With such techniques, newspapers can make vast improvements in the quality of journalism they are practicing.

[4] Ibid.

PART **II**

COPY EDITING
SKILLS

CHAPTER 4

THE EDITING PROCESS

THE COPY EDITOR'S RESPONSIBILITIES

Of all the copy editor's duties, editing for accuracy is probably the most important. A newspaper that is inaccurate soon loses its credibility and, ultimately, its readers.

Good reporting, of course, is the key ingredient in ensuring accuracy. But all who edit the story share that responsibility. Editors ensure accuracy by questioning the reporter about the information obtained and the means of obtaining it, and by checking verifiable facts. Usually the city editor questions the reporter, and the copy editor checks verifiable facts. The spelling of names and the accuracy of addresses can be checked in telephone books, city directories and similar sources. The newspaper's library, almanacs, stylebooks, dictionaries, databases and other references are used to check other facts. The good newspaper provides its staff with these source materials, and the good copy editor uses them frequently.

Ensuring accuracy is important, but the copy editor's job entails much more than that. This chapter and those that follow outline what is expected of the copy editor. In general, though, those responsibilities include:

1. Ensuring accuracy.
2. Trimming unnecessary words.
3. Protecting and polishing the language.
4. Correcting inconsistencies.
5. Making the story conform to style.
6. Eliminating libelous statements.
7. Eliminating passages in poor taste.
8. Making certain the story is readable and complete.
9. Ensuring fairness.

The copy editor who does each of these things in every story will be a valuable addition to the newspaper's staff. The importance of accuracy already has been emphasized, but a brief review of the other responsibilities may be useful.

When unnecessary words are being trimmed, adjectives and adverbs often are suspect. If an event is *very interesting,* it is sufficient to say it is *interesting. Very* is an overworked word that has become almost meaningless. Similarly, *totally destroyed* is worse, not better, than *destroyed.* Meaningless phrases also should be eliminated. *At the corner of Ninth and Elm streets* is no better than *at Ninth and Elm streets.*

To polish the language, the copy editor must know the difference between a conjunction and a preposition and be aware of the perils of misplacing modifiers. The copy editor also must be able to spell and to use words properly. Copy editors, and certainly students in an editing course, would benefit by getting into the habit of using a dictionary and learning to use words properly. Chapter 5 shows how the copy editor deals with the language.

The top-flight copy editor also will recognize inconsistencies within a story. Here is a good example:

> Mrs. John E. Simpson, 81, of 914 E. Texas Ave., died Saturday at Boone County Hospital after an illness of several months.
>   Mrs. Simpson was born in Audrain County Dec. 21, 1910, to the late John and Mary Simpson. . . .

The inconsistency is that Mrs. Simpson likely did not have the same maiden and married names. Therefore, her parents' surname must be checked. The alert copy editor would have detected that possible error and questioned the city desk about it. And, depending upon the year in which the story is written, the age and date of birth may not agree.

Annoying inconsistencies also result from failure to conform to the newspaper's style. The word "style," as used here, refers to the consistency provided by rules of usage and in no way limits a reporter's individual writing style. Style, for example, dictates that the correct spelling is *employee,* not *employe,* which can be found in some dictionaries. It may be annoying to the reader to find the word spelled one way in one story and another way in the next. The importance of style is emphasized in Chapter 6.

The copy editor faces other problems, many of which cannot be solved by consulting dictionaries and stylebooks. One of those problems is recognizing and eliminating libelous statements. Libel laws vary from state to state, so one of the first duties of a newly employed copy editor is to check the laws of the state. A thorough discussion of legal limitations on the press can be found in Chapter 8. By reviewing the law and interpretations of it, the copy editor can usually determine whether a statement is libelous.

More difficult to resolve are questions of good taste. Some newspapers have policies banning profanity of any type; others permit the use of some words but not others. Most editors would object to a story detailing what occurred during a rape; some would not. These are matters of judgment. When in doubt, the wise copy editor will consult a top-ranking editor for a ruling.

The copy editor makes certain the story is readable. Writing that is good, and therefore readable, has five characteristics:

1. It is precise.
2. It is clear.
3. It has a pace appropriate to the content.

4. It uses transitional devices that lead the reader from one thought to the next.
5. It appeals to the reader's senses.

Writing is precise when words are used in the way they should be used, and it is clear when simple sentences and correct grammar are employed. Pacing is a matter of using varied sentence length. The use of short, choppy sentences conveys action, tension or movement. Conversely, long sentences slow the reader. Transitions help the reader tackle the story, and sharp, descriptive words appeal to the reader's senses to bring him or her close to the action.

Good writing employs all these principles. There is no reason why they should be used in novels but not in newspaper stories. The argument that reporters don't have time to produce high-quality writing is a poor excuse, understandable as it may be, for mediocrity. It can be done, and the best newspapers in this country are proving it. The quality of writing depends upon the reporter, but the copy editor can do much to help. Good editing invariably complements good writing. Occasionally, good editing can save mediocre writing. Poor editing can make it worse or destroy it.

Copy editors have no business changing a writer's style. But copy editors have every obligation to insist that the story be correct in spelling, grammar and syntax: It is their duty to make copy compact and readable.

Most copy can be tightened. Even if only a few words in a paragraph are removed, the total saving in space will be considerable. Some stories, notably material from the wires and syndicates, can be trimmed sharply. But the copy editor should not overedit. If a story is so poorly organized it has to be rewritten, the story should be returned to the originating editor. Rewriting is not a copy editor's job. Nor should the copy editor make unnecessary minor changes. Indiscreet butchering of local copy is a sure way to damage morale in the newsroom.

NEWSPAPER WRITING

Newspaper journalism always has attracted good writers. The best today rank with the stars of the past, including such legendary figures as Stephen Crane, Mark Twain and Ernest Hemingway, all of whom began their writing careers as newspaper reporters. As a class, however, reporters are mediocre writers. Much of this mediocrity can be attributed to the deadline pressure under which reporters write, the lack of enthusiasm for the subjects about which they write and the straightjacket of the traditional inverted pyramid style, discussed later in this section.

The deadline pressure will always exist because newspaper production necessitates the setting of deadlines. That's why the pro who can pound out a readable story in a matter of minutes is a valued member of the newsroom staff. Those other excuses for mediocrity, however, fail to stand up under close examination. A wise editor once said: "There are no dull stories, only dull reporters." The message is clear: A good reporter can find a good story in almost any situation. Blaming the event or situation for a mediocre story is inexcusable. Finally, reporters no longer should feel shackled by the inverted pyramid approach to newspaper writing. Other writing styles have gained acceptance nationwide, and the newspaper that ignores them misses the opportunity to keep its readers interested.

The copy editor must have a thorough understanding of newspaper writing styles, or story forms, so that he or she can recognize them quickly. It would be a serious mistake to assume that every story should be written in the inverted pyramid style. Editing to achieve that effect without grasping what the writer is trying to accomplish can destroy a good story. The following discussion outlines and illustrates the most popular forms.

THE INVERTED PYRAMID APPROACH

This classic style, with its crammed leads and recitation of facts in descending order of importance, should not be dismissed. It remains the staple of newspaper writing. Fast-breaking news stories lend themselves to this treatment. Indeed, the form was developed by newspaper writers, who found it worked well in meeting the needs of their fast-paced business.

The inverted pyramid story has three main parts:

1. The lead.
2. Support and development of the lead.
3. Details in descending order of importance.

Typically, stories written in this form have the traditional lead that tells the reader who, what, when, where, why and perhaps how. Here is an example of an inverted pyramid story:

SPRINGFIELD, Mass. (UPI) — A man screaming "I'm the king" slashed his way through a crowded hospital emergency room with a long-bladed paring knife Monday, killed a 6-year-old boy and injured five other people.

Willie Robinson, 42, infuriated when he and his young granddaughter were burned with cleaning fluid during a domestic quarrel at his apartment, stabbed his wife and ran amok at Bay State Medical Center's Springfield Unit a short time later, police said.

"He had a really wild look in his eyes," said Sgt. George Bishop, a hospital security guard. "There was an awful lot of blood."

Robinson had been taken to the hospital by his nephew for treatment of burns, then "went berserk." He wounded five persons in the emergency room and killed Anthony Lombardi, 6, of Agawam, police said.

Police said Robinson stabbed several women and a guard and then pinned the boy down at an ambulance entrance, stabbed him repeatedly and screamed, "I'm the king, I'm the king. Now I've done it. I'm done."

The boy died about two hours later of wounds in the neck, throat and arms.

The boy's mother, Rose Lombardi, 30, was listed in serious condition with multiple stab wounds.

Police said Robinson would be charged with murder and seven counts of assault and battery.

The inverted pyramid was developed to make it easier to trim the story in the composing room as the deadline neared. Because facts were in descending order of importance, trimming from the bottom was simple. Traditional copy-processing procedures made story length estimates imprecise, so trimming frequently was necessary. Computer technology used in modern newspaper plants permits copy editors to determine the exact length of a story before it is typeset, so page layouts can be more precise. This makes it more feasible for newspapers to use alternative writing styles, which, unlike the inverted pyramid, often employ formal closings.

THE NARRATIVE APPROACH

Some newspaper editors believe there is an increasing need to use the narrative, magazine style in newspaper stories. A narrative may have no breaking news at all, but rather a wealth of new and interesting information that will make it news nevertheless.

This concept already has been tried successfully. For example, some news events heavily covered by television have been presented in the narrative rather than the traditional news style. Here is an example of the narrative approach:

MADRID (UPI) — "You will write about me and my photo will be published on every front page," boasted 16-year-old Mariano Garcia. "I will be a great bull fighter one day."

This was his dream and the theme he returned to time and again during our 200-mile drive from Saragossa to Madrid.

It was on Feb. 23 in the outskirts of Saragossa that Mariano had asked me for a ride.

"I want to go to Madrid and start a career as a bull fighter," the boy said in the accents of his native Mancha.

Mariano's was a classic story of Spain: The eager youth deserting the misery of his sunbaked village with its white-washed walls for the danger and glory of the bull ring.

When he learned that I was a newsman, Mariano pulled a pencil stub and sort of calling card out of his pocket. The card bore an amateurish sketch of the Virgin Mary and Jesus. Across it he scrawled his name in bold letters.

"The Virgin and the Christ are my protectors," he said.

Then he talked with wide-eyed dreaminess of how the bull paws the ground with his left forefoot when excited, of his sudden charges, of the secrets of the matador's capework and of the "pata, rabo y orejas" — the hoofs, tail and ears of the bull — the highest honors the fickle Spanish crowd can pay a matador.

For two years, Mariano tried to get a start on the road to fame and fortune. It came not in Madrid, but at San Martin de Lavega.

The bull he met Thursday was six years old, fat, limping, and the sharp tips of his horns had been clipped. But the old bull could be dangerous. He had survived the ring once and remembered well how the matador evaded his charges and the hooking of his horns.

Mariano made three or four passes with his cape. But the bull was old and the boy was young and the fickle crowd was bored.

"Just a meletilla," some shouted, "just a beginner."

Another matador stepped in to divert the bull. But the animal had his eyes fixed on Mariano. Suddenly, he charged the boy and knocked him down.

Then the old bull drove his blunted left horn into Mariano's skull.

It was a quick kill, as the good matador's sword should be quick.

Mariano Garcia's mother and father carried his body in a bloodstained sheet to the local cemetery. And today I wrote the story Mariano promised I would write.

This type of storytelling has the quality once described by Earl J. Johnson of UPI: "to hold the reader's interest and stimulate some imagination to see, feel and understand the news."

THE PERSONALIZED APPROACH

Business and financial news may not be the most glamorous of subjects for most readers, but *The Wall Street Journal* knows how to make such stories compelling. Here's an example of the *Journal's* personalized approach:

Home on the Range Is a Part-Time Deal for Many Cowboys

They Keep Cows Just for Fun, Helping Keep Prices Low; Job After Banker's Hours

By Marj Charlier
Staff Reporter of The Wall Street Journal

HUNTLEY, Mont.—C.T. Ripley has a redwood ranch house with cowhides adorning the walls and floors. He also has a red pickup truck, with a color-matched stock trailer and six cowboy hats, for whatever the occasion demands.

"I am a cowboy," he says. "That's all I've ever wanted to be."

In truth, he is an oil-refinery employee. But on the side for the past couple of years, he has been putting together his 200-acre "Almosta Ranch." Now he is ready to buy some cattle. He will probably lose money on them, but there is the income from the job sustaining him and the romance of the open range spurring him. He will do it anyway.

Such part-time ranchers are a big problem for full-time cattlemen, many of whom are losing their shirts. The would-be cowboys add up to too many cows, standing the law of supply and demand on its head.

Demand for red meat has tumbled the past decade, depressed by health concerns and recession-induced penny-pinching. As a result, the price ranchers command for cattle has fallen 25 percent, adjusted for inflation. Cattle-herd liquidations would seem to be in order, to bring supply in line with demand and strengthen prices. Some cows have been culled, but analysts suggest the herds must be cut much more to ensure long-term profits.

Small herds compound the price problem. More than 80 percent of the nation's herds have fewer than 100 head of cattle, kept mostly by part-time farmers and those who make their living raising grain. Many of these maintain their livestock, despite the low prices, because cattle aren't their main source of income. Some cattle also are kept at a loss because they provide a tax shelter against other income.

The bottom line: Cow-calf operators (the cowboys who keep beef cows that produce calves for sale to feed lots) have sustained losses eight out of the last 10 years. . . .

The *Journal*'s personalized approach is part of a well-designed formula that newspaper has popularized. It is a four-step process:

1. Focus on the individual.
2. Transition to the larger issue.
3. Report on the larger issue.
4. Return to the opening character for the close.

To tell the part-time ranchers' story in the inverted pyramid formula probably would have been less effective.

THE CHRONOLOGICAL APPROACH

American newspapers of the Colonial period often used the chronological approach in their news accounts. This approach should be used sparingly because it can be boring, but occasionally it can be effective. A detailed account of a gunman's siege may lend itself to this treatment. So may a reconstruction of a pilot's frantic final moments before an airplane crash or a step-by-step account of how a legislative bill was altered to appease lobbyists.

When the chronological approach is used, the formula works this way:

1. A summary lead.
2. Transition to the chronological account.
3. The chronological account.
4. A closing summary or reversion to the inverted pyramid.

One good time to use the chronological approach is when the subject of an interview relates a complicated series of events. There's nothing wrong with allowing the subject to tell the story with a minimum of interference from the writer. Here's an excellent example from United Press International:

COLUMBIA, S.C. (UPI)—The 5-foot waves sloshed over her face, the chilly water of Lake Marion numbed her body, and for a moment Lynne Heath thought about giving up and drowning. But her stubborn temper took over and she kept struggling toward shore.

"I fussed at God. I didn't want to die that way," Ms. Heath, 20, said in an interview Sunday.

"My father is dead, and I talked to him. I told him, 'Hey Dad, put in a good word for me with God. I'm too young to die.' I was stubborn."

The interview was the first time Ms. Heath has talked with the news media about the boating accident March 14 in which her fiance and two other people died. Ms. Heath managed to survive by swimming 90 minutes in the 52-degree water of Lake Marion until she reached shore.

Ms. Heath, her fiance, Kevin Brown, 22, Kevin Morris, 20, and assistant county solicitor Harrison Heller III, 29, were on a fishing trip on the huge lake about a mile from shore when the wind picked up and the water became rough.

The gas tank in the 16-foot fiberglass boat shifted, Ms. Heath said, and the boat took on water and quickly sank.

Heller—who could not swim—was the only one wearing a life preserver. The other preservers went down with the boat.

Ms. Heath said they looked around for something—flotsam or a stump or anything to hold onto—but there was nothing but high waves whipping across the 20-foot-deep water.

"I didn't realize how much danger we were in," she recalled. "Kevin (Brown) looked back at Kevin Morris. He couldn't have lived with himself if he had not gone back to help. Please tell everyone that he went back to help the others.

"I looked at him and I said, 'It's all right. I love you.' The look on his face is one I'll never forget.

"I started swimming toward some houses I had seen on shore. I would swim a little way and the waves would push me back. Waves would come over my head and you would have to hold your breath and then just keep going.

"I have never been a strong swimmer, but I was determined to make it. I swam with the back stroke awhile, the breast stroke, the side stroke. I saw white birds flying over and it made me mad because I wondered why I couldn't just fly out there.

"The sun was shining and it made me feel better. I knew I had to get out of my clothes and shoes. I took off my tennis shoes and my jeans were waterlogged and heavy. I had trouble getting them off.

"I had Girl Scout training and so I tried to make my jeans into a life preserver, but the zipper wouldn't work.

"Soon I had stripped down to my purple tube top and panties. I am 5-foot-2½ and I weighed 122 then. I weigh 112 now. Maybe the baby fat helped with hypothermia.

"At one point I was fixing to give up and I said no, 'My mom will have a nervous breakdown.'

"I'm very stubborn and I have a very hot temper. I think it was my temper. I was mad.

"Finally, after 90 minutes, I got to this beach," she said. "I sat there for about 10 seconds and got my legs to stop shaking so badly. Then I started half crawling and running to the houses about a mile down the beach.

"Briars ripped at my legs but I didn't care. When I got to the house I found these six steep steps. I ran up and just fell in through a screen door."

Mr. and Mrs. Gilbert Minor, a retired couple, wrapped her in a blanket and gave her hot black coffee with lots of sugar while she blurted out the story and asked that authorities be called to help the others.

"We all know it was a miracle," said her mother, Rebecca.

Heller's body has been recovered, and Brown and Morris are presumed drowned.

The writer provides a strong introduction for three paragraphs and then uses the fourth as a transition. The chronological account, much of it direct quotes, begins with the fifth paragraph. Finally, the author provides a summary paragraph. The success of this story is striking evidence that the chronological approach should not be dismissed.

THE FIRST-PERSON APPROACH

The first-person approach also should be used sparingly, but on the right occasion it is effective to have the writer become a part of the story. The first person can be used when the reporter is an eyewitness to an event. It also can be used in participatory journalism, when reporters become ambulance attendants or police officers for a day.

HONING THE LEAD

The lead of a story is its most important element because the lead's quality may well determine whether the reader is hooked or skips the story in favor of another. Editors hesitate to impose formulas for writing by limiting sentence length, but on one point they are almost unanimous: The lead of a story must be short. How short? A Hearst editor demanded short leads and finally got one of only one word. The *Chicago Tribune* applauded this three-word lead: "Money and race." An even better one read: "Are nudes prudes?"

Ralph McGill, late editor of the *Atlanta Constitution,* liked what he called a flawless lead in the Bible: "There was a man in the land of Uz whose name was Job." That all time best seller probably has another of the best leads ever written: "In the beginning God created the heaven and the earth."

Columnist Tom Fesperman uses short leads and short sentences to move his readers along:

> There was a quail whose name was Hercules.
> Don't ask me how he got that name. I have spotted a lot of quail in my time, and I wouldn't call any of them Hercules.
> Even so. Let us get on with the story.
> It is not exactly accurate to say that Hercules was born in Arizona. It's more exact to say he was hatched. . . .

The copy editor's eye brightens when he or she reads leads that rank with these classics:

> Only in Russia could Peter and the Wolf die on the same night. (Stalin's death)
> Today the Japanese fleet submitted itself to the destinies of war—and lost.
> They're burying a generation today. (Texas school explosion)
> The moon still shines on the moonshine stills in the hills of Pennsylvania.
> Fifty thousand Irishmen—by birth, by adoption and by profession—marched up Fifth Avenue today.

Most lead problems arise when reporters try to see how much they can pack into the lead. More often, they should try to see how much they can leave out:

ORIGINAL

EDITED

The former girlfriend of a man charged with killing a local bartender almost four years ago testified Monday that she has never seen another man who claims he killed the victim and that she was with him that night.

A man who says he actually committed the murder for which another man is on trial was contradicted in court Monday.

—*Roy H. Copperud*

Columbia Gas Transmission Corp. has started discussions with its subsidiaries and major customers that could result in increasing the supply of natural gas to its Kentucky subsidiary—and thus to industrial users in the central and northeastern parts of the state who now face a total cutoff of supplies this winter.

Columbia Gas Transmission Corp. has started a search for ways to save industrial users in central and northeastern Kentucky from a threatened total cutoff of gas this winter.

—*Wallace Carroll*

One way to avoid long, cluttered leads is to substitute simple sentences for compound ones:

LONDON—Thirty-five years ago today, a 27-year-old princess was crowned Queen Elizabeth II, and Britain, in an outpouring of emotional fervor unmatched since, hailed her coronation as the beginning of a new Elizabethan era of splendor and achievement.

LONDON—Thirty-five years ago today, a 27-year-old princess was crowned Queen Elizabeth II. Britain, in an outpouring of emotional fervor unmatched since, hailed her coronation as the beginning of a new Elizabethan era of splendor and achievement.

The lead should be pruned of minor details that could come later in the story if they are needed:

Donald E. Brodie, son of William Brodie, for more than three decades a member of the display advertising department of the News, and Mrs. Brodie, 106 W. 41st St., was graduated from Jefferson Medical College last week.

Donald E. Brodie, son of Mr. and Mrs. William Brodie, 106 W. 41st St., was graduated from Jefferson Medical College last week. For more than three decades, William Brodie was a member of the display advertising department of the News.

The lead need not be long to be cluttered and unreadable:

First National is one of four American banks, and the American Express which issues travelers checks throughout the nation.

First National, three other American banks, and the American Express Co. issue travelers checks throughout the nation.

LEADS THAT MISLEAD

A good lead contains qualities other than brevity. It must inform and summarize. It must be straightforward; it cannot back into the action. It sets the mood, the pace and the flavor of the story. It accomplishes what the term implies: It guides, directs, points to and induces. If it is a suspended-interest lead, it must be so tantalizing and intriguing that the reader cannot help but continue.

In an effort to get the maximum punch in the lead, the overzealous reporter may overstate. When this happens, the lead is unsupported by the story or ignores facts contained in it. It stretches and therefore distorts. It is the type of lead that reads, "All hell broke loose in city hall last night." Then the final sentence reads, "When the dispute subsided, members of the council shook hands, and the mayor adjourned the session."

No matter how appealingly you wrap up the lead, it is no good if it gives a wrong impression or tells a lie. The "souped-up" lead invites a sensational headline. If the copy editor lets the overextended lead stand, then tries to top the lead with a calm headline, the editor is likely to have the headline tossed back with the suggestion that more punch be put into it.

Akin to the sensationalized lead is the opinion lead. This type of lead offers a judgment rather than fact. Often it fails to distinguish between mere puffery and news: "Construction features described as newer in concept than space travel will be part of the easy-to-shop-in Almart store to open soon on the Kirkwood Highway."

DON'T BACK INTO IT

John Smith returns home from a meeting and his roommate asks, "What happened at the meeting?"

"Well," replies John, "Jim Jones opened the meeting at 8 and Bill Prentice read the minutes of the previous meeting, and . . . "

"Good night, John."

Too many news leads read like secretarial reports, and that is especially true of leads on speech stories. Few care that a nursing consultant spoke at a group's "regular monthly meeting" or care to know the title of the talk. Readers want to know *what* that person said. That's the news. They won't wade through three paragraphs to learn in the fourth paragraph that "the epileptic child should be treated as a normal person." The lead should get to the point of the story immediately. Like this:

ORIGINAL	EDITED
Dean F. Snodgrass of the University of California's Hastings College of Law says the American Bar Association's longtime ban on news photographs in courtrooms is archaic and unrealistic.	The rule against news photographs in courtrooms is archaic and unrealistic, a law school dean says. *–AP Writing Committee*

INDIRECT

An Atlanta businessman who joined two anti-black, anti-Jewish groups and turned over information to the FBI today associated a man on trial for dynamiting the Jewish temple with race-hating John Kasper.

DIRECT

A man on trial for dynamiting the Jewish temple was linked today with race-hating John Kasper by an FBI undercover agent.

INACTIVE

A top-ranking rocket AFD space weapons expert coupled a disclosure of his resignation from the Air Force today with a blast at the senior scientists upon whom the services rely for technological advice.

ACTIVE, TIGHT

A top-level Air Force space weapons expert blasted civilian scientists today and said he has resigned.

CLICHÉ LEADS

Clichés, because of their familiarity, often produce leads that sound like many the reader has read before. The result is a "so-what?" attitude:

Quick action by two alert police officers was credited with saving the life of. . . .
Police and volunteers staged a massive search today for a man who. . . .

SAY-NOTHING LEADS

If a say-nothing lead causes the copy editor to ask, "So what else is new?" the chances are the readers will have the same reaction.

DETROIT—Somber was the word for the memorial services to American dead of the War of 1812 Sunday.
Fire so hot it burned the mud guards off and melted a small section of an aluminum trailer damaged the trailer. . . .

This is almost like writing, "Fire so hot that it burned the roof and walls and destroyed all the furnishings damaged the house of John Doe. . . ."

ILLOGICAL LEADS

Frequently, illogical leads occur when the writer presents the idea backward or uses a non sequitur, a phrase that is nonsensical or defies logic.

State police attributed an auto collision and the alertness of witnesses to the rapid apprehension of Benjamin Petrucci. . . .

Either the apprehension was attributed to the collision and the alert witnesses or the collision and the witnesses were credited with the apprehension. Other examples:

Hoping to encourage transient parking at its facilities, the city parking authority voted Monday to increase rates at two lots.

Charging more for parking hardly seems to be the way to encourage more of it.

Three small brothers died last night in a fire that burned out two rooms of their home while their father was at work and their mother was visiting a neighbor.

Note how much clearer the revision is: "Left unattended, three small brothers perished in a fire last night that destroyed two rooms of their home. Their father was at work and their mother was visiting a neighbor.

EXCESSIVE IDENTIFICATION

Another problem is excessive identification, sometimes even preceding the name:

Former Assistant Secretary of State for Latin American Affairs Lincoln Gordon said today. . . .

This results in unnecessary clutter in the lead. Long titles should follow names.

TOO MANY STATISTICS

Burdensome statistics or numbers also may clutter the lead. Including those statistics later in the story may help alleviate problems such as these:

At 7 p.m. Monday 60 persons fled a three-story apartment building at 2523 E. 38th St. when a carelessly discarded cigarette sent smoke billowing through the building.

Louis Ezzo, 29, of Plainville, a school bus driver, was charged by state police with speeding and violation of a statute limiting school bus speeds to 40 miles an hour at 3:30 p.m. Tuesday on I-95 Groton.

A 14-year-old boy fired three shots into a third-floor apartment at 91 Monmouth St. Friday to climax an argument with a 39-year-old mother who had defended her 9-year-old daughter against an attack by the boy.

OVERATTRIBUTION

Sometimes attribution isn't needed in the lead. Including it there merely creates clutter:

Mimi La Belle, Blanktown exotic dancer, was arrested on a charge of indecent exposure last night, officers George Smith and Henry Brown said Monday.

UNDERATTRIBUTION

On other occasions the attribution must be included in the lead. An Associated Press reference book comments, "Don't be afraid to begin a story by naming the source. It is awkward sometimes, but also sometimes is the best and most direct way to put the story in proper perspective and balance when the source must be established clearly in the reader's mind if he is properly to understand the story." An example:

All Delawareans over 45 should be vaccinated now against Asian flu.

The attribution should have been in the lead because this is opinion, the consensus of a number of health officials.

SECOND-DAY LEAD
ON A FIRST-DAY STORY

Every veteran wire editor knows that frequently a wire story's first lead is better than its second, third or fourth. A lead telling the reader an airliner crashed today, killing 50 passengers, is better than a later lead reporting that an investigation is under way to determine the cause of an airline crash that killed 50 passengers. If the first lead tells the story adequately, why replace it with a second and often weaker lead?

The first lead:

HOLYOKE, Mass. — At least six persons — four of them children — perished early today when a fire, reportedly set by an arsonist, swept a five-story tenement.

The second lead (with a second-day angle):

HOLYOKE, Mass. — The body of a little boy about 2 years old was recovered today, raising the death toll in a tenement house fire to seven.

And the third lead (back on the beam):

HOLYOKE, Mass. — Seven persons — five of them children — perished when a general alarm midnight blaze, believed set, destroyed a five-story tenement.

Conversely, a first-day lead sounds like old news when placed on a second-day story. Copy editors allow such mistakes to appear in print when they fail to keep up with the news. It is important that copy editors read the newspaper each day. Those who don't fail to recognize whether the story is the first on the subject or a followup. That may make a big difference in the way the lead and headline are written.

EDITING THE STORY

Most experienced editors suggest that the editing process be divided into three distinct steps:

1. Read the story.
2. Edit it thoroughly.
3. Reread the story.

Copy editors frequently skip the first step or abbreviate it by scanning the story for the gist of the news. To do so may be a mistake because intelligent editing decisions cannot be made unless the copy editor understands the purpose of the story and the style in which it is written. That understanding is developed with a quick but thorough reading.

Some editors try to skip the third step, too. They do so at the risk of missing errors they should have detected the first time or those they introduced during editing. Few sins are greater on the copy desk than to introduce an error during editing. The more times a story is read, the more likely errors will be detected.

Unfortunately, deadline pressures sometimes dictate that step one or three, or both, be skipped. When this is done, it becomes increasingly important for the copy editor to do a thorough job the first time through the story.

To illustrate the editing process, let's see how one copy editor edited this story on the defeat of a bill in the Missouri General Assembly

This alert copy editor recognized immediately that, while the lead was well-written, it also was inaccurate. The state's streets and stores are not deserted on Sundays. The reporter, reaching for a bright lead, overstated the case.

Because the story is from the newspaper's state capital bureau, it needs a dateline, which the copy editor inserted. The second paragraph became the lead, and the third paragraph was tightened and combined with the second. Note that the editor struck the phrase "with two members present but not voting." In many states there is a difference between present but not voting and abstaining. An abstention allows the legislator to change his or her vote later; present but not voting does not. The copy editor decided that in this case it wasn't important, so the phrase was deleted.

The story is confusing as written, probably because the reporter was too close to the subject to realize that readers would have difficulty following its meaning. The editor clarified fuzzy passages, tightened the story and distinguished between the amendments that were adopted and defeated before the bill itself was defeated.

The editor deleted the next-to-last paragraph because the legislator quoted used a colloquialism that may have been offensive to some readers. Because it added nothing to the story, it was deleted.

The last paragraph illustrates how important it is to use common sense

BLUE LAW

]state capital bureau[

~~Missouri's city streets and stores will continue to be deserted on Sundays, at least for another year.~~

JEFFERSON CITY (—)

(The House Tuesday afternoon rejected a bill that would have ~~sub-mitted the~~ *submitted* repeal of the states blue laws to the voters in November.)

The measure was ~~soundly~~ defeated 97-53 ~~with two members present but not voting.~~

The ~~state's~~ blue laws, or Sunday closing laws, prohibit ~~the~~ *Sunday* sales of nonessential ~~chosen merchandise~~ *goods*, including automobiles, clothing, jewelry and hardware ~~items~~.

During a ~~lengthy~~ debate ~~that lasted four hours~~ [foor = hour], the original bill was amended ~~to place~~ *One amendment would have placed* [twice. several times] the issue on ~~this~~ November ballot, *and another would have required*

~~The bill also was amended to require~~ *decide whether to* that counties and cities ~~exercise local option to approve~~ repeal ~~of blue~~ *the* laws ~~locally if the~~ *within their jurisdictions,* ~~measure was approved by voters in Nov.~~

Several amendments were defeated *One* ~~that~~ would have required employers to ~~pay as much as twice the wages per hour~~ *increase wages for* to employes *who* working *ed* on Sundays. *Another would have set a*

~~Rep. James Russell, a Florissant Democrat, included in one amendment the proviso that employers be fined~~ $1,000 *fine* for each violation of the wage requirements. ~~His amendment lost.~~

Another *defeated* amendment ~~introduced by Rep. Jerry McBride, St. Louis, would~~ *would* have levied a ~~1¢~~ *1=cent* excise tax on retail businesses open on Sunday. Proceeds ~~seeds~~ from this were to have gone to city and county treasuries.

~~The McBride amendment also was defeated.~~

~~During debate~~ much of the support for blue law repeal came *m* from urban representatives whose ~~constituents~~ *districts* include large retail chain stores and businesses that supported repeal ~~of the existing law~~ during committee hearings.

~~In the end, the majority of the house agreed with Rep. Walter Meyer D. Bellefontaine Neighbors, that "this bill is all screwed up."~~

~~Local~~ *Area* Democratic ~~Reps.~~ Ray Hamlett of Ladonia, Joe Holt of Fulton and John Rollins of Columbia, and Republican ~~Reps.~~ Larry Mead and Harold Reisch all voted in favor of putting repeal on the ballot.

Figure 4–1. An edited story.

58

when editing. Conformity to the stylebook would have called for the identification of each legislator by party affiliation and district number. Because
there are five of them, the paragraph would have been difficult to read. The
editor decided that the legislators' hometowns gave more information to
the reader than the district number, and grouping by party affiliation made
the paragraph less awkward than it would have been if the editor had followed
stylebook practice.

Such editing helps the reader make sense of the story. As a result, it is
good editing.

CHAPTER 5

PROTECTING THE LANGUAGE

ABUSING ENGLISH

Newspapers, because of their mass appeal, have a significant impact on the development—and deterioration—of English usage in the United States. If the quality of English usage is deteriorating, as many experts have charged, then newspapers must share the blame.

The copy editor plays a major role in protecting the language against abuse. One who knows how to spell, makes certain a story is written in proper English, recognizes and clarifies fuzzy passages, and protects the meaning of words is a valuable member of the staff. The copy editor who neglects those chores contributes to the erosion of the language and, ultimately, to the detriment of communication. Clear writing, and correct spelling and grammar contribute to the ready communication of ideas.

Edwin Newman, television commentator and author of *Strictly Speaking* and *A Civil Tongue,* deplores the degradation of the language and asks, "Will America be the death of English?" He argues that it may be too much to hope for the stilted and pompous phrase, the slogan and the cliché to be banished, but he argues that they should not dominate the language.

The message was even more forcefully put by Wallace Carroll, former editor and publisher of the *Winston-Salem Journal & Sentinel:*

> The bastardization of our mother tongue is really a disaster for all of us in the news business. The English language is our bread and butter, but when ground glass is mixed with flour and grit with the butter, our customers are likely to lose their appetite for what we serve them.
>
> Our job is to interpret—to translate. Yet our translators—that is our reporters and copy editors—find it more and more difficult to do this basic job of translation. To begin with, they reach us from universities that are tending to become glorified jargon factories, and for four years or more they have been immured in a little cosmos where jargon is too often mistaken for knowledge or wisdom.[1]

Carroll is correct in his assessment, but it is important to remember that language is always changing. As columnist James J. Kilpatrick writes:

[1] *The Bulletin of the American Society of Newspaper Editors,* May 1970, p. 2.

Ours is a constantly changing language. In speech, as in anything else, the acceptability of change is a matter of personal taste. [Some object] to "host" as a verb—"Johnny Carson hosted the show." I, too, would object. Neither have I yielded to "chair," as in "He chaired the committee." Yet my ear is no longer offended by "to service," "to intern," "to model," "to vacation."[2]

Despite this, it is not the job of the copy editor to initiate change in the language. That role is better left to others. Copy editors serve their readers best by ensuring that copy conforms to accepted standards. With that in mind, let's review some of the common problems of spelling, grammar and usage.

SPELLING

One reason so many misspelled words escape the attention of the copy desk is that copy editors are unable to recognize incorrect spelling, even of simple words. Here is a list of the most frequently misspelled words:

accede	Canada geese	firefighter
accommodate	caress	fraudulent
accumulate	cave-in	fulfill
adherence	chaperon	
admissible	cigarette	gaiety
advertent	commitment	goodbye★
advertise	consensus	grammar
adviser★	consistent	greyhound
all right	consul	grisly
alleged	controversy	guerrilla
allotted, allotment	council	
appall	counsel	hangar (aircraft
asinine		shelter)
ax★	demagogue	hanger (hanging
	descendant	device)
balloon	dietitian	harass
battalion	disastrous	hemorrhage
bellwether	dissension	hitchhiker
berserk	drunkenness	
blond (adj., noun for		impostor
male)	embarrass	incredible
blonde (adj., noun for	emphysema	indestructible
female)	employee★	indispensable
boyfriend	exhilarating	irresistible
buses (vehicles)		
busses (kisses)	feud	judgment★

★ Preferred spelling. Words in parentheses also indicate common newspaper usage.

[2] James J. Kilpatrick, syndicated column for the *Washington Star* Syndicate, August 1969.

kidnapped*

lambastes
largess
liaison
likable
liquefy

mantel (shelf)
mantle (covering)
marijuana
marshal

nerve-racking

occasion
occurred

papier-mache
parallel
paraphernalia
pastime
penicillin
percent*
percentage
permissible
personnel

picnicking
pinscher
playwright
politicking
pompon
preceding
principal (main)
principle (concept)
privilege
procedure
prostate
publicly

quandary
questionnaire
queue

rarefy
reconnaissance
restaurateur
rock 'n' roll (rock-
    and-roll)

sacrilegious
seize
separate
siege
sizable

skillful
stationary (not
    movable)
stationery (writing
    material)
strait-laced
strong-arm
subpoena
summonses
supersede

teen-age (adj.)
teen-ager (noun)
theater*
tumultuous

vacuum
vice versa
vilify

weird
whiskey* (whisky
    for Scotch)
wield
wondrous

X-ray (noun, verb
    and adj.)

Good editors learn to check all words about which they have doubts. The best have more doubts than the worst.

GRAMMAR

Grammatical problems help to destroy a newspaper's credibility among its well-educated readers. Grammatical errors can ruin otherwise clear writing or distort the meaning of a sentence. Let's review the parts of speech:

THE PARTS OF SPEECH

To understand the English language and how it works, one must first know the eight parts of speech. They are *verbs, nouns, pronouns, adjectives* (including the articles), *adverbs, prepositions, conjunctions* and *interjections*. Let's review the uses of each.

Verbs

A verb is a word or group of words that expresses action or state of being. There are two kinds of verbs, finite and non-finite (also called verbals). The finite verb works with the subject of the sentence to give a sense of completeness. A non-finite verb works as a nominal, much like a noun, or as a modifier. Compare the two:

FINITE	NON-FINITE
The police *charged* him with robbery.	The police, *having charged* him with robbery . . .

Let's discuss finite verbs now and take up the verbals later.

Person and Number   Finite verbs can be distinguished by *person* (first, second and third) and *number* (singular and plural). Most verbs have a different form only in the third person singular of the present tense:

	SINGULAR	PLURAL
FIRST PERSON	I drink	we drink
SECOND PERSON	you drink	you drink
THIRD PERSON	he (she, it) *drinks*	they drink

An exception is the verb *to be:*

	SINGULAR	PLURAL
FIRST PERSON	I *am*	we are
SECOND PERSON	you are	you are
THIRD PERSON	he (she, it) *is*	they are

Verbs also frequently have *auxiliary,* or helping, verbs. These can be:

1. Modal auxiliaries. Examples of these auxiliaries, which are added to the main verb, are *will, would, can* and *must:* He *will go* to the store.
2. Perfect auxiliaries. These consist of a form of the verb *have* followed by a verb with an *-en* or *-ed* ending: He *has walked* to the store (present). He *had walked* to the store (past).
3. Progressive auxiliaries. These consist of a form of the verb *be* followed by a verb with an *-ing* ending: He *was going* to the store.
4. Passive auxiliaries. These consist of a form of the verb *be* followed by a verb with an *-en* or *-ed* ending: He *was driven* to the store.

Moods, Voices and Tenses   Other properties of verbs, in addition to person and number, are *moods, voices* and *tenses*. The three moods, *indicative, imperative* and *subjunctive,* indicate differences in the intention of the writer or speaker. The indicative mood is used to make an assertion or to ask a question:

- The man *drove* to the store.
- Where *is* he *going?*

The imperative mood is used for commands, directions or requests:

- Command: *Drive to the store.*
- Direction: *Take* the next right turn.
- Request: Please *drive* me to the store.

The subjunctive mood expresses a condition contrary to fact: "If I *were* wealthy, I would quit work." In this case, the speaker indicates an absence of wealth, so the expression is contrary to fact. The present tense forms of the subjunctive are *(if) I be, (if) you be, (if) he, she or it be, (if) we be, (if) you be* and *(if) they be.* The past tense forms are *(if) I were, (if) you were, (if) he, she or it were, (if) we were, (if) you were* and *(if) they were.* Unlike other verbs, which differ in the third person singular of the present tense, the subjunctive remains the same: *(if) he drive,* not *if he drives.*

  Journalists prefer the *active voice* of verbs to the *passive voice* because in the active voice the subject of the sentence does the acting:

  The *president fired* the secretary of state.

In the passive voice, the subject of the sentence is acted upon:

  The *secretary of state was fired* by the president.

The passive voice therefore diverts attention from the person doing the acting to the person or thing being acted upon. In some cases, the writer or editor may find that preferable:

  The *president was shot* today by a man who dislikes his foreign policy.

Clearly, in such a case the person acted upon is more important than the person doing the acting. But in most cases the active voice is better. It is more direct and less wordy.

  The most common tenses in English are the *present tense,* the *past tense,* and the *future tense.* These three tenses indicate the time *now,* the time *past* and the time *to come.* Tense can also indicate that an action has been completed at some definite time in the present, past or future. This is done by the three *perfect* tenses, which denote perfected, or finished, action or state of being. Finally there are the *progressive tenses,* which indicate action that is continuing or progressing in the present, past or future. Thus, various first-person forms of the verb *to see:*

- Present: *I see*
- Past: *I saw*
- Future: *I shall see*

- Present perfect: *I have seen*
- Past perfect: *I had seen*
- Future perfect: *I shall have seen*
- Present progressive: *I am seeing*
- Past progressive: *I was seeing*
- Future progressive: *I shall be seeing*
- Present perfect progressive: *I have been seeing*
- Past perfect progressive: *I had been seeing*
- Future perfect progressive: *I shall have been seeing*

Because the progressives are wordy and awkward, they are seldom used. On occasion, however, they are helpful in indicating degrees of past or ongoing action. A verb that in its own meaning already expresses continuity does not need a progressive form. Thus, it is unnecessary to write, "I am living in Utah." In this case, "I live in Utah" is adequate. But compare these sentences:

> She *drove* to the store.

> She *was driving* to the store.

The second accurately stresses the continuity of the action.

Irregular verbs do not add *-ed* or *-d* to form the past tense and past participle. Some examples:

INFINITIVE AND PRESENT TENSE	PAST TENSE	PAST PARTICIPLE
begin	began	begun
break	broke	broken
come	came	come
eat	ate	eaten
do	did	done
fly	flew	flown
have (has)	had	had
leave	left	left
lie	lay	lain
sit	sat	sat
tear	tore	torn
win	won	won

Verbs also are classified as *transitive* and *intransitive* to describe their use in a sentence. Transitive verbs require objects to complete their meaning:

> The president *fired* the *secretary of state*.

Without the object, *secretary of state,* the sentence would be incomplete.

Intransitive verbs make assertions without requiring objects:

The moon *shines*.

The cowboy *is* on his horse.

Many verbs can be either intransitive or transitive. An example:

Intransitive: She *breathes*.

Transitive: She *breathes* foul air.

Used intransitively, the verb indicates that the woman is alive. Used transitively, it refers to an experience she is having.

Verbals   Verbals are verbs that have lost their ability to act as predicates in a sentence. Instead, they act as nouns, adjectives or adverbs. There are three kinds of verbals, *infinitives, present participles* and *past participles.*

Infinitives begin with the word *to.* Here are examples of infinitives in context:

To forgive is divine. (present, active voice)

I always seem *to be forgiving* you. (present progressive, active voice)

She was happy *to have been forgiven.* (perfect, passive voice)

An active verb can have two types of participles, present and past. The present participle, such as *milking,* expresses action in progress. The past participle, *milked,* expresses finished action. *Having milked* is a modified form of the past participle known as the perfect participle. The passive forms are *being milked* for the present, *milked* for the past, and *having been milked* for the perfect participle.

When they are not part of a verb phrase, participles are used as adjectives and nouns. Here is an example of a participle used as an adjective:

Freedom *Enlightening* the Nation is the name of the statue on the campus. (*Enlightening* modifies Freedom.)

A present participle that functions as a noun is called a *gerund.* An example:

Acting like a gentleman is *acting* properly. (The first *acting* is a gerund used as the subject of a sentence. The second is used as a predicate noun.)

Nouns

A noun names a person, place or thing. There are two kinds of nouns: *proper nouns* are titles for specific persons, places and sometimes things; *common nouns* are generic names such as *dog* or *wood.* Proper nouns are capitalized; common nouns are not. An example:

New York *City* is the nation's largest city.

The *city* was built beside the river.

In the first sentence, *city* is part of a title and therefore must be capitalized. In the second sentence, *city* is used as a common noun.

Nouns can be either singular or plural. Usually, the plural is formed by adding *-s* or *-es* to the end of the word: *jeep, jeeps; box, boxes.* But words ending in *y* and *f* sometimes change before a plural ending: *hoof, hooves; sky, skies.* Unfortunately, that's not always true: *roof, roofs.* Check a dictionary if you are in doubt. A complicating factor is that some nouns have irregular plural forms: *sheep, sheep; goose, geese.* And some nouns normally occur in the singular only: *dust,* not *dusts; courage,* not *courages.*

Nouns can also be possessive. Newspapers observe these rules for forming the possessive case:

1. Plural nouns not ending in *s* take *'s: the alumni's contributions, women's rights.*
2. Plural nouns ending in *s* take only an apostrophe: *the girls' pony, the ships' wake.*
3. Nouns plural in form but singular in meaning take only an apostrophe: *measles' effects, mathematics' rules.*
4. Singular nouns not ending in *s* take *'s: the church's needs, the girl's toys, Marx's theories.*
5. Singular common nouns ending in *s* take *'s* unless the next word begins with *s: the hostess's invitation, the hostess' seat.*
6. Singular proper nouns ending in *s* take only an apostrophe: *Ceres' rites, Socrates' life.*

For other rules that pertain to possessives, consult the wire service stylebooks.

Nouns have several possible uses in sentences. They can be used as:

1. The subject, object or complement of a verb or verbal.
2. The object of a preposition.
3. A modifier following another noun, called an *appositive:* my brother *Wesley.*
4. A modifier before another noun: a *windshield* wiper.
5. The modifier of an adjective or verb:
   They were *battle* weary. (modifies the adjective *weary*).
   They left *Monday.* (modifies the verb *left*).

Pronouns

A pronoun takes the place of a noun in a sentence. It often refers to a noun, a noun phrase or even a complete sentence mentioned earlier. The word to which the pronoun refers is known as the *antecedent* of the pronoun. Some examples:

The man hit *his* head on the door. (*His* refers to *the man.*)

I have suggested to my brother, *who* lives in Phoenix, that we consider a joint vacation. (*Who* refers to *my brother.*)

The Atlanta Braves have a good team this year. That means the Braves could win the pennant. (*That* refers to the full sentence establishing that the Braves have a good team.)

There are several types of pronouns: *personal, relative, interrogative, demonstrative, indefinite* and *intensive.*

Personal pronouns have *case,* either *nominative, possessive* or *objective; person,* either *first, second* or *third;* and *number,* either *singular* or *plural:*

FIRST PERSON

CASE	SINGULAR	PLURAL
Nominative	I	we
Possessive	my, mine	our, ours
Objective	me	us

SECOND PERSON

CASE	SINGULAR	PLURAL
Nominative	you	you
Possessive	your, yours	your, yours
Objective	you	you

THIRD PERSON

CASE	SINGULAR			PLURAL
	Masculine	Feminine	Neuter	
Nominative	he	she	it	they
Possessive	his	her, hers	its	their, theirs
Objective	him	her	it	them

Relative pronouns are used to introduce adjectival or noun clauses:

The butter, *which* he bought yesterday, is already gone. (adjectival clause)

Whatever he bought yesterday is already gone. (noun clause)

The relative pronouns are *who, whom, whose, that, which, whoever, whomever, whatever* and *whichever.* Sometimes the relative pronoun can be omitted from an adjectival clause:

The butter he bought yesterday is already gone.

Interrogative pronouns are used to introduce questions. They are *who, whom, whose, which* and *what:*

Who will win the marathon?

Whose shirt is that in the washing machine?

The demonstrative pronouns, *this, these, that* and *those,* indicate nearness to or distance from the speaker:

This is my best chance to succeed.

Those are mine.

Indefinite pronouns have vague or unknown antecedents. They include words such as *somebody, everyone, whoever, all, each* and *either:*

Somebody stole my laundry basket.

Each of the girls in the class is smart.

Intensive pronouns, which end with *self* or *selves,* repeat and intensify the noun antecedent:

I shot *myself* in the leg.

Jim *himself* will pitch the ninth inning.

Myself should not be used in place of *me:*

Professor Barrett gave A's to Sandra and *me.* (not *myself*)

The *nominative, objective* and *possessive* cases mentioned earlier have various uses. The nominative pronouns (*I, we, you, he, she, it, they, who* and *whoever*) serve as the subjects of sentences or clauses—even when the verb is deleted—and act as subject complements following forms of the verb *to be:*

Marilyn and *I* are close friends. (subject of a sentence)

Marilyn and I, *who* are close friends, will go to the party together. (subject of a clause)

She is a better mathematician than *he.* (subject of a clause with the implied verb *is*)

It is *I.* (subject complement following a form of the verb *be*)

The pronouns in the objective case are *me, us, her, him, them, who* and *whomever.* The objective case is used to express the object of a verb, verbal or preposition, and the subject of the infinitive:

She forced *me* to take the Fifth Amendment. (object of verb)

Many of *us* coal miners have black lung disease. (object of preposition)

She ranked him as high as *me*. (object of *ranked* in understood clause, *she ranked me*)

The Tigers wanted *him* to be traded to the Red Sox. (subject of infinitive)

In the possessive case, also known as the *genitive*, pronouns show possession either in combination with specific nouns (as *regular possessives*) or alone (as *independent possessives*):

REGULAR POSSESSIVES	INDEPENDENT POSSESSIVES
my	mine
our	ours
your	yours
her	hers
his	his
its	its
their	theirs
whose	whose

Some examples of usage:

I think *my husband* will mow the grass today. (regular)

I like *mine* better. (independent)

Regular possessives can also show possession with gerunds, which act as nouns:

Her dropping the course was ridiculous, the professor said.

Adjectives

Adjectives add to the meaning of nouns or pronouns. In this sense an adjective describes, limits or modifies the noun or pronoun to make it clearer. The two major kinds of adjectives are *descriptive* and *limiting*. An adjective that answers the question *what kind?* is descriptive:

The *handsome* man stepped out of the coach.

Handsome in the sentence above is a *common adjective*, one of three kinds of descriptive adjectives. Others are *participial adjectives* (the *dried* fruit) and *proper adjectives* (the *Indian* princess). A descriptive adjective sometimes is used to complete the meaning of the verb *to be* or any of its forms. When used that way, it is known as a *predicate adjective*. Other verbs, including *seem, look, feel* and *taste*, also may take predicate adjectives:

The milkshake tastes *sweet*.

A descriptive adjective sometimes can act as the subject of a sentence when the article *the* is placed in front of it:

> The *loneliest* call the hot line regularly.

A limiting adjective, tells how many, how often, what number or what amount:

> The *five* generals paid homage to George VI.

The articles—*a, an* and *the*—form a special group of limiting adjectives.

All adjectives except the four *demonstrative* ones, *this, that, these* and *those,* change form to show difference in amount or degree. There are three degrees of comparison, *positive, comparative* and *superlative.* Most adjectives of more than one syllable form the comparative by using *more* or *less* in front of the adjective. Similarly, the superlative of multisyllable words is formed by using *most* and *least:*

POSITIVE	COMPARATIVE	SUPERLATIVE
thorough	more thorough	most thorough
willing	more willing	least willing

The endings *-er* or *-est* are added to most adjectives of one syllable to form the comparative and superlative:

POSITIVE	COMPARATIVE	SUPERLATIVE
clear	clearer	clearest
strong	stronger	strongest

Some words, however, have irregular comparisons: *good, well; more, most; better, best.*

Adverbs

Adverbs change or add to the meaning of verbs, adjectives or other adverbs. They help the words they modify, just as adjectives help nouns. Adverbs are classified three ways by use. *Simple* adverbs are used solely to modify:

> She looked *happily* at her elder son.
>
> He was *perfectly* happy.
>
> We were waiting *quite* contentedly.

Conjunctive adverbs are used to connect main clauses:

> He took the bottle home; *however,* he did not drink.

The conjunctive adverbs include *therefore, consequently, moreover, nevertheless, accordingly, otherwise* and *wherefore*. And, finally, *interrogative* adverbs introduce a question:

When did he take the big step?

Adverbs also are classified by time, place, degree, manner and assertion. For details of those usages, consult a grammar book.

Like adjectives, some adverbs have comparative and superlative forms:

POSITIVE	COMPARATIVE	SUPERLATIVE
fast	faster	fastest
soon	sooner	soonest
little	less	least
well	better	best

Prepositions

A preposition is a connecting word that shows a relationship between its object and some other word in the sentence. Common prepositions include *in, on, at, by, against, above, upon, from, of, without, under, over, through* and *during*. There are many others.

The object of the preposition must be in the objective case, except when the object is a double possessive:

The museum has several hats *of Washington's*.

The object may be a noun, an adjective used as a noun, an infinitive, a participle or a clause. All, however, must be used as nouns.

Conjunctions

Another connecting word is the conjunction, which is used to connect words, phrases, clauses and sentences. *Coordinating conjunctions* connect two words, phrases, clauses or sentences that are grammatically equal. Two independent clauses connected by a coordinating conjunction form a *compound sentence:*

John will attend Harvard, *and* Mary plans to go to Yale.

Note that a coordinating conjunction must be preceded by a comma.

The coordinating conjunctions include *and, both, as well as, either, or, neither, nor, but, yet, so* and *so that*. Conjunctions that come in pairs, such as *either* and *or* and *neither* and *nor*, are known as *correlative conjunctions*.

A *subordinating conjunction* joins a subordinate clause to the principal clause of a sentence. Common subordinating conjunctions include *when, as, since, before, after, until, where, because, if, unless, although, though, even if, that, so that* and *in order that*.

Sentences with clauses joined by subordinating conjunctions are called *complex sentences.* In these constructions, the joined clauses are not grammatically equal:

She can ride horses better *than* I can.

In this case, *than* connects the main clause, *She can ride horses better,* to the subordinate clause, *than I can* (*ride horses* is understood).

Interjections

An interjection is an exclamation that expresses surprise, pain or some other intense emotion. It has no grammatical relation to other words and can be used alone. Some examples: *Ouch!, Whew!, Darn!, Help!* and *Oh!*

USAGE

Knowing the parts of speech is essential to understanding the English language, but that alone is not enough. The real difficulty lies in trying to make words and sentences work together to convey meaning. Often, what *sounds* correct may not *be* correct because of common misuse. Let's examine some of the common misuses of the language.

SUBJECT-PREDICATE DISAGREEMENT

The editors of *After the Fact,* internal publication of the *Louisville Courier-Journal,* lamented, "Everybody knows that subjects and verbs should come in matched pairs: singulars together and plurals together. But, sadly, we let too many unmarriageables slip into the paper." Some examples:

There are two things that either Sloane or Hollenbach have. . . .

The thought is: " . . . things that Sloane has or that Hollenbach has." Remember, when nouns are connected by *either . . . or, neither . . . nor* or *or* ONLY the noun closest to the verb should be considered in deciding whether a singular or plural verb is required. If the final noun in the subject is singular, use a singular verb, and vice versa.

. . . the continuing lag in industrial production and the rise in unemployment is a result of inflation.

Lag and rise *are . . .*

An American Bar Association accreditation team, in addition to a citizens' panel, have both recommended this.

Team is the subject; the verb must be *has*. Parenthetical matter should be ignored in selecting the number of the verb.

It's moved to a point where the anxiety and the concern is unrealistic.

Anxiety and concern *are*...

The monotony of the concrete walls painted in dull green and blue are broken only...

Monotony *is*...

A two-thirds vote by both houses of Congress and ratification by three-quarters of the states is necessary.

Vote and ratification *are*...

NON SEQUITURS   omit

A non sequitur is an error in logic; the phrase means "it does not follow":

A guard at the Allied Kid Co., he died at 7:10 a.m., about five minutes after one of the youths implicated in the attack was taken into custody.

This implies that guards die at 7:10 a.m. Can we infer that workers die at 8:10 and executives at 9:10?

Worn on a chain with swivel and button, this model retails at $39.95.

How much does it cost if I just carry it loose in my pocket?

"Because breath is so vital to life," Burmeister explained, "the field of inhalation therapy and the development of breathing equipment have become increasingly important in medical science today."

It may be true that these things are increasingly important, but not because breath is vital to life. Breath was just as important to life 3,000 years ago as it is today.

Stored in an air-conditioned room in lower Manhattan, the tapes contain information on the reading habits of one million Americans.

The nature of the information on these tapes is not in any way related to the place of their storage or the condition of the air there. An easy way to edit this sentence is to start with the subject: "The tapes, stored in an air-conditioned room in lower Manhattan, contain information...."

Planned by Jones, Blake and Droza, Detroit architects, the new school has 18 classrooms in addition to such standard facilities as cafeteria and library.

This implies that it's a natural thing to expect a school planned by that particular firm to have 18 classrooms and the other features.

Completed three years ago, the plant is 301 feet by 339 feet and is a one-story structure containing. . . .

A plant of exactly that size could have been completed 50 years ago or yesterday.

This particular error crops up most frequently in obituaries:

Unmarried, Jones is survived by his mother, Mrs. . . .

Born in Iowa, he worked on two newspapers in Illinois before coming to St. Louis.

DANGLING MODIFIERS

The dangling modifier is one of the most common errors committed by beginning writers and by all who write in a hurry. The writer knows what is intended but doesn't say it, forcing the reader to rearrange the sentence to grasp its meaning. Some examples:

If convicted of the assault and battery charge, a judge may impose any sentence he sees fit on the defendants.

"If convicted" applies to the defendants, not to the judge.

Besides being cut on the left cheek and bloodied in the nose, Zeck's purse was attached for $825.

Already hospitalized a month, doctors estimate it will be three or four months before he is out again.

An E-shaped building, the fire started in the southwest wing.

A "natural" fertilizer, he predicted that it would solve many problems.

After blowing out the candles atop his birthday cake in three puffs, a movie camera flashed old fight films on the screen near the bar.

The fluoroscopic system makes moving pictures and tape recordings of the mouth and throat while speaking, chewing and swallowing.

Short and readable, I finished it off in about 45 minutes.

MISUSE OF RELATIVE PRONOUNS

No one can say what the most common grammatical errors in news writing are, but near the top must be the misuse of the relative pronoun.

Leon Stolz of the *Chicago Tribune* advised reporters and copy editors, "If you have trouble deciding whether the relative pronoun should be who or whom, you can usually find the right answer by remembering that *who* is nominative, like the personal pronouns *he, she* and *they. Whom* is objective, like *him, her* and *them.* Turn the clause into an independent sentence and substitute a personal pronoun for the relative pronoun."

Applying the Stolz formula:

After his decision to cancel the trip, he sent most of the officials who he had invited to attend.

He invited *they* to attend?

The repeal gives property owners absolute freedom in deciding who they will rent or sell to.

They will rent to *they?*

Miss Barbara Warren, who he met while they were medical students at Passavant Hospital. . . .

He met *she?*

In his last eight games, covering 13⅔ innings, the skinny Texan, who teammates call "Twiggy," has held opponents scoreless.

They call *he* Twiggy?

The paper said two residents of the housing project were known to have been a young man whom they said looked like the description of the sniper.

They said *him* looked like the description of the sniper?

Reporters and copy editors frequently have trouble distinguishing between *that* and *which. That* is preferred when introducing restrictive (essential) clauses that refer to inanimate objects, places, ideas and animals; *which* introduces nonrestrictive (nonessential) clauses, which are nondefining and parenthetical. Two examples:

The river that flows northward through Egypt is the Nile.

The Missouri River, which flows into the Mississippi at St. Louis, is cleaner than it was 10 years ago.

Note that nonrestrictive clauses are set off with commas.

WORD CLUTTER

Clutter words dirty a newspaper, waste space and get in the reader's way. Every day, stories die because strings of clutter words didn't die at the typewriter or on the copy desk.

Reporters should be whacked when they write:

> She was on the operating table from 8 p.m. *Monday night* until 5 a.m. *Tuesday morning.*

Night and *morning* are *redundant* because *p.m.* and *a.m.* mean the same thing.

> For mankind, *the biologists who study genetics* seem to offer . . .

Try *geneticists.*

> He was a Democratic nominee for *U.S.* Congress from the 7th *Congressional* District but lost in the *final* election to *incumbent* Rep. Donald W. Riegle, Jr.

Not everyone can get four redundancies into one sentence.

> He said the USDA is *currently* spending . . .

> Justice said Double Spring had been *in the process of* phasing out its operation. . . .

> Hayley has some 30 *different* (fish) tanks in his home.

> Retired Adm. Jackson R. Tate slipped away to a secret retreat yesterday for his *first meeting* with the daughter *he has never met.* . . .

Compression, a shortcut to ideas, is one of the cardinal virtues of good writing. "The field is 50 feet in length" should be "The field is 50 feet long." "He is said to be resentful" means simply, "He is said to resent."

Pacing is gained by substituting short words for long words and single words for phrases: *big* for *enormous, find* for *discover, approving* for *applying its stamp of approval, Smith's failure* for *the fact that Smith had not succeeded, field work* for *work in the field.*

Compression eliminates the superfluous: "pledged *to secrecy* not to disclose," "wrote a formal letter of resignation' (*resigned*), "read from a *prepared* statement," "go into details" (*elaborate*). A few words may say a lot; a lot of words may say little.

Most experienced copy editors can add to this list of circumlocutions:

A bolt of lightning (lightning)	A period of several weeks (several weeks)
A great number of times (often, frequently)	A small number of (few)
A large number of (many)	A sufficient number of (enough)

Absolute guarantee
(guarantee)
Accidentally stumbled
(stumbled)
Advance planning (planning)
Advance reservations
(reservations)
All of a sudden (suddenly)
As a general rule (usually)
Assessed a fine (fined)
At a later date (later)
At the hour of noon (at noon)
At the present time (now)
At 12 noon (at noon)
At 12 midnight (at midnight)
At the conclusion of (after)
At the corner of 16th and Elm
(at 16th and Elm)

Bald-headed (bald)

Called attention to the fact
(reminded)
Climb up (climb)
Commute back and forth
(commute)
Completely decapitated
(decapitated)
Completely destroyed
(destroyed)
Completely surrounded
(surrounded)
Consensus of opinion
(consensus)
Cost the sum of $5 (cost $5)

Despite the fact that (although)
Disclosed for the first time
(disclosed)
Draw to a close (end)
Due to the fact that (because)
During the winter months
(during the winter)
End result (result)
Entered a bid of (bid)
Exact replica (replica)
Exchanged wedding vows
(married)

Few in number (few)
Filled to capacity (filled)
First priority (priority)
First prototype (prototype)
For a period of 10 days (for 10
days)
Foreign imports (imports)
Free gift (gift)
Free pass (pass)

General public (public)
Grand total (total)

Heat up (heat)
Hostile antagonist (antagonist)

Incumbent governor
(governor)
In addition to (and, besides,
also)
In back of (behind)
In case of (if, concerning)
In order to balance (to
balance)
In the absence of (without)
In the event that (if)
In the immediate vicinity of
(near)
In the near future (soon)
In the not too distant future
(eventually)
Introduced a new (introduced)
Is going to (will)
Is in the process of making
application (is applying)
Is of the opinion that
(believes)

Jewish rabbi (rabbi)

Kept an eye on (watched)

Large-sized man (large man)
Lift up (life)

Made good his escape (escaped)
Major portion of (most of)
Married his wife (married)

Merged together (merged)
Midway between (between)

New bride (bride)
New construction
(construction)
New innovation (innovation)
New record (record)

Off of (off)
Old adage (adage)
Old cliché (cliché)
On account of (because)
On two different occasions
(twice)
Once in a great while (seldom,
rarely)

Partially damaged (damaged)
Partially destroyed (damaged)
Past history (history)
Period of time (period)
Placed its seal of approval on
(approved)
Possibly might (might)
Postponed until later
(postponed)
Prior to (before)
Promoted to the rank of
(promoted to)

Qualified expert (expert)

Receded back (receded)
Recur again (recur)
Reduce down (reduce)
Refer back (refer)
Remand back (remand)

Revise downward (lower)
Rise up (rise)
Rose to the defense of
(defended)

Self-confessed (confessed)
Short space of time (short
time)
Since the time when (since)
Sprung a surprise (surprised)
Started off with (started with)
Strangled to death (strangled)
Summer season (summer)
Sworn affidavits (affidavits)

Tendered his resignation
(resigned)
There is no doubt that
(doubtless)
Total operating costs
(operating costs)
True facts (facts)

Underground subway
(subway)
United in holy matrimony
(married)
Upward adjustment (increase)

Voiced objections (objected)

Went up in flames (burned)
Whether or not (whether)
Widow of the late (widow)
With the exception of (except)

Young juveniles (juveniles)

WRONG WORDS

Good reporters are meticulous in presenting the facts for a story. Others are not so precise in their choice of words. By habit, they write *comprise* when they mean *compose, affect* when they want *effect, credible* for *creditable.* They use *include,* then list all the elements.

Each time a word is misused it loses some of its value as a precision tool. AP reported that "U.S. officials connived with ITT." There was no connivance, which means closing one's eyes to wrongdoing. The precise word would have been "conspired," if, indeed, that is the charge.

Note these examples that got by the copy desk:

> He has been an "intricate part of the general community." . . . (The writer meant *integral,* meaning essential.)

> The two officers are charged with dispersing corporate funds. . . . (The word is *disburse*—to pay out, to expend. *Disperse* means to scatter in various directions; distribute widely.)

> A story indicating that a man might not be qualified for his job says: "Miller refutes all that," and then he says why he is capable. (*Denies* would have been much better.)

> A football pass pattern was referred to as a "flair out." (*Flair* means a natural talent or aptitude. The word is *flare* or expansion outward in shape or configuration.)

> Mrs. Reece, a spritely woman . . . (She may be a sprite—an elf or pixie—but what the writer probably meant was *sprightly*—full of life.)

> His testimony about the night preceding the crime was collaborated, in part, by his mother. . . . (*corroborated,* perhaps?)

> The MSD could be the biggest benefactor in Kentucky under a . . . reimbursement program. (It should be *beneficiary,* one who receives; *benefactor* is the giver.)

Other terms frequently misused:

- Adopted, passed—resolutions are adopted or approved; bills are passed. In legislative jargon, *passed* also can mean passed by for the day or for that meeting.
- Aggravate, irritate—the first means to make worse. The second means to incite or provoke.
- Amateur, novice—an *amateur* is a nonprofessional. A *novice* is a beginner.
- Amount, number—*amount* indicates the general quantity. *Number* indicates an enumerable quantity.
- Avenge, revenge—*avenge* for another. *Revenge* for self.
- Bale, bail—a farmer's hay is *baled;* water is *bailed* out of a boat; a prisoner is released on *bail.* (*Bond* is cash or property given as a security for an appearance or for some performance.)
- Biannual, biennial—the first means twice a year. The second means every two years. The copy editor could help the reader by substituting "every six months" for *biannual* and "every other year" for *biennial.*
- Bills, legislation—"The president announced he will send Congress legislation aimed at liberalizing trade with Eastern Europe." *Legislation* is the law enacted by a legislative power. The president, of course, is not such a power. What he sends to Congress is proposed legislation or bills.
- Canvas, canvass—the first is a cloth. The second means to solicit.

- Celebrant, celebrator—a *celebrant* presides over a religious rite. A *celebrator* celebrates.
- Center around—something can be centered in, centered at or centered on, but it cannot be centered around.
- Collision—"Cars driven by Robert F. Clagett and Mrs. Lois Trant were damaged yesterday when they collided on Denison Avenue. Stonington police reported that Mrs. Trant stopped her car before making a turn into Isham Street and it was hit in the rear by the other vehicle." Two objects can *collide* only when both are in motion and going—usually but not always—in opposite directions. It is not a *collision* when one car is standing still.
- Compared with, compared to—the first uses specific similarities or differences: "He *compared* Johnson with Wilson." The second notes general or metaphorical resemblance: "You might *compare* him to a weasel."
- Comprise, compose—*comprise* is not synonymous with *compose,* but actually almost its opposite. "The secretaries of State, Defense, Interior and other departments compose the cabinet." That is, they constitute it. "The cabinet comprises the secretaries of State, Defense, Interior and other departments." That is, it includes, embraces, contains them.
- Concert, recital—two or more performers give a *concert.* One performer gives a *recital.*
- Continuous, continual—if it rains steadily every day for a week it rains *continuously.* If it rains only part of every day for a week it rains *continually* or intermittently.
- Ecology, environmental—*ecology* is concerned with the interrelationship of organisms and their environment. *Environmental* refers to conditions or forces that influence or modify surroundings.
- Farther, further—the distinction is between extension of space and expansion of thought.
- Flaunt, flout—the first means to wave or flutter showily. The second means to mock or treat with contempt. "The students *flouted* the authority of the school board."
- Flounder, founder—horses *flounder*—struggle, thrash about—in the mud. Ships *founder* or sink. Of course, horses can founder when they become disabled from overeating.
- Grant, subsidy—a *grant* is money given to public companies. A *subsidy* is help to a private enterprise.
- Grizzly, grisly—"Miss Karmel begins her work in a valley of shadows that deepen and darken as she heaps one grizzly happening upon the next." One *grizzly* heaped upon the next produces only two angry bears. The word the writer wants is *grisly.*
- Half-mast, half-staff—masts are on ships. Flagstaffs are mounted on buildings or in the ground.
- Hardy, hearty—a story of four visiting policemen from Africa said they expressed appreciation for their hardy welcome. If that's what they said, they meant *hearty.*
- Hopefully—incorrect for "it is hoped" or "I hope." It really means, "in a hopeful manner."

- Impassable, impossible—the first is that which cannot be passed. The second is that which can't suffer or be made to show signs of emotion.
- Imply, infer—the speaker does the *implying,* and the listener the *inferring.*
- Mean, median—*mean* is the average. If the high is 80 and the low is 50, the mean is 65. *Median* means that half are above a certain point, half below.
- Oral, verbal—all language is *verbal*—"of words." But only *oral* language is spoken.
- People, persons—*person* is the human being. *People* are the body of persons— "American people." There is no rule saying a large number can't be referred to as *people*—"61 million people."
- Sewage, sewerage—*sewage* is human waste, sometimes called municipal or sanitary waste. *Sewerage* is the system to carry away sewage. They are sewerage (not sewage) plants. Industrial waste is the waste from factories. Some cities have storm sewers to carry away rain water and sanitary sewers for sewage.
- Sustenance, subsistence—"The two survived despite little besides melted snow for subsistence." No wonder they almost starved. The word is *sustenance.*
- Tall, high—properly, a building, tree or man is *tall.* A plane, bird or cloud is *high.*

READER-STOPPERS

An ear for language is as important as an eye for grammar. "This doesn't sound right," the copy editor protests after spotting fuzzy passages. Careful reading of copy and careful editing will enable the copy editor to ferret out unclear or nonsensical expressions.

> As explained by one engineer to Reed, one of the reasons for the high cost of repairing the streets is that the space between the concrete and the ground presents problems of pumping liquid concrete between.

We can only hope that Reed understands.

> Gangs of white rowdies roamed the area last night attacking cars bearing blacks with baseball bats, bricks and stones.

Who had the bats?

> Three counties, Meigs, Pike and Vinton, get more than 85 percent from the state. Morgan gets 90.3 percent.

How many counties?

> Many of the 800 executives and clerical people will be transferred, and some probably will be eliminated.

That's rough on people.

> Victims in the other cars were not hurt.

Then why were they victims?

> Monday will be the first day of a new way of delivering an expanded hot-meal program to senior citizens in Genesse County.

Would the "program" or the "meals" be delivered?

> The delegation . . . was welcomed by 20,000 mostly black supporters.

What color was the other part of each supporter?

> Many of the players hovered around 5 feet 2.

They must have looked funny up in the air like that.

> Indignant at being arrested after waiving extradition, Graham lashed out. . . .

Was he indignant because of the facts leading to his extradition, or to his arrest?

> A misplaced time element leads to awkward construction.

> Parents protesting the closing of Briensburg School Monday tried to. . . .

Did they protest Monday only? Was the school closed Monday? Or did they "try to" Monday?

OMISSION

> Dodson told police he had awakened and found his wife missing.

He didn't wake up and find her missing. He woke and found that his wife was missing.

> Robert Lowell, Pulitzer Prize-winning American poet who refused a White House invitation to express his disapproval of American policies, has been nominated. . . .

The writer meant to say Lowell refused the invitation because of his disapproval.

WRONG WORD ORDER

> An insufficient water supply problem for firefighting at Fitch Senior School will be discussed next Thursday.

Try this: 'The problem of insufficient water supply for firefighting at Fitch . . ."

> White segregationists waving Confederate flags and black integrationists marched past each other Tuesday.

Or did white segregationists waving flags march past black integrationists Tuesday?

> Joseph H. Hughes, Jr. of Los Angeles wrote to many of his late son's, Coast Guard Ensign Joseph H. Hughes III, friends.

Translation: "wrote to many friends of his late son. . . ."

CONFUSING ANTECEDENT

> Miss Adele Hudlin agreed to give the dog a home, even though she already had two of her own.

Does she have two homes or two dogs?

> They (the Smiths) have been married 24 years and have two children. Both are 53.

MISUSE OF ADJECTIVES

Informative, rather than merely descriptive, adjectives strengthen nouns: "7-foot Steve Stipanovich" is more effective than "towering Steve Stipanovich."

Many adjectives are redundant, editorial, incorrect or misplaced:

- Redundant—armed gunmen, chilly 30 degrees below zero, exact replica, foreign imports.
- Editorial—blistering reply, cocky labor leader, so-called liberal, strong words.
- Incorrect—"Whirring or grinding television cameras": television cameras are electronic devices and do not whir or grind. "A Pole with an unpronounceable name": every name is pronounceable by somebody. "An unnamed man": every man has a name; the adjective should be *unidentified*.
- Misplaced—"Unfair labor practices strike": the practices, not the strike, are unfair. "The treacherous 26-mile Arkansas down-river race": the river, not the race, is treacherous.

Searching for the right word takes time. Editors urge copy editors to omit an adjective rather than rely on a shoddy one.

CLICHÉS

A good writer uses a fresh and appropriate figure of speech to enhance the story. The copy editor should distinguish between the fresh and the stale. This isn't always easy because some words and phrases are used repeatedly in the news report.

The Associated Press ran almost 400,000 words of its copy through a computer to determine which of the tired words and phrases were used most frequently. The result: *hailed, backlash, in the wake of, informed, violence flared, kickoff, death and destruction, riot-torn, tinder dry, racially troubled, voters marched to the polls, jam-packed, grinding crash, confrontation, oil-rich nation, no immediate comment, cautious (or guarded) optimism, limped into port.*

Copy editors can add to the list of tired expressions:

Acid test
Area girl
Average (reader, voter, etc.)

Banquet (never a dinner)
Belt tightening
Bitter (dispute)
Blistering (accusation)
Bloody riot
Bombshell (announcement, etc.)
Boost
Briefing
Brutal (murder, slaying)

Cardinal sin
Caught the eye of
Controversial issue
Coveted trophy
Crack (troops, etc.)
Cutback

Daring (holdup, etc.)
Deficit-ridden
Devastating (flood, fire)
Devout (Catholic, etc.)
Do your own thing
Dumped

-ees (trainees, escapees)
Experts
Eye (to see)
Eyeball to eyeball

Fiery holocaust
Fire broke out, swept
Fire of undetermined origin
Foot the bill
Freak accident

Gap (generation, credibility, etc.)

Hammer out
Hard-core, hard-nosed
Hike (for *raise*)
Historical document
Hobbled by injury
Hosted
Hurled

Identity crisis
Initial (for *first*)
In terms of
-ize (finalize, formalize)

Junket

Keeled over

Led to safety
Luxurious (apartment, love nest, etc.)
Made off with
Miraculous (cure, escape, etc.)
Momentous occasion

Name of the game

Opt for
Overwhelming majority

Passing motorist
Plush (hotel, apartment, etc.)
Police were summoned
Pressure (as a verb)
Probe

Relocate (for *move*)
Reportedly, reputedly

Seasoned (observers, etc.)
Senseless murder
Shot in the arm
Staged a riot (or protest)
Standing ovation
Stems from
Stinging rebuke
Sweeping changes
Swing into high gear

Task force
Tense (or uneasy) calm
Terminate (for *end*)
Thorough (or all-out)
    investigation
Timely hit
Top-level meeting
Tragic accident
Turn thumbs down

Uneasy truce
Unveiled
Upcoming

Vast expanse
Verbalize
Violence erupted
Violent explosion

Whirlwind (tour, junket)

Young boys

KNOW THE IDIOM

Careless use of the idiom (the grammatical structure peculiar to our language) occurs frequently in the news report. Usually the fault lies in the prepositions or conjunctions.

Three times as many Americans were killed than [*as*] in any similar period.

It remains uncertain as to when the deadline for the first payment will be. (Omit *as to.*)

She had always been able to get through the performance on [*of*] this taxing role.

The economist accused him with [*of*] failing to make a decision. (You charge somebody with blundering, but you accuse him of it.)

He said the guns are against the law except under [*in*] certain specified situations. (But *under* conditions or circumstances.)

Dressen is no different than [*from*] other experts. (*Different* may be followed by *than* when introducing a clause: "The patient is no different than he was yesterday.")

Five men were pelted by [*with*] stones.

The reason for the new name is because the college's mission has been changed. (*Is that* the college's mission has been changed.)

He said he would not call on [*for*] assistance from police except as a last resort. (Call the police or call on the police for assistance.)

But at other times the fault lies in entire phrases which must be used verbatim to be idiomatic:

These men and women could care less about Bush's legislative magic. (The correct phrase is "couldn't care less.")

Gerunds, but not present participles acting as adjectives, require the possessive:

It was the first instance of a city [*city's*] losing its funds.

He said he didn't know anything about Hollenbach [*Hollenbach's*] interceding in his behalf.

An example of a present participle used in a similar context is

I do not like the man standing on the corner.

The possessive is not required because *standing on the corner* is used to identify *man*.

JARGON

A university press release announcing a significant engineering meeting on the campus reported that one of the major papers would be on "the aerodynamic heating of blunt, axisymmetric, re-entry bodies with laminar boundary layer at zero and at large angles of yaw in supersonic and hypersonic air streams." To the consumer of news, that title is *gobbledygook*. Translated, the topic is "how hot a space ship gets when it swings back into the air around the earth."

Doctors, lawyers, educators, engineers, government officials, scientists, sociologists, economists and others have their professional jargon or shoptalk peculiar to the profession. Sometimes this jargon is used to impress the uninitiated; sometimes it is a cover-up.

A judge's ruling on a case involving an actress contained this sentence: "Such vanity doubtless is due to the adulation which the public showers on the denizens of the entertainment world in a profusion wholly disproportionate to the intrinsic contribution which they make to the scheme of things." That's pretentious verbosity. So, too, is this from an educator:

The educator will hold a practicum for disadvantaged children who are under-achieving in reading.

Try "Slow learners who can't read."

Translation is needed when a story on education contains "professional terms" such as *paraprofessionals, academically talented, disadvantaged* (culturally deprived, impoverished students) and *ungraded* and *nongraded classrooms.*

In a special study of state wire reporting, the Associated Press found that unintelligible jargon appeared in legislature stories (*resolves, engrossment, tucked in committee*), in alphabet-soup references to agencies and organizations (SGA, the UCA, CRS, LTA and MMA), in Weather Service forecasts and in market reports. AP then noted, "Neither weather reports nor markets are sacrosanct to editorial pencils."

The copy editor can help the reader by substituting simple words for technical terms and by killing on sight words like *implement* and the *-ize* words.

Here are translations of some technical terms that frequently appear in the news report:

TERM	TRANSLATION
Motivated or motivationed	Moved
Object	Aim
Mentality	Mind
Percentage	Part
Assignment	Task or job
Astronomical	Big

Some common euphemisms:

TERM	TRANSLATION
Container	Can
Continental breakfast	Juice, roll and coffee
Dialogue, conversation	Talk, discussion
Planned parenthood	Birth control
Revised upward	Raised
Withdrawal	Retreat

SLANG

Many editors will agree with this advice from the Associated Press: "Use of slang should be a rarity in the news report." Some editors might even dream that use of slang can be reduced in sports stories, in the signed columns, in comic strips and in ads.

Slang in direct quotations helps reveal the speaker's personality. The reader expects the gangster to use terms of the underworld. He does not expect the reporter to resort to slang such as "The Brinton household is a go-go preparing... for guests."

Some slang words should be avoided because they are offensive ("cops" for *policemen,* "gobs" for *sailors,* "wops" for *Italians*): others are avoided because they reveal a writer's carelessness ("got clobbered" for *was defeated*).

A few examples from a wire service show how a copy editor can overcome the slang:

> "The Supreme Court ruled today that a lower court goofed." What's wrong with the proper word *erred?*

> A Los Angeles story spoke of a couple's getting "a few belts in one of the local bars." What's wrong with *drinks* if that's what they got?

> A Washington reporter wrote that "well-heeled admirers of the senator have shelled out $7,000." We suppose that *well-heeled* means wealthy and that *shelled out* means contributed.

PARALLELISM

Similar ideas or elements in a sentence should be phrased in a similar structural or grammatical form. You would say, "I like gardening, fishing and hunting," not "I like gardening, fishing and to hunt." In the following, the word *requiring* makes a nonparallel construction: "Instead of requiring expensive cobalt drill bits, disposable brass pins are used."

Comparisons should compare similar things. Here is a sentence that compares an apple (the increase) with a pumpkin (the sales): "Consolidated sales of Cottontex Corp. for the first six months of this year were $490 million, an increase of $27 million compared with the first half of last year." Use "an increase of $27 million over the previous year's first half." "The soldier was ragged, unshaven, yet walked with a proud step." Make it read, "The soldier was ragged and unshaven, yet walked with a proud step."

MIXED METAPHORS

> Legislative Hall here was swarming with lobbyists as the second session of the 121st General Assembly got under way Monday.
>
> With lawmakers treading water while awaiting Gov. Elbert N. Carvel's state and budget messages, due Wednesday, lobbyists had a field day.

In two paragraphs the story pictured Legislative Hall as a beehive, a swimming pool and an athletic field.

> Breaking domestic ties with gold would make the nation's gold stock a real barometer of international fever for gold.

Do you shove that barometer under your tongue or what?

> They hope to unravel a sticky turn of events that was further complicated recently.

Did you ever try to unravel glue, molasses, maple syrup or other similar strings or yarns?

MOCK RURALISMS

Here is some advice from Leon Stolz of the *Chicago Tribune:* "If you hold your quota to one mock ruralism a century, your readers will not feel deprived." Expressions such as "seeing as how" or "allowed as how" are supposed to give a folksy touch. They don't. They merely make the writer sound stupid.

FOREIGN WORDS

When copy editors come across foreign expressions in the news report they should be sure of the spelling, the use and the translation. Unless it is a commonly known expression, the copy editor provides the translation if the reporter has not done so. The number in Latin words can cause trouble. For instance, *data* is plural and *datum* is singular. But *datum* is rarely used and *data* can be either singular (as a synonym for information) or plural (as a synonym for facts). *Trivia* is always plural; *bona fides* is always singular. *Media, criteria, insignia* and *phenomena* are plural.

A foreign expression has its place in the report if it supplies a real need or flavor or has no precise native substitute (*blasé, chic, simpatico*).

Copy editors frequently are confronted with problems of translation, not as a rule directly from a foreign language but from a foreign correspondent's translation. Translations made abroad are often hurried; many are the work of men and women more at home in another language than in English. The translations may be accurate but not idiomatic. Some examples:

An AP dispatch telling of a factory explosion in Germany read, "Most of the victims were buried when the roof of a large factory hall came down following the explosion. . . . The blast . . . damaged five other halls. . . . " What is a factory hall? The copy editor would have saved readers a puzzled moment if the dispatch had been changed to read, "Most of the victims were buried when the factory roof fell on them. The blast . . . damaged five other sections of the plant."

CHAPTER 6

STYLE AND MORE

Newspapers adhere to rules of style to avoid inconsistencies that would annoy the reader. The writing in newspapers, like the writing in good books, must be clear, concise and free of irritating inconsistencies. Adherence to style rules gives the newspaper a sense of consistency that would be absent if *goodbye* were used in one story and *goodby* in the next. Style books provide guidance in spelling, word usage, punctuation, titles and many other areas.

Most newspapers follow style rules developed jointly by the Associated Press and United Press International (see Appendix I). Each agency issues its own stylebook, but almost all rules are consistent as a service to those who subscribe to both. Newspapers have embraced these rules as their own, although most have exceptions. A few papers, primarily small dailies and weeklies, follow no stylebook at all.

Style rules should not be confused with individual writing styles; the two in no way conflict. Individual writing styles can and should be developed within the constraints of style rules.

The AP and UPI stylebooks are voluminous, and few have the ability to memorize their content. But it helps to learn as much of their content as possible to minimize time spent referring to them. The best way to learn the rules of style is to study Appendix I. This chapter is designed to supplement that material.

IDENTIFICATIONS

Shakespeare knew the value of a name. In *Othello* he had Iago say, "But he that filches from me my good name / Robs me of that which not enriches him / And makes me poor indeed." A name misspelled is a person misidentified. Of all the errors a newspaper is capable of making, one of the most serious is a misspelled or a misused name. In radio and television it is the mispronounced name.

One of the important roles of the copy editor is to make sure that all names in the copy are double-checked. The proper form is the form the person uses. It may be Alex rather than Alexander, Jim rather than James, Carin rather than Karen. The individual may or may not have a middle initial, with or without a period. Former President Harry S. Truman had no middle name. Some newspapers once used his middle initial without a period, but most now include it. Truman expressed indifference to the issue. Men's first names are seldom used alone, except in sports copy. The same should be true for first names of women.

Anyone resents an attempt at cleverness when a name is involved. Such "cuteness" should be felled on sight:

> Orange County will have a lemon as district attorney. Jack Lemon was elected to the job Tuesday.
>
> Of the five patrolmen on the staff, two are crooks.

The last name was Crook.

A short title generally precedes a name, but a long title follows. It is Harley F. Taylor, principal of Philip C. Showell School, rather than Philip C. Showell School Principal Harley F. Taylor.

Nor should the story make the reader guess at the identification. Here is an example:

> Albert A. Ballew took issue with Mayor Locher today for announcing in advance that the post of administrative assistant in the Safety Department will be filled by a black.
>
> The president of the Collinwood Improvement Council commended the mayor for creating the post, but added. . . .

Now then, who is the president of the Collinwood Improvement Council? Will readers assume it is Ballew? The solution is simple: "Ballew, president of the Collinwood Improvement Council, commended the mayor. . . . "

In recent years newspaper editors have grappled with the difficult problem of whether to abandon use of the courtesy titles traditionally given to women. Most newspapers use the last name only to refer to men on second reference but use the courtesy titles *Miss, Mrs.* or *Ms.* on second reference to women. Feminists and others argue that men and women should be treated equally in news columns and insist that newspapers abandon this practice. For editors caught in the middle of this debate, it is a no-win situation. If they continue to use courtesy titles, feminists and others protest. If they drop courtesy titles, older people, in particular, are offended. Many elderly women prefer to be called *Miss* or *Mrs.* followed by a family name. They consider it demeaning to be called by the last name only. The number of people who object to this practice is not large, however, so many editors have decided to drop courtesy titles altogether. A few newspapers, including the *Kansas City Star,* have done the opposite by using courtesy titles for men as well as women.

It is unlikely that courtesy titles will disappear altogether. In a story about a married couple, it is useful to distinguish between the two on second and subsequent references by using, for example, *Mr. Rodriguez* and *Mrs. Rodriguez.* Using first or given names would be cumbersome and in some cases may give the reader the impression that the reporter is "talking down" to the couple. Some newspapers also use courtesy titles in obituaries and editorials.

Newspaper style may dictate that titles belonging to certain positions be non-sexist (*chairperson* for *chairman*), but even this rule could lead to the absurd (*personkind* for *mankind*). The AP stylebook disallows these forms unless they are formal titles.

Editors can be fair to both sexes by eliminating purely sexist adjectives and by using plural pronouns when possible.

Newspaper style calls for females to be called girls until they are 18 and women thereafter. Males are boys until they are 18 and men thereafter. Appropriateness should determine whether males and females 18 and older or even those under 18 should be referred to by the familiar given name.

A married woman's original name can cause trouble: "He married the former Constance Coleman in 1931." This is incorrect; Constance Coleman was Constance Coleman when he married her. He married Constance Coleman. His wife is the former Constance Coleman.

Woman is used as a general descriptive possessive—woman's rights. *Women's* is used as a specific—women's club (but Woman's Christian Temperance Union). It is women fliers, Young Women's Christian Association, women workers, but woman suffrage. It is never *the Smith woman.*

Foreign names are tricky. In Spanish-speaking countries, individuals usually have two last names, the father's and the mother's—Adolfo Lopez Mateos. On second reference, Mateos should be used.

Newspapers have adopted the official Chinese spelling known as Pinyin. Thus, *Foochow* becomes *Fuzhou.* Familiar names of places and people, including Peking and Mao Tse-tung, still take the familiar American spelling.

In Arabic names, *al* generally is hyphenated—al-Sabah, al-Azhar. Some Arabs drop the article—Mamoun Kuzbari, not al-Kuzbari, but it should be used if the individual prefers. Compound names should be left intact—Abdullah, Abdel, Abdur. Pasha and Bey titles have been abolished. Royal titles are used with first names—Emir Faisel, Sheik Abdullah. *Haj* is used with the first name in both first and subsequent references—Haj Amin al-Hussein, Haj Amin.

The *U* in Burmese names means uncle, our equivalent of *Mr.*, or master. *Daw* means *Mrs.* or *Miss.* Many Burmese have only one name—*U Thant.* If a Burmese has two names, both should be used—*U Tin Maung, Tin Maung.*

Some Koreans put the family name first—*Park Chung Hee.* The second reference should be *Park,* not *Chung Hee,* the given name.

Many Indonesians have only one name—*Sukarno,* not *Achmed Sukarno.*

Swedish surnames usually end in *-son,* and Danish names usually end in *-sen.*

TRADE NAMES

Few editors have escaped letters that begin something like this: "Dear Sir: The attached clipping from your paper of July 14th contains a mention of our product and we very much appreciate this unsolicited publicity. However, the name of our product was used with a lowercase 'c.' As you know. . . . "

Makers of trade-name products want to protect their rights under the Lanham Trademark Act of 1947 and insist that in any reference to the product name the manufacturer's spelling and capitalization be used. This is to protect the trade name from becoming generic, as happened to aspirin, cellophane, escalator, milk of magnesia, zipper, linoleum and shredded wheat.

Much of the confusion and protest can be eliminated simply by using a generic term rather than the specific trade name—*petroleum jelly* for *Vaseline, freezer* for *Deepfreeze, fiberglass* for *Fiberglas, artificial grass* for *Astroturf.*

When the product is trade-named and there is no substitute, the trade name should be used, especially if it is pertinent to the story. Withholding such information on the ground of free publicity is a disservice to readers.

Institutions should be labeled correctly—Lloyd's, not Lloyd's of London; J.C. Penney Co. (Penneys in ads, Penney's in other usages); American Geographical Society; National Geographic Society.

RELIGION

Jewish congregations should be identified in news stories as Orthodox, Conservative or Reform. To help readers, the copy editor should insert "branch of Judaism" or whatever other phrase might be necessary to convey the proper meaning.

The terminology of the congregation concerned should be followed in naming the place of worship as a temple or a synagogue. Most Orthodox congregations use *synagogue.* Reform groups use *temple* and Conservative congregations use one word or the other, but *synagogue* is preferred. The generic term is "Jewish houses of worship." It is never *church,* which applies to Christian bodies.

Sect has a derogatory connotation. Generally it means a church group espousing Christianity without the traditional liturgical forms. *Religion* is an all-inclusive word for Judaism, Islam, Christianity and others. *Faith* generally is associated with Protestants. *Denomination* should be used only when referring to the church bodies within the Protestant community.

Religious labels can be misleading. *Jews* and *Judaism* are general terms. *Israelis* are nationals of the state of Israel, and *Jews* are those who profess Judaism. The state of Israel is not the center of or the spokesman for Judaism. Some Jews are Zionists; some are not.

Not all denominations use *Church* in the organization's title. It is the First Baptist Church but the American Baptist Convention. It is the Church of Jesus Christ of Latter-day Saints (but Mormon Church is acceptable); its units are missions, stakes and wards. It is the Episcopal Church, not the Episcopalian Church. Its members are Episcopalians, but the adjective is *Episcopal:* Episcopal clergymen.

Mass may be *celebrated, said* or *sung.* The rosary is *recited* or *said.* The copy editor can avoid confusion by making the statement read something like this: "The mass (or rosary) will be at 7 p.m." The Benediction of the Blessed Sacrament is neither *held* nor *given*; services close with it.

The order of the Ten Commandments varies depending on the version of the Bible used. Confusion can be spared if the commandment number is omitted. Also to be deleted are references to the burning of a church mortgage unless there actually is a burning ceremony. It is an elegant but ridiculous way of saying the mortgage has been paid off.

The usual style in identifying ministers is *the Rev.*, followed by the individual's full name on first reference and only the surname on second reference. If the minister has a doctorate, the style is *the Rev. Dr.*, or simply *Dr.* on subsequent references. *Reverend* should not be used alone, nor should plural forms be used, such as the Revs. John Jones and Richard Smith. Churches of Christ do not use the term *reverend* in reference to ministers. They are called *brothers.*

Rabbis take *Rabbi* for a title.

Priests who are rectors, heads of religious houses or presidents of institutions and provinces of religious orders take *Very Rev.* and are addressed as *Father.* Priests who have doctorates in divinity or philosophy are identified as *the Rev. Dr.* and are addressed either as *Dr.* or *Father.* For further guidance, consult the stylebook, which contains rules pertinent to usages in all religions.

The words *Catholic* and *parochial* are not synonymous. There are parochial schools that are not Catholic. The writer should not assume that a person is a Roman Catholic simply because he is a priest or a bishop. Other religions also have priests and bishops.

Not all old churches merit the designation of *shrine.* Some are just old churches. *Shrine* denotes some special distinction, historic or ecclesiastical. Usually, shrines are structures or places that are hallowed by their association with events or persons of religious or historic significance, such as Lourdos or Mt. Vernon.

Use *nun* when appropriate for women in religious orders. The title *sister* is confusing except with the person's name (Sister Mary Edward).

DEATH STORIES

People die of heart *illness,* not "failure"; after a *long* illness, not an "extended" illness; *unexpectedly,* not "suddenly"; *outright,* not "instantly"; *following* or *after* an operation, not "as a result of" an operation; *apparently of a heart attack,* not "of an apparent heart attack." A person *dies of* a disease, not "from" a disease.

The age of the person who died is important to the reader. The copy editor should check the age given with the year of birth. Generally, the person's profession or occupation, the extent of the illness and the cause of death are recorded, but without details. The length of the story is dictated by the fame of the person. Winston Churchill's obit ran 18 pages in *The New York Times.*

A person *leaves* an estate; that person is *survived* by a family. A man is survived by his *wife,* not his widow. A woman is survived by her *husband,* not her widower. A man or woman is survived by children if they are children and by sons and daughters if they are adults.

If the family requests that the story include the statement that memorial donations may be made to a particular organization, the statement should be used. Whether such a statement should contain the phrase "in lieu of flowers" is a matter of policy. A few papers, in deference to florists, do not carry the phrase, but that practice is widely discredited as currying favor with advertisers.

A straightforward account of a death is better than a euphemistic one. The plain terms are *died,* not "passed away" or "succumbed"; *body,* not "remains" or "corpse"; *coffin,* not "casket"; *funeral* or *services,* not "obsequies"; *burial,* not "interment," unless interred in a tomb above the ground. Flowery expressions such as "two of whom reside in St. Louis" and "became associated with the company shortly after college" show no more respect for the dead than do the plain expressions "live in St. Louis" or "went to work for the company."

Few stories in a newspaper are more likely to be written by formula than the obituary. There isn't much the desk can do about the conventional style except to contrast it with those that take a fresh approach. Here is a lead from an Associated Press story:

NEW YORK (AP)—If you are a movie fan, you will remember Mary Boland as the fluttery matron, the foolishly fond mother, the ladylike scatterbrain.

The character actress who died Thursday at 80 was none of these in real life.

The copy editor should be on guard for the correct spelling of all names used in the death story and for slips such as "cemetary" for *cemetery* and "creamation" for *cremation.* Errors are inexcusable:

A postmorten failed to disclose the cause of death because the girl's body was too badly decomposed.

The correct spelling is *post-mortem,* or, preferably, use *autopsy.*

Thousands followed the cortege.

The thousands must have been *in,* not "following," the cortege (the funeral procession). Even after death, a medal won by a serviceman is awarded to him. It may be *presented* to his widow, but it is not *awarded* to his widow.

If the service is at a mortuary, the name of the mortuary should be included for the convenience of mourners. A funeral service is *at* a place, not *from* it. A funeral mass usually is *offered;* a funeral service is *held.* Even so, *held* often is redundant: "The service will be at 2 p.m. Thursday...."

The passage should leave no doubt for whom the service was held. This one did: "Services for 7-year-old Michael L—, son of a Genoa Intermediate School District official who was struck and killed by a car Monday in Bay City, will be held...."

People are *people,* not "assaults" or "traffic deaths" or "fatals" or "dead on arrivals":

A youth stabbed at a downtown intersection and a woman pedestrian run down by a car were among assaults on six persons reported to police during the night.

Hugo man among nine traffic deaths

Dead on arrival at Hurley after the crash was Oscar W . . .

The events in a person's life that should be included in the obituary pose a problem for the desk. One story told of a former school administrator who died at 87. It said he had been the first principal of a high school and had served in that capacity for 17 years. Then the story noted that he resigned two months before he was found guilty of taking $150 from the school yearbook fund and was fined $500. Should an account of a minor crime committed a quarter century ago be included in the obituary? To those who knew the former principal intimately, the old theft was not news. Those who didn't know him personally probably would not care about the single flaw in an otherwise distinguished career. Sometimes, however, it is necessary to include unsavory details in obituaries. Good editors do not hesitate to do so.

MEDICAL NEWS

Reporters and copy editors have no business playing doctor. If a child is injured in an accident, the seriousness of the injury should be determined by medical authorities. To say that a person who was not even admitted to the hospital was "seriously injured" is editorializing.

Hospitals may report that a patient is in a "guarded condition," but the term has no meaning for the reader and should be deleted. The same goes for "he is resting comfortably."

One may not sustain a "fractured leg," which seldom causes death, but one may sustain a heart attack. A person may suffer a *fracture of the leg* or a *leg fracture* or, better still, simply a *broken leg*. Injuries are *suffered* or *sustained*, not *received*.

A story described a murder suspect as "a diabetic of the worst type who must have 15 units of insulin daily." The quotes were attributed to the FBI. An editor commented, "In my book, that is a mild diabetic, unless the story means that the suspect is a diabetic who requires 15 units of regular insulin before each meal. A wire service should not rely on the FBI for diagnosis of diabetes and the severity of the case."

Doctor and *scientist* are vague words to many readers. *Doctor* may be a medical doctor, a dentist, a veterinarian, an osteopath, a minister or a professor. The story would be clearer if it named the doctor's specialty or the scientist's specific activity, whether biology, physics, electronics or astronautics.

Medical doctors diagnose the *illness*, not the patient. The proper term to use in determining the remedy or in forecasting the probable course and termination of a disease is *prognosis*.

Mothers are *delivered*; babies are *born*.

Everyone has a temperature. *Fever* describes above-normal temperature.

Everyone has a heart condition. It is news only if someone's heart is in bad condition.

"The wife of the governor underwent major surgery, and physicians reported she apparently had been cured of a malignant tumor." It is unlikely that any doctor said she was *cured* of a malignant tumor. They avoid that word with malignant growths.

"A team of five surgeons performed a hysterectomy, appendectomy and complete abdominal exploration." Why the unnecessary details? It would have been enough to say, "Five surgeons performed the abdominal operation."

Unless they are essential to the story, trade names of narcotics or poisons should be avoided. If a person dies of an overdose of sleeping pills, the story should not specify the number of pills taken.

Also, use *Caesarean section* or *Caesarean operation*.

Usually, no sane person has a leg broken. Use the passive voice: "Her leg was broken."

Use the expression *physicians and dentists,* not *doctors and dentists.* The second suggests that dentists are not doctors.

A doctor who specializes in anesthesia is an anesthesiologist, not an anesthetist.

A person may wear a sling on his or her right arm. That person doesn't wear his or her right arm in a sling.

"He suffered a severed tendon in his right Achilles' heel last winter." It was the Achilles' tendon in his right heel or his right Achilles' tendon.

"A jaundice epidemic also was spreading in Gaya, Indiana health officials said. The disease claimed 30 lives." Jaundice is not a disease but a sign of the existence of one or another of a great many diseases.

Technical terms should be translated:

TERM	TRANSLATION	TERM	TRANSLATION
Abrasion	Scrape	Suturing	Sewing
Contusion	Bruise	Hemorrhaging	Bleeding
Lacerations	Cuts	Obese	Overweight
Fracture	Break	Respire	Breathe

WEATHER

An editor said, "Ever since the National Weather Service started naming hurricanes after females, reporters can't resist the temptation to be cute." He then cited as an example the lead, "Hilda—never a lady and now no longer a hurricane—spent the weekend in Louisiana, leaving behind death, destruction and misery." That, the editor said, is giddy treatment for a disaster causing 35 deaths and millions of dollars in property damage. The potential for passages in poor taste is not lessened by the fact that men's names are now used for hurricanes, too.

Another editor noted that a story referred to "the turbulent eye of the giant storm." Later in the story the reporter wrote that the eye of the hurricane is the dead-calm center.

A story predicted that a hurricane was headed for Farmington and was expected to cause millions of dollars in damage. So the Farmington merchants boarded their windows, the tourists canceled their reservations, and the hurricane went around Farmington. This is the trouble when an editor lets a reporter expand a prediction into a warning.

The headline **Freeze tonight expected to make driving hazardous** was based on this lead: "Freezing temperatures forecast for tonight may lead to a continuation of hazardous driving conditions as a result of Monday night's snow and freezing rain." The story did not mention that there would still be dampness on the ground when freezing temperatures arrived. There wasn't, and driving was unimpeded.

A lead said, "One word, 'miserable,' was the National Weather Service's description today of the first day of spring." The head was **Snow predicted; it's spring, miserable.** It was the weatherman's prediction, not his description. The sun stayed out all day, the clouds stayed away, and readers of the paper must have wondered where this forecaster was located.

Temperatures can become *higher* or *lower,* not "cooler" or "warmer."

In flood stories, the copy should tell where the flood water came from and where it will run off. The expression *flash flood* is either a special term for a rush of water let down a weir to permit passage of a boat or a sudden destructive rush of water down a narrow gully or over a sloping surface in desert regions, caused by heavy rains in the mountains or foothills. It is often used loosely for any sudden gush of water.

Weather stories, more than most others, have an affinity for the cliché, the fuzzy image, overwriting, mixed metaphors, contrived similes and other absurdities.

"A Houdini snow did some tricks Thursday that left most of the state shivering from a spine-tingling storm." Houdini gained fame as an escape artist, not as an ordinary magician. Did the snow escape, or was it just a tricky snow? After the lead, the 22-inch story never mentioned the angle again. *Spine-tingling* means full of suspense or uncertainty or even terror. Sports writers are fond of using it to describe a close game, called a *heart stopper* by more ecstatic writers, often in conjunction with a *gutsy performance.* If a cliché must be used, a very cold storm is *spine-chilling,* not "spine-tingling."

"Old Man Winter Wednesday stretched his icy fingers and dumped a blanket of snow on the state." How would reporters ever write about the weather without Old Man Winter, Jack Frost, Icy Fingers and Old Sol? Why do rain and snow never *fall?* They are always "dumped."

"At least two persons were killed in Thursday's snowstorm, marked at times by blizzard-like gales of wind." By Weather Service standards, this is an exaggeration and a contradiction. By any standard, it is a redundancy. A blizzard is one thing. Gales are something else. Gales of wind? What else, unless maybe it was gales of laughter from discerning readers.

An editor's moral: Good colorful writing is to be encouraged. But a simply written story with no gimmicks is better than circus writing that goes awry. To quote a champion image-maker, Shakespeare, in Sonnet 94, "Lilies that fester smell far worse than weeds."

Blizzards are hard to define because wind and temperatures may vary. The safe way is to avoid calling a snowstorm a *blizzard* unless the Weather Service describes it as such. Generally, a blizzard occurs when there are winds of 35 mph or more that whip falling snow or snow already on the ground and when temperatures are 20 degrees above zero Fahrenheit, or lower.

A severe blizzard has winds that are 45 mph or more, temperatures 10 degrees above zero or lower and great density of snow either falling or whipped from the ground.

The Weather Service insists that ice storms are not sleet. Sleet is frozen raindrops. The service uses the terms *ice storm, freezing rain* and *freezing drizzle* to warn the public when a coating of ice is expected on the ground.

A *cyclone* is a storm or system of winds rotating about a moving center of low atmospheric pressure. It is often accompanied by heavy rain and winds.

A *hurricane* has winds above 74 mph.

A *typhoon* is a violent cyclonic storm or hurricane occurring in the China Seas and adjacent regions, chiefly from July to October.

Here is a handy table for referring to wind conditions:

Light	up to 7 mph	Strong	25 to 38 mph
Gentle	8 to 12 mph	Gale	39 to 54 mph
Moderate	13 to 18 mph	Whole gale	55 to 75 mph
Fresh	19 to 24 mph		

The word *chinook* should not be used unless so designated by the Weather Service.

Temperatures are measured by various scales. Zero degrees Celsius is freezing, and 100 degrees Celsius is boiling. Celsius is preferred over the older term *centigrade*. On the Fahrenheit scale, 32 degrees is freezing, and 212 degrees (at sea level) is boiling. On the Kelvin scale, 273 degrees is freezing, and 373 degrees is boiling. To convert degrees Celsius to Fahrenheit, multiply the Celsius measurement by nine-fifths and add 32. To convert degrees Fahrenheit to Celsius, subtract 32 from the Fahrenheit measurement and multiply by five-ninths. Thus, 10 degrees Celsius is 50 degrees Fahrenheit. To convert degrees Kelvin to Celsius degrees, subtract 273 from the Kelvin reading. (Kelvin is used for scientific purposes, not for weather reporting.)

Avoid these weather clichés:

Fog rolled (crept or crawled) in	Mercury dropped (dipped,
Fog-shrouded city	zoomed, plummeted)
Winds aloft	Rain failed to dampen

Biting (bitter) cold   Hurricane howled
Hail-splattered   Storm-tossed

DISASTER

Conjecturing about possible damage to settlements from forest fires is as needless as conjectures on weather damage. The story should concentrate on the definite loss. Stories of forest fires should define the specific area burned, the area threatened and the type of timber. Be wary of death estimates because officials tend to overstate during the initial shock of the event.

Most stories of earthquakes attempt to describe the magnitude of the tremor. One measurement is the Richter scale, which shows relative magnitude. It starts with magnitude 1 and progresses in units with each unit 10 times stronger than the previous one. Thus, magnitude 3 is 10 times stronger than magnitude 2, which in turn is 10 times stronger than magnitude 1. On this scale the strongest earthquakes recorded were the South American earthquake of 1906 and the Japanese earthquake of 1933, both at a magnitude of 8.9. Intensity generally refers to the duration or to the damage caused by the shock.

In train and plane crashes the story should include train or flight number, the place of departure, the destination and times of departure and expected arrival. Airplanes may collide on the ground or in the air (not "midair"). Let investigators *search* the wreckage, not "comb" or "sift" it.

In fire stories, the truth is that in nine of 10 cases when people are "led to safety," they're not. Except for an occasional child or infirm adult, they simply have the common sense to leave the building without waiting for a firefighter to "lead them to safety."

In both fire and flood stories the residents of the area are rarely taken from their homes or asked to leave. Instead, they're always told to "evacuate" or they're "evacuated." What's wrong with *vacate?*

Eliminate terms such as *three-alarm fire* and *second-degree burns* unless they are explained.

"An estimated $40,000 worth of damage was done Jan. 29. . . . " Damage isn't worth anything. Quite the contrary.

"The full tragedy of Hurricane Betsy unfolded today as the death toll rose past 50, and damages soared into many millions." *Damage* was the correct word here. You collect *damages* in court.

Avoid these disaster clichés:

Rampaging rivers   Tinder-dry forest
Weary firefighters   Raging brush fire
Fiery holocaust   Traffic fatals or triple fatals
Flames licked (leaped, swept)   (police station jargon)
Searing heat

LABOR DISPUTES

Stories of labor controversies should give the reasons for the dispute, the length of time the strike has been in progress and the claims by both the union and the company.

Copy editors should be on guard against wrong or loaded terms. Examples: In a *closed shop* the employer may hire only those who are members of the union. In a *union shop,* the employer may select employees, but the workers are required to join the union within a specified time after starting work. A *conciliator* or *mediator* in a labor dispute merely recommends terms of a settlement. The decision of an *arbitrator* usually is binding. There is a tendency in labor stories to refer to management proposals as "offers" and to labor proposals as "demands." The correct word should be used for the correct connotation.

Strikebreaker and *scab,* which are loaded terms, have no place in the news if used to describe men or women who individually accept positions vacated by strikers. The expression "honored the picket line" frequently appears in the news even though a more accurate expression is "refused (or declined) to cross a picket line."

Union leader is usually preferred to *labor leader.* A *longshoreman* is a waterfront leader. A *stevedore* usually is considered an employee.

On estimates of wages or production lost, the story should have authoritative sources, not street-corner guesses. An individual, however voluble, does not speak for the majority unless authorized to do so. Statements by workers or minor officials should be downplayed until they have been documented.

If a worker gets a 10-cent-an-hour increase effective immediately, an additional 10 cents a year hence and another 10 cents the third year, that worker does not receive a 30-cent-an-hour increase. The increase at the time of settlement is still 10 cents an hour. It also is common to read, "The company has been on strike for the last 25 days." No. The employees are on strike. The company has been struck.

Criminal court terms should not be applied to labor findings unless the dispute has been taken to a criminal court. The National Labor Relations Board is not a court, and its findings or recommendations should not be expressed in criminal court terminology. In most settlements, neither side is "found guilty" or "fined." A finding or a determination may be made, or a penalty may be assessed.

FINANCIAL NEWS

A news release from a bank included the following: "The book value of each share outstanding will approximate $21.87 on Dec. 31, and if the current yield of 4.27 percent continues to bear the same relationship to the market price it should rise to $32 or $33, according to . . . " The copy editor changed the ambiguous *it* to *the book value.* Actually, the release intended *it* to refer to the market price, which shows what can happen when copy editors change copy without knowing what they are doing.

Another story quoted an oil company official as saying that "the refinery would produce $7 million in additional real estate taxes." It should have been obvious that this was a wholly unrealistic figure, but for good measure there was an ad in the same paper that placed the total tax figure at about $200,000 and read, "The initial installation will add about $7 million a year to the economy of the state, not including taxes."

A story and headline said the interest on the state debt accounted for 21 percent of the state government's spending. An accompanying graph showed, however, that the figure was for debt service, which includes both interest and amortization, or payments on principal.

All who edit copy for financial pages should have at least elementary knowledge of business terms. If they can't distinguish between a balance sheet and a profit-and-loss statement, between earnings and gross operating income, and between a net profit and net cash income, they have some homework to do.

This reality was emphasized by a syndicated financial columnist who cautioned business news desks against using misleading headlines such as **Stocks plummet—Dow Jones average off 12 points.** It may be a loss, the columnist noted, but hardly a calamity. The Dow Jones Industrial Average may indicate that the market is up, but in reality it may be sinking. Freak gains by a few of the 30 stocks used in compiling the Dow average may have pushed up that particular indicator. Nor does a slight market drop call for a headline such as **Investors lose millions in market value of stocks.** They lost nothing of the sort. On that day, countless investors the nation over had substantial paper profits on their stocks. If they sold, they were gainers on the buying price in real terms; if they held, they had neither gains nor losses.

The Dow Jones average is one of several indexes used to gauge the stock market. Each uses its own statistical technique to show market changes. The Dow Jones bases its index on 30 stocks. It is an index-number change, not a percentage change.

Reporters of dividends should use the designation given by the firm (regular, special, extra, increases, interim) and show what was paid previously if there is no specified designation such as regular or quarterly.

The story should say if there is a special, or extra, dividend paid with the regular dividend and include the amount of previous added payments. When the usual dividend is not paid, or reduced, some firms issue an explanatory statement, the gist of which should be included in the story.

Newswire stylebooks recommend that news of corporate activities and business and financial news be stripped of technical terms. There should be some explanation of the firm's business (plastics, rubber, electronics) if there is no indication of the nature of the business in the firm's name. The location of the company's home office should be included.

Savings and loan firms object to being called banks. Some commercial banks likewise object when savings and loan firms are called banks. There need be no confusion if the institution is identified by its proper name. In subsequent references the words *company* or *institution* are used. Some newspapers permit **S&L firm** in tight headlines. Actually a *firm* is a partnership or unincorporated group. It should not be used for an incorporated company. *Concern* is a better word for the latter.

Jargon has no place in the business story. "Near-term question marks in the national economy—either of which could put a damper on the business expansion—are residential housing and foreign trade, the Northern Trust Co. said in its December issue of *Business Comments.*"Are near-term question marks economy question marks? If so, can they put a damper on anything? Isn't all housing residential?

> Major producers scrambled today to adjust steel prices to newly emerging industry-wide patterns. . . . The welter of price changes was in marked contrast with the old-time industry practice of posting across-the-board hikes.
>
> This approach apparently breathed its last in April when it ran into an administration buzzsaw, and a general price boost initiated then by United States Steel Corp., the industry giant, collapsed under White House fire.

Readers of financial pages read for information. False color is not needed to retain these readers. This story should have been edited heavily on the desk:

> Stock of the Communications Satellite Corp. went into an assigned orbit Friday on three major stock exchanges, rocketing to an apogee of $46 a share and a perigee of $42 and closing at $42.37, unchanged.
>
> It was the first day of listed trading on the exchanges. The stock previously was traded over-the-counter.
>
> The countdown on the first transaction on the New York stock exchange was delayed 12 minutes by an initial jam of buy and sell orders. . . .

PERCENTAGES AND NUMBERS

Two types of errors appear frequently in stories dealing with percentages. One is the failure to distinguish between percentage and percentage points; the other lies in comparing the change with a new figure rather than the original one. For example, when a tax rate is increased from $5 per $100 of assessed valuation to $5.50, the increase is 10 percent. New figure less old figure, divided by old figure:

$$\$5.50 - \$5 = .50; \frac{.50}{\$5} = .10 \text{ or } 10 \text{ percent.}$$

"Jones pointed out that the retail markup for most other brands is approximately 33 percent, whereas the markup on Brand J is 50 percent, or 17 percent higher." No. It is 17 percentage points higher but 51.5 percent higher. Divide 17 by 33.

"Dover's metropolitan population jumped from 16,000 just 10 years ago to more than 23,000 last year, an increase of better than 70 percent." Wrong again. It's a little less than 44 percent.

Is the figure misleading or inaccurate? The story said, "A total of $6,274 was raised at each of the four downtown stations." This adds up to $25,096. The writer intended the sentence to mean, "A total of $6,274 was raised at four stations." A not-so-sharp copy editor let this one get by: "Almost 500,000 slaves were shipped in this interstate trade. When one considers the average price of $800, the trade accounted for almost $20 million."

Are terms representing figures vague? In inheritance stories, it is better to name the amount and let the reader decide whether the amount is a "fortune." One of the wire service editors noted, "Fifteen thousand might be a fortune to a bootblack, but $200,000 would not be a fortune to a Rockefeller."

For some reason, many stories contain gambling odds, chances and probabilities. When a princess gave birth to a son, reporters quickly latched on to the odds on his name. Anthony was 1–2, George was even money, and Albert was 3–1. One headline played up the third in the betting. The name chosen was William. All this shows the foolishness of editors who play into the hands of gamblers. If odds must be included in the story, they should be accurate. The story said that because weather records showed that in the last 86 years it had rained only 19 times on May 27, the odds were 8–1 against rain for the big relay event. The odds mean nothing to readers except to those who like to point out that in the story just mentioned the odds actually were $3^{1}/_{2}$–1.

"Dr. Frank Rubovits said the children came from a single egg. He said the chance of this occurring 'probably is about 3 million to 1.' " He meant the odds against this occurring. The chance of this occurring is 1 in 3 million.

"The Tarapur plant will be the world's second largest atomic generator of electricity. The largest will be the 500-ton megawatt plant at Hinkley Point in Britain." A 500-ton megawatt plant makes no sense. What the writer meant was a 500-megawatt plant.

Some readers may rely on the idiom and insist that "five times as much as" means the same as "five times higher than" or "five times more than." If so, five times as much as $50 is $250 and five times higher than $50 is still $250. Others contend that the second should be $300. If earnings this year are $3^{1}/_{2}$ times as large as last year's, they are actually $2^{1}/_{2}$ times larger than last year's.

Insist on this style: 40,000 to 50,000 miles, not 40 to 50,000 miles; $3 million to $5 million, not $3 to $5 million.

"The committee recommended that a bid of $26,386.60 be accepted. After recommending the higher bid, the committee also had to recommend that an additional $326.60 be appropriated for the fire truck, because only $26,000 was included in the budget." The sum is still $60 short of the bid.

Equivalents should be included in stories that contain large sums. Most readers cannot visualize $20 billion, but they can understand it if they are told how much the amount would mean to each individual.

Here is one editor's advice to the staff:

We can do a service for those important people out there if we use terms they are most acquainted with. For example, to most of our readers a ton of corn is more easily visualized if it is reported as bushels, about 36 in this case. We normally report yields and prices in bushels and that is the measurement most readers know. The same goes for petroleum; barrels is probably more recognizable than tons. When the opportunity presents itself, translate the figures into the best-known measurement.

Nothing is duller or more unreadable than a numbers story. If figures are the important part of the story, they should be related to something—or at least presented as comparisons.

Two of the most common mathematical errors in news copy are the use of millions for billions and vice versa and a construction such as "Five were injured . . . " when only four names are listed.

SHIPS AND BOATS

Do not use nautical terms unless they're used properly. "Capt. Albert S. Kelly, 75, the pilot who manned the Delta Queen's tiller Monday . . . " What he manned was the helm or wheel. Few vessels except sailboats are guided with a tiller.

A story referred to a 27-foot ship. Nothing as small as 27 feet is a *ship*. *Ship* refers to big seagoing vessels such as tankers, freighters and ocean liners. Sailors insist that if it can be hoisted onto another craft it is a boat, and if it is too large for that it is a ship. Specific terms such as *cabin cruiser, sloop, schooner, barge* and *dredge* are appropriate.

"A rescue fleet ranging from primitive bayou pirogues to helicopters prowled through the night." That should send the copy editor to a dictionary so the editor can explain to readers that a pirogue is a canoe or a dugout. Better yet, simply use the more common term.

"The youths got to the pier just before the gangplank was lowered." When a ship sails, the gangplank is *raised*.

Commercial ships are measured by volume, the measurement of all enclosed space on the ship expressed in units of 100 cubic feet to the ton. Fuller description gives passenger capacity, length and age. The size of vessels is expressed in tonnage, the weight in long tons of a ship and all its contents (called displacement). A long ton is 2,240 pounds. All this is confusing to many readers. Copy editors should translate into terms recognized by readers, who can visualize length, age and firing power more readily than tonnage: "The 615-foot Bradley, longer than two football fields, . . . "

A knot is a measure of speed, not distance (nautical miles an hour). A nautical mile is about $1\frac{1}{7}$ land miles. "Knots per hour" is redundant.

Some readers may understand when the story says, "The limestone carrier was en route home in ballast." All will understand if the story says simply that the ship was going home empty.

SPORTS

Some of the best writing in American newspapers appears in the sports pages. So does some of the worst.

Sports pages should be, and are, the liveliest in the paper. They have action photos, a melange of spectator and participant sports and an array of personalities. Sports writers have more latitude than do other reporters. The good ones are among the best in the business; the undisciplined ones are among the worst.

Attractive pages and free expression mean little if the sports section is unintelligible to half the paper's readers. Too often, the editing reflects the attitude that if readers don't understand the lingo they should look elsewhere in the paper for information and entertainment.

The potential for readers of the sports section is greater than ever because of the growing number of participants in golf, bowling, fishing, boating and tennis. The spectator sports, especially automobile racing, football, golf, basketball, baseball and hockey, attract great audiences, thanks to the vast number of television viewers. Thus the sports pages, if edited intelligently, can become the most appealing section in the paper. But first, writers and copy editors must improve their manners.

A report of a contest or struggle should appeal to readers if it is composed in straightforward, clear English. The style can be vigorous without being forced. Sports fans do not need the sensational to keep their interest whetted. Those who are only mildly interested won't become sports page regulars if the stories are confusing.

KNOW THE GAME

One of the elementary rules in sports writing is to tell the reader the name of the game. Yet many stories talk about the Cubs and Pirates but never say specifically that the contest is a baseball game. Some writers assume that if the story refers to the contest as a "dribble derby" all sports page readers must understand that the story concerns a basketball game.

The story may contain references to parts of the game yet never mention the specific game. Here is an example:

Three Teams Tied in Sliceroo

Three teams tied for low at 59 in the sweepstakes division as the 11th annual Sliceroo got under way Thursday at Lakewood Country Club.

Deadlocked at 59 were the teams of...

In the driving contest, it was...

In the putting and chipping contest...

A best ball is set for Friday and a low net for Saturday, final day of the Sliceroo. A $5,000 hole-in-one competition on the 124-yard 11th hole is set for both final days.

Golfers will understand the story. But nongolfers, even many who enjoy watching golf matches on television, should be told outright that the story concerns a golf tournament. The added information would not offend the golfers. It might encourage a non-golfer to read on.

Some stories fail to state categorically who played whom. The writer assumes that if the opponents' managers are named, all hard-core sports readers will recognize the contestants. Perhaps so, but the casual reader might like to know, too. The caption under a two-column picture read, "They can't believe their eyes. Coach Andy S—, left, and Manager May S—, right, showed disbelief and disgruntlement as the Braves belt Pitcher Don C— for five runs in the eighth inning of their exhibition baseball game Wednesday at Clearwater, Fla. The Braves won, 10–2." Now, whom did the Braves play?

Not all readers understand the technical terms used to describe a sports contest. It might be necessary to explain that a seeded team gets a favored placement in the first round, and that if Smith beats Jones 2–1 in match play it means that golfer Smith is two holes ahead of golfer Jones with only one hole left to play and is therefore the winner. The name of the sport should be used in reference to the various cups. The Davis Cup is an international trophy for men tennis players. The Heisman Trophy is an award presented annually to the outstanding college football player in the nation. America's Cup refers to yachting, and America Cup to golfing.

UNANSWERED QUESTIONS

Answering more questions is one way to win more readers for the sports department. The key questions frequently overlooked are how and why. Why did the coach decide to punt on fourth down instead of trying to make one foot for a first down? How do tournament organizers get the funds to award $200,000 in prizes?

"The shadow of tragedy drew a black edge around a golden day at Sportsman's Park Thursday, bringing home the danger of horse racing with an impact that cut through the $68,950 Illinois Derby like a spotlight in darkness." So, what happened?

The best training for copy editors on the sports desk is a stint on the news copy desk. But before they go on the sports desk they should become familiar with the intricacies of all sports so they can catch the technical errors in sports copy. Here are examples:

"Center fielder Tony Cafar, whose fine relay after chasing the ball 'a country mile' held Ripley to a triple . . . " Unless Tony also made a throw of "a country mile," another player, a shortstop or second baseman, made the relay throw after taking a good throw from Tony.

When a writer covering a basketball game refers to a "foul shot," the reference should be deleted on the sports desk rim. The fouled player gets a free throw from the free-throw line, not the foul line or the charity line.

The copy editor also has to be alert for some of the wild flights of imagination used by sports writers. "The Tar Heels hurdled their last major

obstacle on the way to an unbeaten season but still had a long row to hoe."
Is this a track meet or a county fair?

The following passage is a sure way to discourage sports page readers:

> His trouble in Sunday's 27–6 victory over the Dallas Cowboys before 72,062, largest crowd ever to see the Chiefs, was the reason Moore was in the trenches to receive a shattering kick with 6:24 left in the game.

This example suggests another tendency in sports copy—turning the story into a numbers game. Box scores, league standings and records have a place in the sports story, but generally they should have a subordinate rather than a dominant role.

ABBREVIATED SPORTS

The addiction to abbreviation is strong in both sports copy and headlines. **Broncos get first AFC win over NFC** announces a headline. It means that Denver's professional football team scored the first victory of the season by an American Football Conference team over a National Football Conference team.

"COLOR" IN SPORTS

An editor told his colleagues, "There is nothing more exciting than a good contest. There is nothing duller than reading about it the next day." Yet many spectators who watch a Saturday contest can't wait to read about it the next morning. What were the coaches' and players' reactions to the game? What was the turning point? How long was the pass that won the game? What's the reporter's comment on the crowd's behavior?

So if there is an audience for the report of a contest, the story needs no special flourishes. Loaded terms such as "wily mentor," "genial bossman," "vaunted running game," "dazzling run" and "astute field general" add little or nothing to the story. Adjectives lend false color. The Associated Press reported a "vise-tight race," "the red-hot Cardinals" and the "torrid 13–4 pace" as if these modifiers were needed to lure readers.

If all copy editors were permitted to aim their pencils at copy submitted by the prima donnas of the sports world, there would be no sentences like the following ones:

"Jones, who has been bothered by a sore rib this spring, played eight innings Tuesday, collected two singles and drove in a run." He didn't collect them; he hit them.

"Ortiz threw his first bomb in the second round when he nailed Laguna with a left and right to the jaw." How can you nail something with a bomb?

"Left-hander Glavine, who started on the mound for Atlanta, recovered from a shaky start and pitched six-hit ball for eight innings before a walk and a botched-up double play caused the manager to protect a 4–1 lead, as a result of a three-run homer by Dave Justice in the seventh." The sentence is hard to understand because it is overstuffed and because the facts are not told in chronological order. Revised: "Left-hander Glavine started on the mound for Atlanta. He recovered from a shaky start and pitched six-hit ball for eight innings. Then a walk and a missed double play caused the manager to bring in a new pitcher. Atlanta was leading, 4–1, as a result of a three-run homer by Dave Justice in the seventh."

Here is how to tell a story upside down: "Waldrop's 17-yard explosion for his eighth touchdown of the season punctuated a 65-yard march from Army's reception of the kickoff by a courageous Falcon team, which had gone ahead for the second time in the game, 10–7, in the ninth minute of the final period."

SYNONYM SICKNESS

Not even the best editing can convert some sports writers into Homers and Hemingways. At least, though, copy editors can try to help writers improve their ways of telling a story.

Copy editors can excise clichés such as "paydirt," "turned the tables," "hammered (or slammed) a homerun," "Big Eight hardwoods," "circuit clout," "gridder," "hoopster," "thinclads," "tanksters," "sweet revenge," "rocky road," "free loads" (free throws), "droughts" (losing streaks), "standing-room-only crowds," "put a cap on the basket," "as the seconds ticked off the clock," "unblemished records," "paced the team," "outclassed but game," "roared from behind," "sea of mud," "vaunted defense," "coveted trophy" and "last-ditch effort."

They can insist on the correct word. Boxers may have *altercations* (oral) with their managers. They have *fights* with other boxers.

They can tone down exaggerated expressions like "mighty atom of the ring," "destiny's distance man" or "Northwestern comes off tremendous effort Monday" (Northwestern tried hard). They can cut out redundancy in phrases such as "with 30,000 spectators looking on."

They can resist the temptation to use synonyms for verbs *wins, beats* and *defeats:* annihilates, atomizes, batters, belts, bests, blanks, blasts, boots home, clips, clobbers, cops, crushes, downs, drops, dumps, edges, ekes out, gallops over, gangs up on, gouges, gets past, H-bombs, halts, humiliates, impales, laces, lashes, lassoes, licks, murders, outslugs, outscraps, orbits, overcomes, paces, pastes, pins, racks up, rallies, rolls over, romps over, routs, scores, sets back, shades, shaves, sinks, slows, snares, spanks, squeaks by, squeezes by, stampedes, stomps, stops, subdues, surges, sweeps, tops, topples, triggers, trips, trounces, tumbles, turns back, vanquishes, wallops, whips, whomps and wrecks.

They will let the ball be *hit,* not always banged, bashed, belted, blooped, bombed, boomed, bumped, chopped, clunked, clouted, conked, cracked, dribbled, drilled, dropped, driven, hacked, knifed, lashed, lined, plastered, plunked, poked, pooped, pumped, punched, pummeled, pushed, rapped, ripped, rocked, slapped, sliced, slugged, smashed, spilled, spanked, stubbed, swatted, tagged, tapped, tipped, topped, trickled, whipped, whistled, whomped and whooped.

They will let a ball be *thrown* and only occasionally tossed, twirled, fired and hurled.

They will let a ball be *kicked,* occasionally punted and never toed or booted.

They will resist the shopworn puns: Birds (Eagles, Orioles, Cardinals) soar or claw; Lions (Tigers, Bears, Cubs) roar, claw or lick; Braves (Tribesmen, Indians) scalp or tomahawk; Mustangs (Colts, Broncos) buck, gallop, throw or kick.

They will insist on neutrality in all sports copy and avoid slanting the story in favor of the home team.

They will not string modifiers endlessly: "The Pistons won 29 and lost 40 under the guidance of the then only 24 years old DuBusschere."

LIFESTYLE

One of the brighter changes in newspapers in recent years has been the transformation of the society pages, with their emphasis on club and cupid items, to the family or lifestyle section, which has a broader-based appeal.

Such sections still carry engagement announcements and wedding stories, but their added fare is foods, fashions, finance, health, education, books and other cultural affairs. They are edited for active men and women in all ranks, not solely for those in the top rank of society.

The better editors regard readers of lifestyle sections as alert individuals who are concerned with social problems such as prostitution, racism, civil disorders, prisons, alcoholism and educational reforms. Such editors strive to make their pages informative as well as entertaining.

Some papers now handle engagements, weddings and births as record items. And a few charge for engagement and wedding stories and pictures unless the event is obviously news, such as the wedding of Prince Charles. Most, however, recognize the value of these items and continue to publish them as news.

To add some spice to its pages devoted to wedding accounts, the Gannett Rochester Newspapers started a "Wedding Scrapbook" page in its Saturday section, "Brides Book for Greater Rochester." Included were features on how the couple met, amusing incidents of the participants on the way to the ceremony and pictures of the couple in faraway places.

Wedding and engagement stories are with us to stay, but some customs, such as not giving the bridegroom much recognition, may change. This point was delightfully argued by Paul Brookshire in his column in the *South Dade* (Homestead, Fla.) *New Leader.* Here are some excerpts:

> In these days when the world is quaking in its boots and news of great significance is daily swept into newspaper trash cans for lack of space, it is sickening to read paragraph after paragraph about some little girl changing HER name to HIS.

The groom? He apparently wasn't dressed at all . . . if he was even there. But Mother and Mother-in-Law? Yes. They were fashion plates in beige ensembles and matching accessories or something.

I ask you. Is it a wedding or a fashion show?

If it is a fashion show, why isn't it held in a hotel ballroom and why isn't the groom given a tiny bit of credit for showing up with his clothes on?

The blackout of the bridegroom in wedding accounts is an unpardonable sin. If the groom is mentioned at all he is afforded as much space as an atheist gets on the church page.

And pictures. Did you ever see a photograph of a bridegroom? Maybe in the Post Office but not in the newspaper.

I'm going on record right now in favor of wedding announcements being run as legal notices—payable in advance by the father of the bride.

Better still, if the bride insists on giving a minute, detailed description of every inch of clothing she happens to have on her person, I suggest she take out a paid display advertisement.

In this manner, trade names may be used and shops that sold the girl all her glorious gear could get equal space on the same page.

Newspapers would reap untold profits from this arrangement and readers might be able to get some world news for a change instead of bouffant skirts highlighted with tiers of lace and aqua frocks with aqua tipped orchids and maize silk linen ensembles with . . . whatever you wear with maize silk linen ensembles.

Even though many newspapers have changed the society section to a lifestyle section, some retain a static style, especially on engagement and wedding stories. Wedding story leads too often read like these:

First Methodist Church in Littleton was the setting for the double-ring wedding rites of . . .

Miss Cynthia Jones has become the bride of Joe Smith, it was announced by her parents . . .

After a wedding trip to Las Vegas, Nev., Mr. and Mrs. Jones will live in . . .

All Saints Roman Catholic Church was the setting for the single-ring rites . . .

Newspapers continue to use the following:

* Stock words and phrases—holy matrimony, high noon, exchanged nuptial vows.
* Descriptive adjectives—attractive, pretty, beautiful, charming, lovely.
* Non sequiturs—"Given in marriage by her parents, the bride wore a white silk organza gown with a sabrina neckline and short sleeves." "Wearing a gown of white lace cotton over taffeta with empire waistline, square neckline and short sleeves, the bride was given in marriage by her father."
* Details—gown and flower descriptions and social affiliations that reflect status.
* Circumlocutory headlines—**Betrothal told, Holy vows exchanged, Wedding ceremonies solemnized.**

Excerpts from an error-filled account of a wedding reveal the unbeliev-
able triteness of such stories:

> A petite white United Methodist Church nestled below the towering Rocky
> Mountains in Lyons, Colo., was the setting for the marriage of Shirley Ann
> M— and Wesley William B— on Aug. 4. A happy sun brought warmth and
> color through the old-fashioned peaked stained glass windows at precisely 3
> p.m. when Gloria L . . . played The Wedding March, and guests stood from
> hand-carved oak seats, curved into an intimate half-circle to witness the double-
> ring ceremony. . . .
>
> The Rev. D. L. N— officiated at the afternoon ceremony amid arrange-
> ments of mint-green carnations, white gladiolas, and white daisies with giant
> white satin bows which adorned the altar. Pews were delightfully enhanced with
> waterfall baskets of fresh greenery and wild mountain flowers plucked early that
> morning from beside the St. Vrain River and tied with lime and powder blue
> satin ribbons. . . .
>
> The bride tossed her bouquet from the stairway and "went away" all dressed
> in white and yellow.

Talented copy editors will not allow writers to single out women's
achievements with sexist terms such as housewife (rather than homemaker)
and woman doctor (simply use doctor). They will delete phrases like "is
affiliated with," "refreshments will be served," "featured speaker," "special
guests," "noon luncheon," "dinner meeting." They will refuse to let a person
"host (or hostess) a party," "gavel a meeting" or "chair a committee."

They will not let reporters go out of their way to use *female, feminine*
and *ladies* in all manner of sentences where the word *women* would be proper
and more appropriate, if, indeed, even that word is necessary.

They will catch slips such as "Mrs. Richard Roe, nee Jane Doe." *Nee*
means "born" and people are born only with their surnames. The first (not
Christian) name is given later.

They will remain on guard for awkward sentences:

> Do you keep track of your weight and lose the first 5 or 10 pounds too
> much?

> Seniors realize the importance of proper dress more than younger stu-
> dents, but after a while they catch on.

All copy for lifestyle sections, as well as for the other sections of the
paper, should be edited for its news value. This should apply to the syndicated
features as well as to the locally produced copy. Similarly, the headlines should
reflect as much care and thought as do those on Page One.

CHAPTER 7

THE COPY EDITOR
ON GUARD

BEWARE OF THE HOAX

Readers of *USA Today's* LIFE section probably were intrigued to read this item, picked up from the Associated Press, about the latest romance of actress Elizabeth Taylor:

NEW LIZ LOVE?: Elizabeth Taylor may leave a California hospital in two weeks, but maybe not alone. The Associated Press says a biopsy performed on the star Sunday showed no new signs of lung infection. Taylor spokeswoman Lisa Flowers told the AP that the actress, 58, is fighting severe depression, and has decided to make public her romance with 23-year-old Julian Lee Hobbs. "Julian was out of the picture for so long. . . . She is blooming again, like a rose," Flowers told the AP, adding the couple met in 1988 and plan to travel to Switzerland.

USA TODAY
©Copyright 1990 Gannett Co., Inc.

The next day, readers learned the truth:

CORRECTION: An Associated Press story saying that Elizabeth Taylor is in love with a 23-year-old, quoted Monday in *USA Today,* was a hoax perpetrated by an unknown woman posing as a Taylor publicist, the star's spokeswoman says.

The Associated Press and *USA Today* weren't the first victims of such hoaxes. Virtually every newspaper has been victimized at one time or another. Such incidents emphasize the importance of good journalistic technique, particularly the practice of knowing to whom one is talking. Hoaxes usually begin when an individual calls or stops by a newspaper claiming to be someone he or she is not. Good reporters will verify the identity of anyone they do not know; failing to do so is the surest way to fall victim to a hoax.

The importance of following that rule is clear in the case of a hoax perpetrated on the *Star Tribune, Newspaper of the Twin Cities* in Minneapolis–

St. Paul. The *Star Tribune* ran an eight-paragraph story quoting Richard L. Thomas, president of First Chicago Corp., a large bank holding company, as saying his company was interested in purchasing troubled First Bank Systems of Minneapolis for $20 to $22 a share. That day First Bank stock jumped sharply higher before First Chicago issued a statement denying that Thomas had talked to the Minneapolis paper. The whole story, it turned out, was a hoax.

"We have absolutely no idea" who the imposter was, said Larry Werner, *Star Tribune* assistant managing editor for business. The problem began when the imposter called a real-estate reporter to talk about an earlier story written by a reporter with a similar name. The real-estate reporter tried to transfer the call, but the caller refused, saying he had already been transferred too often. The real-estate reporter gave his notes to the other reporter, who wrote the story. Neither bothered to call First Chicago to confirm that Thomas had actually made the call. A lesson was learned—the hard way.

A newspaper relies on its reputation for credibility, and incidents such as these tend to erode readers' confidence. Editors must always be alert to the possibility of a hoax and raise questions if a story seems suspicious.

Longtime editors know that some hoaxes have a way of reappearing from time to time in various parts of the country. These include:

• The story of 16-year-old baby sitter who adhered to a freshly painted toilet seat for hours. A doctor administered to her, tripped and knocked himself out. Both were carried off in an ambulance for repairs and both sued the family who engaged the sitter.
• A driver who was flagged by a stalled motorist needing a push. Told she would have to get up to 35 mph to get the stalled car started, she backed off, gunned the motor and rammed his car at 35 mph.
• The sheriff who was called to a farm to investigate the theft of 2,025 pigs and discovered that only two sows and 25 pigs were missing. The farmer who reported the loss lisped.
• A farmer armed with a shotgun who went to a chicken house to rout a suspected thief. The farmer stumbled, and the gun went off, killing all his hens.
• The story, usually from some obscure hill hamlet in the east of Europe or in Asia, of an eagle carrying off a 3-year-old child.
• A Sunday driver who called police to report that someone stole the steering wheel and all the pedals from his car. A squad car was sent to the scene, but before police arrived, the man called back and said, "Everything is all right. I was looking in the back seat."
• Someone reports he has found a copy, in near perfect condition, of the Jan. 4, 1800, issue of the Ulster County *Gazette*. The paper is prized not only for its age but because it contains a statement made by the U.S. Senate to President John Adams following the death of George Washington 21 days earlier. It refers to Washington as "Father of our country." Few copies of the original exist, but there are many reproductions.
• A story from Harrisburg, Pa., told about six students permanently blinded by looking at the sun after taking LSD. It was not until after the story had

received wide play and had been the subject of editorials and columns that the hoax was discovered.

- A group of young stockbrokers got credit for plotting a hoax against New York newspapers during the depression days of the 1930s. They created a fictitious football team at a fictitious college, and every Saturday during the fall they phoned in the results of the fictitious football game. The hoax was uncovered near the end of the football season when the fictitious college team began appearing in the ranks of the untied and undefeated teams.
- The bricklayer story makes the rounds periodically, usually with a change in locale. The story may have been reworked from a vaudeville gag of earlier days. It is recorded by a British accent comedian as a monologue under the title of "Hoffnung at the Oxford Club." Fred Allen used it as a skit on one of his radio shows in the 1930s. In 1945 the story was retold in an anthology of humor edited by H. Allen Smith. Three versions had their setting in Korea, Barbados and Vietnam. In World War II the "bricklayer" was a sailor on the USS Saratoga requesting a five-day leave extension. Here is the Barbados version, courtesy of UPI:

LONDON (UPI)—The Manchester Guardian today quoted as "an example of stoicism" the following unsigned letter—ostensibly from a bricklayer in the Barbados to his contracting firm:

"Respected Sir,

"When I got to the building, I found that the hurricane had knocked some bricks off the top. So I rigged up a beam with a pulley at the top of the building and hoisted up a couple of barrels full of bricks. When I had fixed up the building, there was a lot of bricks left over.

"I hoisted the barrel back up again and secured the line at the bottom, and then went up and filled the barrel with the extra bricks. Then I went to the bottom and cast off the line.

"Unfortunately, the barrel of bricks was heavier than I was, and before I knew what was happening the barrel started down, jerking me off the ground. I decided to hang on and halfway up I met the barrel coming down and received a severe blow on the shoulder.

"I then continued to the top, banging my head against the beam and getting my fingers jammed in the pulley. When the barrel hit the ground it bursted its bottom, allowing all the bricks to spill out.

"I was now heavier than the barrel and so started down again at high speed. Halfway down, I met the barrel coming up and received severe injuries to my shins. When I hit the ground I landed on the bricks, got several painful cuts from the sharp edges.

"At this point I must have lost my presence of mind, because I let go the line. The barrel then came down, giving me another heavy blow on the head and putting me in the hospital.

"I respectfully request sick leave."

Perhaps, as one editor has suggested, the original version dealt with the building of the Cheops pyramid or the Parthenon. The story seems to have magic appeal for reporters and copy editors.

Some others, though not hoaxes, are impossible or misleading:

- A man received a series of summonses to pay a tax bill. The notices said he owed $0.00 in taxes and $0.00 in penalties. He was warned that his personal belongings would be attached if he didn't pay. He sent the tax office a check for $0.00 and got a receipt for that amount. Sometimes the yarn is applied to the non-payment of a non-charge from an electric company and a threat to cut off service unless the bill is paid—or to a tuition demand on a student studying at a college on a tax-free scholarship.
- A fake story may be hard to detect. This fraud got by the desk of a New York newspaper: "The thallus or ruling monarch of the principality of Marchantia will arrive here today on a two-day visit as part of a State Department tour."
- Newspapers have worn out the gag about the man who answered "twice a week" opposite "sex" on a census questionnaire. Others that newspapers could do without include:

> Undercover investigators said Monday that they ended a suburban sex ring where housewives worked as call girls to supplement the family income.

> Smith will help to direct a volunteer effort embracing several thousand housewives, who will be calling on their neighbors for contributions.

> In Germany Thursday, Mrs. R— issued a statement to the German press agency in which she denied ever having improper relations with men other than her husband while in Washington.

Impossible or misleading stories and hoaxes aren't the only items that trip up editors who let down their guard. There are many others, some of which are outlined in the sections that follow.

PERILS OF THE SUPERLATIVE

Writing that something is the "first," "only," "biggest," "best" or "a record" seldom adds to a story. Often it backfires.

When President Lyndon Johnson rode in a Canadian government plane, one wire service said he was the first American president to travel aboard an airplane of a foreign government. He wasn't. President Dwight Eisenhower flew in a Royal Air Force Comet from London to Scotland in 1959 to visit Queen Elizabeth.

Another wire service characterized Gouverneur Morris as "the penman of the Constitution" and Lewis Morris as the "only New York signer of the Declaration of Independence." The man who penned the Constitution was Jacob Shallus, and there were four New York signers of the Declaration of Independence.

A California obituary identified a woman as the "first postmistress" in the nation. A Missouri story reported the closing of America's "shortest commercial railroad." Both statements were disproved.

The Associated Press described Herbert Lehman of New York as the "first person of the Jewish faith ever to hold a Senate seat." The AP had to acknowledge that it was wrong by at least six men and more than 100 years. Jewish senators who preceded Lehman were David Levy Yulee of Florida, Judah P. Benjamin of Louisiana, Benjamin F. Jonas of Louisiana, Joseph Simon of Oregon, Isidore Raynor of Maryland and Simon Guggenheim of Colorado.

When United Press International described the Flying Scotsman, a famous British locomotive, as the first steam locomotive to exceed 100 mph, railroad buffs hurried to set the record straight. Records show that on May 10, 1893, the New York Central No. 999 was timed unofficially at 112.5 mph on a one-mile stretch between Batavia and Buffalo. On March 1, 1901, the Savannah, Florida and Western (later part of Atlantic Coast Line, later Seaboard Coast Line) No. 1901 was timed at 120 mph. On June 12, 1905, the Pennsylvania Special traveled three miles near Elida, Ohio, in 85 seconds for an average of 127 mph.

A story from Louisville described a conviction as the first under a new law barring interstate shipment of gambling material. Two months earlier two men had been convicted under the same law. A Billy Graham rally was described as having the largest audience for a single meeting. But a Rosary Crusade in San Francisco had been attended by 500,000, a bigger crowd than Graham's.

All these are examples of abused statistics that invade the news report. One story indicated that New York City has 8 million rats. Another quoted the American Medical Association as saying that only 5 percent of Americans dream in color. How can anyone know such exact figures? Highway deaths may increase from one year to the next, but one possible explanation may be that there are more vehicles on streets and highways. Highway deaths on holiday weekends are higher than normal because such weekends often are longer. "The toll has dropped so that last year there were only 81 traffic deaths here, an all-time low." Since when? 1942? 1776? 1900? "The ships were built in record time." What was the previous record?

All superlatives should be checked. If they cannot be verified, at least they can be softened: "One of the most despicable crimes in the world . . . "; "One of the hardest-working actresses in Germany. . . . "

MISQUOTATIONS

A careful copy editor would be wise to keep a quotation reference at hand while handling copy containing references to often-repeated quotations or attribution of such quotations.

Such a reference will stop reporters from attributing "Go west, young man" to Horace Greeley. The advice was given by John Babson Lane in

1851. Greeley used the expression in an editorial in the *New York Tribune* but amplified it: "Go west, young man, and grow up with the country."

Charles Dudley Warner, not Mark Twain, should get credit for "Everybody talks about the weather, but nobody does anything about it." Bill Nye, the humorist, originated the saying, "There are just two people entitled to refer to themselves as "we"—one is the editor, and the other is the fellow with a tapeworm." Mark Twain later revised the statement: "Only presidents, editors, and people with tapeworms have the right to use the editorial 'we.' "

Voltaire is wrongly credited with the quotation. "I may not agree with what you say, but I will defend to the death your right to say it." Most likely it is a paraphrase of Voltaire's "Think for yourselves, and let others enjoy the privilege to do so too." Gen. John J. Pershing did not exclaim, "Lafayette, we are here!" It was uttered by Charles E. Stanton, chief disbursing officer of the American Expeditionary Forces.

Careless writers attribute the "gilded lily" business to Shakespeare. But what Shakespeare wrote was, "To gild refined gold, to paint the lily." Similarly, the Bible does not say that money is the root of all evil. It says, "Love of money is the root of all evil." Music doesn't have charms to soothe the savage beast. Congreve said, "Music hath charms to soothe the savage breast." And Thomas Hardy did not refer to "the maddening crowd" but to "the madding crowd."

Up to the time of his death, a South African dentist, Philip Blaiberg, had survived with an implanted heart. In an account of Blaiberg's death, a UPI reporter wrote that Blaiberg's last act was to scribble a quote from the Persian poet Omar Khayyám: " . . . for I shall not pass this way again." A Connecticut editor questioned the attribution, causing UPI to send out a correction. The probable author is Stephen Grellet and the usually accepted full quotation is, "I shall pass through this world but once. If, therefore, there be any kindness I can show or any good thing I can do, let me do it now. Let me not defer or neglect it, for I shall not pass this way again."

A sports column tribute concluded, "In the words of the late Grantland Rice: 'When the great scorer comes to write beside your name,/It's not whether you won or lost but how you played the game.' " What Rice really said was, "When the One Great Scorer comes to write against your name—/He marks—not that you won or lost—but how you played the game." Reporters should never quote poetry from memory. When poetry shows up in a piece of copy, the copy editor should assume it's wrong and look it up.

The story quoted a structural linguist's feelings about people who object to ending sentences with prepositions: "You remember what Winston Churchill said when an aide corrected a line in one of Churchill's speeches because it ended in a preposition? Churchill told the aide: 'This is an outrage up with which I will not put.' " Churchill was misquoted. What he said (and even this may be apocryphal) was, "This is the type of arrant pedantry up with which I shall not put."

A column criticizing the overuse of the word *gourmet* said, "I am reminded of the line of poetry which told of the moth flitting its wings signifying nothing." Was it perchance not a poem but a Shakespeare play, and not a moth flitting its wings but "a tale told by an idiot, full of sound and fury, signifying nothing"?

"We've come a long way since Commodore Vanderbilt said, 'The public be damned.' " But the commodore never said it. It was William H. Vanderbilt, son of Cornelius, the so-called commodore, who made the remark.

"Robert Burns, the old Scotchman, said: 'Oh that we would see ourselves as other see us.' " Burns was a distinguished poet, hardly the "old Scotchman." Careful writers prefer *Scot* or *Scotsman* to *Scotchman,* as do the Scots themselves. The actual quotation: "Oh wad some power the giftie gie us/To see oursels as others see us!"

CHANGING QUOTES

Copy editors often have to decide whether to make corrections in direct quotations. Should they correct the syntax of the speaker? If the goof is within quotation marks, should it remain? Did the speaker use poor English or did the reporter write poor English? Do the persons quoted get a friendly or an unfriendly pencil on the desk? Perhaps it was the writer rather than the speaker who used poor grammar. Usually the language is corrected in direct quotes unless, as one editor commented, it is done with malice aforethought when "we want to show someone ain't no good at talking," or the speaker is expected to abuse the language or a speaker, such as the president, makes a slip of the tongue. Some editors, however, insist that the quotation marks be deleted, even when the quotation is changed only slightly.

ATTRIBUTIONS

Copy editors will save reporters from attribution logjams if they remember this question: Is it clear who is talking? If the reporter shifts to a second speaker, the story should identify the new speaker immediately, not at the end of the quotation. The reader assumes the first speaker is still talking.

Sometimes the source cannot be named, yet the statement is newsworthy. The editor assumes readers understand this when a story contains phrases like "a spokesman," "a usually reliable source," "a government official" and "it was learned." Many editors prefer not to use quotation marks around either fact or opinion ascribed to an unnamed source. Some editors understandably deplore the faceless source protection. These editors say, in effect, that if a government official with a special interest in Latin American affairs terms a resolution "worse than useless," why can't the fearless official be named? By withholding identity, papers shamelessly do other people's bidding.

Nonattribution denies the reader a very essential fact—often *the* essential fact—the source of the information, of the idea, of the speculation, of the proposal, of the supposition—even, sometimes, of the accusation. "Republican

State Headquarters issued a statement today blasting. . . . " This is a statement of faceless political critics. Such statements should be attributed either to individuals or to official party organizations that are willing to stand behind them. There's no such organization as Republican State Headquarters.

Another potential difficulty arises in the choice of synonyms for *said*. Do "added," "pointed out," "offered," "admitted," "disclosed," "noted," "revealed," "indicated," "conceded," "explained" or "cited the fact that" give the quotation an editorial tone?

Do the synonyms for *said* convey a hint of doubt as to the veracity of the credited source ("according to," "said he believes")? "According to" actually refers to the content, not to the speaker: "According to the mayor's letter . . . ," not "According to the mayor. . . . "

Does the writer use gestures for words?

"We're gonna put on a show, too," grinned Wags.

"Now I can invite my friends to play on the grass," Donna beamed.

"The bill will be paid," the official smiled.

"I heard something pop in my shoulder," he winced on his way to the dressing room.

No matter how good a grinner or wincer, how bright a beamer or how broad a smiler, you just can't grin, wince, beam or smile a quote. If it's a quip, that should be obvious from the context. If it isn't, saying so won't make it so. An exclamation mark may be used after a brief expletive, but it looks silly after a long sentence.

Said is a simple verb that usually is preferable to others used in an effort to convey determination, skepticism and wit. Usually the quoted matter can speak for itself. Many of the best writers use *said* almost exclusively. *Said* used repeatedly can give emphasis; it is not weakened by repetition.

And then there are the problems associated with quotations themselves. For example, does the quoted word invite the reader to disbelieve the statement?

"Father Divine's blond wife was at his bedside, along with his 18 'secretaries.' " By placing quotes around *secretaries*, the writer expressed an opinion, not a fact.

Do scattergun quotations bewilder the reader?

"The actress said she would wed Wilding 'at the end of the week.' "

"The blood-covered body of a 'brilliant' 19-year-old Williams College sophomore was found today—a rifle nearby—in a fraternity house room. Police Chief George A. Royal said it was 'apparently murder.' "

Is the source given immediately in a controversial quotation?

When the information is disputable, the source should come at the beginning; it should not be appended to the statement. "The administration budget has imposed a tremendous burden on consumers, Sen. Jane Doe contended in calling for revisions." Change it to read, "Sen. Jane Doe called for revisions and contended that the administration budget has imposed a tremendous burden on consumers."

Does the quotation reveal precisely what the speaker said? "Stewart still maintains 'he called it as he saw it.' " You can't quote someone in the third person.

Does an awkwardly split quote interrupt the speaker? " 'He,' said Jones, 'needs a wig.' "

Are the circumstances of the statement clear? Was the statement made in an interview, a report, a letter, a public speech? Was it in English originally, or has it been translated? Was it prepared or extemporaneous? Was it made over a network or a single station? What network? What station?

Is that attribution overworked? In some crime or accident stories, phrases such as "police said" or "Patrolman Jones reported" are used in almost every sentence. A blanket attribution such as "police gave this account of the accident" would ease the monotony for the readers.

TELL THEM, DON'T TEASE THEM

News is regarded one way in the newspaper office and another way by its readers. In the news room the reporter is constantly admonished to "keep 'em short." "How much do you have on that hotel death?" the city editor asks. "Enough for about 14 inches," answers the reporter. "Hold it to 7," orders the superior. "We're short on space today."

So the reporter prunes the story to 7 inches. The story reaches the copy desk and an editor goes to work to make it even tighter.

All this, of course, is unknown to the reader who sits down to enjoy the newspaper. A headline catches the eye: *80-foot fall at hotel ends actor's grim joke.* The reader begins the story: " 'Watch me do a trick,' said the 26-year-old actor to his companion, and he stepped out the eighth-floor window of their downtown hotel early Sunday." Muses the reader, "I was downtown early Sunday morning. I wonder what hotel it was and what time?" The story doesn't answer his questions. It does identify the victim. Also his companion. Near the end of the story is a brief description of the companion, Paul Lynde: "Lynde is a widely known actor, investigators said." "Funny I never heard of him," the reader again muses. "Wonder what he appeared in?"

This was the story as sent by the Associated Press. For the morning papers the story failed to identify the hotel, did not give the time of the fall and identified Lynde only as a widely known actor. Readers of afternoon papers got some of the missing details. The hotel was the Sir Francis Drake, the time was "the wee hours Sunday morning" and Lynde was identified as a comedian who appeared in the Broadway and film versions of "Bye Bye Birdie" with Dick Van Dyke and in the movie "Under the Yum Yum Tree" as Imogene Coca's henpecked husband.

The ability to give details is the newspaper's great advantage over its competitors in other media. Readers relate to the news. The more involved they become in the events, the more avid they become. In short, they demand the whole story down to the last detail. If the story says, 'Hastings Banda, the leader of Nyasaland, received his education in Ohio," the reader wants to know, "Where in Ohio?" "At what university?" "When?" The reader relates to the news. "I wonder if that's the same Banda I knew when I was at Ohio State in the 1950s."

A wire story about a plane crash in New York City said the 79 passengers included "two young opera singers en route to a South Carolina concert, prominent Southern businessmen, and a former Virginia college beauty queen." The story as sent drew this protest from a client's managing editor: "Who the people are who die in these crashes is a point of interest equal to or more than the circumstances of the crash. We all identify with them—where they are going, where they are coming from. I want to know what opera those opera singers were going to sing in."

A story related that a man had gone to court to fight for a seat in the legislature, but it did not tell to which party he belonged. Another told of a woman mugged while waiting for a bus at Delaware and Woodlawn avenues, but did not give the time of the incident, which would be of interest to those who ride the bus.

In a story about an airplane crash, the cost of the plane is an important piece of information and should be included.

One paper ran a story about a drunk chimpanzee that supposedly escaped and created havoc around the countryside by trying to break into homes. But the story failed to tell who owned the chimp, what he was doing in the county, how he got anything to drink and what finally happened after a game warden arrived on the scene. These were basic questions the reporter forgot to answer. The copy editor should have checked.

Another paper had a three-column picture and story about consecration ceremonies at the Cherry Hill Methodist Church's new "Harlan House." The story told that Harlan House was named for "Miss Mollie" Harlan, that the Rev. Dr. Darcy Littleton took part in the ceremonies, that "Miss Mollie" is now buried in the Cherry Hill Cemetery, that Littleton is now with Goodwill Industries in Wilmington, that G. Harlan Wells spoke and that the Rev. R. Jerris Cooke conducted the service. But when all this was said and the picture was examined, readers were still left to guess what Harlan House is or who Mollie Harlan was that the house should be named for her. Was she related to G. Harlan Wells?

A paper reported in detail the arrest of a minister on charges of operating a motor vehicle without a license, failure to carry a car registration card, disorderly conduct and disobeying a police officer. When three of the four charges were dismissed, the story failed to tell why. Answer: It is standard procedure to dismiss the license and registration charges when a driver has simply forgotten to carry the documents.

A Page One story told the fascinating details of a divorce decree upheld by the state Supreme Court but failed to mention the names of the parties in the case.

Another story gave an account of the Senate's 78-8 approval of the president's trade bill but failed to tell who the eight opponents were and, even worse, how the senators from the paper's state voted on the measure. This was a revolutionary trade measure that had been in the news for months and was finally opposed by only eight senators. Wasn't anyone who handled the story curious about their names?

A story in March said, "The Bahais will celebrate New Year's eve at the Bahai center. There will be readings and music." The story read, "New Year's Day tomorrow is known as Naw-Ruz." Couldn't the reporter have dropped the music and the readings and told instead who Bahais are and what the heck New Year's Day is doing in the middle of March?

A skindiver stayed under water for 31 hours and spent much of his time reading a paperback book. There was no word to explain what kept the pages from disintegrating. (The paper was a glossy stock.)

A woman won a fat prize in a magazine advertising contest. There was no hint what she did to win, a point made more important by the statement that the woman could neither read nor write.

Another story concerned a judge who reversed his own conviction of a union leader for breach of the peace. The reversal, said the story, was based on "new evidence" but failed to tell readers the nature of the new evidence.

The story said that 105 of the 120 blacks enrolled at Northwestern marched out of a building singing. It failed to mention the songs they sang, a detail that might have shed more light on their behavior.

If any part of the story is confusing, the copy editor should supply explanations. Obviously, the explanation should not be as hard to understand as the phrase itself. For instance:

> Congress in 1946 waived government immunity to suits in tort (a civil wrong in which a legal action may lie) and permitted suits on tort claims against the United States.

The parenthetical explanation hardly aids most readers. If an explanation is required, it should be one that really helps:

> As a rule, sovereign government may not be sued by its citizens unless the government consents. In 1946 Congress gave blanket permission to citizens to sue the U.S. government if they thought it was responsible for injuries to them or their property.

The story of a boy who died, apparently of suffocation after he choked on a hot dog in his home. Police said the boy left the table after dinner and was found choking in his bathroom. His mother slapped him on the back in a vain attempt to dislodge the obstruction. Firefighters took him to a hospital where he was pronounced dead. A few lines of first-aid instruction at the end of the story might have saved other lives.

A woman who was hospitalized twice in a short time asked to be transferred from one hospital to another to be near her husband. What ailed hubby? It wasn't explained.

The Royal Navy dropped the unit *fathom* and started measuring depths in meters. The story told all about it. All, that is, except how deep a fathom is.

A story contained the statement "where family income is below federal poverty levels" but neglected to tell the readers what the poverty level is by federal standards.

"A bell captain in a midtown hotel was arrested for scalping World Series tickets." Why the reluctance to name the hotel? A directive reminded editors, "In these days, when GIs, businessmen, students, school teachers et al. are traveling throughout the world, such identification is often of interest to many readers. The part of town where a news event occurs is sometimes pertinent too in stories from the big cities that are frequented by travelers."

Here is a complete story as one newspaper printed it:

TALLAHASSEE—The simmering feud between Republican Gov. Claude Kirk of Florida and his Democratic cabinet erupted into a full scale shouting battle today, and Kirk ordered an end to weekly cabinet meetings for the first time in state history.

Cabinet members immediately declared they would go on meeting anyway.

The stormy session began with the cabinet refusing to spend $35,000 on a federal liaison office that Kirk wants to open in Washington.

Some readers must have wondered how a Republican governor came to have a Democratic cabinet, what officials belong to the cabinet, what can be accomplished by cabinet meetings not attended by the governor and whether the weekly meeting is required by law.

The first rule in writing or editing a story is to ask yourself: Who will read the item and what will they most want to know about the subject? Both the writer and the copy editor should pare the story for word economy. They should not pare it for fact economy.

EXTRANEOUS FACTS

News presents the pertinent facts. Every story should answer all the questions the reader expects answered. If a big story returns after having been out of the news, it should contain a short background or reminder. Readers don't carry clips to check background.

Robert J. Casey, an author and former reporter for the defunct *Chicago Daily News,* once observed, "Too many facts can louse up a good story." If a fact isn't vital in telling the news, it should be omitted. It is an example of string saving. Stray bits have a way of bringing trouble. A buried reference to a 30-year-old hanging "from an apple tree on Joe Smith's farm" brought a libel suit. Joe Smith was still living; the hanging wasn't on his farm. The reference added nothing to the story but taught the editor a lesson.

This could be held to a paragraph or two; it is not worth five column inches of type:

Robert F. Kelley today was named chairman of this year's Democratic Jefferson-Jackson Day dinner.

The appointment was announced jointly by Democratic State Chairman John M.C— and National Committeeman William S. P—.

Kelley, administrative assistant for 12 years to ex-Sen. J. Allen F— Jr. in Washington, said he will name a dinner committee, site, date and speaker in a "few days."

The Jefferson-Jackson Day dinner, traditionally held in late April or early May, is the largest meeting of its kind held by the Democrats each year.

Kelley said he already is trying to line up a "nationally known" speaker for the occasion.

Kelley, now associated with the legal department of the D—Co., has been a member of the dinner committee for several years. This is his first assignment as chairman of the affair.

Kelley was a vice chairman of last year's Community Fund drive and has a wide background in party and civic affairs.

He is a past president of the Delaware State Society and the Administrative Assistants and Secretaries Club in the nation's capital.

MORE PRECISION

A school board (or board of education) is a group of individuals elected by the citizens to direct the operation of the school system. It is not a place, not an office, not a building, not the school system.

"He studied French under E. B. DeSauze, the retired supervisor of the school board's language department." De Sauze was supervisor of foreign languages for the public schools. The school board has no language department.

It is the American Museum of Natural History, not the Museum of Natural History in New York City, and the Smithsonian Institution, not the Smithsonian Institute.

The U.S. Supreme Court did not ban prayers in school. The court banned the requirement that children pray any particular prayer, or the writing by public authorities of a required prayer. The decision had to do with public schools. It did not interfere with required prayers in church-operated schools.

Gas and *gasoline* are not synonymous. Gas is either natural or manufactured. Some explosions are caused by gas, some by gasoline. The story and headline should contain the precise term. Similarly, in stories of food poisoning, the copy should specify whether the story is referring to canned or bottled foodstuffs.

Reporters and headline writers are fond of writing that taxes will "eat up" a will or a fortune or an estate. Taxes may deplete the bank account, but they can't eat up anything.

"A defective 20mm cannon . . . suddenly fired and the shell killed one airman and injured another." The writer should have said *unexpectedly* rather than "suddenly," a *shell* rather than "the shell," and *bullet, slug* or *projectile* rather than "shell."

Pistol is a general term for a small firearm. It can be single-loading, or a revolver or an automatic. Clip-loading pistols are sometimes called automatics, but they are usually semiautomatics or self-loaders. The barrel diameter of rifles and pistols is expressed in calibers (.22). A shotgun bore is expressed by its gauge (12-gauge) except for the .410.

"A 20-year-old robber was dead as the result of a gun battle in which 14 shots were fired at point-blank range." "Point-blank range" is an archaic expression based on the firing of cannon. Because the expression is meaningless to today's readers, why use it?

ETHNIC GROUPS

"It is perhaps the most cosmopolitan area in the city, stronghold of the Poles and densely populated with other ethnic groups including Czechs, Bohemians, Slovaks and some Italians," one story reported. But Czechs and Bohemians are one and the same people. The Czech lands include Bohemia and Moravia. Some Bohemians prefer to be called Czechs. Slovaks are a separate people, although there is a strong language affinity. There is a difference between a Slovak and a Slovenian, as any editor would soon realize should the two be confused.

Wire service copy sometimes fails to explain terms common in one section of the nation but not in another. For instance, readers may deduce that *bracero* is a Mexican laborer. If the word can't be explained, it should be eliminated so as not to puzzle readers who don't know Spanish.

An executive city editor gave the copy chief trouble for failure to catch the idiocy of an "anti-Soviet" play written in the czarist days. Even though *Soviet* technically refers to an organizational system within the Communist structure, it is now generally accepted as a reference to the U.S.S.R. Russia, of course, is only one of the republics in the Soviet Union.

Britain or *Great Britain* refers to the largest of the British Isles and consists of England, Scotland and Wales. *United Kingdom* should be used when England, Scotland, Wales and Northern Ireland are meant. A Briton is a native or subject of Britain. Despite the fact that other nationals of the United Kingdom may be annoyed when *England* is used as the equivalent of *Britain* or the *United Kingdom,* the use of *England* in the wider sense is acceptable.

STEREOTYPES

The copy editor must be on guard against unnecessary stereotyping in copy. People have become increasingly sensitive to demeaning and derogatory labels, and the editor has been forced to confront them in copy. The copy editor guards against conscious and unconscious semantic bias. To do that requires an awareness of stereotypes.

People live in two worlds: the one they experience directly and the one they know about from other sources. There is no doubt that the first world is smaller and that the second is created largely by the mass media. Thus, what Walter Lippmann called "the pictures in our heads"—our view of reality—are formed largely by information channeled to us through the media. For that reason alone, the process of stereotyping is insidious because it tends to distort our view of reality.

A stereotype is a standardized mental picture representing an oversimplified opinion, emotion, attitude or uncritical judgment of a person, group, race, issue or event. It often results in demeaning or ridiculing the subject.

We stereotype out of necessity; stereotypes provide us with a shorthand way of looking at the world. For example, we might form a stereotype based on personal experience: Whenever certain weather conditions have appeared, it has rained. So when we feel high humidity and see dark clouds, we carry umbrellas. This oversimplified reaction to an event makes our lives easier. We can react to the situation without thinking. In this example, what we believe to be true is grounded in fact, or at least in personal experience; it usually has rained on us under these conditions. So not all stereotypes are without basis in fact. Nor are they all dangerous. In this example, we might be inconvenienced if it did not rain and we had to carry umbrellas all day, but that is all.

Most stereotypes, however, are not this innocuous.

Language reflects the prejudices of society. Casey Miller and Kate Swift make the point that English, through most of its history, evolved in a white, Angle-Saxon, patriarchial society. Its vocabulary and grammar therefore frequently reflect attitudes that exclude or demean minorities and women.[1]

Words are so much more than they appear to be. As semanticists tell us, words represent attitudes and beliefs. The words chosen by an individual say as much about the individual as anything else.

When we stereotype, we label (people especially), and once we do that, the label tends to attract more attributes than it should. Like a snowball rolling down a hill, the label becomes all-encompassing. The words and images that are caught up in it classify people indiscriminately:

Women . . . are fragile. Mexicans . . . are lazy. Blacks . . . are on welfare. Indians . . . are drunks. Professors . . . are absent-minded. Old people . . . are senile.

When people are stereotyped according to race, that is racism. In the last decade or so, the general public has begun to be aware that language also stereotypes according to sex, which is sexism. Even newer in the public consciousness is ageism, stereotyping according to age.

While there is little excuse for reporters to let their stereotypes spill over into their writing, there is less excuse for copy editors to pass copy with racist, sexist or ageist assumptions and statements. For the copy editor, these "isms" ought to be added to the list of "red flags"—those things in copy, headlines, cutlines, even the premise of a story itself—that cause the editor to step back, to wonder why.

As Miller and Swift write, "The need today . . . is to be in command of language, not used by it, and so the challenge is to find clear, convincing, graceful ways to say accurately what we want to say."[2]

[1] Casey Miller and Kate Swift, *The Handbook of Nonsexist Writing* (New York: Lippincott & Crowell, 1980), p. 3.
[2] Ibid., p. 8.

RACISM

There was a time when racism in newspapers was blatant; racial identifications were mandatory. Certain stories were not written because of the race of the participants; others were written for the same reason. Generally, that no longer is the case. Racism in the media, as in much of society, has become subtle.

That is not to say that it is impossible to find examples of blatant racism.

A story about a bomb threat to a northern Wisconsin high school included this: "According to the complaint filed at the Minocqua Police Department, (the secretary) reported that the threat came from a male Indian's voice." Just how does a male Indian sound?

The *Chicago Tribune*, not too many years ago, described the subject of one of its stories as "the well-dressed, articulate black man." The implication was that it was out of the ordinary for a black man to be well-dressed and articulate.

Subtle racism is more difficult to identify.

A story from *The New York Times* News Service about an explosion at a day-care center in a black section of Atlanta included this:

" 'I heard a real loud boom and I ran out the door and saw the smoke and dust and ran down here," said Eugene Drewery, 30, an unemployed construction worker.... " It might be suggested that it was necessary to describe the man as unemployed to explain why he was home in the middle of the day. It is, however, sexist to assume a young man should not be home during the day and irrelevant to the story to include his job status. Instead, the reader is helped to make an unjustified connection between the man's race and the fact of his unemployment.

A writer in the *Star Tribune, Newspaper of the Twin Cities,* used the following anecdote to begin his story about a high school celebrating its state basketball championship:

> One of the posters done up Sunday for the celebration honoring North High School's boys' basketball team was misspelled.
>
> The one that said "Team Minneapolis" was all right and so were the ones that said "State Champs!" and "Polar Power," but over on the front wall of the gymnasium, right underneath the big polar bear, was a banner proclaiming *"Congradulations."*
>
> One of the women helping with the decorations spotted the error. "Oh, no," she said, "that's what they'll show on TV."
>
> Before long a new poster, with the blue tempera paint that spelled "Congratulations" still dripping, was taped up over the old one.
>
> Image is important to the people of North High School, because this school in the heart of one of the city's poorest neighborhoods has had such a bad image for so long. But on this afternoon of celebration after an evening of achievement, the people of North High were talking of pride in their community, their school and, of course, their basketball team....

A copy editor headlined the story: **North High spirit triumphs over spelling.**

A week later, the paper's reader representative explained in his column what an eye-opener the story proved to be for the *Star Tribune,* which received numerous complaints about the headline and the story from members of the North High community, teachers and students. The Minneapolis Urban League requested and received a meeting with *Star Tribune* staff members involved in the story. As the newspaper's ombudsman explained to his readers:

> The meeting . . . forced some of us to decide that the headline and, by extension, the story did indeed display an insensitivity both to the feelings of the North High community and to the danger of reinforcing stereotypes.
>
> [The] assistant managing editor of the *Star Tribune* reflected after the meeting that [the reporter] "wrote in good faith a story in which he made choices of material that he thought told the story of a school with image problems trying to cope with those problems on a day of pride and triumph. But he produced a story that did almost precisely the opposite in the eyes of lots and lots of readers. The headline exacerbated the problem. . . ."
>
> But the *Tribune's* real failure was not so much in the writing of the story as in not taking a second step, said [the assistant managing editor]. Some editor should have looked at the story with an awareness of the stereotypes and the danger of reinforcing them. That editor should have anticipated the effect of the story and ordered changes."

SEXISM

Like racism, sexism appears in both blatant and subtle forms. Unlike racism, however, blatant sexism is common in most American newspapers.

It has been and remains common to describe women in news stories in ways that men making news seldom have been described, even though, for example, the stylebooks of the Associated Press and United Press International clearly state that "women should receive the same treatment as men in all areas of coverage."

Irrelevant descriptions of women's appearances remain. Note the incongruity of these two consecutive paragraphs:

> At 8:58 p.m. Nancy Reagan—wearing a red dress and large gold earrings—was greeted by an ovation as she entered the gallery.
> Two minutes later, Reagan entered the chamber to an explosion of applause.

Apparently it was unnecessary to describe the president's attire.

UPI carried the practice to extremes when Joan Kennedy received her master's degree. Wrote UPI, "Mrs. Kennedy, dressed in black cap and gown, marched under the sunny skies with some 400 other graduates. . . ."

Copy editors must recognize slanted adjectives and descriptive phrases that serve only to reinforce sexual stereotypes:

> Patricia Brennan, an auburn-haired 24-year-old with the look of a mischievous tomboy, claims she never stood in front of the Post Office and yelled, "Nah, nah! Anything you can do we can do better."

Alcott shared the opening day lead with Barbara Moxness. . . . The personable 24-year-old brunette from Santa Monica, Calif., started the day four strokes ahead. . . .

Nancy Freitas, 32, a blonde with green eyes and a preference for strictly feminine, tailored attire, is the new general manager of the San Diego Breakers of the International Volleyball Association.

One of the most common problems faced by newspapers is how to refer to women in stories. Many newspapers have dropped the traditional practice of using courtesy titles for women, but the use of such titles remains common. One exception is on sports pages, where it is more common to treat men and women similarly—without courtesy titles. Whatever a newspaper's policy, the copy editor should ensure consistent treatment.

It is incorrect to write Mrs. Mary Smith because she is not married to Mary; she is either Mary Smith or Mrs. John Smith. It is unacceptable to treat men and women of equal position differently, as in the story that made these identifications: "Ms. Long, 29, is a physician. . . . " and "Dr. Stanley Mohler. . . . " Equivalent terms should be applied to men and women in a story or headline: lady/gentleman; woman/man; girl/boy. This headline, then, should have been unacceptable:

**Lady doctors
and male nurses**

**Male nurse walks tightrope
of compassion and tradition**

These headlines should not have been written either:

**Brattleboro Man Found Dead
Montpelier Girl Found Dead**

He was 18; she was 26.

There are times when a copy editor might question the entire approach a reporter has taken in a story on the basis that it only reinforces sexual stereotypes, much as the Minneapolis reporter was cited for reinforcing racial stereotypes.

For example, a reporter began her story this way: "Mothers aren't the only ones who can tell us how to eat properly. A computer can, too." And so could a father. But this reporter reinforces the prevailing stereotype that it is the mother's role to look out for the needs of children. Further, there is a more subtle implication that a computer can replace a mother. The story easily could have been made more acceptable; the copy editor could have changed the lead to read, "Parents aren't the only ones. . . ."

A similar sexist role is prescribed by the writer whose lead read: "The women were not the only ones who enjoyed themselves at the . . . Homemakers School last night. . . . The men and children had a good time, too, sampling the good food. . . . "

How many stereotyped images can you identify in this lead, which shows that men also can be victims of reportorial sexism?

It's your weekly trip to the hairdresser. Your hair has been shampooed, cut, colored and curled, and you're ready to bake under the dryer. As you sit there, reading your latest issue of Vogue magazine, you turn to your neighbor to discuss the newest trends in skirt length.

Suddenly, you realize you're face to face with a man—and he's in curlers.

You can react three ways.

You can blush and wish you were dead.

You can quickly end the conversation and wish you'd worn makeup.

You can keep talking and wonder if he's dating anyone.

AGEISM

Ageist stereotypes have been around as long as those based on race and sex. One that comes immediately to mind is the "Confucius say . . ." variety—the wisdom of old age. Only now, however, are people beginning to explore the implications of stereotypes about aging and the aged, and the complex set of problems they have helped to create.

Common stereotypes portray the old as poor, isolated, sick, unhappy, rigid, reactionary, unproductive, and grandparently.

The Gray Panthers, activists who serve as advocates for the old, designed their Media Watch Project to allow viewers to identify and publicize ageist stereotypes in television programming and commercials. They urge alertness to several stereotypes:

- Physical appearance: face always blank or expressionless; body always bent over and infirm.
- Clothing: men's baggy and unpressed; women's frumpy and ill-fitting.
- Speech: halting and high-pitched; stubborn, rigid, forgetful.

The Gray Panthers also warn of distortions, in which old age is depicted either as an idyllic or a moribund stage of life, and omissions, in which the concerns and positive aspects of aging are omitted.

The sensitive copy editor will be alert for ageism in copy and headlines.

In this example, from a story about a visit to central Missouri by Clare Booth Luce (see Figure 7-1), both ageist and sexist stereotypes are evident. An alert copy editor deleted the paragraph from the story.

"She remained standing during the reception, even though she is frail since cataract surgery a few years ago. Her eyes are still bright blue, and her beauty shines despite her years. The attitude of the young college men attested to her attractiveness—they all wanted to kiss her."

Apparently, age alone sometimes is enough to qualify one as grand-motherly or grandfatherly. A headline on a sports page announced: **Local Grandmother Wins Bowling Tourney**. In the story, no mention was made of grandchildren. The woman was, however, identified as being 58. Another

Figure 7-1.   Stereotypes exist in newspapers. An account of the visit of Clare Booth Luce prompted ageist and sexist stereotypes that were deleted by the copy editor. [Photo courtesy of the Columbia Missourian]

reporter wrote that "Cora is a grandmotherly sort" without elaborating on just what that said about Cora. And the copy editor who asked in a headline, **"Can one live happily ever after retirement?"** implied that retirement rarely is a time of happiness.

UNACCEPTABLE LABELS

Editors increasingly are being called upon to be more sensitive to the labels they place on people or groups of people. The terms *Negro* and *colored*, once common in U.S. newspapers, have disappeared in favor of *black*. Now the term *African American* is gaining favor. Similarly, *Indian* is being abandoned for the more precise term *Native American*.

Our language is full of derisive terms for people. Such terms often, but not always, are directed at minorities (*Jap, wetback, wop*). Examples of such derogatory terms aimed at the majority are *WASP* (for white Anglo-Saxon Protestant) and *honky* (a derisive term directed toward whites by blacks).

Some words (*codger, gaffer, deaf and dumb*) are offensive to some groups but commonly appear in print. Other negatives are aimed at a person's sexual preference (*dyke, queer, faggot*) or background (*redneck, hillbilly*).

A few terms may not seem at first glance to be offensive but are if one is aware of their backgrounds. An example is *basket case,* a term that began as British army slang for a quadruple amputee but has come to be used indiscriminately for those who are incapacitated.

Sensitivity to others is essential if the newspaper is to retain its credibility with all readers. Such terms have no place in newspapers.

TASTE

An editor of a morning newspaper said his newspaper likes to protect those who read during breakfast against the incursions of unpalatable news. How then, he asked, did this sentence get to the breakfast table: "Plans to take still another sample were canceled when Hutchinson become ill and threw up." Actually, he *vomited*. Had the story said he became nauseated, anyone who is familiar with 10½ beers—Hutchinson's load in less than 2½ hours—would have gotten the point.

The *Los Angeles Times* and other metropolitan newspapers have adopted a screen code to control and avoid lewd advertising in entertainment copy. One of the advertising executives of the *Times* said, "It is not our intention to be either picayunish or prudish in our evaluation, but we are convinced that moral and social values have not decayed as frequently as portrayed, and we trust that together we can find a better standard of values in the area of good taste." Among subjects banned are bust measurements, compromising positions, double meaning, nude figures or silhouettes, nymphomania, perversion, and suggestive use of narcotics, or alcohol. Words avoided include *cuties, girlie, lust, nymph, party girls, play girls, scanty panties, sexpot, strippers* and *third sex*.

The caution should apply equally to amusement promotion copy and to all other copy. Both wire services direct their editors to downplay anatomy. Copy editors should apply heavy pencils to stories about the "10 best undressed women" and about an actress hired because of her uncommonly ample bosom. Better yet, those stories should not be used.

There is no need to run everything turned in as news by the staff, the wire services or the syndicates. There is an obligation to print the news. There also is an obligation to edit it.

Some vulgarisms get into the report, usually when they are said by a public figure at a public gathering and in a justifiable news context. Most member papers used the following lead from London even though the AP headed the dispatch with a cautionary note: " 'Gentlemen,' said Prince Philip, 'I think it is time we pulled our fingers out.' "

But the editor of a Dayton, Ohio, newspaper was forced to resign when management panicked because 50 callers protested after the editor had approved the inclusion of dialogue, including words connoting sexual intercourse, in a Page One murder story. The fact that the dialogue was from a direct transcript of testimony during the hearing had no effect on management's decision. Nor did the fact that 110,000 or so other readers didn't complain.

Is *s.o.b.* milder than the full expression? If the president of the United States refers to a syndicated columnist as an "s.o.b.," that's news. The columnist in question passed off the slur by saying the president obviously meant "sons of brotherhood." Another president used the phrase "sons of business."

When Jack Ruby shot Lee Harvey Oswald, accused of assassinating President John F. Kennedy, Ruby is purported to have exclaimed, "I hope I killed the son of a bitch." The quote appeared in the news dispatches from Dallas. There was a day when editors would have substituted dashes or asterisks for the words. Some bannered the quote, but with initials: **Jack Ruby—"I hope I killed the s.o.b."**

Frankness used in good taste is preferable to yesterday's euphemisms, such as "social disease" for *syphilis*, "intimate relationship" for *sexual inter-*

course, "assault" for *rape.* Why refer to washrooms and toilets in public buildings, such as schools, as "bathrooms"? Ever try to take a bath in one?

This story was published in a daily under a two-column headline:

Coed Reports Rape

An 18-year-old university student claimed she was raped early Sunday morning by a man she met in a local nightclub, sheriff's officers said.

The woman said she was drinking and dancing with the man at the Sweet Lass lounge before accepting a ride to the man's apartment. The man invited her to his apartment for some drugs, she told officers.

When the couple arrived at the apartment, the man invited the woman into the bedroom and the woman accepted. The man then partially undressed the woman (she completed the undressing) and attempted to have sexual relations with her, she said.

The woman told police she said no to the man but did not resist his advances.

After a brief period, the woman said the man "gave up, rolled over and went to sleep."

While the man slept, the student said she got dressed and went to her dormitory. Because of her intoxicated condition, the woman said she was unsure whether the sexual act was completed.

The reporter should never have submitted this non-story. The story should never have passed the city desk and certainly should have been challenged on the copy desk. No one was arrested or charged, so there was no news value. It is, at best, but idle chatter and has no place in a newspaper.

EDIT TO THE FINAL STOP

One of the most common problems found in newspapers is the failure of editors to make stories consistent from top to bottom. The most common example is the story with numbers that don't add correctly:

The United Way on Monday awarded $23,000 in supplemental funds to three agencies.

. . . The additional funds will go to the Boy Scouts, $11,000; the Girl Scouts, $9,000; and the Salvation Army, $4,000.

Here are some other classic examples:

"Tanglewood Barn Theater ended its regular season with a bang in its production of 'Wonderful Town' Wednesday night." Last paragraph: "The show will be repeated at 8:15 p.m. through Sunday."

"His companion said Fennell dived from the boat, swam away, went under and never came up." Last paragraph, "Interment will be in Mt. Zion Cemetery." What was to be buried in lieu of the body that never came up?

"The largest single cost of the trial was jury expenses, which total $3,807."
Later: "Another cost was $20,015 paid to extra guards and bailiffs."

A story concerned a robber. Part of it went like this: "The suspect apparently hid in the store when it closed at 9 p.m. About 11 p.m. he confronted a security guard, Paul H. Hogue, 57, of 5625 Lowell Blvd., as he was turning off the lights in the budget store of the basement." Last paragraph: "According to parole officials, Hogue's parole was suspended June 6 for failure to report and he was being sought as a parole violator." A correction sufficed in this case, but a correction does no credit to the reporter or to the copy editor.

The editor who edits to the final stop and who is ever alert to the kinds of problems described in this chapter will be a valued member of the newspaper's staff. By doing the job properly, that editor will be building credibility for the newspaper, not contributing to the demise of that credibility.

CHAPTER 8

LEGAL LIMITATIONS ON THE PRESS

The editor who lives in constant fear of a damage suit, the copy editor who snitts libel in every story and thereby tries to make the safe safer and the reporter who thinks it is cute to refer to an inept council member as a simian have no place on a newspaper. The first procrastinates and vacillates, the second makes the copy vapid, and the third lands the publisher in court.

Neither the reporter nor the copy editor need be a lawyer, but both should know enough about the legal aspects of journalism to know when to consult a lawyer. Some of these trouble spots are discussed in this chapter.

The press can use its immense freedom vigorously. Only when it abuses its freedom does it face punishment.

We need no license to establish a press and start publishing. Nor must we submit copy to any censor before or after publication. We can criticize the government and its officials severely and have no fear that the doors to the newspaper will be padlocked. In our system, no government—federal, state, county or municipal—can be libeled. The newspaper is not a public utility. It can reject or accept any story, advertisement, picture or letter it wishes.

We do not have to beg or bribe officials to get a quota of newsprint. The newspaper does not depend on government advertising (except for the possible exception of legal advertising). We do not face the threat of withdrawal of the government's privileges should we disagree with its policies.

Courts generally cannot exercise prior restraint to prevent publication of information, although one lower court did in the *Pentagon Papers* case, and the Supreme Court declined to review a judge's prior restraint on Cable News Network's decision to broadcast tapes of former Panamanian dictator Manuel Noriega's conversations with his lawyer. Punishment, if any, comes after publication. Long ago we rejected the notion that the greater the truth, the greater the libel. We can report, portray or comment on anyone who becomes newsworthy. Not even the president is immune from press coverage.

References to a half-dozen U.S. Supreme Court decisions will indicate the scope of the freedom the press enjoys. Some early cases helped to establish the principles that truth is a defense in libel and that the jury may determine both the law and the fact. The court has prohibited a discriminatory tax on the press. The court has told judges that neither inherent nor reasonable tendency is sufficient to justify restriction of free expression and that contempt of court is to be used only when there is a clear and present danger of interfering with the orderly administration of justice. The court has held that comment on or about public officials is privileged, even if false, provided there is no "actual malice." The court defined actual malice as publication with knowledge that the information is false or with reckless disregard of whether it is false. This privilege now covers public figures—those in the public limelight—as well as public officials.

This brief review is intended to remind editors of the unusual liberties we enjoy. It should not deter editors and publishers from maintaining a constant vigil to preserve and extend these freedoms. We still have the problems of news management at all levels of government. We still have some judges and attorneys who would dry up most news of crime until after the trial. In some jurisdictions we still cannot use cameras in the courtroom. We still have those who would like to censor what we read, hear or view. We still wrestle with the problem of what constitutes obscenity and who is to decide what is obscene. Worst of all, we have many in our society who care little about press freedom. If these people could have their way, they would return to 16th-century England and the Court of Star Chamber where any criticism of the realm was promptly punished. What some people don't realize is that the freedom to read, to listen and to view is their right, not the special privilege of any commercial enterprise.

THE LIBEL HAZARD

Publishers and broadcasters face risks far greater than do most other professional or business executives. More than a century ago a London editor, John T. Delane of the *Times,* said, "The Press lives by disclosures." All disclosures are hazardous. If errors occur, they are public and may subject the error maker to liability.

The day is rare when any publisher or broadcaster doesn't commit errors—wrong facts, wrong names and identifications, wrong addresses, wrong dates, wrong spelling or pronunciation, wrong grammar or wrong headlines. Fortunately, only a handful of such errors are serious enough to prompt lawsuits.

Few libels are deliberate. Almost all result from erroneous reporting, misunderstanding of the law or careless editing.

MISUNDERSTANDING THE LAW

In an attempt to foster understanding of the law, here is a review of some common misconceptions:

1. There is a common assumption that if a statement originated from an outside source, it is safe. That is wrong because a newspaper or broadcast station is responsible for whatever it publishes or broadcasts from whatever source—advertisements, letters, feature stories.
2. There is a feeling that if a person is not named, he or she may not sue. That is not true because a plaintiff sometimes can be identified by means other than name.

3. There is a feeling that if the harmful statement concerns a group, individual members cannot sue. That is wrong because some groups are small enough (juries, team members, council members) that each may have a case.

4. Another common error is misjudging the extent of privilege in an arrest. Statements by the police as to the guilt of the prisoner or that the prisoner "has a record a mile long" are not privileged, although some states do grant a privilege to publish fair and accurate stories based on police reports. All persons are presumed innocent until they are proved guilty.

CARELESSNESS IN REPORTING AND EDITING

These situations may prove to be dangerous:

1. Mistaken identity. Similarity of names doesn't necessarily mean similarity of identity. People in trouble often give fictitious names. Identification should be qualified by phrases explaining the situation such as "who gave his name as...," "listed by police as..." or "identified by a card in her purse as...." In listing addresses in crime and court stories, some papers use the block instead of a specific number. Several families might live at the same address.

2. Clothing the damaging statement with *alleged* or *allegedly*. Qualification with these words carries little protection.

3. "Needled" headlines. Qualifications are difficult in a headline because of the limited character count. It is wrong to assume that as long as the story is safe the head can take liberties. Many readers read only the headline. A picture caption also may be libelous. Within the story itself, statements usually cannot be taken out of context to create a libel. The story usually must be considered in its entirety.

4. The assumption that a person with an unsavory reputation can't be libeled. A man may be a notorious drunk, but that doesn't necessarily make him a thief.

5. Confession stories used before the confession has been admitted as evidence in court. In pretrial stages, this poses dangers. It is better to say merely that the prisoner has made a statement.

6. The assumption that any statement one person makes about another is protected if the reporter can prove that the first person actually made the statement about the second. That is not true in most states. If A reports that B is a liar, the reporter must be prepared to prove not that A made the statement, but that B is, in fact, a liar.

LIBELOUS STATEMENTS

The legal definition of libel is damage to a person's reputation caused by bringing that person into hatred, contempt or ridicule in the eyes of a substantial and respectable group. Anything is a newspaper is libelous if it damages a living person's reputation or has an adverse effect on that person's means of earning a living. The same applies to businesses and to institutions.

A story is defamatory if it accuses a living person of a crime or immorality or imputes a crime or immorality; if it states or insinuates that a person is insane or has a loathsome or contagious disease; if it tends in any way to subject the victim to public hatred, contempt or ridicule or causes others to shun that person or refuse to do business with that person; or if it asserts a want of capacity to conduct one's business, occupation or profession.

Wrong assumptions sometimes can make a statement defamatory. A person who sets fire to a dwelling is not necessarily an arsonist. A person who kills another is not necessarily a murderer. Some items in a newspaper are false but not necessarily defamatory. A false report that a man has died usually is not libelous.

A statement may cause someone pain and anguish, but mere vituperation does not make a libel; it must be substantial. It is not enough that the statement may disturb that person. It must damage that person in the estimation of those in the community or of those with whom the person does business.

Libel can be avoided if the staff exercises responsibility in accuracy, exactness and judgment. But even when libel does occur, it need not terrify the staff. Some cases are not serious enough to entice a lawyer to take the case to court.

Only the person libeled has cause for action. Relatives, even though they may have suffered because of the false and defamatory statements, have no recourse in libel. The offended person must bring suit within the statutory period (ranging from one to six years depending on the jurisdiction). If the person should die before or during the trial, there may be no continuation of the case by survivors.

A person who has been libeled may ask the publication to print a correction. This could satisfy the individual because it tends to set the record straight. In states having retraction laws, the plaintiff can collect only actual damages—and no punitive damages—if the retraction is made on request and within a certain time limit.

Sometimes newspapers offer to run a correction, possibly offer a nominal payment, and then obtain a release from further liability. This procedure saves the time and cost of a trial and may eliminate the possibility of major judgments against the newspaper.

Suppose the plaintiff insists on taking the rascal editor into court. The plaintiff must hire a lawyer and pay the filing fee. The person should be advised of the defenses available to the newspaper—constitutional defense, truth, privilege and fair comment. Because libel concerns reputation, the plaintiff's reputation, good name and esteem can be put at issue. A person with a skeleton in the closet may hesitate to have the past revealed in court. A public figure or public official will have the burden of proving the material was published with actual malice.

Suppose the plaintiff wins in lower court. That person may get damages of hundreds of thousands of dollars—or only a few cents. If the defending publisher loses, an appeal is likely, even to the U.S. Supreme Court if the question involves a constitutional issue. Is the plaintiff able to pay appeals court costs if the case is lost? As a final protection, most publishers buy libel insurance.

Most of the larger dailies have their own lawyers to advise them on sensitive stories. Some lawyers urge, "When in doubt leave it out." But the publisher's attitude is, "This is something that should be published. How can it be published safely?" On extra-sensitive stories in which the precise wording has been dictated by an attorney, the desk should make no changes. The headline must be as carefully phrased.

Libel may involve businesses as well as individuals. A corporation, partnership or trust or other business may be damaged if untrue statements tend to prejudice the entity in the conduct of its trade or business or deter others from dealing with it. Non-profit organizations likewise may collect damages resulting from a publication that tends to prejudice them in the public estimation and thereby interferes with the conduct of their activities.

LIBEL DEFENSES

CONSTITUTIONAL

In a landmark decision in 1964, the U.S. Supreme Court ruled that the constitutional provisions of the First and Fourteenth Amendments could be used as a defense against libel if the defamatory words were used to describe the public acts of public officials and were published without actual malice (New York Times Co. v. Sullivan, 376 U.S. 254, 1964).

The court argued that "debate on public issues should be uninhibited, robust and wide-open, and that it may well include vehement, caustic and sometimes unpleasantly sharp attacks on government and public officials."

In the *Times* decision the court defined actual malice as knowledge that a statement is false or reckless disregard of whether it is false. The burden of proving actual malice was placed on the plaintiff.

The ruling was later extended to include public figures, those in the public eye but not in public office, who thrust themselves into the vortex of public debate (AP v. Walker, 383 U.S. 130, 1967) or pervasive public figures (Curtis Publishing Co. v. Butts, 388 U.S. 130, 1967).

It was used to permit robust discussion in criminal libel cases (Garrison v. Louisiana, 379 U.S. 64, 1964) and in privacy cases where the issue is in the public interest (Hill v. Time, 385 U.S. 374, 1967).

Finally, the *Times* rule was extended to include private persons involved in public interest issues (Rosenbloom v. Metromedia, 403 U.S. 29, 1971).

In 1974 the court overturned the Rosenbloom plurality decision and ruled that the Constitution does not require private persons involved in public issues to prove actual malice in suits seeking actual damages for defamation (Gertz v. Welch, 418 U.S. 323, 1974).

One effect of the Gertz decision was to permit the states to make their own interpretation of libel defense standards for private individuals seeking actual damages. Since the ruling, 22 jurisdictions have given private individuals more protection against damaging statements than accorded to public officials or public figures. Those jurisdictions are Arizona, Arkansas, the District of Columbia, Hawaii, Illinois, Kansas, Kentucky, Maryland, Massachusetts, Michigan, Minnesota, New Hampshire, New Mexico, Ohio, Oklahoma, South Carolina, Tennessee, Texas, Utah, Washington, West Virginia and Wisconsin. In these jurisdictions the negligence test is applied. It requires reporters to use the same care in reporting and writing as any reasonable reporter would use under the same or similar circumstances.

Four states—Alaska, Colorado, Indiana and Texas—use the same standards for private citizens as for public figures and public officials. New York requires private citizens to prove that the reporter exercised "grossly irresponsible conduct." Standards have not yet been set in other states.[1]

TRUTH

Truth is an absolute defense to libel. The truth must be as broad and as complete as the publication upon which the charge was made. Truth offered in evidence need not mean the literal accuracy of the published charge but rather the substance or gist of the charge.

A defending publisher who relies on a document as evidence to show truth must be sure the document can be produced at the trial and be admitted in evidence. A publisher who relies on a witness to give testimony as to truth must be assured the witness is qualified to testify. To take an extreme example, a publisher could not rely on the testimony of a doctor when that testimony would violate the doctor-patient relationship.

PRIVILEGE

Reports of judicial, legislative and executive proceedings—federal, state or municipal—may be published and successfully defended on the grounds of qualified privilege. The qualifications are that the report be fair, substantially accurate, complete or a fair abridgment.

For example, a food inspector may make an official report to a board of health describing conditions found at a certain establishment. The information, even though false, may be reported safely as long as the newspaper's account is full, fair and accurate. If truth is required in the newspaper account, then privilege would be worthless as a defense. What a food inspector may say about Sunday school teachers at a meeting of a service club is not privileged. Only statements made by the official acting in an official capacity can be defended as privileged.

Statements of attorneys, except those made in a courtroom, or by civic organization officials usually are not privileged, nor are press releases from government bureaus.

In many states the mere filing of a complaint, petition, affidavit or other document is not privileged. Anyone can go to the court clerk and

---

[1] The Missouri Group, *News Reporting and Writing* (New York: St. Martin's Press, 1988).

file a complaint containing false, scandalous and damaging statements about another merely upon payment of a filing fee. Proof that libelous statements are contained in the document is not a basis for privilege in many states.

FAIR COMMENT AND CRITICISM

Newspapers are free to discuss public affairs and to comment on the conduct of all public officials, even a low-ranking park board member. This defense has three qualifications: (1) The comment is founded on facts or what the publisher had reasonable grounds to believe are facts. (2) The comment is not made with intent to damage. Here, the burden of proof is on the plaintiff. (3) The comment does not involve the private life or moral character of a person except when it has a direct bearing on qualifications or work.

Those who put themselves or their work before the public are subject to public assessment of their performance, however strong the terms of censure may be. Decisions of the U.S. Supreme Court suggest that, short of malice and reckless disregard of the truth, all debates on public issues should be uninhibited, robust and wide-open, and that such debates may well include vehement, caustic and sometimes unpleasantly sharp attacks on government and public officials. The same freedom could very well apply to comments on anyone in the public eye. The only limitation on the press is that the comments cannot be based on misstatements.

This should not be construed as license. Character and public reputation are priceless possessions and are not good hunting grounds simply because a person holds public office, aspires to public office or in any manner offers talents to the public. There is a difference between assessing the fitness of a candidate or commenting on the products of a public performer and a reckless attack on character and reputation.

CORRECTIONS

The publication of a correction technically admits the libel and therefore negates truth as a defense. But when the defense of truth is not clearly evident, the publisher should make the decision to correct.

When made, the correction should be full and frank and displayed as conspicuously as the article complained of.

A reporter obtained her story over the phone from the judge's secretary. She took her notes in shorthand. When she transcribed her notes, she mistook DWS (driving while under suspension) for DWI (driving while intoxicated) and thus wrote falsely that a certain person had pleaded guilty to driving while intoxicated. Even if this story had been edited by another, it is unlikely the copy editor would have caught the error. The paper should have printed a correction to indicate lack of malice (ill will or intent to damage) and to escape punitive damages should the injured person sue for libel.

But the follow-up story was not a clear correction, and this should have been caught by a copy editor. The headline read **Ex-sheriff's patrolman admits count.** The lead: "A man who five months ago was suspended from the Franklin County Sheriff's Patrol was arraigned in Municipal Court here yesterday, pleading guilty to driving for the past nine years on a suspended license." Later, the story said that the patrolman had been dropped from the force for "misuse of authority" and then qualified that statement with another to the effect the patrolman had to resign on order of the Office of Strategic Information, Fort Ethan Allen, Vt.

The patrolman sued for libel. The defense tried to argue that the crime of driving while the license was suspended was as serious as the crime of driving while intoxicated and therefore the newspaper should not be held accountable for a minor error. The jury disagreed and returned a judgment of $3,500 for the former patrolman.

RIGHT OF PRIVACY

A libel action is brought to protect a person's reputation against defamation. A privacy action is brought to protect a person's right to be left alone. The distinction between the two is not as clear as it once was because privacy is now being used as an alternative to libel or in conjunction with libel.

The right of privacy is an expanding legal doctrine that is so vague and has such ill-defined limits that the press has difficulty in knowing where it stands legally.

Violation of the right of privacy encompasses four torts:

1. Intrusion on the plaintiff's seclusion or solitude, or into private affairs.
2. Public disclosure of embarrassing private facts about the plaintiff.
3. Publicity that places the plaintiff in a false light in the public eyes.
4. Appropriation, for the defendant's advantage, of the plaintiff's name or likeness.

Newspaper accounts generally concern newsworthy subjects who have forfeited, voluntarily or involuntarily, their rights of privacy. The right of privacy does not protect a person or that person's actions if they are a matter of legitimate public interest. Newsworthiness is based on three basic components: public interest, public figures and public records.

Generally, a person who voluntarily participates in a public event abandons the right of privacy. Thus, a newspaper may legitimately display the types of persons who join the Easter parade. But a newspaper in Alabama had to pay damages to a woman photographed while her skirts were blown above her head by an air jet in a fun house at a country fair. She was recognizable because her children were with her.

Some risk is involved in printing photographs taken of people without their consent in their homes or in hospital beds. Pictures showing ways to beat the summer heat may be humorous to readers but not to the hefty woman fanning herself under a tree in her own back yard.

Truth usually is not accepted as a defense in a privacy invasion case, but truth, combined with publishing information released to the public in official court records, is a defense. In other words, the defense is adequate if the information is truthful, comes from an open public trial or comes from court documents that are open for public inspection. Another defense against "private facts" invasion of privacy is that the information is in the public domain because it is widely enough known.

The definition of newsworthiness is so broad and its use as a defense against "private facts" invasion of privacy is so powerful that some scholars wonder if "private facts" invasion of privacy still exists. Newsworthiness, however, is not a defense to intrusion into seclusion.

Appropriation of name or likeness is an expanding threat. Plaintiffs have won appropriation of voice suits, and more jurisdictions are permitting surviving relatives to bring privacy actions against the exploitation of the names or likenesses of deceased relatives.

JUVENILE DELINQUENTS

It is not illegal for a newspaper to publish the name of a juvenile. But some states do not allow officials to release news or pictures of juveniles, defined in most states as anyone under the age of 18. Many officials insist that names of juvenile offenders be withheld on the theory that there is greater opportunity for rehabilitation if the youth is not stigmatized by publicity that may affect him or her for years.

In some states the children's code gives exclusive jurisdiction to the juvenile court over offenders under 14, regardless of the acts committed, and gives concurrent jurisdiction to the district court over youngsters between 16 and 18, unless the crime involved is punishable by either death or life imprisonment if committed by an adult. In murder cases involving youths 14 and over, the district court has original jurisdiction.

Coverage of juvenile matters may be allowed under the following circumstances:

1. *Public hearings.* A U.S. Supreme Court decision extends to juveniles the same guarantees to due process of law provided adults in criminal proceedings. The juvenile has the same rights against self-incrimination, to representation and even to a jury trial. Even in juvenile court, the youngster has a right to a public trial if requested. But after the finding of the jury at a public trial, the juvenile could still be placed before a juvenile court for disposition, out of sight of the press and the public.

2. *Permission of the court.* If the code permits it, the judge may, at his or her discretion, allow coverage concerning the hearing of a juvenile. Frequently, the judge of a juvenile court allows reporters to attend juvenile court sessions but does not permit identification

of the youthful offender. There may be publication of news of such cases, provided that any reference to any child involved is so disguised as to prevent identification.

3. *Traffic cases.* Names of persons of any age may be used in traffic cases.

Copy editors should be alert to the distinction between a juvenile and a minor. In most states a minor is defined as anyone under the age of 21, although some states have reduced the age of majority to 18.

PLAGIARISM AND COPYRIGHT INFRINGEMENT

Plagiarism and copyright infringement are still other areas of concern to the copy editor. Only news stories, not the news itself, can be copyrighted. Even if a newspaper does not protect itself by copyrighting the entire paper or individual stories, it still has a property right in its news and can prevent others from "lifting" the material.

It is assumed that copy editors will be so thoroughly familiar with the contents of opposition papers that they will be able to spot material that copies or paraphrases too closely the work of others.

If a wire service sends out a story based on the story of another member or client, copy editors should not delete the wire service credit to the originator of the story. Nor should they delete any credit on stories or pictures. They may, if directed, compile stories from various sources into one comprehensive story, adding the sources from which the story was compiled.

If their own paper publishes a story to be copyrighted, copy editors should ensure that the notice is complete—the notice of copyright, the copyright date and who holds the copyright.

In editing book review copy, copy editors should have some notion of the limits of fair use of the author's quotations. The problem is relatively minor because few copyright owners would object to the publishing of extracts in a review, especially if the review were favorable. If the review has to be trimmed, the trimming probably would come in the quoted extracts.

LOTTERIES

A lottery is any scheme containing three elements—consideration paid, a prize or award and determination of the winner by chance. This includes all drawings for prizes and raffles, and games such as bingo and keno. It is immaterial who sponsors the scheme. Pictures and advertising matter referring to lotteries and similar gift enterprises are barred from the mail.

Newspapers may not be permitted to announce them or to announce results. Federal law now exempts newspapers in states with legal lotteries as long as they confine themselves to reporting state lotteries. Stories also may be used in cases in which something of news value happened as a result of the lottery. An example would be a story concerning a laborer who became wealthy overnight by having a winning ticket on the Irish Sweepstakes. This would probably be considered a legitimate human interest story rather than a promotion for horse races and lotteries.

CRIME AND COURTS

No longer do American editors play crime by the standards of past generations. They print crime news, but they do not rely on crime stories, even a sex-triangle murder, to boost street sales. Topics such as space and ocean exploration compete with crime for the attention and interest of today's more sophisticated readers.

Crime is a part of the news record, however, and will be carried if newspapers are to fulfill their obligations to readers. Unless they have unusual angles, minor crimes generally are merely listed. When presented in detail, the crime story should be written with the same thoroughness and sensitivity that experts give other subjects. Some observers argue that newspapers should offer more news of criminal court activities—but with the constructive purpose of showing the community the origins and anatomy of crime and how well or how poorly the justice system is functioning.

Copy editors who handle crime stories should make sure that their reports contain no prejudicial statements that could deprive the defendants of fair trials. Their headlines should avoid labels.

One editor admonished his staff, "We should be sensitive about assumption of guilt, not only to avoid libel but to avoid criticism and a bad impression on readers." The caution was occasioned by this lead: "With the dealer who sold a .32-caliber pistol to Mrs. Marian C apparently located, Shaker Heights police today were using handwriting expert Joseph Tholl to link the accused slayer of Cremer Y, 8, to the weapon purchase." The whole tone of this lead is an assumption of guilt and the effort of police to pin the crime on somebody. It should have said the police were trying to determine whether Mrs. C was linked to the gun purchase—not trying to link her.

Here is a conviction lead:

FAYETTEVILLE, N.C. (AP)–Two Marines are being held without bond after terrorizing a family, stealing a car, and trading shots with officers.

They were identified as . . .

They told officers after their Saturday capture they were members of the National Abolitionist Forces, which they described as a militant black group.

In reference to this story, the general news editor said in part, "We do not have a formal set of guidelines for handling crime news, but this story certainly does not conform to regular AP practice. It makes us authority for that statement that the two men held had terrorized a family, stolen a car and traded shots with officers. All we should have said was that they were charged with doing all those things, and who had made the charge."

CORRECT TERMINOLOGY

Newsworthy crimes and trials are covered in detail so that essential information may be conveyed to the public.

Copy editors have to have some knowledge of legal terms and the legal process if they are to make the story and headline technically correct yet meaningful to the layman. *Arrested* is a simple verb understood by all readers. It is better than *apprehended* or *taken into custody*. It is equal to *captured*. A person who is cited, summoned or given a ticket is not arrested.

An *arraignment* is a formal proceeding at which a defendant steps forward to give the court a plea of guilty or not guilty. It should not be used interchangeably with *preliminary hearing,* which is held in a magistrate's court and is a device to show probable cause that a crime has been committed and that there is a likely suspect.

Bail is the security given for the release of a prisoner. The reporter reveals ignorance when writing, "The woman is now in jail under $5,000 bail." She can't be in jail under bail. She can be free on bail, or she can be held in lieu of bail.

A *parole* is a conditional release of a prisoner with an indeterminate or unexpired sentence. *Probation* allows a person convicted of some offense to go free, under suspension of sentence during good behavior, and generally under the supervision of a probation officer.

The word *alleged* is a trap. Used in reference to a specific person (Jones, the alleged gambler), it offers little or no immunity from libel. Jones may be charged with gambling or indicted for gambling. In both instances, *alleged* is redundant. The charge is an allegation or an assertion without proof but carries an indication of an ability to produce proof.

A jail sentence does not mean, necessarily, that a person has been jailed. The individual may be free on bail, free pending an appeal or on probation during a suspended imposition of sentence.

Listing the wrong name in a crime story is the surest route to libel action. Thorough verification of first, middle and last names, of addresses and of relationships is a necessity in editing the crime story.

Names of women or children in rape cases or attempted rape cases generally should not be used. Nor should the story give any clue to their addresses in a way by which they can be identified. Increasingly, feminists are arguing that rape victims' names should *not* be withheld. They argue that rape victims have no reason to feel shame.

Sentences may be consecutive or concurrent. If a man is sentenced to two consecutive three-year terms, he faces six years of imprisonment. If his sentences are concurrent, he faces three years. But why use these terms? The total sentence is what counts with the readers and the prisoner.

If a man has been sentenced to five years but the sentence is suspended, he is given a suspended five-year sentence, not a five-year suspended sentence.

Juries are of two kinds—investigative (grand) and trial (petit). If a grand jury finds evidence sufficient to warrant trial, it issues a *true bill* or indictment. If sufficient evidence is lacking, the return is a *no-bill* or *not-true bill.* "Jones was indicted" means as much as "the grand jury indicted Jones." To say "the grand jury failed to indict Jones" implies it shirked its duty.

A *verdict* is the finding of a jury. A judge renders decisions, judgments, rulings and opinions, but seldom verdicts, unless the right to a jury trial is waived. Although verdicts are returned in both criminal and civil actions by juries, a guilty verdict is found only in criminal actions. Judges declare, but do not order, mistrials. Attorneys general or similar officials give opinions, not rulings.

Corpus delicti refers to the evidence necessary to establish that a crime has been committed. It is not restricted to the body of a murder victim; it can apply as well to the charred remains of a burned house.

Nolo contendere is a legalistic way of saying that a defendant, although not admitting guilt, will not fight a criminal prosecution. *Nolle prosequi* means the prosecutor or plaintiff will proceed no further in the action or suit. Most readers will understand the translation more readily than the Latin expression.

The Fifth Amendment guarantees the due process of law protection for all citizens. The report should not suggest that the use of this protection is a cover-up for guilt. Phrases such as "hiding behind the Fifth" should be eliminated.

The story should distinguish between an act itself and an action. *Replevin,* for example, is an action to recover property wrongfully taken or detained. Trouble will arise if the copy editor lets the reporter translate the action too freely: "Mrs. March filed the replevin action to recover furniture stolen from her home by her estranged husband." So, too, with the tort of *conversion.* "Wrongful conversion" may imply theft, but neither the copy nor the head should convey such implication.

Keeping track of the plaintiff and the defendant should pose no problem except in appellate proceedings in which the original defendant may become the appellant. The confusion is not lessened by substituting *appellee* and *appellant.* The best way is to repeat the names of the principals.

In some civil suits the main news peg is the enormous sum sought by the plaintiff. Whether the same angle should be included in the headline is questionable. In some damage claims the relief sought is far greater than the plaintiff expects to collect. The judgment actually awarded is the news and the headline.

MISUSED TERMS

Copy editors can "tidy up" the crime and court report by watching for the following:

All narcotics are drugs, but many drugs are not narcotics.

A defendant may plead guilty or not guilty to a charge or a crime. There is no such plea as innocent, but "not guilty by reason of insanity" is a plea. A defendant may be judged not guilty by reason of insanity. He is not innocent by reason of insanity. An acquittal means the defendant has been found not guilty. The danger of dropping the *not* has caused some editors to insist on using *innocent* rather than *not guilty,* although some lawyers argue that *innocent* is inappropriate for verdicts.

All lawsuits are tried in courts. *Court litigation,* is therefore redundant.

Statements are either written or oral (not verbal).

"Would-be robber" has no more validity than "would-be ballplayer."

The word *lawman* has no place in the report. It can mean too many things—a village constable, a sheriff's deputy or the sheriff, a prosecutor, a bailiff, a judge, an FBI agent, a revenue agent and so on. It is also sexist. Almost always a more precise word will be found more suitable in a newspaper.

Use *sheriff's deputies* rather than *deputy sheriffs.*

Divorces are granted or obtained. Medals are won or awarded.

"Hit-and-run," "ax-murder," "torture-murder" and the like are newspaper clichés. They should be changed to "hit by an automobile that failed to stop," "killed with an ax," "tortured and murdered."

There's no such thing as an *attempted holdup.* A holdup is a robbery even if the bad guy got nothing from the victim.

Misplacement of words makes the reporter and the copy editor look ridiculous:

"An 80-year-old man . . . pleaded guilty yesterday to reduced charges of attempted indecent and immoral practices in Jefferson Criminal Court."

"Seven persons have been fined . . . for impaired driving in Fenton District Court."

LEGAL JARGON

Legal jargon also should be avoided:

"The case was continued for disposition because the attorney requested no probation report be made on the boy before adjudication."

W.J. Brier and J.B. Rollins of Montana State University studied some Missoula, Mont., adults and their understanding of legal terms. Here are the terms incorrectly defined by more than half the respondents, followed by the correct explanation:

- *Accessories before the fact*—those charged with helping another who committed the felony.
- *Extradition*—surrendered the prisoner to officials of another state.
- *Arraigned*—brought to court to answer to a criminal charge.
- *Indicted*—accused or charged by a grand jury.
- *Civil action*—pertaining to private rights of individuals and to legal proceedings against these individuals.
- *Extortion*—oppressive or illegal obtaining of money or other things of value.
- *Remanded*—sent the case back to a lower court for review.
- *Felony*—a crime of a graver nature than a misdemeanor, usually an offense punishable by imprisonment or death. Misdemeanors, however, can carry sentences of up to one year.

- *Continuance*—adjournment of the case.
- *Writ of habeas corpus*—an order to bring the prisoner to court so the court may determine if the prisoner has been denied rights.
- *Administratrix*—female administrator.
- *Stay order*—stop the action or suspend the legal proceeding.
- *An information*—an accusation or a charge filed by a prosecutor.
- *Venire*—those summoned to serve as jurors.
- *Demurrer*—a pleading admitting the facts in a complaint or answer but contending they are legally insufficient.

Other misunderstood terms include:

- *Released on her personal recognizance*—released on her word of honor to do a particular act.
- *Make a determination on the voluntariness of a confession*—decide whether a confession is voluntary.
- *The plaintiff is . . .* —the suit was filed by . . .

Terms that should be translated include: *bequest* (gift), *debenture* (obligation), *domicile* (home), *in camera* (in the judge's office), *liquidate* (settle a debt), *litigant* (participant in a lawsuit), *paralegals* (legal assistants), *plat* (map), *res judicata* (matter already decided).

Lawyers are fond of word-doubling: *last will and testament, null and void, on or about, written instrument.* Another is *and/or.* "The maximum sentence . . . is a $20,000 find and/or 15 years' imprisonment." The maximum would be the fine and 15 years.

Few readers understand the meaning of the word *writ* (a judge's order or a court order). "In a petition for a writ of mandamus, the new bank's incorporators asked the court. . . . " The copy editor should have changed that to "The new bank's incorporators asked the court to . . . ," or if the term *mandamus* was essential, it should have been explained (a court order telling a public official to do something).

Euphemisms include "attorney" for *lawyer,* "sexually assaulted" or "sexually attacked" for *raped.* Not all jurists, who profess to be or are versed in the law, are judges, and certainly not all judges are jurists.

THREADBARE PHRASES

Here are some threadbare phrases that too often appear in newspapers: *stern warning, brilliant defense, shattered body, police speculated, on the lam, soberly pronounced sentence, robed justices, curfew clamped.*

BE EXACT

A *robber* steals by force. A *thief* steals without resorting to force. Theft suggests stealth. A *burglar* makes an unauthorized entry into a building. If a burglar is caught in the act, pulls a gun on the homeowner and makes off with the family silverware, that person is a robber.

Theft and *larceny* both mean taking what belongs to another. *Larceny* is the more specific term and can be proved only when the thief has the stolen property. Pickpockets and shoplifters are thieves.

Statutory grounds for divorce is redundant. All grounds for divorce are statutory in the state where the divorce is granted.

Charge has many shades of meaning and is often misused. "The psychologist charged last night that black high school students generally do not think of the university as a friendly place." The statement was more an observation than a charge.

Members of the Supreme Court are justices, but not judges or supreme judges. The title of the U.S. Supreme Court's chief justice is Chief Justice of the United States.

Words such as *looted, robbed* and *swindled* should be used properly. It is incorrect to write: "Two men were fined and given suspended sentences yesterday in Municipal Court for stealing newsracks and looting money from them," or "Thieves broke into 26 automobiles parked near the plant and looted some small items." Money or other property is not looted. That from which it is taken is looted. Nor is money robbed. A bank is robbed; the money is stolen. "A man in uniform swindled $1,759 from a woman." No, the person is swindled, not the money.

Some papers object to saying that fines and sentences are *given,* on the ground that they are not gifts.

CHAPTER 9

HANDLING THE WIRE

WIRE SERVICE TECHNOLOGY

Perhaps no area of journalism has been affected more by technological development than the wire services. Both major services in the United States, the Associated Press and United Press International, have invested heavily in computerized equipment that has vastly improved their ability to deliver the news. Most newspaper offices no longer have Teletype machines clattering away to deliver the news at speeds of 50 to 70 words a minute. In their place are computer data links over which AP and UPI transmit stories directly into newspapers' computers at speeds of 1,200 words a minute. Many broadcast stations have high-speed printers to receive copy at that rate, too.

Even the means of transmission has changed. For many years, wire news was transmitted over leased telephone lines in a complicated network that stretched around the world. Today, most of those lines have been replaced by satellite links. The process begins when the wire service beams news material to a satellite orbiting the earth. The signal bounces off the satellite and is picked up by receiving dishes atop newspaper and broadcast station offices. Despite the cost of this sophisticated technology, the wire services have saved millions of dollars in reduced telephone line charges.

Newspapers and broadcast stations have been helped by such developments, too. They get the news faster, cost increases are minimized and reliability is improved. Satellite delivery generally is less subject to interference, and the resulting garbled copy, than telephone transmission.

All this is possible because of the remarkable developments in data transmission that have occurred in the past 20 years. Business and industry, spurred by the need for instant communication with far-flung plants and workers, and the need for the latest information on prices, stock market trends and similar information, led the demand for improved communication. Emergence of the personal computer, improved satellite technology and the shrinking cost of mass data storage have made it possible to do things that once were merely dreams. A traveling salesperson is as close to the office computer as the nearest telephone. With a portable personal computer (some of which fit into a briefcase and weigh less than 10 pounds) and a telephone, that salesperson can report expenses, check for messages from the boss and call up for the latest price of the company's stock. And that's just the beginning. There are literally thousands of databases available to those with the proper security codes.

Some of those databases also provide the user with access to the wire services. News from the Associated Press is offered to subscribers to Dow Jones News Retrieval and CompuServe. News provided that way, however, is not available for broadcast or reprinting; it is intended solely for the individual consumer. Nor is that news indexed by importance, properly sorted or headlined. And it is expensive; those connected to such services pay for access by the minute. For all those reasons, there is ample reason to suspect that consumption of the news by home computer will not replace the services provided by print and broadcast editors—sorting, editing, indexing and headlining the news.

HOW THE SYSTEM WORKS

Stories delivered by the wire services come from several sources:

1. Copy developed by the agencies' own large staffs of reporters, feature writers, analysts, columnists and photographers.
2. Rewrites of stories developed by subscribers. Newspapers or broadcast stations contracting with a wire service agree to make their own news files available to the service, either by providing proofs or computer printouts of stories. Other wire service staffers rewrite from any source available—smaller papers, research reports and other publications.
3. Stringers or correspondents in communities where there is no bureau. Such stringers frequently are newspaper reporters and are called stringers because of the old practice of paying correspondents by their strings of stories represented in column inches.
4. Exchanges with other news agencies, such as foreign agencies.

A reporter telephones a story to the state bureau of AP. If the story has statewide interest, AP files the story on its state wire. If the story has regional interest, the state bureau offers it to a regional bureau, or, in some cases, the state office may offer the story directly to the national desk.

The national desk thus becomes the nerve center for the entire operation of the news agency. That desk collects news from all the state, regional and foreign bureaus, culls the material, then returns it to the regional and state bureaus or to subscribers directly.

The operation sometimes is referred to as a gatekeeping system. A Dutch story, for example, would have to get by the Amsterdam office before it could be disseminated in Holland. The same story would have to clear the London bureau before being relayed to New York and the national desk. That desk then would decide whether the story should be distributed nationally. The desk could send the story directly to newspapers or route it through regional and state bureaus. In the latter cases, the regional bureau would judge whether to transmit the story to a state bureau, and a state bureau would have the option of relaying the story to subscribers. A wire editor then would accept or reject the story. Finally, the reader would become the ultimate gatekeeper by deciding which stories to read and which to ignore.

Small- and medium-sized dailies usually subscribe to only one wire service. Because both agencies cover approximately the same news, the choice for smaller dailies usually rests with the service offering the better state report. But because enough difference exists between the two agencies, larger papers are compelled to subscribe to both services.

Traditionally, the wire service has opened the news cycle with a news budget or summary that indicates to editors the dozen or more top national and international stories that were in hand or were developing.

Today's wire editors may get a four- or five-line abstract of the complete offering—foreign, national, regional and state—transmitted directly to the newspaper's computer. From these abstracts or from VDT directories wire editors select the stories in which they think their readers are interested. Then they retrieve those stories directly from the newspaper's computer.

With high-speed service, the AP and UPI can deliver up-to-the-minute stories that are better written and better edited than those in the past. Wire editors are spared the task of plowing through scores of stories they don't want; they have more time to consolidate the offerings of both major wire services and other news syndicates.

AP and UPI gather news from around the world to serve subscribers both at home and abroad. Both offer general news, features, special interest news (sports, business, religion), analyses or interpretives and pictures.[1]

The primary wire (A wire) originates in New York City or Washington and carries top national and international news. The AP devotes a secondary national wire, or B wire, to national and international news. UPI does the same, but "splits" once an hour allow for transmission of state and regional news.

Separate national wires deliver sports, markets and pictures. Smaller dailies rely primarily on the state wire, a combination of the main news wires, sports, markets—and state or regional news. The state bureau also delivers pictures, both by facsimile transmission and by mail. Both services provide subscribers with individually requested stories. Broadcast stations have access to special radio wires but if they desire, may also have any of the other wires.

HIGH-SPEED CIRCUITS

The wire services' high-speed circuits are referred to variously as dataspeed, DataStream, DataNews or DataFeature. The circuits permit the agencies to hold back stories until they can be wrapped up or be self-contained.

Dataspeed circuits originally were used to transmit tabular matter such as the stock market and sports boxscores. Today the services deliver the national wires, as well as feature syndicated and supplemental copy, on such circuits.

Newspapers receiving high-speed transmissions usually capture everything the wire services transmit directly in a computer. One circuit is used

[1] AP and UPI provide similar services, but they are organized differently. AP is a cooperative owned by its member newspapers and broadcast stations. UPI is a privately owned company.

for almost all the services available, and selector devices are installed at the newspaper to filter out services to which the paper does not subscribe. If a newspaper purchases the A wire, B wire and sports wire, but not the financial wire, the selector blocks reception of financial items. The others are allowed to pass into the newspaper's computer system for storage and later retrieval.

United Press International uses its DataNews circuit for most of its own services and all syndicated copy. Thus, a newspaper client can select which UPI services it wants, and on the same circuit it can receive copy from *The New York Times* News Service, the *Washington Post-Los Angeles Times* Syndicate or many other supplemental services. This "piggyback" feature makes UPI service less expensive than AP service because AP uses two circuits—DataStream for news and DataFeature for supplementals—to transmit the same amount of information. UPI also uses individual selector codes for each client. With this system, when a client asks for an item to be repeated, it can be sent directly to that client without clogging the computer storage facilities of other newspapers with multiple copies of the same story. Both services use separate circuits for high-speed transmission of stock market tables.

Almost all newspapers that subscribe to high-speed services edit those stories on VDTs, but high-speed printers are available for backup in case the newspaper's computer fails.

BUDGETS AND PRIORITIES

The wire services operate on 12-hour time cycles—PMs for afternoon papers, AMs for morning papers. The cycles often overlap so that stories breaking near the cycle change are offered to both cycles or stories early in one cycle are picked up on stories late in the other cycle.

For a morning paper, the wire news day begins about noon with the following:

a200

d lbylczzcczzc

Starting AMs Report, a201 Next

1202pED 03-07

Then follows the news digest (or budget), notifying editors of the dozen or more top news stories in sight (Figure 9-1). An addition to the first budget may come a short time later. The budget is used to give wire editors a glimpse of the major stories forthcoming and aids them in planning space allocations.

Major stories breaking after the budget has been delivered are designated:

FLASH—a two- or three-word statement alerting editors to a story of unusual importance: President shot. On the old teleprinter machines a warning bell signifying a flash brought editors running to the machine. Today a flash

```
        d  lbylczzcczzc
Starting AMs Report, a201 Next
1202pED 03-07


     a201
        r  lbylczzcv
AP NEWS DIGEST
Saturday AMS
 Here are the top news stories in sight for AMs at this hour. The
General Desk supervisor is Ed Dennehy. He may be reached at 212
262-6093 if you have urgent questions about the spot news report.
ECONOMIC-ENERGY
 WASHINGTON - The unemployment rate remained stable at 8.2 per cent
last month, largely because 580,000 persons stopped looking for work,
the labor department reports. New material. With Wirephoto chart
NY15.
 WASHINGTON - The Social Security System is plunging into deficit, an
advisory panel tells Congress, and should be strengthened with
general tax revenues. New material. Wirephoto upcoming.
 DETROIT - With six plants closed this week, Ford soon may step up
production next week to keep pace with General Motors, Chrysler and
American Motors, all of which will have every plant in operation.
Developing, to be announced officially late in afternoon.
 UNDATED - Millions of Americans with visions of ripe red tomatoes
and leafy green lettuce at home-grown costs are planning vegetable
plots this summer. But there are plenty of pitfalls between garden and
table. New, Consumer Scorecard, by Louise Cook.
```

Figure 9-1.   Wire service budget.

is seldom used because a bulletin serves the same purpose and is almost as fast.

BULLETIN—a short summary, usually no more than a lead, of a major story. Again, it is used primarily to alert editors and is not intended for publication unless the bulletin arrives at deadline. A bulletin also may be used to signal corrections such as a mandatory "kill" on a portion of a story that could be libelous.

BULLETIN MATTER—expands the bulletin with more, but brief, details. Unless the deadline is a factor, the wire editor holds up the story for a more detailed account.

URGENT—calls editors' attention to new material or to corrections of stories sent previously.

SORTING THE PIECES

Wire editors have two considerations in selecting wire copy for publication—the significance of the stories and the space allotted for wire copy. If space is tight, fewer wire stories are used and heavier trims may be made on those that are used.

Budget stories usually, but not necessarily, get top priority. When stories listed on the budget arrive, they are so indicated by BUDGET, BJT or SKED, together with the length in words. If such stories are developing or are likely to have additional or new material, the editor places each story in a folder or computer holding queue and concentrates on stories that will stand.

Eventually the stories in the folder or holding queue have to be typeset. This is done by working backward—taking the latest book number and latest time indicator. The fifth and last lead may eliminate the fourth lead but pick up on the third lead and so forth until the story is compact and in order.

The Associated Press has added a feature called DataRecaps to aid wire editors in handling a breaking story. Previously, editors had to assemble the pieces from multiple leads, inserts, subs and adds or wait until space was cleared on the wire for a no-pickup lead. Now the service notifies wire editors a recap is coming, then delivers a complete story at 1,200 words a minute. UPI does much the same with frequent "writethrus."

Starts and stops occur even on copy apparently wrapped up. A story arriving early in the morning describes a congressional appropriation of $5.9 *billion* to provide jobs for the unemployed. Fifty items later editors are informed that the figure should be changed to $6.4 *million*. Still later, New York sends the message that the original $5.9 *million* should stand. Eventually the service again corrects the figure to the original $5.9 *billion*. Such changes pose few problems for the editor if the story has not yet been typeset. The editor simply changes the copy on paper or on the computer screen.

EDITING THE WIRE

On each news cycle, even the wire editors of large newspapers have more stories than they can use. On larger dailies using all the wires from the two major national news agencies, the flow of copy is monumental, even though the wire editor does not have to confront some of the special wires such as sports and markets.

One way to handle this spate of copy is to categorize the news—one queue for stories from Washington, D.C., another for New York and international, another for national, another for regional, another for area copy, and the like. Some computer systems do that automatically.

An advantage of the paper's receiving more than one news service is that the editor can use the story from one service to check facts against the same story from another service, such as casualty figures, proper names and spellings. If there is a serious discrepancy in facts, the editor asks the state or regional bureau for verification.

WIRES MAKE MISTAKES

Two points should be kept in mind as you edit wire copy. The first is that neither wire service tailors copy for a particular newspaper. Abundant details are included, but most stories are constructed so that papers may use the full account or trim sharply and still have the gist of the report.

The second point is that the wire isn't sacred. Both AP and UPI have a deserved reputation for accuracy, impartiality and speed of delivery. They also make errors, sometimes colossal ones.

A source who turned out to be unreliable caused United Press to release a premature armistice story during World War I. A confused signal from a New Jersey courthouse caused AP to give the wrong penalty for Bruno Richard Hauptmann, convicted in the kidnapping and slaying of the Lindbergh child. The state wire, more often than not, is poorly written and poorly edited. Even the wire executives admit they still have bonehead editing and some stories that don't make sense. In both agencies, stories abound with partial quotations, despite repeated protests from subscribers.

Both services have advisory committees, usually composed of managing editors, who monitor writing performance. Here is one example from the APME (Associated Press Managing Editors) writing committee:

DETROIT (AP)—Two Detroit factory workers were killed Wednesday evening on their jobs, Detroit police said today. *(Clearly an industrial accident.)*

The two men, employees of the Hercules Forging Co., were identified as James H—, 51, the father of nine children, and M.C. Mc—, 37, both of Detroit, Mc— may have been struck accidentally, police reported. *(Oh, somebody struck him accidentally, but hit the other fellow on purpose.)*

Police said they had a man in custody and added he would probably be charged in connection with the deaths. *(Let's see, both of them were killed by the same man, but one death may have been an accident, but the suspect is charged with two murders?)*

Police say they interviewed 15 workers at the plant who could give no reason for the shootings. *(Now gunplay gets into this story.)*

Witnesses told police the man confronted H— with a carbine and shot him when he tried to run. He fired a second shot after H— fell, they said.

The third shot, apparently aimed at another workman, hit Mc—, police said. *(Now we are beginning to understand that what started out sounding like an industrial accident has become double murder.)*

PECULIARITIES OF WIRE COPY

At most newspapers, wire copy is edited the same as local copy, but a few peculiarities apply to the editing of wire news. First, wire news, unlike local news, usually carries a *dateline,* which indicates the city of the story's origin.

Despite the name of the device, most newspapers no longer include in the dateline the date the story was written:

OLD DATELINE

OVERLAND PARK, Kan., Jan. 12 (AP)—An apparent good Samaritan who helped start a woman's car talked about how dangerous it was to be out at night then pulled a gun and took her purse, police said. . . .

MODERN DATELINE

OVERLAND PARK, Kan. (AP)—An apparent good Samaritan who helped start a woman's car talked about how dangerous it was to be out at night then pulled a gun and took her purse, police said. . . .

Note that the city of origin is in capital letters and the state or nation is in uppercase and lowercase letters. At most newspapers, style calls for the dateline to be followed by the wire service logotype in parentheses and a dash. The paragraph indentation comes before the dateline, not at the start of the first paragraph.

Stories that contain material from more than one location are called *undated* stories. They carry no dateline but a credit line for the wire service:

By the Associated Press

Arab extremists said today they would blow up American installations throughout the Middle East unless all Americans leave Beirut immediately. . . .

Stories compiled from accounts supplied by more than one wire service carry similar credit lines:

From our wire services

LA PAZ, Bolivia—Mountain climbers experienced in winter climbing tried today to reach the wreckage of an Eastern Airlines Boeing 727, which crashed Monday while approaching La Paz in a snowstorm.

When editors combine stories, they must be sensitive to the fact that wire stories are copyrighted. If material in the story was supplied exclusively by one service, that service should be credited within the text. Combining the stories this way often provides a newspaper's readers with a better story than could be obtained from either of the major services alone. Good newspapers make a habit of doing this frequently.

Wire stories often use the word *here* to refer to the city included in the dateline. If the editor has removed the dateline during the editing process, the city must be inserted in the text. Otherwise, *here* is understood to be the city in which the newspaper is published.

Both major wire services use Eastern time in their stories. Some newspapers outside the Eastern time zone prefer to convert those times by subtracting one hour for Central time, two for Mountain or three for Pacific. When this is done, if the dateline remains on the story, it will be necessary to use phrases such as *3 p.m. St. Louis time* or *3 p.m. PDT* in the text. The newspaper's local style will specify the form to be used.

LOCALIZING WIRE STORIES

Wire stories often become ideas for local stories. If Congress has reduced the amount of money it will provide for loans to college students, a newspaper in a college town may want to contact the college's financial aid officer to determine what effect the measure will have locally.

When the Soviet Union shot down a Korean Airlines plane, the *Columbia Missourian* learned that two people were aboard who had just completed their doctoral degrees at the University of Missouri. Their daughter was with them aboard the jet. Because members of the family had lived in Columbia for several years, many people knew them. As a result, a major international story became a good local story:

Recent University graduates Somchai Pakaranodom and his wife, Wantanee, were on their way back to Thailand after living in Columbia for four years. They never made it.

The couple, along with their 7-year-old daughter Pom, were among the 269 killed when a Soviet jet shot down Korean Air Lines Flight 007 north of Japan.

"We had laughed about the flight schedule," education Professor Dorothy Watson recalled Friday, sitting in her living room where a week earlier she had thrown a going-away party for the Pakaranodoms.

The couple left Columbia Saturday. They were traveling first to Chicago then on to New York to catch the flight to Seoul and eventually on to Bangkok, Thailand.

With the sound of news reports about the crash coming over the television from the next room, Mrs. Watson fought back the tears. "I kept thinking they couldn't possibly be on the plane," she said, "It is just such a waste, so stupid."

At first she didn't connect the crash with her friends.

On Friday, another faculty member called to break the news to her. She said even then she refused to believe it, until Korean Air Lines confirmed the family was on the flight.

Both Fulbright scholars, the Pakaranodoms received their doctoral degrees from the University Aug. 5. Somchai's degree was in agricultural engineering, Wantanee's in reading education. . . .

Localizing wire stories can be done in several ways. The story can be rewritten to emphasize the local angle, a separate local sidebar to the wire story can be written, or a simple insert in the wire story may be sufficient.

NEW LEADS, INSERTS, TAKES

After copy has left the copy desk, changes sometimes have to be made because of new developments, corrections or additional information. Under the traditional system, the routine for new leads and inserts works this way:

Obtain a proof of the story from the composing room. This proof has several designations, including "marker," "Cx" or "fix." Draw a block around the portion of the lead to be deleted and write in the margin: "Kill for new lead." On the remaining portion, write in the margin: "Pickup" (Figure 9-2).

Figure 9-2.   Marking proof for new lead and two insertions.

The new copy will be marked "New lede FARM." At the end of the new lead, write "pickup" and indicate the paragraph where the story resumes: "The trend..." (2nd graf).

Assume two insertions are to be made, one between the fourth and fifth paragraphs, the other between the seventh and eighth paragraphs. Use the proof to show where the inserts are to go, marking one "insert A" in the margin, the other "insert B."

The copy would be marked "insert A fourth graph FARM" and "insert B seventh graph FARM," and each would close with "end insert."

Return both the copy and the proof to the composing room.

If more information is to be added to the end of the story, the copy editor simply uses the notation "Add FARM" on the copy. No proof or marker is necessary.

On computer editing terminals, new leads and inserts, whether from the wires or local generation, are handled at first as separate stories under their own file number if the earlier version has already been typeset. Copy editors set these in the same measure as the earlier story, retain the pickup line so those in the pasteup department can see it, and typeset the later revision—whether add, insert or lead. If the new lead comes in before the story has been typeset, the copy editor can call the lead to the screen, insert the old story into that file, delete what should come out and typeset the story as a unit.

```
m290
FARM 2nd lead 110
   WASHINGTON (AP)--Urban sprawl, highways, parks, airports....
The trend: 2nd graf m283


m295
FARM Insert 70
   WASHINGTON FARM m283, updating, insert after 4th graf:
threat?
   Meanwhile, the total land area in farms also has been,....
Experts in USDA, etc. 5th graf.


m299
FARM  Insert 40
   WASHINGTON FARM m283, further updating, insert after 7th graf:
improved.
   Economic recovery and further industrialization during....
Further, etc. 8th graf.
```

Figure 9-3.   Copy for new leads and inserts. m290 is the book number on the new lead (110 words) of the original story (book number m283). The story picks up at the second paragraph of the original, beginning "The trend..." Copy for the two inserts (70 and 40 words long) indicates the position of the inserts.

If the story has been sent to the typesetter but a copy of the story is in the storage file, the story can be recalled and corrected on a computer terminal. The original story is then put on the screen and merging is accomplished by using the paragraph insert feature. Finally, a copy of the typeset strip can be obtained and indications for new leads and inserts can be made on that proof. Because modern phototypesetters are so fast, some newspapers choose to set the entire story a second time.

A story breaking near deadline may have to be handled in small segments or "takes" to minimize the time needed for typesetting. The first take usually is no more than the lead. It would carry the slug word, for example, MAYOR. If the head size has not been determined, the slug would indicate that the head will come later—HTC or HTK.

The first take ends with "more." The second take is slugged "1st add MAYOR" and similarly is kept open with "more." The process is repeated until the final take, usually so indicated, as "sixth and last add MAYOR." This segment closes with an endmark.

The copy editor keeps notes as the story moves so that the headline can be written as soon as the final take is in.

With the new technology this procedure is no longer as important as it once was because of the speed with which copy can now be written, edited and set into type.

OTHER NEWS SERVICES

Syndication of news by major metropolitan newspapers, a combination of such papers or a newspaper group have made it possible for dailies to give readers a variety and depth of news coverage. Among such news syndicates are *The New York Times* News Service, *Washington Post-Los Angeles Times* Syndicate, and the Copley and Gannett news services. By syndicating their news, the publishers participating in the supplemental services are able to recoup some of the costs of news gathering and, in fact, have been able to expand news coverage.

The wire services similarly offer their own feature syndicates that include news and features from other newspapers (London Express) or from parent corporations (Scripps Howard News Service).

The services mentioned are among more than 200 syndicates offering publishers news, features, pictures, and special services. In addition to giving spot and secondary news, these services provide sports, foods, fashions, bylined columns and features ranging from amateur photography to zoo animals.

PICTURE SERVICES

Both major wire services offer picture service to their subscribers. The Associated Press service, called Laserphoto, uses laser beam technology to scan the

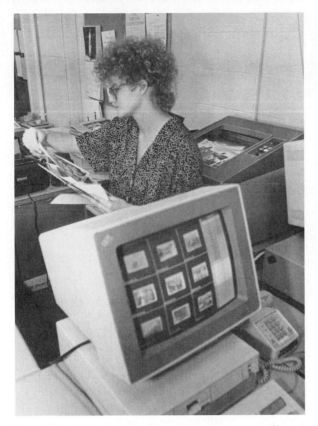

Figure 9-4.   Wirephoto machine. Most newspapers still receive photos on a machine similar to this AP laserphoto device, shown at rear. Soon, most will receive them directly on computer terminals, foreground. [Photo by Jeff Adams]

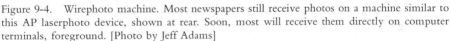

photo at the transmission point, convert it to digital language for telephone or satellite transmission, and, using another laser beam, convert it back to picture form at the newspaper. UPI's service, Unifax II, operates similarly but with a wet-process chemical system similar to those found in some office copiers.

Both wire services are rushing to implement digital delivery of pictures. Digital transmission will greatly speed the dissemination of photos, which in turn will increase the number of pictures a service can transmit each day. Digital processing also will save money. Because digital photos can be captured and stored in a computerized photo desk, images can be previewed on the computer screen. Then editors can print out only those pictures they plan to use, saving thousands of dollars each year in paper and chemical costs.

Digital photo processing also will give newspapers more control over the quality of wire images than is possible now. A photo editor equipped with a digital photo desk can change the contrast or brightness of an image or increase its sharpness. Unfortunately, digital photography also will allow

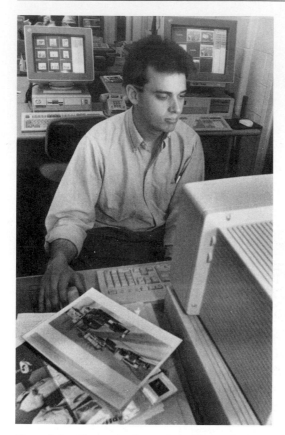

Figure 9-5.   Electronic picture desk. Electronic picture desks such as this one are replacing traditional photo-processing techniques. [Photo by Jeff Adams]

unscrupulous editors to clip the head off one person electronically and place it on the body of someone else. The industry is grappling with the establishment of ethical guidelines that will limit the extent of electronic changes.

We may soon see the day when pictures are not only transmitted in digital form but also taken that way. Various companies are developing digital cameras, and as quality improves, newspapers probably will be among the first industries to embrace them. In the interim, extensive work is being done with still-video cameras, which take the picture in analog form but permit easy conversion of the image to digital data. *USA Today*, in particular, has been an early proponent of such technology.

HEADLINE
WRITING SKILLS

CHAPTER 10

CREATING THE HEADLINE

HEADLINE FUNCTIONS

A copy editor's first task is to correct and refine copy. This means, as outlined in earlier chapters, checking copy for accuracy, clarity, conciseness, tone and consistency of style.

A second task is to write a headline that:

1. Attracts the reader's attention.
2. Summarizes the story.
3. Helps the reader index the contents of the page.
4. Depicts the mood of the story.
5. Helps set the tone of the newspaper.
6. Provides the adequate typographic relief.

Those are the major functions of headlines. Not every headline can accomplish each of those tasks, but editors who write headlines with these goals in mind will write better headlines than those who ignore them.

Good headlines attract the reader's attention to stories that otherwise may be ignored. The day's best story may have little or no impact if the headline fails to *sell* it, or attract the reader's attention. Headlines sell stories in many ways, but often they do so by focusing on how the reader's life will be affected. For example, if the City Council has approved a city budget of $30 million for the coming year, one approach is to headline the story:

Council approves $30 million budget

Another approach, which does a better job of selling the story, might be this:

City tax rate to remain unchanged

That approach answers the questions the reader is most likely to ask about the council's action: How will it affect me?

Some headlines attract attention because of the magnitude of the event they address:

Earthquake in Algeria kills 20,000

Others attract attention because the headline is clever or unusual:

Hunger pangs
Thief finds sandwich goodies,
wine provide appetizing loot

Each story requires a different approach, and the headline writer who is able to find the correct one to attract the reader's attention is a valued member of the newspaper's staff.

Most headlines appear over new stories designed to inform, not entertain, so the headline that simply summarizes the story as concisely and accurately as possible is the bread and butter of the headline writer:

U.S., China to sign major grain deal

Such headlines seldom win prizes for originality or prompt readers to write letters of praise. But a newspaper full of headlines that get right to the point is a newspaper that is easy to read. The reader knows what the story is about and can make an intelligent decision about whether to read more. The headlines summarize the news, much as five-minute radio newscasts do.

If the headlines on a page do a good job of summarizing the stories, the editors have created for their readers a form of index to the page. This also helps the reader determine what to read and what to bypass. In one sense, good headlines help readers determine what *not* to read. And, while that may seem counterproductive to the newspaper's objectives, it is realistic to recognize that a reader will partake of only a small percentage of the newspaper's offerings. Newspapers help make those choices easier by providing a choice of fare, much as supermarket managers offer their customers various brands of green beans. That may not be an appealing comparison to those who view newspapers as entitites above that sort of thing, but it *is* realistic. To ignore that reality is a mistake.

The headline also sets the mood for the story. The straightforward news headline indicates that the story it accompanies is a serious one. Similarly, a headline above a how-to-do-it story should reflect the story's content:

It's easy to save by changing your car's oil

Setting the mood is even more important when writing headlines for humorous stories. One newspaper hurt readership of a bright story during the streaking craze of the early 1970s by using a straight headline:

Judge lectures streaker

The story was a humorous account of the court appearance of a group of college students who had run across a softball diamond in the nude. In the second edition, the headline writer did a much better job:

Streaker gets the pitch
It's a whole nude ball game

The mood was set for the reader to enjoy the story.

Headlines probably reveal as much about the tone, or character, of a newspaper as anything it contains. If the top story on the front page is head-lined **Cops seek lover in ax murder** and the second story carries the headline **Jackie O. flips over new beau,** there can be little doubt about the nature of the publication. Serious tones, as well as sensational ones, can be set with headlines.

Finally, headlines provide typographic relief. They separate stories on the page and relieve the tedium that would exist with masses of text-sized type. This function will be discussed in detail in Chapters 13–16.

HEADLINE STYLES

Styles of headlines, like fashions, change constantly, even though their functions remain the same. Because style is an important factor in determining what can and cannot be included in a headline, it may be useful to review the historical development of headline styles.

Newspapers' first news display lines were short and slender, usually a single crossline giving little more than a topical label: *Latest From Europe.* By adding more lines or by varying the length of the lines, designers created the hanging indention, the inverted pyramid and the pyramid:

```
XXXXXXXXXXXX      XXXXXXXXXXXX        XXXXXX
  XXXXXXXXX         XXXXXXXXX       XXXXXXXXX
  XXXXXXXXX           XXXXXX       XXXXXXXXXXXX
```

Later, by centering the second line and making the third flush with the right-hand margin, they developed the stepline. It became one of the most popular styles of headlines and is still in use at a few newspapers:

Heavy Rain
   Shuts Down
      All Beaches

The next move was to combine these elements—a stepline, an inverted pyramid, a crossline, then another inverted pyramid. The units under the introductory head became known as *banks* or *decks.* An article in *The Quill* cited one found in a western newspaper describing a reporter's interview with Gen. Phil Sheridan in 1883:

FRISKY PHIL

**Gazette Reporter Holds
Interesting Interview
With Hero of Winchester**

*The Great Warrior Receives the
Newspaperman with Open Arms;
He is More or Less Broken up on
   the craft anyway*

**HE TRAVELS IN A SPECIAL
MILITARY COACH AND LIVES
ON THE FAT OF THE LAND**

**Sheridan is Many Miles Away,
but the Champagne We Drank
with him Lingers with Us Still**

*We Feel a Little Puffed
Up Over Our Success At-
tending Our Reception by
Little Phil, But Man is
   Mortal*

**May He Who Watches Over the
Sparrows of the Field Never
Remove His Field Glasses from
the Diminutive Form and Great
   Soul of Phil Sheridan**

Throughout most of America's history newspaper headlines have tended to depict the mood of the times as well as the tone of the paper. **Jerked to Jesus** shouted the *Chicago Times* on Nov. 27, 1875, in headlining the account of a hanging. Some other classics:

AWFUL EVENT

**President Lincoln
Shot by an Assassin.**

The Deed Done at Ford's
Theatre Last Night

The Act of a Desperate Rebel

**The President Still Alive at
Last Accounts**

No Hopes Entertained of His
Recovery

*Attempted Assassination of
Secretary Seward*

Details of the Dreadful Tragedy

The New York Times

AMERICA IS
MISTRESS
OF AIR

**Wright's Machine is
Perfect; Uncle
Sam Buys**

**Overland Trip With
Passenger Succeeds**

**"We Flew Eight Miles an Hour
Coming Back," Says
Lieutenant.**

The Denver Post

PEARY WIRES HE HAS NAILED STARS AND STRIPES
TO THE NORTH POLE AND IS ON HIS WAY HOME

OFFICIAL MESSAGE
SENT ARCTIC CLUB

**Backers Were Momen-
tarily Expecting Veteran
Explorer to Report Suc-
cessful Quest of Goal
Reached by his Rival**

**Latter Sends His Instru-
ments and Records to the
United States for Examin-
ation and Will Prove His**

> Claims Before a Jury of
> Scientists of Two Conti-
> nents-Dispells All Doubt.

The Denver Post

Big type and clamoring messages still weren't enough for some newspapers in the late 1800s. According to Gene Fowler, an executive told the owners of the *Denver Post,* "You've got to make this paper look different. Get some bigger headline type. Put red ink on Page One. You've got to turn Denver's eyes to the *Post* every day, and away from the other papers." So the *Post* ran its headlines in red to catch the readers' attention. The message had to be gripping. According to Fowler's version, Harry Tammen, co-owner of the *Post,* was so incensed over a lifeless banner that he grabbed a piece of copy paper and composed one of his own: **Jealous Gun-Gal Plugs Her Lover Low.** When the copy desk protested the headline wouldn't fit, Tammen snapped, "Then use any old type you can find. Tear up somebody's ad if necessary." Still the desk wasn't satisfied. "It isn't good grammar," the desk chief argued. But Tammen wouldn't budge. "That's the trouble with this paper," he is quoted as saying. "Too damned much grammar. Let's can the grammar and get out a live sheet."

The battle for circulation was hot. So were the headlines. Many were also colorful:

Demon of the Belfry Sent Through the Trap

Dons Planned to Skedaddle in the Night

Does it Hurt to Be Born?

**Conductors Robbing Little Girls
of their Half-Fare Tickets**

Do You Believe in God?

During and after the Spanish-American War some newspapers used as many as 16 decks, or headline units, to describe the story. Frequently the head was longer than the story.

With improved presses and a greater variety of type available, designers were able to expand the headline. Eventually the main Page One head stretched across the page and became known as the *banner, streamer* or *ribbon.* On some papers it was called, simply, the *line.* This headline sometimes called for the largest type available in the shop. When metal type wasn't adequate for the occasion, printers fashioned letters from wood (called *furniture*). A 12-liner meant that the line was 12 picas, or 144 points (two inches).

During this period, the names of headline forms were derived from their use or position on the page. A story placed above the nameplate and banner headline is called a *skyline,* and the accompanying headline is known as a *skyline head.* Sometimes the skyline head stands alone but carries a notation about where the story can be found.

A headline may have several parts—the main headline and auxiliary headlines known as *decks, dropouts* or *banks.* These are not to be confused with *subheads* or lines of type (usually in boldface) sometimes placed between paragraphs in the story.

A *kicker* headline is a short line of display type, usually no larger than half the point size of the main headline and placed over the main part of the headline. On some papers the kicker is termed the *eyebrow* or *tagline.*

A *stet head* is a standing headline such as **Today in history.**

A *reverse plate* headline reverses the color values so that the letters are in white on a black background. A *reverse kicker,* in which one line in larger type is above the deck, is called a *hammer* or a *barker.*

As the tone of the newspaper was moderated after the turn of the century, so were the headlines. Banner headlines still shout the news, occasionally in red ink, but gloom and doom headlines have virtually disappeared. Understating is more likely to be found in headlines today than overstating. Extra editions have been out of date for a long time. And no longer do circulation managers hurry into the city room to demand a banner headline that will increase the newspaper's street sales.

Between World Wars I and II the cult of simplification, known as streamlining, brought changes in the newspaper headline. Designers put more air or white space into the head by having each line flush left, with a zigzagged, or ragged, right margin:

XXXXXXXX   XXXXXX   XXXXXXXX
XXXXXXX   XXXXXXX   XXXXXXX
XXXXX   XXXXXXXX   XXXXXXXX

Urged by this spirit of simplification, they abolished the decorative *gingerbread* such as fancy boxes and reduced the number of banks or eliminated them altogether except for the deck reading out from a major head—called a *readout* or *dropout.* They argued that the *flush left* head was easier to read than the traditional head and that it was easier to write because the count was less demanding.

Another part of the streamlining process was the introduction of modern sans serif typefaces to challenge the traditional roman typefaces such as Century, Caslon, Goudy and Garamond (see Chapter 13). Advocates of the new design contended that sans serif faces such as Helvetica and Univers were less ornate than the roman ones, gave more display in the smaller sizes, contained more thin letters (thus extending the count) and allowed a greater mixture of faces because of their relative uniformity.

Headlines in all-capital letters gradually gave way to capital and lowercase letters, which are easier to read. In modern headline design, only the first word of the headline and proper names are capitalized. This form of headline capitalization is known as *downstyle.*

The wider columns in contemporary newspaper design give headline writers a better chance to make meaningful statements because of a better count in one-column heads. The trend away from vertical makeup and toward horizontal makeup provides more multicolumn headlines on the page. Such *spread heads* can be written effectively in one line.

Traditionally, the headline has headed the column and hence its name. But the headline need not necessarily go at the top of the news column (see Figures 14-23, 14-24 and 14-25).

Increased emphasis on news display in recent years has prompted designers to discard established rules in favor of headline styles that complement the story. Design concepts borrowed from magazines are used increasingly. Thus, newspapers now contain flush-right headlines, hammer heads are proliferating and decks, or dropouts, are returning (Figure 10-1). Through it all, the flush-left headline remains dominant.

THE HEADLINE WRITING PROCESS

Readers read the headline first, then the story. Copy editors work in reverse; they first read the story, then write the headline. This often leads to confusing heads because copy editors mistakenly assume that if readers will only read the story they will understand what the headline is trying to convey. But except in rare cases deliberately designed to tease the reader, the headline must be instantly clear. In most cases, the reader will not read a story simply to find out what the headline means.

Headline writing, then, involves two critical steps:

1. Selecting which details to use.
2. Phrasing them properly within the space available.

The copy editor exercises editorial judgment in completing the first step in the process. Most use the *key-word method* in which the copy editor asks: "Which words must be included in the headline to convey to the reader the meaning of the story?" In its simplest form, this involves answering the question: "Who does what?" Thus, most good headlines, like all good sentences, have a subject and predicate, and usually a direct object:

Tornado strikes Jonesboro

That done, the copy editor tries to make the headline fit. Synonyms may be necessary to shorten the phrase, and more concise verbs may help:

Twister rips Jonesboro

That in simplified form is the essence of headline writing. But it is seldom that easy. All newspapers have rules to define the limits of what is acceptable, and consideration must be given to such factors as the width of

GAME 2: *Rockets don't want a rhinoceros on their backs, so Bird rates special attention from rising star...*

To Weigh 5 Days of Testimony

Zimmerman Case Goes to the Jury

HDC Buys Seven Old Homes on W. Vine, Will Renew Them

To Convert Them to 18 Apartments Under U.S. Rent-Subsidy Plan

Tilt!

EM to bar pinball halls to youths

Police Expand Task Force

Missing Persons Bureau Placed Under Redding's Command

Suicide and euthanasia

Christiaan Barnard tackles controversial subject

Japan's time for expansive ceremony is passing

Hirohito's reign may end era

The summer place

Feeling at home in a second home

Joe Swisher's story

Look into his eyes, listen to his account and then decide for yourself: Is this man a child molester?

TICKS

The Best Defense? A Good, Strong Dose of Prevention

Pressure to phase out local rent control laws

Senate bill ties housing funds to city regulations, but it wouldn't affect L.A.

ROBOTS:
GE Moves Into Automation

Boston has a T(itle) party

76ers blow 3-1 lead, Celtics win East

Animal magnetism

'Be Kind Week' or not, volunteers care for dumped pets

Figure 10-1. Sample headline styles.

the column and the width of the characters in the typeface to be used. In the sections that follow, the complexity of headline writing will become apparent. Through it all, however, it may be useful to keep in mind the two critical steps previously outlined.

THE HEADLINE ORDER

Typically, the copy editor receives a headline order when assigned to edit a story. The editor responsible for layout will have determined the headline size and style based upon the length and significance of the story and its placement on the page. (In some cases, the copy may be marked *HTK,* or "hed to kum," indicating that a layout decision has not been made and therefore no headline size has been determined. When this occurs, the copy editor merely edits the story; the headline will be written later.)

Each newspaper has its own schedule showing headline designations and line count, the maximum number of units that will fit on a line in the specified typeface and size (see Figure 10-2). The practice of designating headlines varies. Here are four methods:

1. *Number designation.* Headlines of one or two columns are assigned a number. A 2 head, for example, might call for a one-column, two-lined head in 24-point Bodoni, capitals and lower case. A 22 head would be the same as a 2 head but in two columns. Sometimes the number corresponds to the type size and style. A 24 head would be in 24 points, and a 25 would be in 24 points italic.

2. *Letter designation.* Here letters are used to show the type family and size. If C calls for 30-point Vogue extrabold, the head might be indicated as follows: 2C=. This means two columns, two lines of 30-point Vogue extrabold. The letter may also indicate the headline style. If D, for instance, means a one-column head in three lines of type, ½ D would be one column in two lines. Or if D is a headline with a deck, the ½ D would be the same head but without the deck.

3. *Designation by numbers and type family.* A designation such as 1-24-3 Bod. means one column, 24 points, three lines of Bodoni; 3-36-1 (or 3361) TBCI means three columns of 36 point, one line of Tempo bold condensed italic. At some papers, the first number designates the column width, the second number the number of lines and the third number the size of type (2/3/36).

4. *Computer code designations.* The code F (for font) 406, could well mean the 400 series (Gothic) and 6 could indicate the size of type (48 point). The code numbers thus identify the size and family of type, line width, number of lines and choice of roman or italic.

Headline Schedule

This headline schedule lists the unit count (maximum count) per line of headlines of the indicated column width and type size. It does not list each headline by number of lines since, for example, the count per line for a 1-24-2 would be the same as that for a 1-24-3.

Bodoni Bold and Bodoni Bold Italic

Headline	Maximum	Headline	Maximum	Headline	Maximum
1-14	21	4-36	39	4-60	23 1/2
1-18	18	2-48	14	5-60	30
1-24	13	3-48	21	6-60	36
2-24	26 1/2	4-48	29	2-72	7
1-30	10 1/2	5-48	37	3-72	14 1/2
2-30	23	6-48	44	4-72	20
1-36	9	2-60	11 1/2	5-72	24 i/2
2-36	19	3-60	17 1/2	6-72	30
3-36	29				

Avoid using headlines not listed above. For example, 14BB would not be used across two columns.

Bodoni Light and Bodoni Light Italic

Headline	Maximum	Headline	Maximum	Headline	Maximum
1-14	22	4-36	42	4-60	25 1/2
1-18	19	1-48	7	5-60	32
1-24	14	2-48	15	6-60	38 1/2
2-24	29	3-48	23 1/2	2-72	7 1/2
1-30	11	4-48	31 1/2	3-72	15 1/2
2-30	24	5-48	40	4-72	21 1/2
1-36	9 1/2	6-48	48	5-72	26 1/2
2-36	20 1/2	2-60	12 1/2	6-72	32
3-36	31	3-60	19		

Poster Bodoni

Headline	Maximum	Headline	Maximum	Headline	Maximum
1-14	16	1-30	8	1-60	4
1-18	13	1-36	6 1/2	1-72	3
1-24	10 1/2	1-48	5		

Note: To figure the maximum count for Poster Bodoni headlines of more than one column, multiply the maximum for one column by the number of columns.

Italic and Roman versions of the same headline type size should count the same.

In all cases, count spaces between words as one-half. Count numerals (except 1), the dollar sign ($), the percentage symbol (%) and devices of similar width as one and one-half (1 1/2).

Figure 10-2. Sample headline schedule.

Here are some of the common abbreviations used in headline designations:

- *X* for extra (VXBI means Vogue extrabold italics)
- *x* for italics (2–30–2) SP *x* means two columns, two lines of 30–point Spartan italics)
- *It., I.* or *ital.* for italics
- *K* for kicker line or eyebrow (2–30–2K)
- *H* for hammer and inverted kicker (3–36–1H); also called barker head
- *J* for jump or runover head
- *RO* for readout, or *DO* for dropout, under a main multicolumn headline
- *W* for wicket head
- *Sh* for subhead
- *R* for roman (VXBR is Vogue extrabold roman)

COUNTING THE HEADLINE

Most newspapers now have computer systems that allow the copy editor to press a button and determine almost instantly whether a headline will fit. This is possible when computers are programmed with the width value of each character available in the typeface. At split-second speed the computer can add the width values of the characters the copy editor has assembled on the computer screen and determine whether that total exceeds the maximum width value of the line in the specified typeface, size and column width (see Figure 10-3). The availability of this feature simplifies the copy editor's work. If it is not available, the copy editor turns to time-tested manual methods of calculation.

The easiest way to count a headline manually is with the typewriter system—one letter for all letters, figures, punctuation and space between words. If a line has a maximum of 18 units as specified by the newspaper's headline schedule (see Figure 10-2) and the head has 15 counts, it will fit, unless it contains several fat letters (such as M and W). In that case, the headline writer recounts the line using the popular Standard Method:

STANDARD HEAD-COUNT METHOD

Lowercase letters	1 unit
Uppercase letters	1 ½ units

EXCEPTIONS

Lowercase f, l, i, t and j	½ unit
Lowercase m and w	1 ½ units
Uppercase M and W	2 units
Spaces	½ unit
Punctuation	½ unit
Uppercase I or L and numeral 1	½ unit

UNISETTER FILMSTRIP FONT WIDTH TABLES
(Note fonts listed in same order as on filmstrip)

Load	UNI Font No & Name		CQ Font No & Sequence

STRIP A
01 Font 1 News #2   032 Sec#1011
02 Font 3 News #2 Bold   033 Sec#1011
03 Font 2 News #2 Italic   313 Sec#1011
04 Font 4 Sans #1   049 Sec#1011
STRIP B
05 Font 5 English Times   705 Sec#1011
06 Font 6 Times Italic   705 Sec#1011
07 Font 7 Times Bold   707 Sec#1011
08 Font 9 Franklin Wide   415 Sec#1000

STRIP C
: Font 1 News #2   (same as strip A)   032 Sec#1011
: Font 3 News #2 Bold   (` `)   033 Sec#1011
: Font 4 Sans #1   (` `)   049 Sec#1011
09 Font 90 Sans #1 Hvy   SPECIAL USE   050 Sec#1011

UNISETTER STRIP 'A1' Sequence # 1011
<F01 T>, Unisetter Font #032
         News #2 (Std TTS Widths)
000 000 . NULL TF
164 021 5.   1 t
157 030 45.   2 o
150 033 35.   3 h
156 033 34.   4 n
188 881 818.   5 =
154 018 25.   6 l
162 027 24.   7 r
147 033 245.   8 g
151 018 23.   9 i
160 033 235.   10 p
143 033 234.   11 c
166 033 2345.   12 v
145 030 1.   13 e
172 027 15.   14 z
144 033 14.   15 d
142 033 145.   16 h
163 027 13.   17 s
171 033 135.   18 y
146 021 134.   19 f
170 033 1345.   20 x
141 033 12.   21 a
167 045 125.   22 w
152 021 124.   23 j
163 033 123.   24 u
161 033 1235.   25 q
153 033 1234.   26 k
124 039 95.   27 T
117 042 845.   28 O
110 045 835.   29 H
116 045 834.   30 N
115 054 9345.   31 M
114 039 825.   32 L
122 045 924.   33 R
107 045 9245.   34 Q
111 024 923.   35 I
120 042 9235.   36 P
103 039 9234.   37 C
126 042 92345.   38 V
105 045 91.   39 E
132 036 915.   40 Z
104 045 914.   41 D
102 042 9145.   42 B
123 033 913.   43 S
131 045 9135.   44 Y
106 042 9134.   45 F
130 045 91345.   46 X
101 042 912.   47 A
127 054 8125.   48 W
112 054 8124.   49 J
125 045 8123.   50 U
121 045 81235.   51 Q
113 045 81234.   52 K
134 054 P2.   53 BLR
056 018 0345.   54 period
054 018 034.   55 comma
060 027 02335.   56 zero
061 027 01345.   57 1
062 027 0125.   58 2
063 027 01.   59 3
064 027 024.   60 4
063 027 05.   61 5
066 027 0135.   62 6
067 027 0123.   63 7
070 027 023.   64 8
071 027 045.   65 9
073 018 0245.   66 Semicolon
072 018 S0245.   67 Colon
044 027 012.   68 Dollar
033 027 S01235. 69 EM leader
032 054 PS025.   70 EM space
034 054 035.   71 EM leader
176 054 PS05.   72 Copyright
032 027 4.   73 Asterix
077 033 80235.   74 Question Mark
001 027 S01345. 75 1/8
002 027 S0125.   76 1/4
003 027 S01.   77 3/8
004 027 S024.   78 1/2
005 054 S05.   79 5/8
006 054 S0123.   80 3/4
007 054 S0123.   81 7/8
037 054 S023.   82 EM Dash
046 042 S045.   83 Ampersand
034 054 S035.   84 EM leader
051 027 015.   85 Closed paren
050 027 S015.   86 Open paren
041 021 S012.   87 Exclamation mark
175 036 P024.   88 Register mark
055 018 014.   89 Hyphen
053 054 S014.   90 Plus sign
033 027 01235.   91 EM leader
177 054 PS0125. 92 Check
137 018 PS0134. 93 Close bracket
136 018 PS0134. 94 Open bracket
010 054 P803.   95 1/3

174 054 PS01345. 96 Solid Star
042 018 S04.   97 Unquote
047 018 04.   98 Quote
011 054 PS0124.   99 2/3
057 027 P0124.   100 Slash
043 054 P03.   101 Number sign
032 054 P025.   102 EM space
174 054 P01345. 103 Open Star
188 887 P8188.   104 Open Brace
173 027 P01.   105 Closed Brace
100 054 P05.   106 At sign
222 054 P0135.   108 Times sign
075 054 P0123.   109 Equals sign
252 054 PS023.   110 Division sign
140 027 P045.   111 Foot mark
230 027 P0235.   112 Inch mark
074 027 PS2.   113 Cents
045 054 PS4.   114 Percent sign
076 027 PS01.   115 Degree mark
233 027 PS012345. 116 EM dash
135 027 P012345. 117 EN bullet
200 054 PS0135. 118 Open box
030 018 0.   thin space
031 027 0234.   EN space
032 054 013.   EM space
040 000 3.   space bar
356 050 0.HALF SIZE PS
357 050 0.HALF SIZE PW
360 050 0.SUP PS
361 030 0.SUP PW
362 030 0.SUP VB
363 050 0.INF PS
364 050 0.INF PW
365 050 0.INF VA
371 014 0.MIN
372 000 0.NOM
373 060 0.MAX
376 000 0.DEVCR
377 000 0.DEVB
END
UNISETTER STRIP 'A3' Sequence # 1011
<F02 T-F01>, Unisetter Font #313
         News #2 Ital (Std TTS Widths)
377 000 0.DEVB
END
UNISETTER STRIP 'A1' Sequence # 1011
<F03 T-F01>, Unisetter Font #032
         News #2 BOLD (TTS Widths)
377 000 0.DEVB
END

UNISETTER STRIP 'A4' Sequence # 1011
<F04 T-F01>, Unisetter Font #049
         Sans #1 (Std TTS Widths)
377 000 0.DEVB
END

UNISETTER STRIP 'B1' Sequence # 1011
<F05 T-F01>, Unisetter Font #705,
         English Times
000 000 ,   NULL TF
164 018 5.   1 t
157 030 45.   2 o
150 030 35.   3 h
156 030 34.   4 n
155 045 345.   5 m
154 015 25.   6 l
162 021 24.   7 r
147 027 245.   8 g
151 015 23.   9 i
160 030 235.   10 p
143 024 234.   11 c
166 027 2345.   12 v
145 024 1.   13 e
172 024 15.   14 z
144 030 14.   15 d
142 02?

?03 027 P0125.   106 Open Star
173 027 P01.   105 Open Brace
100 054 P05.   107 At sign
222 054 P0135.   108 Times sign
079 054 P0123.   109 Equals sign
252 054 PS023.   110 Division sign
140 027 P045.   111 Foot mark
230 027 P0235.   112 Inch mark
074 027 PS2.   113 Cents
045 054 PS4.   114 Percent sign
076 027 PS01.   115 Degree mark
233 027 PS012345. 116 EM dash
135 027 P012345. 117 EN bullet
200 054 PS0135. 118 Open box
030 018 0.   thin space
031 027 0234.   EN space
032 054 013.   EM space
040 000 3.   space bar
377 000 0.DEVB
END

UNISETTER STRIP 'B2' Sequence # 1011
<F06 T-F05>, Unisetter Font #705,
         English Times ITALIC
377 000 0.DEVB
END

UNISETTER STRIP 'B3' Sequence # 1011
<F07 T-F05>, Unisetter Font #707,
         English Times BOLD
377 000 0.DEVB
END

UNISETTER STRIP 'B4' Sequence # 1000 NG
<F09 T-F01>, Unisetter Font #415,
         Franklin Wide
000 000 , NULL TF
164 026 5.   1 t
157 038 45.   2 o
150 039 35.   3 h
156 039 34.   4 n
133 060 343.   5 m
154 018 25.   6 l
162 027 24.   7 r
147 040 245.   8 g
151 018 23.   9 i
160 039 235.   10 p
143 035 234.   11 c
166 036 2345.   12 v
145 037 1.   13 e
172 034 15.   14 z
144 041 14.   15 d
142 041 145.   16 h
163 034 13.   17 s
171 037 135.   18 y
146 025 134.   19 f
170 038 1345.   20 x
141 037 12.   21 a
167 051 125.   22 w
152 021 124.   23 j
165 039 123.   24 u
161 039 1235.   25 q
153 040 1234.   26 k
124 044 95.   27 T
117 050 845.   28 O
110 050 835.   29 H
116 049 834.   30 N
115 060 9345.   31 M
114 040 825.   32 L
122 048 924.   33 R
107 050 9245.   34 Q
111 022 923.   35 I
120 048 9235.   36 P
103 047 9234.   37 C
126 046 92345.   38 V
105 042 91.   39 E
132 046 915.   40 Z
104 050 914.   41 D
102 049 9145.   42 B
123 044 913.   43 S
131 046 9135.   44 Y
106 041 9134.   45 F
130 047 91345.   46 X
101 047 912.   47 A
127 063 8125.   48 W
112 028 8124.   49 J
125 049 8123.   50 U
121 050 81235.   51 Q
113 048 81234.   52 K
077 036 035.   71 Question mark
046 039 8035.   84 Ampersand
041 021 8012.   87 Exclamation mark
137 021 P0134.   93 Closed brackets
136 021 PS0134. 94 Open brackets
042 018 04.   97 Unquote
047 018 804.   98 Quote
030 019 0;   Thin space
031 028 0234.   EN space
032 055 013.   EM space
040 000 3;   Space bar
361 070 00.SUP PW
362 030 00.SUP VB
364 030 00.INF VA
365 030 00.INF VA
371 017 00.MIN
372 000 00.NOM
373 060 00.MAX
377 000 00.DEV B
END

UNISETTER STRIP 'C1'   Same as F01
UNISETTER STRIP 'C2'   Same as F03
UNISETTER STRIP 'C3'   Same as F04

UNISETTER STRIP 'C4'   SPECIAL USE ONLY
<F90 T-F01>, Unisetter Font #050
         SANS #1 HVY
113 048 S1234.   52 K
130 047 S1345.   46 X
377 000 0.DEVB
END

Figure 10-3. Width values programmed into a computerized editing system allow the copy editor to determine whether a headline fits the space available. Here, the editor has composed a headline and dropout and learns that the headline is 10 picas short and the dropout is eight picas short. This is indicated by the right-hand column of numbers preceding the lines. [*Photo by Joe Edens*]

Because of the variation in the widths of letters in different families of type or even within the same family, the Standard Method is not always correct. The letter *i,* for example, is usually thinner than the lowercase *t.* And in some faces *r* is thinner than *d* or *g* and a string of zeroes will likely make the line too long.

That reality led journalism professors at the University of Missouri to develop a more accurate method of counting that has been adopted by many newspapers. If it is used, no headline will be too long, regardless of the type family used. The counts:

MISSOURI HEAD-COUNT METHOD

Lowercase letters	1 unit
Uppercase letters	1 ½ units

EXCEPTIONS

Lowercase i, l	½ unit
Lowercase m, w	1 ½ units
Uppercase I	½ unit
Uppercase M and W	2 units
Spaces	½ unit
Numerals	1 ½ units
Period, comma, quotation mark, hyphen	½ unit
Dollar sign, percentage symbol, dash and question mark	1 ½ units

All headline writers are expected to keep within the maximum count allowable. It is costly and time-consuming to have heads reset. If it appears that the desired head slightly exceeds the maximum count, the writer may provide an optional word as a substitute for a long word. The compositor then can try to fit the head as originally written. If it won't fit, the optional word can be used.

Some desk editors insist that each line of the head, even in a flush-left head, take nearly the full count. Others argue there is merit in a ragged-right edge. In a stepped head the lines cannot vary more than two or three units or the head will not step properly. Unless a special effect is desired, each line should fill at least two-thirds of the maximum type-line width.

The copy editor should not write several heads for the same story and invite the editor to choose. The copy editor should submit only the best head possible within the available count.

FORMING THE HEADLINE

Occasionally the desk editor or some other executive will suggest an angle that should go into the head or call attention to an angle that should be avoided.

Usually, however, headline writers are on their own. They know that within a matter of minutes they must edit the copy and create a headline that will epitomize the story and make a statement in an easy-to-digest capsule.

By the time copy editors have edited the copy they should have an idea brewing for the head. They begin by noting key words or phrases. These are their building blocks.

With these blocks copy editors try to make an accurate and coherent statement. First they try to phrase the statement in the active voice. If that fails, they use the passive. If possible, they try to get key words and a verb in the top line.

Take a routine accident story:

Three Atlantans were killed Friday when their car collided with a garbage truck on Highway 85 at Thames Road in Clayton County.

The victims were: . . .

Patrolman C. F. Thornton said the truck was driven north on Highway 85 by . . .

The auto pulled into the highway from Thames Road and was hit by the truck, Thornton said.

The headline order calls for a one-column, three-line head with a maximum of nine units. In this story the lead almost writes the head. The obvious statement is "Three Atlantans killed as car and truck collide." **3 Atlantans** won't fit, so the writer settles for **3 killed.** For the second line the writer tries **in truck,** and for the third line **car collision.** The headline writer discards **car collision** because it is too long; **car crash** will fit. By changing the second line from **in truck** to **as truck** the writer gains another verb in the third line. The head now reads **3 killed as truck, car crash.**

Key headline words are like signposts. They attract the reader's attention and provide information. Such words, meaningfully phrased, produce effective headlines.

Note how quickly the key words *(Dutch, prince, born)* emerge in the lead of a wire story: "Crown Princess Beatrix gave birth to a son last night and Dutchmen went wild with joy at the arrival of a king-to-be in a realm where queens have reigned since 1890." One copy editor used the key words this way:

Dutch treat
A prince is born,
first in century

Many dull heads can be improved if the writer will make the extra effort. Sometimes the first idea for the head is the best; often it is not. By rejecting the lifeless heads and insisting on better ones, an editor inspires everyone on the rim to try harder. Furthermore, a good performance on news heads is likely to generate better headlines in all departments of the paper.

The job of the copy editor is to create effective headlines for all copy. The big story is often easier to handle than the routine one because the banner story has more action and thus more headline building blocks.

The usual death and wedding stories offer little opportunity for original headlines. There are only so many ways to announce a wedding or a death in a head, and the writer dare not try to be clever in handling these topics. The standing gag on the copy desk is, "Let's put some life in these obit heads." If Jonathan Doe dies, that is all the headline can say, except to include his age: **Jonathan Doe dies at 65** or **Jonathan Doe dead at 65.** If he were a former mayor, that fact would be used: **Jonathan Doe, ex-mayor, dies.**

THE TITLE LESSON

Beginning headline writers might start with what Carl Riblet Jr., an expert on the subject, calls the title lesson. Learners start by listing the titles of all the books they have read. This is to demonstrate that readers can recall titles even if they have forgotten the contents. It also demonstrates the effectiveness of an apt title. A good title helps sell the product, as illustrated by those revised by alert publishers: "Old Time Legends Together with Sketches, Experimental and Ideal" *(The Scarlet Letter),* "Pencil Sketches of English Society" *(Vanity Fair)*, "The Life and Adventures of a Smalltown Doctor" *(Main Street),* "Alice's Adventures Underground" *(Alice in Wonderland).*

The beginner limited to a one-line head with a maximum of 15 or 20 units is forced to pack action into a few words, to merge as many elements as possible from the story, to indicate the tone or mood of the story and finally to compose an interesting statement. Riblet gives this example:

A young man said he and a middle-aged business agent had been drinking in a saloon. They went to the older man's apartment. There they quarreled over a gambling debt. The younger man told police he was threatened with a .30-caliber rifle. In self-defense, he picked up a bow and arrow and shot the older man in the stomach. The younger man tried to pull out the arrow but it broke and the wounded man died.

The copy editor got the story with instructions to write a one-line, 20-count head. He knows the paper's rule that every headline must contain a verb. He wrote: **Business agent slain.** In this instance it would seem wiser to bend the rule and get the key words in the headline: **Bow and arrow killing.** This lesson has practical value in writing the one-line head, such as the banner **Mayor censured** or **Steelers No. 1,** the kicker **Smelly problem** or **Circus magic,** the column heading **The goldkeepers,** the filler head **Postal auction,** or the magazine feature **Acrobat on skis.**

HEADLINE RULES

Practices vary, but on some desks no headline writer is permitted to hang conjunctions, parts of verbs, prepositions or modifiers on the end of any line of a headline. Like many newspaper rules, this one can be waived, but only if an exceptionally better headline can be created.

Rigid rules can bring grief to copy desks. One newspaper group has two ironclad rules: No head may contain a contraction. Every head must contain a verb. This leads to some dull and tortured heads, especially on offbeat feature stories.

The *Los Angeles Times* evidently has no policy against splitting ideas in heads. It may be argued that readers see the one-column headline as a unit and do not have to read each line separately as they would in a multicolumn head. Eventually experiments may be designed to test whether readers can comprehend a split head as easily as they can one that breaks on sense. Until the results of such tests are available, headline writers should phrase headlines by sense. The practice can't hurt them if they join a desk that tolerates splits. A talented copy editor will take no longer on a phrased headline than on a split headline.

Good phrasing in a headline helps the reader grasp its meaning quickly. Each line should be a unit in itself. If one line depends on another to convey an idea, the headline loses its rhythm. It may cause the reader to grope for the meaning. Note the differences in the original and the revised heads:

ORIGINAL	REVISED
Thousands join Easter parade in Philadelphia	**Thousands join Easter parade in Philadelphia**
Men need to sleep longer, report shows	**Men require more sleep, study reveals**
Stay calm, Browns, you'll soon know your title foe	**Just stay calm Browns; you'll know foe soon**
Jones loses new bid for freedom	**Jones again loses bid for freedom**
Four Russia women tour Denver area	**Four women from Russia tour Denver**
Ordnance station to welcome commander	**Naval ordnance station to welcome commander**
U.S. eyeing New Mexico site for nuclear wastes	**U.S. favors New Mexico for nuclear waste burial**
Police work draws in Japanese women	**Police work lures Japanese women**

What follows is a list of headline rules one editor distributed to his staff. He did so with the warning: "Rule No. 1 is that any other rule can be broken if you have a valid reason for doing so." That's good advice, even though many of these rules are common in newsrooms around the country. His list:

• Draw your headline from information near the top of the story. If the story has a punch ending, don't give it away in the headline.

- Build your headline around key words—those that must be included.
- Build on words in the story, paraphrasing if necessary, but it's best to avoid parroting the lead.
- Emphasize the positive unless the story demands the negative.
- Include a subject and predicate (expressed or implied).
- Try to use a verb in the top line.
- Maintain neutrality.
- Remember the rules of grammar and observe them.
- Eliminate articles and most adjectives and adverbs—except in feature headlines.
- Try to arouse the reader's interest. Remember that one function of the headline is to attract the reader to the story.
- Try to capture the flavor of the story.
- Make certain your headline is easy to read.
- Abbreviate sparingly.
- Verify the accuracy of your headline and be certain it has no double meaning.
- Verify that you've written the headline required.
- Verify the count of each line.
- Use short, simple words, but avoid such overworked and misused words as *flay, rap, eye* (as a verb) and *probe*. The use of such words is known as *headlinese*.
- Make the headline definite. Tell specifically what happened.
- If the main element is a characterization, the subsidiary element (dropout or kicker) should support that characterization.
- Never exaggerate. Build the headline on facts in the story. If a statement is qualified in the story, it must be qualified in the headline as well.
- Make the headline complete in itself. Each headline must have a subject and a predicate. The implied verb *is* may be used. (**Note:** In feature headlines, this rule is sometimes violated. You may want to use a headline that is similar in construction to a book or magazine, suggestive of the story rather than a synopsis of it.)
- Never write a headline that begins with a verb and has no subject, such as *Vote against compensation bill*. The result is a headline that commands the reader to do something, a meaning entirely different than the one intended.
- Phrase your headline in the present tense if possible, even though the event has been completed. This form is known as the historical present. Do not, however, link the present tense with a past date, such as *John Doe dies yesterday*. If a past date is so important that it must be used, the verb should be in the past tense. In most cases, the date can be omitted: *John Doe dies of pneumonia*.
- Do not use the present tense to indicate future events unless some word is included to clarify the meaning, as *City Council meets tonight*.
- Don't write a headline after a single reading of the story.
- Don't be afraid to ask questions if you fail to understand the story.
- Don't just fill a line. Say something.
- Don't violate the rules of headline writing just to make a line fit.
- Don't use common last names (*Smith, Jones,* etc.) or other names that are not easily recognized.

- Don't use the speaker's name in the top line. What he or she said is more important.
- Don't use *is* and *are* in the headlines.
- Don't mislead the reader.
- Don't split nouns and their modifiers, verb forms and prepositional phrases over two lines.
- Don't use *said* when you mean *said to be*.
- Don't use *feel* or *believes* or *thinks*.
- Don't pad headlines with unnecessary words.
- Don't use double quotation marks in headlines or in other devices using headline type (kickers or dropouts).
- Don't use slang.
- Don't write question heads.

Some of these rules, and a few this editor missed, merit further explanation.

USE THE PRESENT TENSE

Most news concerns past events. But to give the effect of immediacy, the headline uses the present tense for past events: **British doctors vouch for birth control bill; City has bumper crop of junk cars; Jonathan Doe dies at 65**.

If, however, the headline announces a future event in the present tense, the reader won't know whether the event has occurred or will occur. **Powell's wife tells everything** means that the wife has testified. But if the reader learns from the story that the testimony will not be given until the following day, the reader knows the head was misleading. The head should have read **Powell's wife to tell everything**. The present tense can never be used if the date is included on a past event: **Jonathan Doe dies Wednesday**.

On future events the headline may use the future, *will be;* the infinitive, *to be;* or the present: **Traffic parley opens Monday**. *Scheduled* is a seldom-used headline word because of its length. Convenient substitutes are *set* and *slated* and consequently are worked to death in heads over stories of future events. It happens like this: **Two speakers set,** and the reader wonders, "On eggs?"

HEADLINE PUNCTUATION

The period is never used in headlines except after abbreviations. Instead of full quotation marks, use single quotation marks which take less space and may be more appealing typographically in headline-size type. The comma may replace *and* and a semicolon may even indicate a complete break: **Tumbling spacecraft tangles chute; cosmonaut plummets to death**. The semicolon also indicates a full stop. Unless it is a last resort, neither the dash nor the colon should be used as a substitute for *says*. When used, the colon comes after the speaker, and the dash after what was said: **McCoy: Dual role too big; Dual role too big—McCoy**.

USE ABBREVIATIONS SPARINGLY

Few beginning headline writers have escaped the abbreviation addiction. It occurs when the writer tries to cram too much into the head. The story said a woman under hypnosis had imagined herself as a reincarnation of an 18th-century Bridey Murphy in Ireland. The theory was discounted by a professor of psychology at a state university. This is how a student headlined the story: **CU psych. prof. doubts B.M. story**. A simple head such as **Professor doubts 'Bridey' claims** would have given readers enough information to lead them into the story.

Abbreviations clutter the headline: **Mo. village U.S. choice for Pan-Am**. It could have been written as **Missouri favored as Pan-Am site**.

An abbreviation that has more than one meaning leads to confusion, especially when the headline writer is also guilty of poor phrasing: **Ten girls are added to St. Vincent candy striper unit** or **Ill. man asks Pa. to join Miss. in Mass. protest,** or **Nebron New L.A. Muni Asst. P.J.**. (He was elected assistant presiding judge of the Los Angeles Municipal Court.)

Headline writers frequently overestimate the ability of readers to understand the initials used in the headlines. Some are easily recognized, such as FBI, CIA, NBC. Others aren't, such as AAUW, NAACP, ICBM. On many newspapers the style calls for abbreviations and acronyms without periods in headlines. Other newspapers use periods for two-letter abbreviations, including U.S. and U.N., but TV is a frequent exception.

Some contractions are acceptable in heads; others aren't. *Won't, don't* and *shouldn't* give no trouble, but *she'll, he'll, who're* and the "s" and "d" contractions do: **Triplets 'fine'; so's the mother of 22** or **Mother'd rather switch than fight**. Try to read this aloud: **Anymore service, the town hall'll collapse**.

GRAMMAR IN HEADLINES

Although headline writers must constantly compress statements, they have no license to abuse the language. A grammatical error emblazoned in 48-point type may be more embarrassing than a half-dozen language errors buried in body type. The writer normally would say **Russian girls urged to stop copying Paris.** But the second line was too long so the writer settled for **Russian girls urged 'stop copying Paris.'** A comma should have been used to introduce the quoted clause. Transposing the lines would have produced a better head. A headline read **Jones best of 2 choices, senator says.** He can't be the best if there are only two choices.

One headline read: **Woman reports she is robbed by man posing as inspector.** The present "reports" is correct. However, the second verb should be "was" to show that she is reporting a previous event.

A standing rule on use of proper names in headlines is that the names should be instantly recognizable to most readers. **Union under investigation gave to Tiernan campaign.** Unless this headline is for a Rhode Island paper, most readers won't recognize the name of a former Rhode Island congressman.

Copy editors who can't catch spelling errors have no place on the copy desk. They are a menace if they repeat the errors in the headline, as in these: **Rodeo parade has governor as marshall; Kidnap victim trys to identify captors.**

HEADLINING SPORTS

Sports pages report on contests involving action and drama, and headlines over such stories should be the easiest in the paper to write. Yet, because of the jargon used by sports writers and the numerous synonyms signaling a victory of one team over another, the sports story headline has become a jumble.

A reader says to his companion, "I see that the Jayhawks crunched the Cornhuskers." "Yeah?" asks a University of Nebraska basketball fan. "By how much?" "Ninety-eight to 94," replies the reader. If that's a crunching, what verb describes a 98–38 victory?

The struggle for substitutes for *wins, beats* and *defeats* produces verbs such as *bests, downs, smears* and *swamps.* Presumably, the reader reads a sports page to find out who wins in what races. What does it matter, then, if simple words like *wins* or *defeats* are used over and over? Certainly they are better than editorialized counterparts such as *clobbers, wallops, flattens* and *trounces.*

AVOID SLANG

A straight head that tells the reader precisely what happened is always better than one in which the writer resorts to slang. Slang in heads, as well as in copy, lowers the tone of the paper and consequently lowers the readers' estimation of the paper. The headline, no less than the copy, should speak to the general reader, not to reporters and other specialists.

Here is an object lesson from a San Diego newspaper. The second edition carried a six-column head in the lifestyle section: **Kids going to pot are aided.** Under the head was a three-column cut showing a girl sitting on a bed in a holding room at Juvenile Hall. The picture also revealed a toilet stool in one corner of the room. To the relief of the embarrassed editor, the top line in the third edition was revised to **Teen narcotic users aided.**

DON'T REPEAT WORDS

Another restriction on headline writing is that major words in the headline cannot be repeated except for effect in a feature head. The rule has little logic except to prevent obvious padding, such as **Campus to launch campus chest drive** and **Wind-lashed blizzard lashes plains states.**

If the main head contains a word like *fire,* the readout or dropout could easily include a synonym. *Blaze* would be acceptable; *inferno* would not.

Repetition is sometimes used deliberately to heighten a feature: **Thinkers failures, professor thinks; New look? never! old look's better; Pokey driving sends three back to pokey.**

DOWN WITH HEADLINESE

Faced with the problem of making a statement of a nine-unit line, headline writers have to grab the shortest nouns and verbs possible. They are tempted to use overworked words such as *hits, nabs, chief* or *set* because such words help to make the headline fit. Or they may reach for words with symbolic meanings, such as *flays, slaps, grills, hop* or *probe.* Nothing is "approved"; it is "OK'd" or "given nod." All are headline clichés and have no place in today's newspaper.

The headline should not falsify the story. Many of the headlinese words do, at least by implication. If the story tells about the mayor mildly rebuking the council, the headline writer lies when he or she uses verbs like *hits, slaps, scores, raps, rips* or *flays.* An *investigation* or a *questioning* is not necessarily a "grilling"; a *dispute* is not always a "row" or a "clash." *Cops* went out with prohibition; today's word is *police.*

Others that should be shunned are "quiz" for *question,* "hop" for *voyage,* "talks" for *conference,* "aide" for *assistant,* "chief" for *president* or *chairman,* "solon" for *legislator* or *congressman,* "probe" for *inquiry,* "nabs" for *arrests,* "meet" for *meeting,* "bests" for *defeats,* "guts" for *destroys,* "snag" for *problem,* "stirs" for *incites* and "hike" for *increase.*

During the U.S. involvement in Vietnam, millions of readers must have wondered what headlines were trying to say with the incessant use of "Viet" and its variations. The word was used indiscriminately to refer to North Vietnam, South Vietnam, the Viet Cong, the North Vietnamese army, the South Vietnamese army and the Vietnamese people.

DON'T INVITE LIBEL OR CONTEMPT

Because of the strong impression a headline may make on a reader, courts have ruled that a headline may be actionable even though the story under the head is free of libel. Here are a few examples:

> **Shuberts gouge $1,000 from Klein brothers**
> **'You were right,' father tells cop who shot his son**
> **McLane bares Old Hickory fraud charges**
> **Doctor kills child**
> **A missing hotel maid being pursued by an irate parent**
> **John R. Brinkley—quack**

A wrong name in a headline over a crime story is one way to involve the paper in a libel action.

The headline writer, no less than the reporter, must understand that under our system a person is presumed innocent of any crime charged until proved guilty by a jury. Heads that proclaim **Kidnapper caught, Blackmailers exposed, Robber arrested,** or **Spy caught** have the effect of convicting the suspects (even the innocent) before they have been tried.

If unnamed masked gunmen hold up a liquor store owner and escape with $1,000 in cash, the head may refer to them as "robbers" or "gunmen." Later, if two men are arrested in connection with the robbery as suspects or are actually charged with the crime, the head cannot refer to them as "robbers" but must use a qualifier: **Police question robbery suspects.** For the story on the arrest the headline should say **Two arrested in robbery,** not **Two arrested for robbery.** The first is a shortened form of "in connection with"; the second makes them guilty. Even "in" may cause trouble. **Three women arrested in prostitution** should be changed to **Three women charged with prostitution.**

The lesson should be elementary to anyone in the publishing business, but even on the more carefully edited papers heads are sometimes guilty of jumping to conclusions. This was illustrated in the stories concerning the assassination of President John F. Kennedy. Lee Harvey Oswald was branded the assassin even though, technically, he was merely arrested on a charge of murder. In a statement of apology, the managing editor of *The New York Times* said his paper should not have labeled Oswald an assassin.

In their worst days, newspapers encouraged headline words that defiled: **Fanged fiend, Sex maniac, Mad-dog killer.** Even today some newspapers permit both reporter and copy editor to use a label that will forever brand the victim. When a 17-year-old boy was convicted of rape and sentenced to 25 to 40 years in the state penitentiary, one newspaper immediately branded him *Denver's daylight rapist.* Another paper glorified him as *The phantom rapist.* Suppose an appeal reverses the conviction? What erases the stigma put on the youth by the newspaper?

The copy editor who put quotation marks around **Honest count** in an election story learned to his sorrow that he had committed libel for his paper. The implication of the quotes, of course, is that the newspaper doesn't believe what is being said.

MISCELLANEOUS RULES

Emphasis in the headline should be on the positive rather than the negative when possible. If the rodeo parade fails to come off as scheduled because of rain, the head makes a positive statement: **Rain cancels rodeo parade,** not **No rodeo parade because of rain.** The news value is lacking in the headline that says **No one hurt as plane crashes.** The positive statement would be **90 passengers escape injury as plane crashes into mountain.** Here are three negating words in a headline: **Tax writers veto lids on oil write-off.** Better: **Tax writers leave oil tax as it stands.**

The negative is illustrated in this headline from an English paper: **Only small earthquake; but not many killed.**

This admonition does not apply to feature heads in which the negative helps make the feature: **No laws against drowning, but it's unhealthy;**

Not-so-gay nineties (on weather story); **Laundry gives no quarter until suit is pressed.**

The question head, except on features, is suspect for two reasons: It tends to editorialize, and newspaper heads are supposed to supply answers, not ask questions. If the headline asks the reader a question, the answer, obviously, should be in the story. If the answer is buried deep in the story, the question headline should be shunned. A five-column head asked, **Did Anastasia murder help kill barber shaves?** The lead repeated the same question, but the reader was compelled to look through a dozen paragraphs only to learn that the question referred to a frivolous remark that should have been used only to color the story.

ENJOY THE GAME

It's fun to write headlines because headline writing is a creative activity. Copy editors have the satisfaction of knowing that their headlines will be read. They would like to think that the head is intriguing enough to invite the reader to read the story. When they write a head that capsules the story, they get a smile from the executive in the slot and, sometimes, some praise.

Somerset Maugham said you cannot write well unless you write much. Similarly, you can't write good heads until you have written many. After they have been on the desk for a while, copy editors begin to think in headline phrases. When they read a story, they automatically reconstruct the headline the way they would have written it. A good headline inspires them to write good ones, too.

They may dash off a head in less time than it took them to edit the copy. Then they may get stuck on a small story. They may write a dozen versions, read and reread the story, and then try again. As a last resort, they may ask the desk chief for an angle. The longer they are on the desk the more adept they become at shifting gears for headline ideas. They try not to admit that any head is impossible to write. If a synonym eludes them, they search the dictionary or a thesaurus until they find the right one.

If they have a flair for rhyme, they apply it to a brightener: **Nudes in a pool play it cool as onlookers drool.**

Every story is a challenge. After the writer has refined the story, it almost becomes the copy editor's story. The enthusiasm of copy editors is reflected in a newspaper's headlines. Good copy editors seek to put all the drama, the pathos or the humor of the story into the headline. The clever ones, or the "heady heads," as one columnist calls them, may show up later in office critiques or in trade journals:

Council makes short work of long agenda
Hen's whopper now a whooper
Stop the clock; daylight time is getting off

Lake carriers clear decks for battle with railroads
'Dolly' says 'Golly' after helloful year
Tickets cricket, legislators told
Quints have a happy, happy, happy, happy, happy birthday (First birthday party for quintuplets of Catonsville, Md.)

CHAPTER 11

AVOIDING
HEADLINE PROBLEMS

The headline must be as accurate as the story itself. Like inaccurate stories, inaccurate headlines invite libel suits and destroy one of the newspaper's most valuable commodities—its credibility. Inaccuracy, though, is merely one of many pitfalls in headline writing. Others include overstating, missing the point of the story, taking statements out of context, confusing the reader, attempting poor or inappropriate puns, showing poor taste, using words with double meanings and giving away the punchline of a suspended-interest story. Numerous examples in this chapter point out the danger of careless handling on the copy desk.

MAKING IT ACCURATE

The key to ensuring accuracy is close and careful reading of the story. Erroneous headlines result when the copy editor doesn't understand the story, infers something that is not in the story, fails to portray the full dimension of the story or fails to shift gears before moving from one story to the next. Some examples:

> **Cowboys nip Jayhawks 68-66 on buzzer shot.** The lead said that Kansas (the Jayhawks) beat Oklahoma State (the Cowboys) by two points in a Big Eight conference basketball game.

> **Player shuns rain, wind and the course.** If golfer Gary Player had shunned them, he wouldn't have played. He conquered rain and wind to lick the course.

> **Paducah's bonding law said hazy.** The details weren't hazy; the subject of the story was hazy about the details.

> **3 in family face charges of fraud.** They were arrested in a fraud investigation, but the charges were perjury.

> **Black child's adopted mother fights on.** The child didn't select the mother; it was the other way around. Make it "adoptive."

> **Do-nothing Congress irks U.S. energy chief.** The spokesman criticized Democrats, not Congress as a whole, and the "do-nothing" charge was limited to oil imports.

Four held in robbery of piggy bank. The bank was the loot; the robbery was at a girls' home.

White House hints at ceiling on oil spending. The subject of the story was oil imports.

Greek plebiscite set Dec. 8. The vote was set for Dec. 8. The setting didn't come on that date.

If that pooch bites you can collect $200. The story said the animal had to have rabies for you to collect up to $200.

Didn't like her face, shoots TV announcer. A man fired a gun at her but missed.

Graham backs sterilization view. Although he backed one viewpoint, he criticized the program generally.

Bishop says segregation is justified. The lead quoted the bishop as saying that Christians are not morally justified in aiding segregation.

Schools help pay expenses for Forsyth County's dogs. The story said the dog-tax money helps support the schools.

Civic ballet auditions scheduled Saturday. One listens to auditions; one looks at tryouts or trials.

Youth, 19, breaks parole, subject to whipping post. The story correctly said he had been on probation.

Circus clown's daughter dies from high-wire fall. Second paragraph of story: "The 19-year-old aerialist was reported in good condition at Paterson General Hospital with fractures of the pelvis, both wrists and collarbone."

India-China relations worsen. The story was datelined Jakarta and had nothing to do with India.

Chicago to see outstanding moon eclipse. The story wasn't about a moon eclipse; it was about an eclipse of the sun. And "outstanding" is hardly an appropriate way to describe an eclipse.

Brilliant modern study of Holy Roman emperor. The story was a review of a book on Emperor Hadrian who was born A.D. 76 and died in 138. The Holy Roman Empire lasted from A.D. 800 to 1806.

Israelis release Arabs to regain heroes' bodies. Nowhere does the story call them heroes. The two were executed during World War II for assassinating a British official.

OVERSTATING

Akin to the inaccurate headline is one that goes beyond the story, fails to give the qualifications contained in the story or confuses facts with speculations.

Examples:

West Louisville students at UL to get more aid. The lead said they may get it.

Integration may improve learning, study indicates. But the lead was two-sided, indicating an improvement in one area and a loss in another. The headline should reflect divided results or views, especially in highly emotional news subjects.

Pakistan, U.S. discuss lifting of embargo on lethal weapons. The story said, correctly, that the embargo may be eased. And aren't all weapons lethal?

Arabs vote to support PLO claim to West Bank. The story said that Arab foreign ministers voted to recommend such action to their heads of state. The head implies final action.

Schools get 60% of local property tax. This reflects fairly what the lead said but fails to reveal an explanation, later in the story, that the schools get a proportion of the contributions of various levels of government—federal, state and local. Although the local property tax contributes 60 percent, the amount is far less than 60 percent of the total local property tax.

Here's what happens when a copy editor gets carried away:

Bacon enlivens buttermilk muffins. (The genius who thought of enlivening buttermilk muffins must be assumed to have done so with his tongue in his cheek and a piece of paper in his mouth.)

County heavens to explode with color. (Perhaps a booster head for a fireworks display, but slightly exaggerated.)

COMMANDING

Headlines that begin with verbs can be read as commands to the reader and should be avoided. A New York City newspaper splashed a 144-point headline over the story of the shooting of Medgar Evers, a civil rights advocate. The head: **Slay NAACP leader!** Another head may have given the impression that a murder was being planned: **Slaying of girl in home considered.** In reality, police were trying to determine if the murder took place in the girl's house or in a nearby field.

Here are some examples of heads that command:

**Save eight
from fire**

**Buy another
school site**

**Arrest 50 pickets
in rubber strike**

**Find 2 bodies,
nab suspect**

Assassinate U.S. envoy

EDITORIALIZING

The reporter has ample space to attribute, qualify and provide full description. The copy editor, however, has a limited amount of space in the headline to convey the meaning of the story. As a result, there is a tendency to eliminate necessary attribution or qualification and to use loaded terms such as *thugs, cops, pinkos, yippies* and *deadbeats* to describe the participants. The result is an editorialized headline.

Every word in a headline should be justified by a specific statement within the story. Was the sergeant who led a Marine platoon into a creek, drowning six recruits, drunk? Most headlines said he was, but the story carried the qualification "under the influence of alcohol to an unknown degree."

Consider this common construction: **Author scores federal misuse of strip studies.** The head states as a fact that the federal government is misusing studies on strip mining. The story credited that view only to the author. In other words, the headline states an opinion as a fact.

Even though the headline reports in essence what the story says, one loaded term will distort the story. If Israel, for reasons it can justify, turns down a compromise plan offered by the United States concerning the West Bank problem, the head creates a negative attitude among readers when it proclaims **Israel spurns U.S. compromise.**

It is often difficult to put qualification in heads because of count limitations. But if the lack of qualifications distorts the head, trouble arises. A story explained that a company that was expected to bid on a project to build a fair exhibit was bowing out of the project because the exhibit's design was not structurally sound. The headline, without qualification, went too far and brought a sharp protest from the construction company's president: **Builder quits, calls state world's fair exhibit 'unsound'.**

SENSATIONALIZING

Another temptation of the headline writer is to spot a minor, sensational element in the story and use it in the head. A story had to do with the policy of banks in honoring outdated checks. It quoted a bank president as saying, "The bank will take the checks." In intervening paragraphs several persons were quoted as having had no trouble cashing their checks. Then in the 11th paragraph was the statement: "A Claymont teacher, who refused to give her name, said she had tried to cash her check last night and it had been refused." She was the only person mentioned in the story as having had any difficulty. Yet the headline writer grabbed this element and produced a head that did not reflect the story:

State paychecks dated 1990
**Can't cash it,
teacher says**

MISSING THE POINT

The process of headline writing starts as soon as a copy editor starts reading the story. If the lead can't suggest a headline, chances are the lead is weak. If a stronger element appears later in the story, it should be moved closer to the lead. The point is so elementary that every reporter should be required to take a turn on the copy desk if for no other reason than to learn how to visualize the headline before beginning the story.

Although the headline ideally emerges from the lead, and generally occupies the top line (with succeeding lines offering qualifications or other dimensions of the story), it frequently has to go beyond the lead to portray the full dimensions of the story. When that occurs, the qualifying paragraphs should be moved to a higher position in the story. Example: **U.S. company to design spying system for Israel.** The lead was qualified. Not until the 15th paragraph was the truth of the head supported. That paragraph should have been moved far up in the story.

The head usually avoids the exact words of the lead. Once is enough for most readers. Lead: "Despite record prices, Americans today are burning more gasoline than ever before, and that casts some doubt on the administration's policy of using higher prices to deter use." Headline: **Despite record gasoline prices, Americans are burning more fuel.** A paraphrase would avoid the repetition: **Drivers won't let record gas prices stop them from burning up fuel.** Since the story tended to be interpretive, the head could reflect the mood: **Hang the high price of gasoline, just fill 'er up and let 'er roar.** Most copy editors try to avoid duplicating the lead, but if doing so provides the clearest possible head, it is a mistake to obfuscate.

BORING THE READER

A headline that gives no more information than the label on a vegetable can is aptly known as a label head. Generally these are the standing heads for columns that appear day by day or week by week, like **Social Notes** or **Niwot News.** They tell the reader nothing. They defy the purpose of a display line, which is to lure the reader.

Almost as bad are the yawny, ho-hum heads that make the reader ask, "So what else is new?" The writer who grabs a generality rather than a specific for the head is more than likely to produce a say-nothing head. Such writers prefer **Many persons killed** to **1,000 persons killed.** "Factors" is about the dullest headline word imaginable. **Factors slow car input.** Something is responsible for either output or input. In this case, a parts shortage was the main cause.

Notice how little information is provided in the following samples:

**Financial program
explained**   **Newark
Rotary told
of planning**

Development plans
described

Coroner seeks cause
of why driver died

Class night to be today

Autopsy scheduled
for dead Akronite

Pan Am jet lands safely

Broyhill speaks
at big picnic

Wadsworth derailment
puts 13 cars off rails

Rotarians hear
Korean bishop

Cars collide
at intersection

Meeting to be held

STATING THE OBVIOUS

Readers read newspapers to get the news. If the headline tells them the obvious, they have been short-changed. Here are examples of the obvious statement:

Fall shirts offer new innovations
(Not to be confused with those old innovations.)

Corn field selected
as place for annual
county husking bee

Turkish ship
sinks in water
near Cyprus

Warm house best
in cold climate

Californian, 20,
drowns in water
of Lake Mohave

REHASHING OLD NEWS

Some stories, like announcements, offer little or no news to invite fresh headlines. Yet even if the second-day story offers nothing new, the headlines cannot be a repetition of the first-day story lead.

Suppose on Monday the story says that Coach Ralston will speak at the high school awards dinner. If Ralston is prominent, his name can be in the head: **Ralston to speak at awards dinner.** On Thursday comes a follow-up story, again saying that Coach Ralston will be the awards dinner speaker. If the headline writer repeats the Monday headline, readers will wonder if they are reading today's paper. The desk editor will wonder why copy editors won't keep up with the news. The problem is to find a new element, even a minor one, like this: **Tickets available for awards dinner.** So the dinner comes off on Friday, as scheduled. If the Saturday headline says **Ralston speaks at awards dinner,** readers learn nothing new. The action is what he said: **Ralston denounces 'cry-baby' athletes.** Or if the story lacks newsworthy quotes, another facet of the affair goes into the head: **30 athletes get awards.**

MISSING A DIMENSION

The headline must portray the story in context. That is, the headline should not repeat what was said yesterday or the day before that or a week ago. It may be a second-day story with a fresh angle. To judge the news fairly and accurately, the copy editor must keep up with the news through daily reading of a newspaper.

There is no trick in writing a vague, generalized headline statement. The real art of headline writing comes in analyzing the story for the how, the why or the consequences. If the story has more than one dimension, the head should reflect the full story, not part of it. Take this horrible example: **D.J. company union (IAPE) withdraws COLA provision.** That's three too many abbreviations. Worse, the head fails to capture the real meaning of the story, which was that the union (Independent Association of Publisher's Employees Inc.) reached an agreement with Dow Jones & Co. providing for across-the-board pay increases. In return, the union agreed to withdraw its demand for a cost-of-living adjustment (COLA). And IAPE is an independent union, not a company union.

Other examples?

Report says school 'integration' still not achieved. The report was already several days old. This was a columnist's view of the matter, and it called for something more than a straight news head.

Carroll to use funds for coal-road repair. This was not the news. The governor had said previously that he might use general fund money. The head should have reflected the fact that the governor NOW plans to use road fund money.

Documents link royal family to sex scandal. Somehow the head should have told readers the story did not describe scandals in Britain's present royal family but concerned an unlordly lord in Queen Victoria's court almost a century ago.

Coroner says teeth aid in identifying dead. That was news decades ago. The news, as explained in the story, was about the number of methods used in medical detective work.

Police chase, capture 2 Alabama van thieves. Unless the item is for an Alabama paper, who cares about a run-of-the-mill crime? It turns out the thieves were 12 years old, a fact that should have been in the headline to justify the story.

If only one element emerges in the headline, the head fails to do justice to the story. This headline is weak: **Man injured in accident.** At least one person in a community is injured in an accident nearly every day. The word *man* is a faraway word. *Driver* is closer. *Injured in accident* can be shortened to *injured* if the word *driver* replaces *man.* Now the top line can read: **Driver injured.** A second element in the story shows that he was wearing a seat belt.

Marrying the two ideas produces a head like this: **Injured driver wore seat belt.** The original head is passable but weak. The revised head gives more information and is an attention-getter.

Notice how a good copy editor can make a pedestrian head come alive and have more meaning:

ORIGINAL	REVISED
6 priests lose duties after rap of bishop	**Priests fired after calling bishop callous**
Man says robber returned to house a second time	**Intruder hits, robs man in home, returns later for lost jacket**
Gardening idea from Mexico helps increase tomato output	**Texan doubles tomato crop with Mexican water tip**
Four-car accident Friday	**6 injured as 4 cars collide**
Gary project funded by U.S. closes down	**South Inc. runs out of money, closes in Gary**
Motorist, 59, dies of apparent coronary	**Motorist dies at wheel; car hits telephone pole**
N.U. trustees O.K. new hearing system	**N.U. students get bigger judicial role**
Senate amends bill to cut pay increase for top judges	**Senate amends bill to give top judges 15% pay boost**
Statistics released on test	**Here's that test; can you pass it?**
State approves housing plan	**State approves another dorm**
10¢ fare is urged for the elderly	**10¢ fair is urged for those over 65**
Two persons killed, 6 wounded in attacks by Ulster terrorists	**2 killed, 6 wounded by Ulster terrorists; 6-year toll at 1,238**

MUDDLING THE HEAD

Because many words can be either verbs or nouns, the headline writer should make sure that such words can't be taken either way. The reader will likely ascribe the wrong meaning:

Population growth: doom writers' field day. Cue: "doom" is intended as a noun. **Doom writers capitalize on population growth.**

Study heralds cop selectivity profile. Cue: "heralds" is a verb, "cop" a noun. Better: **Study draws profile of an ideal cop.**

Flourish floors drabness. Cue: The second word is the verb.

Resort wear showing cues orchestra women's benefit. It's anyone's guess what this means with so many words that double as nouns or verbs.

Flexible can not dangerous. Can is a noun here, not a verb.

Project job needs with new method. "Project" is intended as a verb. Perhaps "foresee" would do the trick.

The lack of a verb may force the reader to reread the head:

4 children die in fire while mother away; If the count won't permit "mother is away," the head should be recast: **Mother away; 4 children die in home fire.**

Physican says president well. But "president" appears to be the object of "says," and the head literally says the physician is a capable elocutionist. When the lines are transposed, president is clearly the subject of the implied verb *is:* **President well, physician says.**

Some desk chiefs have an aversion to using auxiliary verbs in heads. Others insist that if the verb is needed to make the head clear, it should be used or the head should be recast. Often the lack of a vital auxiliary verb produces gibberish:

Rookie admits prisoners struck. Thai pleas said less important than U.S. lives. East-west rail service said unfeasible.

Ex-convict fatally shot fleeing cop. Here is the copy editor's thought: "Ex-convict (is) fatally shot (while) fleeing (from) cop." But many readers will follow the normal order of subject, then predicate, so they read "(An) ex-convict fatally shot (a) fleeing cop." Not good, but perhaps passable: **Ex-convict killed while fleeing police.**

Trooper kills man who had slain wife. Does this mean the trooper killed the man who had slain his (the trooper's) wife? Or that the trooper killed a wife slayer? Or that he killed a man whose wife had been slain by someone else?

Official says CIA, FBI may have 'destroyed' files. To most readers this means the two agencies possibly destroyed some secret files. The quotes around "destroyed" suggest that perhaps they didn't destroy the files. The story, though, said that files previously reported as having been destroyed may still be in the hands of the CIA and FBI. A clearer head: **Official says CIA, FBI may hold 'destroyed' files.**

An easy way to get tortured prose in headlines is to clothe nouns in human garb as in this one:

Fear drives guardsmen to panic.

Span crashes hurt four, none serious. (Some writers apparently think a headline provides a license for changing an adverb to an adjective.)

Smoke brings firefighters to Galt house. (If smoke can impel action, it would "send" the firefighters.)

Rains force roads to close; few families to evacuate. (Rains can't force roads; they can force somebody to close the roads.)

Again, a cardinal rule in headline writing is that the headline, standing alone, must be instantly clear to readers. If the headline puzzles them, they assume the story also will be puzzling and will turn to something they can understand. Examples:

Scarcity sandwiches Jim between signs of the times. This makes sense only if readers know that during an inauguration ceremony a student named Jim paraded through the audience wearing a sandwich board sign reading "I need a job."

Next surge in food costs to be mild. If it's mild, how can it be a surge?

Doctor urges sex, abortion rule shifts. What the good doctor said was that sex taboos are out of date.

Out-of-town Busch strike is felt here. Busch refers to a beer.

Water falls; calls build to Niagara. Want to know what idea this head is trying to convey? The water pressure in Penns Grove had fallen and the water company had received many complaints.

5 from Mt. Pleasant win handicapped essay prizes. What's a handicapped essay? Or were the prizes handicapped?

Suit curbing shed, fence sites loses. If readers take long enough, eventually they will understand that someone lost a lawsuit that would have restricted sites for sheds and fences.

Parked car collides with church. A church on wheels, perhaps?

Elm disease is thriving throughout Longmont. Somehow one doesn't normally think of a disease as thriving. Make it "spreading."

WRITING BAD PUNS

The rule is that a pun in a head must be a good one or the impulse to commit it to print should be suppressed. When they're bad they're awful:

**Unbreakable window
solves a big pane**

Battle of Buicks Saturday
**You buffs 'auto' be told;
'Little Indy' revving up**

This story illustrates the danger of trying to be too cute:

The president of the American Foundrymen's Society said in an interview that small, specialized foundries are shrinking in number because of problems concerned with scrap shortages, high material costs and the high price of conforming to anti-pollution laws and other requirements. Although the number of such small foundries is not great, the shrinkage is causing problems for the Defense Department, designers, manufacturers and investors. Overall, the statement said, the foundry business is flourishing as the nation's sixth largest industry in terms of value added.

Some headline writers could not resist the foundry-foundering pun and thus distorted the story's meaning:

America's foundry business is foundering

Foundry business flounders

(This proves that the writer couldn't distinguish between *founder* and *flounder*.)

Other headline writers stressed only one dimension of the story:

Foundries dwindling

**Foundry industry
in big trouble**

**Foundry failures are
accelerating**

**Foundry industry
suffering shrinkage**

A spot survey of papers using the story showed that slightly more than half (58 percent) of the headlines were reasonably fair and accurate:

Small foundries are disappearing

Small foundries having big financial woes

Foundry firms hurt by material scarcity

A few headlines got both dimensions:

Industry, military hurt by foundry ills

A few were incredibly inept:

Foundry institute shrinkage eyed

Amateur boat builders face problems

Industry needs help, ferret out foundry

AVOIDING BAD TASTE

Newspapers must, of necessity, reveal human sorrows as well as joys, afflictions as well as strengths. No story or headline should mock those who have misfortunes. The newspaper belongs in the parlor where good taste is observed.

A story related that a Johannesburg motorist, whose car stalled on railroad tracks, died under the wheels of a train when he was unable to release his jammed seat belt. The victim may have been unknown to readers in an American community, but death is a common tragedy and should be treated with respect, something the copy editor forgot: **Belted to death.**

A minor story told about a man digging his own grave, starving while lying in it for 21 days and dying two hours after being found. The headline: **Down ... and then out.**

Another story related how a woman survived a 200-foot leap from a bridge, suffering only minor injuries. Investigators said the woman landed in about four feet of water near shore. The item was insensitively headed: **Higher bridge needed.**

AVOIDING DOUBLE MEANINGS

A headline is unclear if it can imply more than one meaning. Some readers may grasp the meaning intended; others won't. An ad writer for a coffee company created a double meaning in this slogan: "The reason so many people buy Red & White Coffee is that 'They Know No Better.' "

Boy struck by auto in better condition. Than if he had been hit by a truck?

Rector sees sex as gourmet meal. He said people would be healthier if they looked on sex as a gourmet meal rather than something distasteful.

U.S. to close one Air Force base in Spain: Moron facility will shut in December. The facility is in Moron, Spain.

Rape classes planned. Rape will be the subject of the classes.

YWCA opens public series with abortion. Abortion will be discussed at the first class meeting.

Flint mother-in-law wounded in argument. That's better than being shot in the head.

Place names like Virgin, Utah; Fertile, Minn., and Bloomer, Wis., inevitably invite a two-faced headline if the town is used:

Virgin woman
gives birth
to twins

Man loses hand
in Bloomer

Other geographical terms:

Book in pocket
saves man shot
in South End

Three Boston
waitresses shot
in North End

Unusual family names of officials—Love, Fortune, Dies, Church, Oyster—also invite two-faced headlines:

Oyster probes
unknown jam

Picks Fortune
for Indiana
revenue chief

Wallace attacks
U.S. grant

Fink heads bridge
charity unit

Billy Hooks
patient in Durham

Slaughter re-creates
Constantine's Rome

Presidents and presidential candidates have been victims of two-faced heads:

Ike to get girls' calf

Goose given
to Eisenhower

LBJ giving bull
to Mexican people

Johnson putting rusty
on White House green

Robert Kennedy stoned

Ford, Reagan neck in
presidential primary

Case and *chest* produce these headlines:

Ord Phillips gets
two years in
cigarette case

Chest pleas issued for
mother's milk bank

The worst possible headline verb is *eyes*:

Frear resting,
eyes return

Green eyes
major title

Sidewalks to be eyed
in Elsmere

Alleged Rhodes
perjury said eyed

More double-takes in headlines:

Five nudes pinched
at stag show

Patients feel
doctors' pinch

Suspect's counsel
says: Winsett
quizzed in nude

Andalusia girl
improved after
drinking poison

Swine housing
to be aired

Flies to attend
wedding of son

Top swine prize
to county youth

Boy chasing fox
found rabid

Publisher says
bar endangers
press freedom

Franklin pair
is improved
after shooting

Club to serve
world culture

Governors' seats
held key to South

Relatives served
at family dinner

Expectant mother, 23,
is anxious for facts

Man with two
broken legs saves
one from drowning

Sex educator says
kindergarten's the time

Bed aflame, jumps
from fourth floor

President says women
responding adequately

Colonel's wife found
by body holding knife
in hand

New restrooms
big assets
for shoppers

Wiley tours sewage
plant, gathers
ammunition for fight
against diversion move

Oklahoman hit by auto
riding on motorcycle

Police slay suspect
bound over for trial

Engineers to hear
ground water talk

Local option fast time
offered to skirt problem

Illegitimacy talks

U.S. to fire Europe
into stationary orbit

Two accused
of kidnapping
slain man

State dinner featured
cat, American food

Admiral likes
to make waves

Pennsauken's safety chief
quits blaming politics

Bradley school
getting new head

Youth hangs self in cell
after uncle tries to help

Man on way to Italy
to see family killed

Heroin busts up

Glacier Lake still
up in the air

Man who shot himself
accidentally dies

Chief says U.S.
courts ulcers

Stores on 4th
between Walnut and
Chestnut to dress up rears

Even the lifestyle pages contain two-faced headlines:

Italian cookies
easy to make

Guide, don't push child

Fresh dates are great

Nurses awarded
for poster art

O'Brien peas in squash

Strong attire right
for bill's death

Male underwear
will reveal new
colorful sights

Carries on for husband

Designer's death
blow to theater

GIVING AWAY THE PUNCHLINE

Some stories are constructed so that the punch line comes at the end, rather than at the beginning. Obviously, if the point of the story is revealed in the headline, the story loses its effectiveness. The following story calls for a head that keeps the reader in suspense until the end:

One Saturday afternoon not long ago a night watchman named Stan Mikalowsky was window-shopping with his 5-year-old daughter, Wanda, and as they passed a toy shop the child pointed excitedly to a doll nearly as big as she was.

The price tag was only $1 less than the watchman's weekly pay check, and his first impulse was to walk away, but when the youngster refused to budge he shrugged and led her into the store.

When Stan got home and unwrapped the doll, his wife was furious.

"We owe the butcher for three weeks, and we're $10 short on the room rent," she said. "So you got to blow a week's pay for a toy."

"What's the difference?" said the night watchman. "Doll or no doll, we're always behind. For once let the kid have something she wants."

One word led to many others, and finally Stan put on his hat and stomped out of the house.

Mrs. Mikalowsky fed the child and put her to bed with the doll next to her and then, worried about Stan, decided to go looking for him at the corner bar and make up with him. To keep his supper warm, she left the gas stove on, and in her haste threw her apron over the back of the chair in such a way that one of the strings landed close to a burner.

Fifteen minutes later when the Mikalowskys came rushing out of the bar, their frame house was in flames and firefighters had to restrain the father from rushing in to save his daughter.

"You wouldn't be any use in there," a cop told him. "Don't worry, they'll get her out."

Fireman Joe Miller, himself a father, climbed a ladder to the bedroom window, and the crowd hushed as he disappeared into the smoke. A few minutes later, coughing and blinking, he climbed down, a blanket-wrapped bundle in his arms. . . .

The local newspaper headlined its story with the line that should have been saved for the finish:

**Fireman rescues life-size doll
as child dies in flames**

PART IV

PICTURES, GRAPHICS, AND DESIGN

CHAPTER 12

PHOTOS AND GRAPHICS

THE IMPORTANCE
OF GRAPHIC ELEMENTS

At good newspapers, the days are gone when a city editor would say to a reporter, "That's a good story; now get me a photo to go with it." Today, good newspapers treat graphical elements—photos, charts, graphs and maps— as the editorial equivalents of stories. Accordingly, they are assigned with the same care, and often at the same time, as news and feature articles.

That development came about as newspapers of the 1980s faced the realities of increasing competition for the reader's attention. Editors found that newspapers needed to be more attractive if they were to hold or increase readership. The result was a decade in which newspaper design became almost as important to many editors as content. In general, the size and quality of newspaper photographs increased, and charts, graphs and maps proliferated. All of those elements were increasingly likely to be printed in color.

None of that should be surprising. We live in a visual society in which color and design play important roles. Visual appeal is used to market everything from television to cereal boxes, and newspapers are not exempt. That has necessitated a change in the way almost all newspapers look. The gray, vertical columns of the past have given way to modular design, color, more and larger pictures, charts, graphs and maps. To make those changes, newsrooms have been forced to change their internal structures.

Today, photo editors are key members of the newsroom management team, usually equal in rank to news, city or metropolitan editors. Design desks have been added in many newsrooms to relieve the copy desk of the chore of designing as well as editing (see Figure 12-1). Many metros have gone so far as to appoint assistant managing editors for graphics. And graphic departments, which produce charts, graphs and maps, have sprung from nowhere, even at relatively small dailies.

Not surprisingly, technological advance has helped. Few newsrooms today are without personal computers with design and charting software. These machines allow editors and artists to create graphics that would have taken days to execute through traditional methods.

Now the art of photography itself is about to change as digital cameras threaten to make silver-based photography obsolete. Both local and wire-

Figure 12-1.   Newspapers increasingly use layout and design terminals to design pages. Previously, paper dummies were completed and the composing room executed the design. [Photo by Scott Serio]

service photos are being processed with computers and digital-imaging software (see Figure 12-2). Once again the newspaper industry is embracing technology to help it remain competitive. Most observers agree that the results to date are promising.

No fancy technology, however, can make a bad picture good or help an editor determine whether a graphic accomplishes what it purports to do. This chapter is designed not to make photographers or graphics artists of editors but to give those editors an appreciation of the role of photos and graphics in the appeal of newspapers. Visual literacy is critical to the competent editor.

Rewriting can often turn a poorly written news story into an acceptable one. Little can be done to change the subject matter of clichéd photos—tree plantings, ribbon cuttings, proclamation signings and the passing of checks, certificates or awards from one person to another. Some newspapers use photographs of these situations simply because of the tradition that "chicken-dinner" stuff must be photographed. It is a tradition that should be scrapped, and most good newspapers already have done so.

Only on a rare occasion would a city editor permit reporters to share their time with sports, Sunday supplements or the advertising department. Yet that is what happens on papers with a small staff of photographers.

One consequence is that too often good local news and feature stories are less effective than they could be because they lack the additional information that accompanying pictures could provide. Another is that too often mediocre,

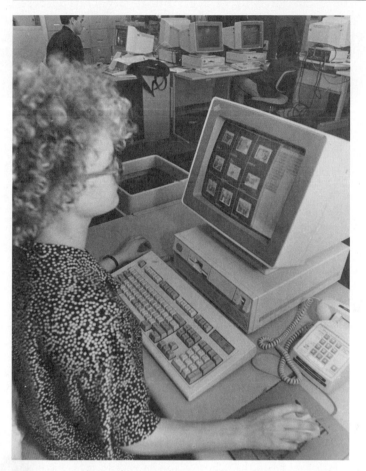

Figure 12-2.   Photo editing workstation. Photo editing increasingly is done at photo editing workstations. Newspaper photography is in the early stages of a transition to computerization. [Photo by Jeff Adams]

space-wasting pictures from the wire services or syndicates are given more attention than they deserve.

A photo editor is almost as essential to a newspaper as a city editor. Some executive—preferably one with a background in photography—should be responsible for assigning photographers to news and feature events. Someone in authority should insist that all photos, including those from news agencies, be edited and that cutlines, or captions, be intelligently written.

If it is a good picture, it should get a good play, just as a top story gets a big headline. If pictures are a vital part of the story, editors should be willing to cut back on words, if necessary, to provide space for pictures. Some events can be told better in words than in pictures. Conversely, other events are essentially graphic, and editors need little or no text to get the message across.

Pictures can "dress up" a page. But if their only purpose is to break up the type, they are poorly used. The large number of pictures used, even on front pages, without an accompanying story suggests that the pictures are being used for their graphic value rather than for their storytelling value. Ideally, pictures and stories should work together.

Still pictures, even action shots, may not be able to compete with television in some ways, but still photography can add color to words and can capture moods. Originality starts with the picture. Its values are interest, composition and quality of reproduction.

A small, poor-quality picture should be rejected because the flaws will be magnified in the enlargement. Facsimile prints may be retouched, but the quality is seldom as good as pictures made from glossy prints. Generally, pictures reproduce better if they are reduced rather than enlarged, but content, not technical quality, should be the factor that determines the play a picture is given.

PHOTOGRAPHER-EDITOR RELATIONSHIPS

An encouraging development in recent years has been the trend toward making photographers full partners in the newspaper editorial process. Historically, photographers have been second-class citizens in the newspaper hierarchy. They have not enjoyed the prestige of the reporter or the copy editor, and with rare exception their opinions have been ignored or have not been solicited.

Many insightful editors have now realized that photographers possess an intangible quality known as visual literacy, a trait sometimes lacking in even the best of wordsmiths. Photographers should have a voice in how their pictures are displayed, and editors who have attempted to give them a voice invariably have been pleased with the results. The number of newspapers using pictures well is increasing each year, although leading picture editors agree that there is ample room for improvement. For every newspaper using pictures well, it is easy to find three still using the line-'em-up-and-shoot-'em approach.

A key to improvement in the quality of a newspaper's pictures is allowing the photographer to become involved in the story from the outset. If possible, the photographer should accompany the reporter as information for the story is gathered. If that is impossible, allowing the photographer to read the story—or to take time to talk with the reporter about the thrust of it—will help ensure a picture that complements the story. Newspapers throughout the country each day are filled with pictures that fail to convey a message because the reporter, photographer and editor failed to communicate.

An important part of this communications process involves writing the photo order, the document given to the photographer when an assignment is made. A photographer for the *Columbia Missourian* once received an order for a picture of an elementary school principal. The order instructed the photographer to meet the principal in his office at 3:15 p.m. and to take a picture of him at his desk. It mentioned that the principal would be unavailable until that time. The story focused on how the principal went out of his way to help frightened first-graders find the right bus during the first few weeks of school. Because the reporter failed to mention that when he wrote the photo order, the photographer followed his instructions exactly. He arrived at 3:15 and took the picture. Only after returning to the office did he learn of the thrust of the story and discover that the principal was "unavailable" 15 minutes earlier because he had been helping students find their buses. The best picture situation had been missed.

Words and pictures are most effective when they work together. For that to happen, reporters, photographers and editors must work together. Often the best approach is to let the photographer read the story and determine how to illustrate it. The photographer, after all, should be the expert in visual communication.

EDITING DECISIONS

Most pictures, like most news stories, can be improved with editing. The photo editor, like the copy editor, must make decisions that affect the quality of the finished product. The photo editor must determine:

1. Which photo or photos complement the written story or tell a story of their own.
2. Whether cropping enhances the image.
3. What size a photo must be to communicate effectively.
4. Whether retouching is necessary.

SELECTION

Picture selection is critical because valuable space is wasted if the picture does nothing more than depict a scene that could be described more efficiently with words. The old adage that a picture is worth a thousand words is not necessarily true. If the picture adds nothing to the reader's understanding of a story, it should be rejected.

Conversely, some pictures capture the emotion or flavor of a situation more vividly than words. In other situations, words and pictures provide perfect complements.

A talented photo editor, experienced in visual communication, can provide the guidance necessary for successful use of pictures. Smaller papers without the luxury of full-time photo editors can turn to their photographers for advice, but often the news editor or copy editor must make such decisions. When that is necessary, an appreciation for the importance of visual communication is essential for good results.

Internal procedures reflect a newspaper's picture selection philosophy. Some allow the photographer to make the decision; the pictures he or she submits to the desk are the only ones considered for publication. This procedure may ensure selection of the picture with the best technical quality, but that picture may not best complement the story. A photo editor, working closely with the photographer, the city editor and copy editors, should have a better understanding of the story and be able to make the best selection. Contact prints, miniature proofs of the photographer's negatives, allow the photographer, reporter and editors to review all frames available so the best selection can be made (see Figure 12-3).

Figure 12-3.   Contact print sheet. Photographers and editors often choose pictures from contact prints of the available negatives.

CROPPING

A photograph is a composition. The composition should help the reader grasp the picture's message clearly and immediately. If the picture is too cluttered, the reader's eyes scan the picture looking for a place to rest. But if the picture contains a strong focal point, the reader at least has a place to start. A prime job of a photo editor, therefore, is to help the photograper take out some unnecessary details to strengthen the overall view.

Certain elements within the picture could be stronger than the full picture. Some photo editors try to find these interest points and patterns by moving two L-shaped pieces of cardboard over the picture. This helps to guide the editor in cropping. The editor looks for a focal point, or chief spot of interest. If other points of interest are present, the photo editor tries to retain them. The editor searches for patterns that can be strengthened by cropping. The pattern helps give the picture harmonious and balanced composition. Among these patterns are various letter shapes—L, U, S, Z, T, O—and geometric patterns such as a star, a circle, a cross or a combination of these.

Because most news and feature photos contain people, the editor strives to help the photographer depict them as dramatically as possible. The editor must decide how many persons to include in the picture, how much of a person to include and what background is essential.

Historically, newspapers have opted for the tightest possible cropping to conserve valuable space. Severe cropping, however, may damage a picture to the point that not printing it would have been preferable. Those who win awards for photo editing appreciate the fact that background is essential to some photographs. As a result, they tend to crop tightly less often than do editors with more traditional approaches to picture editing. In Figures 12-4a and 12-4b, tight cropping allows the reader to see interesting detail. But in Figures 12-5a and 12-5b, tight cropping eliminates the environment and damages the meaning of the picture. Those who can distinguish between these approaches are valuable members of newspaper staffs. They possess visual literacy.

SIZING

The reproduction size of a photograph should be determined by the value of the picture, not the amount of space available. Too often, newspaper editors try to reduce a photograph to fit a space and destroy the impact of the photo in the process. Common sense should dictate that a picture of 15 individuals will be ineffective if it appears as a two-column photo. More likely, such a photo will require three or even four columns of space.

Talented photo editors know that the greatest danger is making pictures too small. If the choice is between a two-column picture and a three-column picture, the wise photo editor opts for the larger size. Pictures can be too large, but more often they are damaged by making them too small. Another alternative may be available. Modern production techniques make it easy for the editor to publish a 2 ½-column photo. Text to the side of it is simply set in a wider measure to fill the space.

Figures 12-4a and 12-4b.   Footprint on the lunar soil. An example of how cropping (b) can bring out an interesting detail in a photograph (a). The close-up view was photographed with a lunar surface camera during the Apollo 11 lunar surface extravehicular activity. [*Photographs courtesy of the National Aeronautics and Space Administration.*]

Figures 12-5a.   Tight cropping can occasionally destroy the impact of a picture.

Sizing of any photograph is an important decision, but sizing of pictures in multi-photograph packages is particularly important. In such packages, one photograph should be dominant. The use of multiple pictures allows the editor flexibility that may not exist in single-picture situations. If a picture editor selects a photo of a harried liquor store clerk who has just been robbed and a photo of the outside of the store where the robbery occurred, the editor has three choices:

1. Devote equal space to the two pictures. This is the least desirable choice because neither picture would be dominant and, consequently, neither would have eye-catching impact.
2. Make the outside shot dominant and the close-up of the clerk secondary. This would work, but the dominant picture, which serves

Figures 12-5b. Here, tight cropping takes the farmer out of his environment by making it difficult or impossible for the reader to determine that the setting is a barn. [Columbia Missourian *photos by Manny Crisostomo*]

merely as a locater, would have little impact. The impact of human emotion, evident in the clerk's face, would be diminished.

3.   Make the facial expression dominant with good sizing and make the outside shot as small as 1½ columns. The outside shot, standing alone, would look ridiculous if used in that size. But used in conjunction with another, larger photo, it would work well.

Dramatic size contrast is an effective device in multi-picture packages (Figures 12-6a and 12-6b). An editor with an eye trained in visual communication understands the usefulness of reversing normal sizing patterns for added impact.

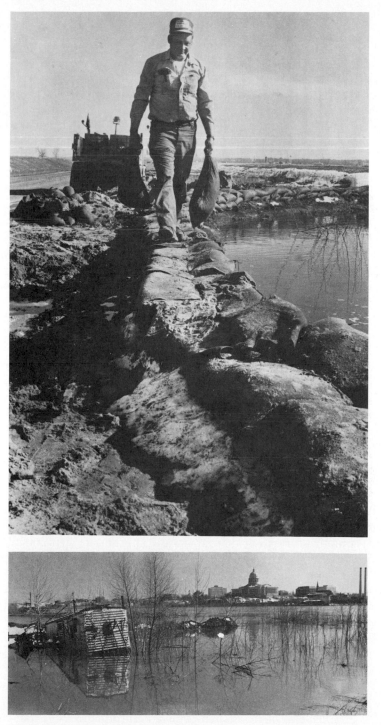

Figures 12-6a and 12-6b.   Many editors would run the overall flooding shot larger than the picture of the farmer laying sandbags in place. The pairing, however, has more impact if the close shot of the farmer is run larger than the scene-setting overall picture. [Columbia Missourian *photos by Lee Meyer and Mike Asher.*]

RETOUCHING

Some pictures can be improved by *retouching,* the process of toning down or eliminating distractions within the frame. Minor imperfections in photos can be retouched with an airbrush, an instrument that applies liquid pigment to a photo surface by means of compressed air. Retouching also can be done by brushing on a retouching liquid or paste, or by using retouching pencils of various colors. Even regular pencils can be used to retouch imperfections in black-and-white photos.

Care must be exercised, however, to ensure that retouching does not change the meaning and content of the photo. Changing a photo to alter its meaning is as unethical as changing a direct quotation to alter a speaker's meaning.

This whole issue has taken on new importance in recent years with the arrival of computerized photo editing. An unscrupulous editor can move one of the Great Pyramids in relation to the Sphinx to improve a picture's composition or place the head of one person on the body of another. Both those things have happened in recent years as magazines and newspapers have grappled with the ethics of changing photographs.

Most good newspaper editors have taken the solid ethical position that nothing more than changing the brightness, contrast or sharpness of a picture should be tolerated. Anything more than that leads to deception, which is sure to destroy a publication's integrity, at least where photographs are concerned.

PICTURES AS COPY

When the picture has been processed, someone—reporter or photographer—supplies the information for the caption, also known as the cutline. The picture and caption information then go to the appropriate department where the editor decides whether to use the picture and, if so, how to display it.

Before submitting a picture to the production department, the editor supplies enough information to get the correct picture in the correct place with the correct caption. A picture, like a story, generally carries an identifying slug. To ensure that the picture will match the screened mechanical reproduction, the cutline, and, if need be, the story, the editor uses a slugline.

A slip of paper clipped on the picture or taped to the back normally contains information such as:

1. The slug, or picture identification.
2. The size of the desired screened reproduction.
3. Special handling instructions.
4. The department, edition and page.
5. The date the photo is to appear.
6. The date and time the picture was sent to the production department.
7. Whether the picture stands alone or accompanies a story.

The picture is then routed directly to the camera room or indirectly through the art department. The caption goes to the composing room. Caption copy contains, in addition to the cutlines, essential directions to match text and picture.

If the picture is to go with a story, the information is carried on both the cutline and the story copy. The reason is obvious. Unless properly slugged, the story may appear on Page 3 and the photo on Page 16.

Sometimes the photo may be separated from the story deliberately. A teaser picture may be used on Page One to entice readers to read the story on another page. If a long story has two illustrations, one illustration often is used on the page where the story begins and the other on the jump page. On major events such as the death of a president, pictures may be scattered on several pages. In that case, readers are directed to these pages with a guideline such as "More pictures on pages 5, 7 and 16."

Sometimes the mechanical reproduction of the photo is made in reverse. The result can be ludicrous, particularly if the picture shows a sign or if the principals are wearing uniforms containing letters or numerals.

The person responsible for checking page proofs makes sure the correct headline is over the correct story and the captions under pictures of a local politician and a jackass are not reversed.

THE ENLARGING, REDUCING FORMULA

At most newspapers, photographers make 8-by-10-inch prints. Photos then are enlarged or reduced as necessary during the screening process. Photos are enlarged or reduced in proportion to their width and depth. A simple method of determining this proportion is to draw a diagonal line from the upper-left to the lower-right corner of the photograph as cropped. It is best to draw this line on the back of the picture to make sure the line is not accidentally reproduced in the newspaper. Then measure the reproduction width along the top of the picture and draw a vertical line at that point. The point where the vertical line intersects the diagonal line indicates the reproduction depth of the picture.

A more common procedure is to measure in pica or inches the width and depth of the photograph as cropped. Because the editor knows the width he or she wants the picture to be when it is reproduced, a proportion wheel (Figure 12-7) allows that editor to determine the reproduction depth quickly. The percentage of enlargement or reproduction is known as the SOR, or size of reproduction. If a photograph is being enlarged, the SOR will be greater than 100 percent. If the photograph is being reduced, the SOR will be less than 100 percent. Knowing this allows the editor to make a quick check to determine if reproduction instructions to the engraver or camera room are correct.

If the picture margins are uneven, the editor may place a sheet of tissue paper over the picture and draw the diagonal and connecting lines on the tissue

Figure 12-7.   Example of disc showing enlargement and reduction ratios. The finder is set at dimensions in Figure 12-7 with 4⅛" on the inner circle matching 3⅜" on the outer circle. The figure 6⁵⁄₁₆" is opposite the inner figure of 7¾" and the SOR, or size of reproduction, is 81 percent. The numerals on the wheel, while marked as inches, also can represent picas if the newspaper uses that unit of measurement in sizing photographs.

to determine reproduction depth. Or the editor may measure the picture area and use a mathematical proportion to determine reproduction depth. Suppose the picture is 48 picas wide and 60 picas deep and the reproduction width is 34 picas. Simple cross–multiplication is used to determine the unknown dimension: 48:34 :: 60:X. The answer is 42½ picas in depth.

If the editor decides to make the picture 34 picas wide and 45 picas deep, then X will be substituted for one of the picture measurements to determine the extent of the crop to produce the 34 by 45 proportion. If X is substituted for the width of the picture, the X:34 :: 60:45. 45X equals 2040, and X equals 45.3. Subtracting 45.3 from 48 shows a crop of 2.7 picas on the width of the picture.

Some picture editors place a plastic sheet over the picture. Column widths and inches are drawn on the sheet, and a string is attached to the sheet in the upper-left corner. By positioning the string from the upper-left to the lower-right corners of the picture, the editor can determine the depth of the enlargement or reduction (Figure 12-8).

PICTURES CAN LIE

The picture editor makes the same kind of editorial judgment about a picture that the city editor and the wire editor make about a local story and a wire story. Does the picture tell the whole story or only part of it? Does it distort,

Figure 12-8.   A clear plastic sheet placed over a photograph enables a photo editor to size a picture quickly. A string attached to the plastic sheet is extended from the upper-left to the lower-right corner of the picture to show its depth in five columns or less.

editorialize, mislead? Does it omit important details or include details that create an erroneous impression? In other words, is the picture loaded?

The point was raised by James Russell Wiggins, former editor of the *Washington Post,* during a lecture at the University of North Dakota. "The camera," he said, "can be a notorious, compulsive, unashamed and mischievous liar."

To illustrate, he said he once declined to print a photograph of President Harry Truman walking across the platform of Union Station before a backdrop formed by a row of caskets just shipped in from the Korean war. "What that camera said was that the Korean war was 'Truman's war,' just what thousands of the president's critics were saying."

He also commented on the distorted portrait of police officers during civil disorders. The pictures may have been representative of the action, but they failed to tell what really happened in perspective and why.

"The camera does not tell the truth," said Wiggins, "and because what it tells is not the whole truth, skepticism about the media rises in the minds of readers who know that police officers, whatever their undoubted faults, are not always wrong."

A picture may be striking and it may be narrative. But if it conveys a false or distorted impression, it would be better left unpublished.

Picture editors often can show subjective judgment in the selection of pictures. Suppose an editor has four or five pictures of a public figure. Some editors will select the more favorable picture; others will pick the less favorable one. Many of the pictures used of former President Nixon, even before his resignation, were editorialized. Pictures of former Presidents Jimmy Carter and Lyndon Johnson were similarly criticized.

TASTE IN PICTURE EDITING

It was a tragic fire in a metropolitan area. A woman and a child took refuge on an ironwork balcony. As firefighters tried to rescue them, the balcony collapsed, sending the woman to her death and the child to a miraculous survival. Photographers took sequence shots of the action (Figures 12-9a and 12-9b). Should a picture editor use the pictures?

Some readers will be incensed, accusing the papers of sensationalism, poor taste, invasion of privacy, insensitivity and a tasteless display of human tragedy to sell newspapers.

Picture editors could reply that their duty is to present the news, whether of good things or bad, of the pleasant or the unpleasant. Defending the judgment to use the pictures on Page One, Watson Sims, editor of the *Battle Creek* (Mich.) *Enquirer and News,* said, "The essential purpose of journalism is to help the reader understand what is happening in this world and thereby help him to appreciate those things he finds good and to try to correct those things he finds bad."

Of the flood of pictures depicting the war in Vietnam, surely among the most memorable were the Saigon chief of police executing a prisoner, terrified

Figure 12-9a. Two of the controversial sequence shots of a fire tragedy in a Boston apartment. Scores of readers protested the use of these widely distributed photos. Most editors defended the use of the pictures. [*Photos by Stanley Forman of the* Boston Herald-American, *distributed by UPI.*]

Figure 12-9b.

children fleeing a napalm attack, and the flaming suicide of a Buddhist monk. Such scenes were part of the war record and deserved to be shown.

Photos of fire deaths may tell more than the tragedy depicted in the burned and mangled bodies. Implicit could be the lessons of inadequate inspection, faulty construction, carelessness with matches, arson, antiquated fire-fighting equipment or the like.

Picture editors have few criteria to guide them. Their news judgment and their own consciences tell them whether to order a picture for Page One showing a man in Australia mauled to death by polar bears after he fell or dived into a pool in the bears' enclosure in a zoo. Of the hundreds of pictures available that day, surely a better one could have been found for Page One. If the scene causes an editor to turn away and say, "Here I don't belong," chances are the readers will have the same reaction. Not all of life's tragedies have to be depicted. The gauge is importance and newsworthiness.

PICTURE PAGES

Some newspapers devote an entire page to pictures with a minimum of text. Some use part of the page for pictures, the rest for text matter. Some pages are made up of unrelated photos; some are devoted to related pictures. Some use part of the page for sequence pictures and leave the remainder for unrelated pictures or text matter. Increasingly, photo pages on a single subject are used to tell a story more forcefully than words can tell it (see Figure 12-10).

Here are a few pointers on picture pages:

1. Three or four large pictures make a more appealing picture page than eight or 10 smaller ones.
2. Let one picture, the best available, dominate the page.
3. Emphasize the upper-left portion of the page either with a dominant picture or a large headline.
4. If the content allows, crop some of the pictures severely to achieve either wide, shallow, horizontal ones or narrow, long, vertical ones.
5. In a picture series or sequence, place a big picture in the bottom right corner of the page. It is the logical stopping point.
6. Let the page breathe. White space makes both the pictures and the text stand out. But keep interior spacing standard and allow white space to bleed to the outside. Trapped interior white space is distracting.
7. Don't align pictures with a T square. An off-alignment often provides extra white space or leaves room for a caption.
8. If a picture page has to be made up in a hurry, pick the best picture, rough-sketch it on a dummy, slug and schedule the picture and get it to the production department. Then edit the other pictures. The cutlines can be written while the editor looks at photocopies of the pictures.
9. Vary picture page patterns. Don't make today's picture page look like last Saturday's.

Above, Landhuis gives some tips to a hired hand before handing over the controls. At left, lifts are too expensive for the farmer, so he depends on the use of his arms.

Handicapped farmer keeps a dream alive

Landhuis says a sure way to check his cows for sickness and stress is to feed them mineral salts from a dish.

Tenacity helps Landhuis farm, raise cattle

By Mitchell B. Chamberlain
Missourian staff writer

As a child, when his friends wanted to become policemen, firefighters, doctors or lawyers, Marion Landhuis dreamed of becoming a farmer.

Ten years ago, after a successful career in a management position for Montgomery Ward and Co. and then at Texaco Inc., Landhuis, then 37, finally exercised his stock options and us-1 his savings to buy a farm with his brother. He raised corn, wheat and soybeans on the 212-acre farm east of Columbia and started a cow-calf operation

Then his dream of farming was nearly shattered.

On Sept. 4, 1980, Landhuis was shot in the back during a robbery in Callaway County. The bullet, which is still lodged in his spine, paralyzed him from the waist down.

For 109 days, Landhuis was hospitalized in Columbia Regional Hospital. "It's difficult to keep your positive disposition when you're utilizing all of your energies just to live," he said.

To get through each day, he takes medication to control the pain. Even with the medication, it requires an enormous amount of tenacity to cope, he says.

Nevertheless, Landhuis is still trying to do some farming on a limited basis. He has a herd of cattle that he tends, and he farms a plot of land north of town. Most of the 212-acre farm has been rented to his neighbor.

Although Landhuis says there is equipment available to aid the handicapped farmer, it is often quite expensive. There are lifts available to help the handicapped farmer onto his machinery and hand controls for locomotion, but most of the equipment is not under warranty, he says.

"Farmers represent about 3 percent of the population," Landhuis says. "Handicapped farmers represent only a very small percentage of this."

"There are so few of us, it is not economically feasible for manufacturers to cheaply produce farm equipment for such a small population."

In general, the handicapped person must be innovative, he says. Many cities are not built with the handicapped in mind.

"Columbia is pretty good to its handicapped citizens," Landhuis says. Many buildings have automatic doors and ramps to aid those in wheelchairs.

But these features represent costly additions that many businesses or communities are not willing to spend, he says, and often the handicapped are overlooked.

Today his smile carefully conceals his pain. Landhuis says he con-

stantly works at keeping a positive attitude.

"Since there is snow on the ground, I can't even feed the cows," he said. "My wife has to do it, and that really hurts me."

The psychological effects of becoming paraplegic can be devastating.

But Landhuis' optimistic outlook on life is his mainstay, he says.

He says he has received a great deal of support from his family. His wife, Pauline, was at his side daily during of his long hospital stay, he says.

Friends have helped support him morally, as well as, financially.

As he recuperated in the hospital, about 20 area farmers used their own equipment to harvest his soybean crop.

Medical bills from Columbia Regional Hospital added up to more than $25,000, a fund was created to pay the expenses because Landhuis did not have any medical insurance.

People from all over the country contributed money, he says.

But even with the support of family and friends, Landhuis' recuperation has been difficult.

There was no apparent progress for the first six months after his injury, he says. Now, progress is slow.

"I'm a realist," he says. "I know I'll probably never be able to walk again, but there are other things to do in life than complain about my situation."

Above, Landhuis stuffs wood for the furnace in a bag as his wife, Pauline, piles it up for him. At right, Marion talks with another bidder at the Columbia sale barn — always trying to keep up with what's new

Photos by Chris Fennewald

Figure 12-10.   Consistent internal spacing is important in producing a strong picture page. White space should bleed to the outside margins.

10. Captions need not appear below the pictures. In fact, a narrow caption beside the picture may be easier to read than a wider one below it.

11. In a sequence or series of pictures, don't repeat in one caption what was said in another.

12. If all the pictures were taken by one photographer or provided by one wire service, a single credit line on the page will suffice. Too many credits give the page a bulletin-board effect.

13. In a photo-essay page, keep the captions as brief as possible. Usually, the pictures tell most of the story, especially if the headline has established the theme.

14. Headlines generally are more effective at the left or right of the page or under the main pictures. Occasionally the head may be overprinted on the main picture if the type does not rob the picture of important details.

CAPTION GUIDELINES

Picture texts are known by many names—cutlines, captions, underlines (or overlines), legends. A caption suggests a heading over a picture, but most editors now use the term to refer to the lines under the picture. *Legend* may refer either to the text or to the heading. If a heading or catchline is used, it should be under, not over the picture.

The copy editor "sells" the reporter's story by means of a compelling headline. By the same token, the picture editor can help control the photographic image with a caption message. The primary purpose of the caption is to get the reader to respond to the photo in the manner intended by the photographer and the picture editor.

Readers first concentrate on the focal point of the picture, then glance at the other parts. Then, presumably, most turn to the caption to confirm what they have seen in the picture. The caption provides the answers to questions of who, what, where, when, why and how, unless some of these are apparent in the picture.

The caption interprets and expands upon what the picture says to the reader. It may point out the inconspicuous but significant. It may comment on the revealing or amusing parts of the picture if these are not self-evident. The caption helps explain ambiguities, comments on what is not made clear in the picture and mentions what the picture fails to show if that is necessary.

The ideal caption is direct, brief and sometimes bright. It is a concise statement, not a news story. It gets to the point immediately and avoids the "go back to the beginning" of the background situation.

If the picture accompanies a story, the caption doesn't duplicate the details readers can find in the story. It should, however, contain enough information to satisfy those who will not read the story. Ideally, the picture and the caption will induce readers to read the story. Normally the caption of a picture with story is limited to two or three lines.

Even when the picture relates to the story, the caption should not go beyond what the picture reveals. Nor should the facts in the caption differ from those in the story.

Captions stand out in the newspaper's sea of words and strike the reader with peculiar force. Every word should be weighed, especially for impact, emotional tone, impartiality and adherence to rules of grammar and the accepted language.

Anyone who tries to write or rewrite a caption without seeing the picture risks errors. The writer should examine the cropped picture, not the original one. The caption has to confine itself to the portion of the picture the reader will see. If the caption says a woman is waving a handkerchief, the handkerchief must be in the picture. In a layout containing two or more pictures with a single caption, the writer should study the layout to make sure that left or right or top or bottom directions are correct.

Although no one should try to write a caption without first looking at the picture, pictures frequently have to move to the production department quickly. The editor removes the captions (from wire-service and syndicated pictures) and jots down the slug and size of the pictures and any revealing elements in the pictures that might be added to the cutlines. A photocopy of the picture may be made. Time permitting, a proofsheet showing pictures and their captions should be given to the photo editor.

When the caption has been composed, the writer should compare the message with the picture. The number of people in the picture should be checked against the number of names in the caption. Everyone appearing prominently in the picture should be identified. If a person is so obscured in the crowd that the person is not easily identifiable, that fact need not be brought to the reader's attention.

WRITING THE CAPTION

Here are some tips on caption writing:

1. *Don't tell the obvious.* If the person in the picture is pretty or attractive, that fact will be obvious from the picture. The picture will tell whether a man is smiling. It may be necessary, however, to tell why he is smiling. An explanation need not go as far as the following: "Two women and a man stroll down the newly completed section of Rehoboth's boardwalk. They are, from left, Nancy Jackson, Dianne Johnson and Richard Bramble, all of West Chester." An editor remarked, "Even if some of the slower readers couldn't have figured out the sexes from the picture, the names are a dead giveaway."
2. *Don't editorialize.* A writer doesn't know whether someone is happy, glum or troubled. The cutline that described the judge as "weary but ready" when he arrived at court on the opening day of trial must have made readers wonder how the writer knew the judge was weary.

3. *Use specifics rather than generalities.* "A 10-pound book" is better than "a huge book." "A man, 70," is more descriptive than "an old man."

4. *Omit references to the photo.* Because the readers know you are referring to the photograph, omit phrases such as "is pictured," "is shown" and "the picture above shows."

5. *Use "from left" rather than "from left to right".* The first means as much as the second and is shorter. Neither *left* nor *right* should be overworked. If one of two boys in a picture is wearing a white jersey, use that fact to identify him. If the president is in a golf cart with a professional golfer, readers shouldn't have to be told which one is the president.

6. *Avoid "looking on."* One of the worst things you can say about a person in a photo is that he or she is "looking on." If that is all the person is doing, the photo is superfluous. Perhaps something like this will help: "William McGoo, background, is campaign treasurer."

7. *Don't kid the readers.* They will know whether this is a "recent photo." Give the date the photo was taken if it is an old photo. Also, let readers know where the picture was taken—but not how. Most readers don't care about all the sleet and snow the photographer had to go through to get the picture. Also, readers aren't stupid. If the caption says three persons in a Girl Scout picture are looking over a drawing of a new camp, readers aren't fooled if the picture shows two of the girls behind the drawing; they obviously can't be looking it over. If a special lens was used, resulting in a distortion of distance or size, the reader should be told what happened.

8. *Write captions in the present tense.* This enhances the immediacy of the pictures they accompany. The past tense is used if the sentence contains the date or if it gives additional facts not described in the action in the picture. The caption may use both present and past tenses, but the past time-element should not be used in the same sentence with a present-tense verb describing the action.

9. *Make sure the caption is accurate.* Double-check the spelling of names. The paper, not the photographer, gets the blame for inaccuracies. Caption errors occur because someone, the photographer or the reporter accompanying the photographer, failed to give the photo desk enough, or accurate, information from which to construct a caption. Apparently assuming that any big horn is a tuba, a caption writer wrote about a horn player with half his tuba missing. His editor was quick to reprimand, "Umpteen million high school kids, ex-bandsmen and musicians in general know better."

10. *Double-check the photo with the caption identification.* The wrong person pictured as "the most-wanted fugitive" is a sure way to invite libel.

11. *Be careful.* Writing a caption requires as much care and skill as writing a story or a headline. The reader should not have to puzzle out the meaning of the description. Notice these jarring examples:

Fearing new outbreaks of violence, the results of Sunday's election have been withheld.

Also killed in the accident was the father of five children driving the other vehicle.

Yum! Yum! A corn dog satisfies that ravishing fair appetite. (The word, obviously, was *ravenous,* not *ravishing*.)

Don't hit the reader over the head with the obvious. If the photo shows a firefighter dousing hot timbers after a warehouse fire and a firefighter already has been mentioned in the text, it is ridiculous to add in the caption that "firefighters were called."

12. *Avoid last-line widows or hangers.* The last line of the caption should be a full line, or nearly so. If the writer knows the number of characters per pica in the type used for the caption, the writer can set the margin stops so that each line corresponds with the type line. Captions written on computers can be composed to check line endings. When the lines are doubled (two 2-columns for a four-column picture), the writer should write an even number of lines.

13. *Captions should be humorous if warranted by the picture.* Biting humor and sarcasm have no place in captions.

14. *The caption should describe the event as shown in the picture, not the event itself.* Viewers will be puzzled if the caption describes action they do not see. Sometimes, however, an explanation of what is not shown is justified. If the picture shows a football player leaping high to catch a pass for a touchdown, viewers might like to know who threw the pass.

   A wire service delivered a combination of three pictures showing the vice president as he played in a celebrity golf tournament. He missed a putt, then buried his head in his hands. But golfers looking closely saw the third picture obviously was not taken on the green, and that while the man had a putter in two pictures he held a wood in the third. The caption should have explained that after he missed the putt he grabbed another club, walked off the green and then showed his displeasure with the miss.

15. *Update the information.* Because there is a lapse between the time a picture of an event is taken and the time a viewer sees the picture in the newspaper, care should be taken to update the information in the caption. If the first report was that three bodies were found in the wreckage, but subsequently two more bodies were found, the caption should contain the latest figure.

   Or, for a picture taken in one season but presented in another, the caption should reflect the time difference. An example: "Big band singer Helen O'Connell, left, reminisces with Pat and Art Modell backstage at Blossom Music Center this summer..." Reading that on Dec. 1, it is difficult to decide when it happened, especially with a present-tense verb and frost in the air.

16. *Be exact.* In local pictures, the addresses of the persons shown may be helpful. If youngsters appear in the picture, they should be identified by names, ages, names of parents and addresses.

Potential pies

Although it's more than a month until jack-o'-lanterns will be needed for the festivities of Allhallows eve, the seasonal harvest of pumpkins has begun in the fields of Valley View Farms in Adams County.

Onion harvest

Onions previously dug from the ground were being topped and boxed by a six-man crew working at the Yosh Nigo farm on U.S. 50, near Uranium Downs this morning. Onions are among the last of the season's crops which farmers are hastening to gather while the weather is still good.

Sentinel photo by Dennis Hogan

HIGH-RISE EXCITEMENT—Fans on balconies watch first lap of qualifying race for the Long Beach Grand Prix. Brian Redman won main event in a Lola before an estimated 75,000 spectators.
DETAILS IN SPORTS SECTION

Times photo by Jack Murphy

The way it was, then...

No, this wasn't taken from last night's bout in Manila when champion Muhammad Ali faced Joe Frazier for the third time. This shot was taken during the 15th round of their first meeting in March, 1971, when and the heavyweight title. During their second encounter, in January 1974, there were no knockdowns and very little else. Ali was a 2-1 favorite around the world to win, but in Manila the odds dropped to 6-5 for Ali. (Defender photo)

Sargent Shriver

All weld and good

Sparks fly as Larry Page welds a latch on the door of a boxcar. He was working yesterday in the Penn-Central Railroad yards outside of Jeffersonville. Ind.

Figure 12-11.   Caption styles. Edmund Arnold, an authority on typography, argues that when display is added to the caption, readership increases as much as 25 percent.

17. *Credit the photographer.* If the picture is exceptional, credit may be given to the photographer in the caption, perhaps with a brief description of how he or she achieved the creation. On picture pages containing text matter, the photographer's credit should be displayed as prominently as the writer's. Photo credit lines seldom are used on one-column or half-column portraits.

18. *Pictures without captions.* Although pictures normally carry captions, mood or special-occasion pictures sometimes appear without them if the message is obvious from the picture itself. Not all who look at pictures will also read the captions. In fact, the decline is severe enough to suggest that many readers satisfy their curiosity merely by looking at the picture.

19. *Creating slugs.* In writing a series of captions for related shots, use only one picture slug, followed by a number—moon 1, moon 2 and so on.

20. *Know your style.* Some papers use one style for captions with a story and another style for captions on pictures without a story (called *stand-alones* or *no-story*). A picture with a story might call for one, two or three words in boldface caps to start the caption. In stand-alones a small head or *catchline* might be placed over the caption (Figure 12-11).

21. *Give the location.* If the dateline is knocked out in the caption, make sure that the location is mentioned. Example: "GUARDING GOATS—Joe Fair, a 70-year-old pensioner, looks over his goats Rosebud and Tagalong, the subject of much furor in this northeastern Missouri community, boyhood home of Mark Twain . . . ." The Missouri community was Hannibal, but the caption didn't say so.

22. *Rewrite wire-service cutlines.* The same pictures from news agencies and syndicates appear in smaller dailies as well as in metropolitan dailies. Some papers merely reset the caption supplied with the pictures. Most, if not all, such captions should be rewritten to add to the story told in the picture and to indicate some originality on the paper's part.

23. *Watch the mood.* The mood of the caption should match the mood of the picture. The caption for a feature photo may stress light writing. Restraint is observed for pictures showing tragedy or dealing with a serious subject.

WORKING WITH GRAPHICS

THE ROLE OF GRAPHICS

Photographs help the reader gain a visual appreciation of reality; graphics help the reader understand the massive, the intangible or the hidden. A map of part of the city is usually a better locator than an aerial photo of the same area. A chart often helps the reader track trends over time. An artist's cutaway can show the undersea levels of a sinking ship.

Information graphics, as these devices are known, have appeared with increasing regularity in newspapers and magazines, large and small, in recent years. Personal computers are ideal for creating such graphics quickly and inexpensively, and newspapers rushed to embrace them in the 1980s. Suddenly, publications that once had only photographers and artists added graphic designers to create charts, graphs and maps. Contests added categories for graphic design, and the Society of Newspaper Design was formed. Clearly, the 1980s was a decade of unprecedented emphasis on graphics and design.

Many believe that transformation was sparked by the arrival of *USA Today* in 1979, and there is no doubt that newspaper set new standards for the use of color and graphics. Colorful charts, graphs and maps played a key role in the concept of *USA Today,* which the Gannett Co. designed for the busy reader. Charts, graphs and maps are a good way of communicating lots of information in a hurry, and *USA Today's* editors were quick to embrace them. The newspaper's colorful weather map was emulated by papers worldwide (see Figure 12-12).

But *USA Today* was far from alone in adopting information graphics. *The New York Times* and other prestigious newspapers began publishing full-page graphics on section fronts, *Time* magazine produced startling graphics under the genius of Nigel Holmes, and syndicated services of graphics material proliferated. Both the Associated Press and United Press International greatly increased the quality and quantity of graphics moving on the photo wires. The AP and Knight Ridder Newspapers even created separate delivery services just for information graphics.

Figure 12-12.   The USA Today weather map. [Courtesy of USA Today]

Like photographs, however, information graphics can be good or bad. Confusing charts, graphs and maps hinder readers rather than help them. Graphics that are too busy may obfuscate rather than enlighten.

TYPES OF INFORMATION GRAPHICS

Illustrations help the reader understand complex things or concepts, including information that may be extremely difficult or impossible to describe in words. They take many forms, from the simple illustration to the complex diagram.

Maps, of course, help the reader locate things. Local maps help the reader locate places within the city. Maps of counties, states, regions or nations help readers locate sites with which they may not be familiar (see Figure 12-13). Good graphics departments maintain computerized base maps of various

Figure 12-13.   A map. One form of information graphic. [Courtesy of Newspaper Enterprise Association.]

0   15 miles

Figure 12-14. Secondary window within a map. [Courtesy of Newspaper Enterprise Association]

Hot, Hot, Hot! The discomfort index

Relative Humidity	Air Temperature (Degrees Fahrenheit)										
	70	75	80	85	90	98	100	105	110	115	120
	Heat Index										
0%	64	69	73	78	83	87	91	95	99	103	107
10%	65	70	75	80	85	90	95	100	105	111	116
20%	66	72	77	82	87	93	99	105	112	120	130
30%	67	73	78	84	90	96	104	113	123	135	148
40%	68	74	79	86	93	101	110	123	137		
50%	69	75	81	88	96	107	120	135			
60%	70	76	82	90	100	114	132				
70%	70	77	85	93	106	124					
80%	71	78	86	97	113	136					
90%	71	79	88	102	122						
100%	72	80	91	108							

Source: The World Almanac   **NEA GRAPHICS**

As temperatures rise, humidity increasingly becomes a factor in reducing the body's ability to cool itself. The discomfort index measures what various temperatures and humidities "feel like" to the average person.

Figure 12-15. A table. Tables are a form of information graphic used to convey numerical information graphically. [Courtesy of Newspaper Enterprise Association]

Figure 12-16. A bar chart. A form of information graphic used to help the reader visualize quantities. [Courtesy of Newspaper Enterprise Association]

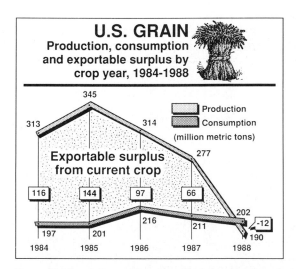

Figure 12-17. A fever chart. Quantities over time are depicted in these graphics. [Courtesy of Newspaper Enterprise Association.]

FEDERAL GOVERNMENT:
Religions of congressmen (9-15-88)

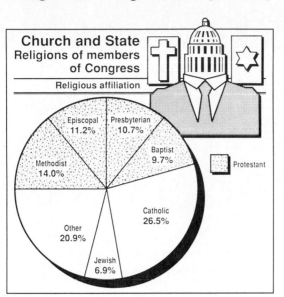

Figure 12-18.   A pie chart. These information graphics help the reader visualize the division of the whole into components. [Courtesy of Newspaper Enterprise Association]

locales. When an event occurs, it is a simple matter to add specific locator information to the base map to create a helpful aid for the reader. Secondary windows within maps sometimes are used to pin down specific areas within geographic regions or to show the location of the specific region within a larger area (see Figure 12-14).

The *table* is used to display numerical information graphically (see Figure 12-15). Tables are useful when lots of numbers are involved as in precinct-by-precinct election results.

Bar charts help the reader visualize quantities (see Figure 12-16) while *fever charts* show quantities over time (see Figure 12-17). *Pie charts* are used to show the division of the whole into components (see Figure 12-18).

All these devices are tools the editor uses to help convey information to readers. Some information is conveyed best in words, some in pictures and some in information graphics. The editor who knows when to choose each of those devices helps to create an easy-to-read publication.

CHAPTER 13

TYPOGRAPHY IN THE ERA OF DESKTOP PUBLISHING

INTRODUCTION

Typography is the art of selecting, spacing and using type. It is also the means of changing ideas into printed form for others to share. The main purpose of this chapter is to provide editors, whose job it is to help clarify ideas, with basic information about typography because they have so many opportunities to make decisions involving type.

Most editors do not choose type for the main body of news. That decision is most likely made when the newspaper was first published, and it is rarely changed. But daily they have much discretion in choosing the type styles for headlines and feature stories. Hundreds of types are available on desktop computers for that purpose.

In deciding on a type style, the editor should have four main goals:

1. To choose a type that is easy to read.
2. To choose one whose style harmonizes with the story content.
3. To choose an attractive type.
4. To use the type in ways that facilitate reading (not impede it).

Indeed, simply by avoiding decisions that impede reading, one can go a long way toward facilitating it.

Younger newspaper readers tend *not* to spend a great deal of time reading or thinking about the news. Much recent speculation has been devoted to making changes in newspaper type and layout to motivate them to read newspapers more often. Unfortunately, an editor cannot motivate readers to read simply by selecting a certain typeface or using it in a special way. Other factors are more important than type in encouraging reading. One is the news content. Readers tend to read only those items that interest them or seem important. But in many instances the correct type, spaced properly, can make a news article easier and faster to read. That's the editor's chance to use typographic principles to facilitate reading.

DESKTOP PUBLISHING HAS
COMPLICATED THE USE OF TYPE

Setting type by inputting words on a computer keyboard represents a relatively new technology for editors. Today, a reporter can typeset a story instantaneously. If the editor dislikes the reporter's choice of type, he or she can quickly change the typeface size and line spacing. Other changes are possible as well. So today's editor works in an era of "change and speed." However, the selection of type still requires care, good artistic judgment and some common sense about which changes maximize readability.

Therefore, the focus of this chapter is not simply on learning typographic principles but on learning to decide among the many alternatives that desktop publishing offers.

The material in this chapter is written under the assumption that readers of this text will know how to set type on a computer and be able to use these principles whenever they have an opportunity to use that equipment.

WHAT EDITORS SHOULD
KNOW ABOUT TYPOGRAPHY

The following is a list of concepts that editors should know about typography, as a minimum:

What a typeface is
How to measure type
How to differentiate typefaces
How typefaces differ
    by letter construction
    by general style (roman, italic, sans serif, text, script, cursive, square serif)
    by size
    by weight
    by family (style characteristics)
How to use type effectively
How to choose a type size
How to choose a type family
How to choose a type weight
How to choose a special style
How wide a line should be
Which line spacing (leading) to choose
What principles of type selection to follow
How to develop artistic judgment

What problems arise in setting type on a desktop computer
    Screen sizes that are not equivalent to printed sizes
    "Cute" typeface selections
    Too many type choices
    Use of tonal screens underneath type
    Effect of paper choices on type
    Page "weight"

WHAT IS A TYPEFACE?

Type is often referred to as a *typeface*. That term began to be used when type was a piece of metal on top of which was its "face" in raised form. The era of metal type was also called the hot-type era because all type metal had to be heated to more than 500 degrees and then poured into a mold from which the letters were cast. *Hot type* has long since been replaced by cold type, and we live in a cold-type era. *Cold type* is set without heat. Type set on a computer desktop operation is a form of cold type.

Typeface

Type size

Figure 13-1.   A piece of metal type showing the "typeface."

SPECIFYING TYPE

An editor specifies a particular typeface when preparing copy to be set in at least five ways: by point size, by family, by weight, by letter width and by style, as shown in Figure 13-2.

GENERAL TYPE MEASUREMENTS

Most type measurements are carryovers from the old days of hot type and are identical to those used by traditional printers. Although desktop computers allow measurement in inches, many people retain the printers' practice of measuring in picas and points. Following are the basic traditional measurements:

- *Points*—72 points equal an inch (a point is 1/72 of an inch). All type is measured in points. An editor can specify 12-point or six-point type or any point size. Type may even be quite large, such as 120-point type. It also is correct to specify such large type by its height in inches, such as six-inch or eight-inch type.
- *Picas*—Six picas equal one inch (a pica is 1/6 of an inch). Twelve points equal one pica. The width of a line of type is usually expressed in picas, for example, *14 picas* or *35 picas wide*.
- *Page measurements*—These are usually measured in inches. For example, a page may measure 7 by 10 (or 7" × 10") inches. (Width is usually expressed first and length second).

DIFFERENTIATING TYPEFACES

Five ways in which typefaces differ and sample specifications

How these could be specified:	*(1)* By Point Size	*(2)* By Type Family	*(3)* By Weight	*(4)* By Width	*(5)* By Style
Example 1	24 pt.	Bodoni	Lightface	Regular	Italic
Example 2	60 pt.	Century	Boldface	Condensed	Roman

Figure 13-2.   Basic information that should be on type specification sheets.

DIFFERENCES IN LETTER DESIGN

One way typefaces differ is in their use of *serifs*. The body type in most newspapers have serifs. A serif is a relatively fine line at the bottom and top of letters like *d, h, i, l, m, n, p, r, u, x* and *z*. They also appear on capital letters.

Type letters also differ in their use of thick and thin elements, which can be placed in slightly different positions on each letter. Figure 13-3 illustrates the differences between three typefaces. The type user, however, should not pay too much attention to slight variations of single letters but should concentrate on their appearance in mass form, as in a typical newspaper paragraph. A paragraph (of about 50 words) can show the editor what the mass effect really looks like.

DIFFERENCES IN TYPE FAMILY

Just as members of the same human family tend to have similar facial characteristics, so do members of a type family. A type family includes all variations of a given type with common characteristics. Some type families have many variations; others have few. Figure 13-4 shows one of the large families of typefaces.

DIFFERENCES IN TYPE WEIGHT

Type may be differentiated by the weight of the letter. Most typefaces are manufactured in lightface and boldface. Some faces are manufactured in medium, demibold heavy, and ultrabold as well. The terminology here tends to be confusing. One manufacturer titles its medium-weight type *demibold,* whereas another calls a corresponding type *medium.* The terms *heavy, bold* or *black* also may mean the same thing. Figure 13-5 shows common examples of type weights.

DIFFERENCES IN LETTER WIDTH

Most typefaces are manufactured in normal (or regular) widths. Regular widths are used in most reading matter. But wide and narrow widths also are available. Type manufacturers have created extra-condensed, condensed, expanded and extended typefaces in addition to regular. These extra widths, however, are not manufactured in all type sizes or families. Therefore, it is necessary to check your newspaper's headline schedule to see if a desired width is available (see Figure 13-6).

DIFFERENCES IN TYPE STYLE

There are a number of ways to differentiate type by style. Each of them helps the editor find some unique quality in most typefaces. Here are a number of style differentiations and classifications:

Seven general styles:
    Roman
    Italic
    Sans serif
    Text
    Script
    Cursive
    Square serif

Differences Between Typefaces

Shown below are three typefaces often used on desktop computers. Study the differences and read the comments.

Here is an example of 24 pt. Bookman
Here is an example of 24 pt. Times
Here is an example of 24 pt. Palatino

COMMENTS:

a. The letters in one typeface are designed to be wider than others.
b. Some letters in one face are taller than others.
c. Compare the design of an "e" or "a" in each typeface. Note the differences.
d. Each typeface has its own set of peculiar characteristics.
e. Note the mass effect of each typeface below.

HOW SAMPLE TYPEFACES (ABOVE) LOOK IN PARAGRAPHS

10 pt. Bookman

Typefaces have been designed to have unique characteristics. In selecting typefaces for a story, think of the connotation (or feeling) of the typeface and its relationship to the story. Is one typeface better than another? Some typefaces are warmer, more legible, more powerful or more delicate. Some are more feminine or masculine.

10 pt. Times

Typefaces have been designed to have unique characteristics. In selecting typeface for a story, think of the connotation (or feeling) of the typeface and its relationship to the story. Is one typeface better than another? Some typefaces are warmer, more legible, more powerful or more delicate. Some are more feminine or masculine.

10 pt. Palatino

Typefaces have been designed to have unique characteristics. In selecting typeface for a story, think of the connotation (or feeling) of the typeface and its relationship to the story. Is one typeface better than another? Some typefaces are warmer, more legible, more powerful or more delicate. Some are more feminine or masculine.

FIGURE 13-3.   Some of the more important ways typefaces differ.

Helvetica Hairline

Helvetica Light

Helvetica Regular

Helvetica Medium

Helvetica Demi-Bold

Helvetica Bold

Helvetica X-Bold

Helvetica Bold Condensed

Helvetica X-Bold Condensed

Helvetica Bold Condensed

Helvetica X-Bold Condensed

Helvetica Medium

Helvetica Bold

Figure 13–4.   Some members of the Helvetica family.

Bauer Beton Light

Bauer Beton Medium

Futura Demibold

Bauer Beton Bold

BERNHARD GOTHIC HEAVY

Bernhard Gothic Extra Heavy

Bauer Beton Extra Bold

Futura Ultrabold

Figure 13-5. Various weights of typefaces.

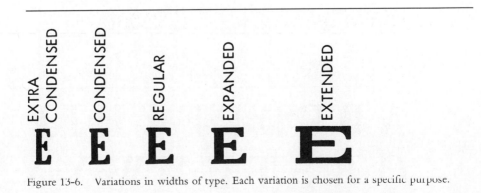

Figure 13-6. Variations in widths of type. Each variation is chosen for a specific purpose.

Two very broad styles:	Oldstyle Modern (sometimes called transitional)
Two more broad styles:	Traditional Contemporary
Company of production:	Each manufacturing company may make the same type family

The most common means of classification divides type into broad categories termed *roman, italic, text, sans serif, script* and *cursive,* sometimes called the *races* of type. It is best to think of these classifications as style characteristics that help in differentiating and identifying typefaces. Square serif is sometimes added to make a seventh style.

Roman Type

Roman type (see Figure 13-7) has a vertical shape; it has serifs; it usually has combinations of thick and thin elements in each letter (called *stem* and *hairline*, respectively). Some type experts consider all vertical letters to be roman, even those without serifs or with no variations in the width of letter elements (stem and hairline). This form of classification, therefore, may be confusing to the beginner because the roman designation will have two purposes: one to distinguish it from sans serif and the other to distinguish it from italic. For simplicity's sake, it is best to use the classification as first described.

Italic Type

Italic types are characterized by their slanted letter shapes. Although italic types were originally designed to print many letters in relatively little space, their use today is limited to citations or words that must be emphasized. They are also used in headlines and body types. Today, italic types are designed to accompany roman types, to provide consistency in the family of design. Figure 13-8 shows an italic type of the same family.

A B C D E F G H I J
Q R S T U V W X Y

Figure 13-7.   A roman typeface.

ABCDEFGHIJKLMNO pqrstu

Figure 13-8.   Italic versions of the Bodoni family.

Sans Serif (or Gothic) Type

In America, printers use two terms to identify typefaces with no serifs. One is *sans serif:* the other is *Gothic.* The terms *sans serif* comes from the French word *sans,* meaning "without," or *without* serifs. The other term, *Gothic,* is a misnomer. Originally, Gothic type meant the churchy-looking types Americans often called "Old English." But today printers use the term *Gothic* also to refer to serifless type (see Figure 13-9).

Text Type

Text type is often incorrectly called Gothic because it looks like the Gothic architecture of the Middle Ages. But printers call it text because it appears to have a texture, like cloth, when printed in large masses. These letters were originally drawn with a broad-nibbed pen and were created to show a minimum of curves. Today the type is used for church printing or conservative headlines. Students should never have text set in all capital letters for two reasons: (1) It was never written that way originally, having always appeared in capital and lowercase letters; (2) it is difficult to read when set in all capital letters (see Figure 13-10).

Script Type

Script letters resemble handwriting. Although the type designers have tried to make it appear as if all the letters are joined, small spaces can be seen between them. Some script letters appear to have been written with a brush, others with a calligraphic pen. Like text type, script type should never

24 point Microgramma Bold (Foundry)

ABCDEFGHIJKLM

24 point Futura Bold (Foundry)

ABCDEFGHIJKLMNOPQR

Figure 13-9.   Different styles of sans serif typefaces. There are many variations, all called sans serif.

HARD TO READ

Easier to read

Figure 13-10.   Cloister text typeface set in all caps and lowercase. "Text" should never be set in all caps. (Note: the printers' use of the word "text" is different from artists' usage. Printers call a churchy-looking face text because when seen en masse, it has a texture.)

be prepared in all capital letters because it is hard to read in that form (see Figure 13-11).

Cursive Type

Although cursive type styles look much like script typefaces, they are easily differentiated by their ornateness. Cursives are used mostly in advertising but occasionally for compartmentalized headlines on the Lifestyle page (see Figure 13-12).

OLDSTYLE VERSUS MODERN TYPEFACE

Editors may note that some typefaces are labeled "oldstyle" or "modern." The term "oldstyle" may be interpreted literally because it is a style desig-nation. But the term "modern" may be misleading. Modern type does not refer to contemporary times, but to style, and both styles are being designed today.

HARD TO READ

Easier to read

Figure 13-11.   Brush script also should never be set in all caps. Notice how hard it is to read in all caps.

ABCDEFGHIJKLMNOPSI
abcdefghijklmnopqrstuvwxyzabcdefg 12345

Figure 13-12.   A cursive typeface.

HOW TO MEASURE TYPE
FROM A PRINTED PAGE

There is no problem in measuring a piece of metal type, but because metal type is a thing of the past, editors must be able to measure type from a printed page, as in a type specimen book or another newspaper. Specimen books usually indicate the size of typefaces, but occasionally they do not.

Type Shoulders

Printed type is difficult to measure because one has to account for the space underneath the lowercase letters (see Figure 13-13). This space is called a *shoulder*, and it is there to allow for descenders of letters such as *g, p, q* and *y*. But shoulders vary from typeface to typeface. Some have large shoulders, others have small ones. How can the shoulder space be determined?

To dramatize the problem Figure 13-14 shows imaginary lines by which letters are created on a piece of metal type. These lines are called (1) base line, on which all letters other than *g, p, q* and *y* rest; (2) cap line, to which most capital letters and tall letters rise; (3) lowercase line, where small letters align (called the x-height of letters); and (4) descender line. Each line helps in aligning letters.

In measuring the letter *h,* one must allow room for the shoulder underneath the letter. The ascender rises above the lowercase line, but there is no descender below the base line. Thus, when one wants to measure type from a printed page, one must allow space for the descenders. To accurately determine ascender space one simply looks for a capital letter or one with a high ascender. If it is necessary to measure the point size of a line of capital letters, one would take the space normally used for descenders into consideration (see Figures 13-15 and 13-16).

PROFITS

Figure 13-13.   It is difficult to measure this line of type because it does not show descenders.

Figure 13-14.   Drawing of a letter showing the imaginary lines that define ascenders, descenders, and x-height.

Figure 13-15.   How to measure type: measure the distance between the top ascender and lowest descender.

Figure 13-16.   Why printed type is so difficult to measure. Each of these *E*'s is 48 points high, but the shoulder space (or descender space) of each varies.

AN INTRODUCTION TO LEADING

The space between lines of body type is called *leading* (pronounced *ledding*). Remember that leading for body type usually has been determined at the time that a newspaper creates its basic design. Therefore, computer typesetters may be preset to control the amount of line spacing that the designer recommended. The machine automatically provides the leading desired.

However, one should not assume that because the leading has been preset, it never can or should vary. In most newspaper operations, provisions have been made for changing the leading occasionally to meet certain needs, most often in feature stories and/or special kinds of stories. When editors want to feature a momentous story, then additional leading should be used. Leading usually makes lines of type easier to read because it gives readers more white space between lines, which helps readers focus their eyes on the type.

Also, when lines of type are 20 picas or longer and the shoulders of typefaces are very short, some leading should be used.

What then are the leading options? If a newspaper uses no leading at all, that practice is called setting type "solid." (Actually there is a tiny bit of space between lines of type when it is set solid, caused by the descender space at the bottom, or shoulder, of each letter.)

Options range from one–half–point to six–point leading for body type, and the range is extended from three to about 12 points of leading for headlines. The only way to know how type will look after it is leaded is to set a sample paragraph or two and study its readability. See Figure 13-17 for samples of alternative leading.

Also see the discussion of spacing in newspaper typography that follows.[1]

SPACING IN NEWSPAPER TYPOGRAPHY

Good typography depends so much on the manner in which words and lines are spaced that a separate discussion is in order here. There are a number of different places in newspaper layout where type spacing is very important.

LINE SPACING

The principle of making each line of type an easy eyeful can be aided by the generous (but not too generous) use of space between the lines. This provides a "right-of-way" for the eye along the top and bottom of each line. Types with short ascenders and descenders and large lower case letters need more space between lines than faces with long ascenders and descenders and small lower case letters. A fairly safe rule is to let the spacing between the lines approximately equal the space between the words.

The above paragraph is set with generous spacing (3-point leads) between lines, while *this* paragraph is set with no leads and is consequently tougher ploughing for the eye. The type is the same size but looks smaller. Educated instinct will in time tell you the difference between jamming and scattering type lines.

Figure 13-17.   The top paragraph has been leaded three points. The bottom has been set solid, meaning that there is no leading between lines. Leaded lines usually are easier to read than solid.

---

[1] Don Herold, *ATA Handbook,* Advertising Typographers Association of America Inc., p. 24.

Heat Wave Hits Cities Near Coast

Figure 13-18.   Headlines usually are easier to read when leaded. These lines are too close.

These places are

1.   Between the lines of a headline.
2.   Between a headline and the story below.
3.   Between a headline and the story above.
4.   Between body type and illustrations or ads.
5.   Between paragraphs.
6.   Between subheads and body type above and below.
7.   Between words.
8.   Between letters.

HEADLINE

The research on line spacing is inconclusive. Yet there is a feeling that lines with generous space between them are easier to read than those tightly spaced. However, too much space between the lines of a headline is undesirable. One must judge whether all lines can be read as a single entity (desirable) or as a collection of individual lines (undesirable). When there is too much space, each line receives too much emphasis (see Figures 13-18 and 13-19).

The responsibility for maintaining good headline spacing lies not only with the printer, typesetter or pasteup person, but with the editor as well.

BETWEEN A HEADLINE AND THE STORY BELOW

One of the most unattractive ways of placing headlines on top of stories is to have little or no space underneath the head. The objective is to position

Heat Wave Hits Cities Near Coast

Figure 13-19.   Two points of leading between lines helps readability.

the headline so that it gets attention and does not crowd the first line of the body copy underneath. The amount of space underneath a head depends on the depth of shoulder that accompanies the headline typeface. If the shoulder is large, then little extra space is necessary. If it is small, additional space is required. Essentially, there ought to be about 12 points of space between the baseline of the type and the top of the first line underneath for typefaces from 14 points to about 36. Typefaces larger than 36 points may need two to four points of space in addition to the 12 points previously mentioned. Smaller headlines may need only eight to 10 points of space between the baseline and the top of the line underneath (see Figure 13-20).

This same principle of spacing applies to standing heads. Such heads also need adequate space above and below them.

BETWEEN A HEADLINE AND THE STORY ABOVE

A general rule of thumb about the spacing of headlines is that there should be at least $1\frac{1}{2}$ times as much space above as below. This is to make it clear that a story above is not part of the headline below. In bygone days, stories ended with a "30" dash. Today, white space is substituted for the dash. But the reader must never be confused by spacing. Therefore, a generous amount of space should be placed above headlines. For larger-sized headlines, from 36-point type and larger, this space may be as much as two picas. For smaller sizes (14 to 36-point type) the space above the head may be anywhere from 18 points to two picas (see Figures 13-20 and 13-21).

BETWEEN BODY TYPE AND ILLUSTRATIONS OR ADS

An area of typography that is overlooked many times in the contemporary newspaper is the spacing of type on top of illustrations and ads (and sometimes below illustrations). The problem usually is that the type is positioned too close to these elements (see Figure 13-22). As a result, the reader's attention is diverted from news copy to either an illustration or an ad. Again, as a rule

Bob Mann stages rally to take Pensacola lead

PENSACOLA,FLA. (AP) - Bob Mann fired seven birdies and one eagle for a 9-under par 63 Saturday to take a

Mann, shared the National Team Play title with Wayne Levi, but he has never won an individual title on three

Figure 13-20.   Headline is too close to body type.

The size, timing and details of the
tax cut envisioned by many Senate
Democrats would be set by the
Finance Committee.

Smith's view

WASHINGTON (AP) - Senator
Thomas Smith said today he sees
no possibility that a tax cut will be
enacted in the near future.
Criticizing Republican senators
for trying to push through a tax cut
in the Senate Monday, Smith said
it was "very unstable."

Figure 13-21.   There should be more space above and less space below a headline. In this example,
one should remove some space underneath the head.

of thumb, there ought to be no less than one pica space separating elements,
and more if possible. The one pica of space allows both the story and the
illustration below to get the attention each deserves. Furthermore, space of
more than one pica between body type and illustrations simply looks much
more attractive than less than one pica of space.

BETWEEN PARAGRAPHS

It has been the practice in setting type not to place any space between paragraphs of a story. However, when a particular story is a bit short for the
column space allotted (in pasting the news on a page), it is a common practice to place extra space between each paragraph to lengthen the story.

It is recommended, however, that one or two points of space be deliberately placed between paragraphs in order to make the story easier to read,
especially if it is long. Paragraph spacing tends to bring more light into a
story and give the reader short pauses while reading paragraphs. There is no
research to prove the value of this extra space between paragraphs, but a long
story is usually more attractive with extra paragraph spacing than without. It
is a matter of artistic judgment for the most part.

ABOVE AND BELOW SUBHEADS

When subheads are used between paragraphs of a long story, there should
be more space above the subhead than below. Generally, about four points
are placed above and two points below. The purpose of this spacing is to

Figure 13-22. Body type is too close to the advertisement. This presents the reader with a crowded environment. It may be somewhat difficult to read.

allow the subhead to be seen and perform its function. Subheads are used to break up the large masses of type in a long story. Without subheads, this type has a gray, boring appearance that tends to discourage the reader. With subheads, the gray area is broken up somewhat, and the type looks more interesting. Furthermore, a subhead allows the reader a half-second breather before continuing. If a story is interesting, subheads may not be needed. But not all stories can be equally interesting to all readers, and there is logic in adding subheads. The space above and below a subhead should help rather than hinder reading. Generally, a subhead is added to a story about every fourth or fifth paragraph (see Figure 13-23).

WORD SPACING

Spacing between words should be narrow rather than wide. When narrow word spacing is used, it often helps the reader see more words at one sighting and therefore speeds up the reading process. However, there ought to be enough space between words for the reader to recognize where one word ends and another begins. Phototypesetting sometimes increases the space between words too much (see Figure 13-24). Of course, the other extreme of long words in narrow line widths is also undesirable. These gaps of white space slow down the reading because the words must be read individually instead of in groups. Generally, the space between words should be about one-third the size of type used. Nine-point type would have three-point word spacing.

LETTERSPACING

Letter spacing usually is done for headlines that are too short. Added spacing between letters makes the line appear longer. Letter spacing usually is not

---

Dets. Joseph McSorley, Bernard Joseph and Howard Baynard.

The three teachers were arraigned before Municipal Judge Ralph Dennis.

Police said they presented a search and seizure warrant to Miss Pincus at 6:30 P. M. Monday at her second floor apartment. They said they found a package wrapped in foil allegedly containing hashish lying on a table.

WAITED FOR SECOND

Miss Pincus attended the University of Wisconsin.

The officers said they then spent several hours in Stetzer's

It was estimated that as much as 20 acres might be needed for such facilities.

OPPOSITION VOICED

Any use of park land for school purposes, however, would have to be approved by the park commission, which has demonstrated strong opposition to the plan.

The only site among the four suggested which the Board of Education could purchase through condemnation is the Five Points tract.

Tate opposes use of this land, however, because its private use could mean attrac-

Figure 13-23.   Space is also needed above and below a subhead, but a little more is needed above the subhead.

While in Urbana-Champaign, the students will learn how to convert the computer language of their experiments into the language of the supercomputer; and compete for a year's worth of on-line time to complete their experiments.

Figure 13-24.   Too much space between some words.

programmed for body type on desktop computers but it is possible. It was easily done when type was set on a Linotype. If letter spacing needs to be done, no more than one point should be added between the letters in headlines under 14 points. Two points of space may be added between type that is over 14 points high, and even more for large type. Generally, letter spacing should be avoided, if possible, because it tends to call attention to the words that receive the extra space. The reader may stop and notice that a word has been spaced out. Any time the reader is made to stop the flow of reading, typography is relatively poor.

TYPE SELECTION PRINCIPLES

To use type effectively, editors must be able to differentiate type. That isn't all that is required, but it certainly is the first step along the way. What follows are some basic principles on making intelligent type selections and then arranging the type in the most readable manner.

CHOOSE LEGIBLE TYPEFACES

Any typefaces selected for printing must be legible. That is, every letter must be easily deciphered. When a typeface is not legible, readers may read a lowercase *c* for an *e*, or perhaps be confused by any letters that look like other letters. Illegible type may require readers to spend extra time trying to figure out the meaning of words. If the news is fascinating, readers will read a story regardless of its type's legibility.

Newspaper editors tend to use the most legible type for their main news. The place where less legible type could appear would be feature story headlines and/or body types where an editor is looking for some unique typeface that would call the reader's attention to the story or perhaps fit its unique nature.

When the more legible types are selected and reading becomes easier, readers may be able to read more of what has been written in the amount of time normally allocated for reading newspapers. Whether they *will* read more depends on factors other than typography.

Almost all typefaces in common printing use today are *somewhat* legible. It isn't necessary to consult research to learn which types are most legible, because legibility isn't an "either/or" evaluation. It is a matter of choosing the best available alternative. Shown below are two typefaces: Caslon and Galia. Readers might well say both are legible, but there is no question that Caslon is much more legible than Galia. Perhaps a short headline of Galia may cause no reading difficulties, but Caslon could be used in short or long headlines and still be readable (see Figure 13-25).

CHOOSE ATTRACTIVE TYPEFACES

Of the thousands of typefaces available for printing, some are much more attractive than others. In order to decide which typeface is most attractive, editors should have a sense of artistic appreciation and good taste. Editors will sometimes select a typeface that is cleverly designed but not the most attractive choice available. When artists are asked which typefaces are most attractive, they tend to select very simple, plain typefaces rather than clever or ornate ones.

CHOOSE THE BEST TYPE SIZE AND WEIGHT

It is important to consider point size and weight at the same time one selects a typeface.

To determine the size and weight needed for type, one must take into account the column width in which type is to be set. A 36-point headline set in a one-column width rarely looks readable. The problem is that only one short word could be set in a one-column space. That's hardly a headline worth having, unless it is a "hammerhead" (a one-word headline used in conjunction with other, longer headlines underneath to tell a striking fact about a piece of news).

The editor should therefore decide how many words of any size type are needed within a given column width. This is easy to determine with a computer. When no computer is available, the editor has to count the number

Education

EDUCATION

Figure 13-25. Legible versus less legible type. The bottom typeface, however, may be used occasionally for a special purpose when surrounded with enough white space. It has some use when a few words are needed to attract attention.

of characters of a given typeface that can be set within a desired column width. How many words of a headline should appear on one line is a matter of editorial judgment.

A second consideration is the type weight that is appropriate for the type size. Headlines may be too small and insignificant in lightface type but look very nice in boldface of the same size. Therefore, the editor has to balance type size and weight at the same time in order to make an intelligent choice. Sometimes an editor can achieve the effect of more weight by using larger typefaces even though they are set in lightface letters. More often, however, a larger and bolder typeface is needed to get the reader's attention. Readers tend to skim headlines as they look for interesting stories. Editors can help readers in this task.

CONSIDER THE AGE OF THE POPULATION

As the population of the United States continues to get older, readers may have difficulty reading newspapers because the type is so small. For that reason, the editor should pay special attention to both body type and accompanying headline type sizes. What is the optimum?

There is no valid research on the subject, so correct type sizes are a matter of opinion. Generally, body-type sizes run from about nine points to about 11 points. Recommended body-type sizes for older readers are from 10 to 14 point with extra leading between the lines.

In attempting to decide on the proper size of body type, the editor should ask, how large is the body of the type size now being used? If the type has a large body and very little shoulder, then larger typefaces may not be needed. But if the type now being used has a small body and large shoulder, larger sizes may be required.

Headline point sizes depend on how many column widths the head covers. Headline sizes may be as follows:

	HEADLINES: PRESENT SIZES	HEADLINES: NEWER SIZES
1 column width	14 to 18 points	16 to 20 points
2 column widths	18 to 24 points	20 to 30 points*
3 column widths	24 to 36 points	30 to 42 points*
4 column widths	36 to 48 points	42 to 60 points*

Many, though not all, condensed typefaces are poor choices for headlines and hardly ever appropriate for body type because they are difficult to read. Some type designers have chosen condensed typefaces for headlines as a means of making the type sizes larger and still retaining the same number of words as regular type. This is supposed to make the headlines more readable for older people (see Figure 13-26).

* A slightly condensed type may be required here, but not extra-condensed.

Colorful, detailed Indian fashions find Western fans

Her designs are a kaleidoscope of color. Sequins, mirrors, brocade or intricate embroidery accent each piece differently and—if the crowds can be a gauge—successfully.

"I'd like to communicate all the moods and colors of Asia

Going to greater lengths

Those unpredictable British designers take the lead in feminine, wearable fashions.

By Pat Morgan

Writing from London

We have seen fashion's future, and it is long.

After an extended infatuation with skirts that could seemingly go no snorter, but always did, several

new look.

This could be the season to change all that, however.

With the mostly fanciful, and virtually unwearable, clothing presented during the recent runway shows in Italy—the European country that traditionally offers the most classic, tailored styles—

Figure 13-26.   Some condensed type is difficult to read quickly.

That idea can easily be challenged if the typeface is too condensed. The reason is that few adult readers have an opportunity to read much condensed type in print anywhere: not in books, magazines, newspapers or advertisements. Therefore, they are not used to reading it. On the other hand, if the choice of condensed type is not extreme, older readers' eyes may become acclimated to the narrowed letters with little difficulty.

A much better alternative, however, is a typeface that is not condensed but has somewhat narrowed lowercase letters. The best of these is Times Roman, but another possibility is Century Schoolbook.

It is important to note that even when condensed type is mixed into a primarily roman headline schedule, the combination can be difficult to read.

AVOID UNUSUAL TYPEFACES

Any typeface that calls attention to itself is usually undesirable. The only exception would be one- or two-word headlines that sometimes appear on feature stories and are surrounded by generous amounts of white space. They can be suitable. The extra white space seems to allow readers a little more time to decipher the words than is needed for ordinary letters.

But occasionally letters are selected for their novelty rather than their suitability and seem amateurish rather than professional choices.

AVOID ALL CAPITAL HEADLINES

Type set in all capitals is usually more difficult to read than type set in caps and lowercase or "downstyle" (only the first letter is in caps). Most readers read by recognizing word shapes of caps and lowercase letters with their ascenders and descenders. All capital letters have none of these differences, and readers must put the letters together to form words: a slower process. See Figure 13-27 below that graphically shows the problem. Also see Figure 13-28.

SELECT THE BEST TYPE FAMILY

Which type family is best for a headline on a particular kind of story? There usually isn't much choice in most newspaper offices. One selects from whatever is available. But even with a limited number of choices, there may be good or bad options from which an editor may choose. So the answer is that the type selected ought to match the nature of the story, if possible.

Matching a typeface to the nature of a story is based on the connotation of each type family. Type families differ just as humans do. Therefore, it is necessary to know the connotations of each typeface that a newspaper owns. It is not a difficult task to evaluate most of these connotations (see Figure 13-29).

AVOID TYPE THAT CAUSES FATIGUE

Although an editor may select a legible type for a story, that type may cause readers' eyes to tire.

Figure 13-27.   Why caps are read slower: the reader has to place each letter together to form a word. In lowercase, the shape of the word is recognized and helps identify it.

CAPS VS. LOWER CASE

There is little doubt that lower case letters are more easily read than caps. Some typographers like to avoid capitals, even in headlines.

In fact, the recognizability of words seems to lie chiefly in the upper half of the lower case letters as illustrated below:

11. Frank had been expecting a letter from his brother for several days;
so as soon as he found it on the kitchen
table he ate it as quickly as possible.

11. Frank had been expecting a letter from his brother for several days,
so as soon as he found it on the kitchen
table he ate it as quickly as possible.

Figure 13-28.   The legibility of type seems to lie in the upper half of lowercase letters.

One kind of type that is considered to be particularly fatiguing is sans serif. Sans serif typefaces in headlines seem to cause no fatigue problems because letters are fairly large and there is a generous amount of space around headlines. But sans serif typefaces, especially in the lightweight versions, tend to be so monotonous in color that they are boring.

Another kind of type that falls into the same category is condensed body type. Letters that look "squeezed" tend to be harder to read in mass and tend to be fatiguing.

The solution to reader fatigue, of course, is to avoid those typefaces. However, for certain purposes, they look attractive, and some editors might want to use them anyway. If a sans serif or condensed face must be used in large quantities, then they can be made more readable by adding more space between the lines. This will let the reader see the words in a more contrasting environment.

CHOOSE TYPE WITH THE RIGHT CONNOTATION

Most typefaces in existence have some connotation that should be known by the person making type selections. *Connotation* answers the question of how readers will discern meaning. Typefaces can be warm, cold, strong, weak, feminine or masculine, to name only a few connotations. The connotation of type, matched with the nature of a particular story, enables type to add to or distract from the news. Some typefaces have very little connotation and neither add nor distract. It is also possible that two or more persons can look at the same typeface and disagree about its connotation. But most often there is little disagreement about connotation.

The person making a type selection may sometimes have to spend some time searching for an appropriate face for a story. At other times, it is easy and quick to find what one is looking for. See Figure 13-29 for the connotations of various typefaces.

TYPOGRAPHY ON A DESKTOP COMPUTER

THE HIGH RESOLUTION TYPE PROBLEM

Many persons who use desktop computers are unaware of the problems related to good typography. They usually think that the desktop computer produces rather nice-looking printed type that is equivalent or nearly equivalent to type from a phototypesetting machine. But the user of the desktop simply has not developed a sharp enough perception of the difference between typical desktop printing and fine typography set on a high-resolution machine like the Linotronic phototypesetter. There's a big difference.

Most desktop computer printers produce type at 300 dots per inch (dpi). At that rate, type looks superficially like phototypesetting, but on closer examination it is a poor reproduction because most phototypesetters print some-

Elegance
Clearcut Initial—French Script

MODERNISM
Kabel Light

DIGNITY
Forum

UNUSUALNESS
Newfangle

Antiquity
Satanick

NATURE
Sylvan

Sincerity
Baskerville

STRENGTH
John Hancock

Distinctiveness
Civilité

CHEAPNESS
Mid-Gothic

Figure 13-29.   The connotations of some different typefaces.

where around 1,200 dpi. In typefaces smaller than 18 points, the dots that make up a single letter are invisible. It will take a strong magnifying glass to see them. But in larger typefaces, they tend to be visible, especially in very large typefaces. Many companies now have a Linotronic machine that can produce type up to 2,540 dpi. Therefore the publisher can buy additional equipment to smooth out these irregularities (called "jaggies"), but often find it too expensive, and continue on with 300 dpi. While 300-dpi type is better than dot-matrix printing, it is not in nearly the same league as the higher dpi printing (see Figure 13-30).

High-quality typography is not possible if the type resolution is only 300 dpi. Some smaller newspapers use the 300 dpi type with virtually no complaints because their readers do not know or care about the difference.

But some publishers produce type on their desktop machines and then have it reproduced at a higher dpi level by companies that turn out camera-ready copy*at the high-resolution levels for a fee.

Shall the typesetter use the highest level of type resolution? For a newspaper where quality printing is a standard to be upheld, the answer is yes. Some newspapers cannot afford such a high standard. Many readers don't care as long as the type is large and clear enough without more resolution.

KERNING

Kerning is the process of eliminating unsightly space between certain kinds of letters, such as *A, F, L, T, V.* For instance, when a capital *T* and *A* are placed side by side, the space underneath the right side of the *T* and the space on the left side of the *A* combine to make an unsightly amount of space and may even slow the reading process by a small amount.

A desktop computer can reduce this space by one-half to one point. A few computers can reduce this space by 1/100th the width of a character.

Figure 13-30.   Type with and without the jaggies.

* Camera-ready copy is ready to be photographed and converted into a printing plate from which thousands of copies can be reproduced.

So kerning, whether done manually or automatically, makes type somewhat more attractive. The laser printer that can reduce the kern space by 1/300th is not up to professional standards, but this quality will be increased as improvements are made on desktop equipment. Nevertheless, it is probable that many readers miss the nuances of kerning in small type (such as under 18 points). When a computer program like Quark Express is used, the typist can press a key that allows the computer to automatically kern letters or can press another key to have the computer kern letters at a desired level. Many newspaper computer operators allow the computer to do kerning automatically.

DESKTOP TYPE PRINTED
OVER TINT SCREENS

One of the newspaper typographic techniques that became popular even before desktop publishing was that of printing type over a tint screen. A tint is a colored mass of dots over which type is printed. It is often used in boxes. The objective is to make a certain story more noticeable. In the present desktop age, the technique has become even more popular. The problem with this technique is that unless the tint is very light (gray or a light color), type can be very difficult to read. Unreadable tint boxes are often seen in newspapers. An editor who wants to use a screened background tint should always place it over a very light screen, using a light color such as yellow or orange or a very light gray. If this admonition is ignored, all the best efforts at increasing readability will have been defeated (see Figure 13-31).

APPROPRIATE USE OF CONTRAST

Attractive typography often brings contrast to a page. Contrast is achieved by selecting typefaces in sizes and weights that make some type print a bit heavier and some print lighter or by using italic with roman headlines or serif with san serif heads. The editor should strive for pleasant, attractive contrast rather than strong, overbearing contrast, however. Too much contrast is as bad as no contrast.

OFFBEAT TYPEFACES

Many people who are setting type on a desktop computer for the first time are excited at having the opportunity to choose from so many different type options. Some will inevitably be attracted to offbeat typefaces. (An offbeat typeface is not commonly used and tends to be garish.) Some people think that these typefaces will add a dash of charm to a feature article, and indeed they may. Most often, however, offbeat typefaces call too much attention to themselves and not necessarily to the ideas. Therefore, the editor who chooses typefaces for headlines should not make it a practice to select offbeat faces.

Last week's commodity prices

By The Associated Press

■ Corn and oat futures advanced but wheat and soybeans retreated on the Chicago Board of Trade.

Wheat for delivery in May settled Friday at $2.82½ a bushel, down from $2.87¾ a week earlier; May corn rose to $2.39¼ a bushel from $2.38½; May oats rose to $1.28 a bushel from $1.27; May soybeans slipped to $5.64 a bushel from $5.64½.

■ Live cattle futures fell but other livestock and meat futures advanced on the Chicago Mercantile Exchange.

June live cattle fell to 74.92 cents a pound from 75.25 cents; May feeder cattle rose to 89 cents a pound from 88.77 cents; June hogs rose to 57.62 cents a pound from 57.47 cents; May frozen pork bellies rose to 61.10 cents a pound from 59.27 cents.

■ Precious metals fell on New York's Commodity Exchange.

June gold dropped to $356 a troy ounce from $358.30; May silver dipped to $4.003 a troy ounce from $4.024.

■ Heating oil advanced but other energy futures retreated on the New York Mercantile Exchange.

Light sweet crude oil for June delivery fell to $21.18 barrel from $21.27; June home heating oil rose to 55.91 cents a gallon from 55.13 cents; June unleaded gasoline fell to 69 cents a gallon from 71.21 cents; June natural gas dropped to $1.343 per 1,000 cubic feet from $1.35.

Public Aid in area counties

The percentage of residents in east central Illinois counties who receive aid (Aid to Families with Dependent Children, food stamps, Medicaid, etc.) from the state Department of Public Aid.

	1988	1989
Champaign	4.7%	5.0%
Coles	7.0%	7.4%
Douglas	5.2%	5.4%
DeWitt	6.1%	5.8%
Edgar	8.5%	9.4%
Ford	5.8%	5.8%
Iroquois	5.2%	6.0%
Moultrie	4.6%	4.7%
Piatt	5.2%	5.2%
Vermilion	10.4%	10.9%

Source: Illinois Department of Public Aid

Poverty threshold

The following are the maximum incomes for households to be considered in poverty by federal guidelines.

Household size	Annual income
1	$6,620
2	$8,880
3	$11,140
4	$13,400
5	$15,660
6	$17,920
7	$20,180
8	$22,440

Source: U.S. Department of Health and Human Services

Figure 13-31.   Dark gray or color tints underneath type may make it difficult to read.

DEVELOPING ARTISTIC JUDGMENT

The best way to understand type is to be able to differentiate the many kinds of existing typefaces. Unless the slight variations in letter shapes are known, one typeface may appear as good as another. Once the differences in typefaces have been learned, however, the editor can develop an aesthetic sense for what looks attractive in print, based on some elementary artistic principles.

Developing a sense of artistic judgment in type is best done by studying type in print, no matter where it appears. For example, beautifully set type often appears in a magazine, a book or a financial report. If one works at developing a sensitivity to what looks good in print, one will be alert to such printing. Then it is advisable to make a mental note of the way type was set or why it looks so good. An editor may adjust these techniques to the newspaper environment, if at all possible. In this manner an editor uses type to aid communication. The editor should also know and keep up with typographic research. Almost every year, there are new studies that can add to one's knowledge of how to use type. While research cannot answer whether one typeface is more appropriate than another for a headline, there are many helpful things to be learned from research. In fact, as more studies are conducted, some of the older ideas on using type will be rejected or replaced.

CHAPTER 14

AN INTRODUCTION TO NEWSPAPER LAYOUT

HOW IMPORTANT IS NEWSPAPER LAYOUT?

Students often ask, "How important is newspaper layout and design?" The answer usually is, "It's very important because layout represents the package, and packaging sells the newspaper." That assertion may have been true at some time in the history of the newspaper business, but it is not true today. Layout should not be thought of as a major way to sell newspapers but as a way of making reading easier and more pleasant. To put layout in the correct context, think of it as a means of facilitating reading.

Content (the news) is more important than form (the layout). It is content that sells newspapers. Most people buy newspapers because they like the coverage of the news, the thoroughness of the writing, the integrity of the newspaper or some other quality. Good layout may also be appreciated but not as a primary consideration.

So newspaper layout is very important today but not as simple packaging. It is important because it is of benefit to readers. When newspaper management provides an attractive and efficient layout, it tells readers that the publisher and editors are concerned about facilitating their reading. That's good marketing.

Because layout is important, editors and others involved with the preparation of the paper must have a good foundation in the theory and practice of layout and design.

IS THERE A DIFFERENCE BETWEEN LAYOUT, MAKEUP AND DESIGN?

Students may be confused by terms such as makeup, layout and design. They all mean the same thing but may be used in different ways. Layout was formerly called makeup, and in some newspaper plants it still is. The more current term is *layout*. The term *design* is often used as an omnibus word to describe the layout of an entire newspaper. But it sometimes is used to describe the action of laying out either a page or an entire newspaper. The best way to understand these terms is to hear or see them in the context of a sentence. It is correct to use them interchangeably, and this should not be a stumbling block for students.

THE OBJECTIVES OF
NEWSPAPER LAYOUT AND DESIGN

Five major objectives should guide an editor in working effectively with newspaper layout and design:

1. Layout should organize the news.
2. Layout should create an attractive page.
3. Layout connotations should be consistent with the nature of stories.
4. Layout should be interesting.
5. Layout should reflect the current scene.

LAYOUT SHOULD REFLECT
THE ORGANIZATION OF NEWS

Good layout may be defined as a plan for bringing order to an entire newspaper or a specific page. Every layout should show how the news has been organized for the day so that readers can know which stories are most and least important. Readers who spend a great deal of time reading will have to spend less time searching for stories of interest if the organization of the paper is clear and simple.

One element of organization is story placement throughout the newspaper. The layout staff should place stories adjacent to other, similar stories in certain sections of the paper.

Organization also covers each individual page, where stories often are graded from the top down in importance. This does not mean that important stories cannot be placed at the bottom, because occasionally, for variety's sake, an important story is placed there. But layout personnel have many ways of telling readers which stories are most important: by placing them at or near the top of a page, by placing them in boxes, and by setting their headlines in large type.

Another dimension of this same objective is the need to help readers follow a story when it is continued from column to column and page to page. Under intense pressure to get the paper out, the layout personnel may place the last six inches of a story in an obscure column or position that does not help the reader. Good layout avoids this.

LAYOUT SHOULD MAKE
A PAGE APPEAR ATTRACTIVE

Because attractiveness is a major cultural value, good layout should be attractive to most readers. We all like things that look nice, and we use this principle in selecting beautiful clothes, furniture and cosmetics that enhance personal appearance. An attractive layout invites readers to come into a page and read the news. An unattractive layout could do the opposite.

Readers will often skim a page before reading it. In other words, they may be looking for an interesting story, and a skim may save time in finding it. But pages that are *too dark*, or *too light*, may not be read. Of course, scintillating news stories of great importance may be strong enough to motivate a reader to read a page regardless of the impediments. We know that devoted readers to poorly designed newspapers often defend their paper's design with great fervor because they have become acclimated to it. They don't recognize poor design, and they perceive only their favorite paper. Even in this situation, readers will often approve of a new and easy-to-read layout if they can be shown that it is indeed better than the old one. It may simply take persuasion to get them to appreciate an improved layout.

LAYOUT CONNOTATIONS CAN COMPLEMENT STORIES

Occasionally, a layout can match the nature of a story. For example, various artistic devices can be used to surround stories for Thanksgiving Day, Christmas, political or sporting events.

STYLING DEVICES CAN CREATE INTERESTING LAYOUTS

To avoid creating a monotonous page, a layout editor can vary story shapes or lay stories out into strongly vertical or horizontal shapes. Stories can be boxed, run over colored tints, run with multiple photographs. All these are styling devices to avoid boredom. After many years of reading a newspaper, readers may simply wish for some variety, even though they may not write to the editor. Slight layout variations may be just what are needed to avoid dull-looking pages.

LAYOUT SHOULD REFLECT THE CONTEMPORARY SCENE

Some of the great graphic designers of our century have noted that design should reflect contemporary culture. For newspaper design, this is important because news is the essence of the contemporary scene. It seems illogical to place contemporary news in an old-fashioned format.

One may then ask, "Are there various degrees of contemporary design, and if so, which is the best?" The answer may be indeterminate. But most designers would agree that some degree of contemporary design belongs in a newspaper layout. Nevertheless, there are always some readers, perhaps a small number, who dislike modernism in almost everything and possibly in design as well.

IS THERE ONE "BEST"
NEWSPAPER DESIGN IN AMERICA?

There is no single design that can be called the "best" in America. A study of a large sample of American newspapers would show that many different styles are in use, with some common characteristics among all. *USA Today* is widely imitated but not necessarily because it is best. It simply calls attention to itself, a quality that many editors want.

Because there is no "best" design, there is room for innovation. The main value of knowing that there is no best design is that leaders in our business ought to have a certain amount of tolerance in judging the work of layout editors. In the old days of makeup there were very strict makeup rules that had to be followed slavishly. Any deviation from those rules was judged to be bad design. More tolerance would allow more experimentation in design. However, discipline is needed—not everything goes.

DESIGN RESEARCH IS NEEDED

The consequence of more tolerance in design is that there is a pressing need for design research. Artists typically dislike the regimen of research imposed on an activity like art because they assume that it will restrict their freedom. But when design is intended for a specific purpose like improving the readability of the news, research is necessary to overcome the habit of making quick judgments that "this layout is good and the next one is bad." Research can provide more definitive answers to the question, "What is good design?" At present, many design judgments are totally subjective.

GRAPHIC REPSONSIBILITIES
OF LAYOUT EDITORS

Although the objectives of layout and design are quite clear, they may not provide enough details about the specific objectives that editors face when laying out a page. A layout editor has the following responsibilities:

1. Telling readers which stories are most important.
2. Helping readers follow stories from column to column.
3. Helping readers know on which page a story is continued and where the continuation appears.
4. Helping readers know which other stories are related to the one being read.
5. Helping readers know which pictures are related to which stories.
6. Helping readers know where stories end and new ones begin.
7. Keeping readers from losing interest in long stories.
8. Setting type large enough, in the best typeface, in an optimum line width, and with optimum line spacing to maximize readability.
9. Making the entire page interesting—not just the top.
10. Helping readers with limited time find the stories they want.

PRINCIPLES OF ARTISTIC DESIGN
APPLIED TO NEWSPAPERS

The application of artistic design principles can help layout editors achieve their objectives and carry out their responsibilities. The newspaper is a graphic art form, using words, pictures, color, lines and masses subject to the same principles of artistic design as other graphic art forms. The principles most applicable to newspapers are known as balance, contrast, proportion and unity.

BALANCE: A MEANS OF
MAKING THE PAGE APPEAR RESTFUL

Balance means equilibrium. It means that a page should not be overwhelmingly heavy in one section or extremely light in another. An unbalanced page may give readers a vague feeling of uneasiness because of the concentration of weight in only one or two sections of the page. Most readers do not know whether a page is balanced or unbalanced. They are not artists and do not care about the principles of artistic design. Yet they often know that a certain page "feels" better to read than do other pages. The most frequent cause of imbalance in newspaper design is making a page top-heavy by placing large and bold headlines at the top while using almost insignificantly light headlines at the bottom. Another cause of imbalance is the practice of placing a large, dark picture at the top without having one of similar size or weight at the bottom. As a result, readers' eyes tend to gravitate toward the bolder sections of the page and away from the lighter portions. Assuming that every element on a page has value, an unbalanced page, theoretically, is more difficult to read than a balanced page.

Balance in newspaper design is achieved by visually weighing one element on a page with another on the opposite side of the page, using the optical center as a fulcrum. The optical center is a point where most persons think the true mathematical center is located. It is a little above and to the left of the actual mathematical center (see Figure 14-1). This practice does not lead to precise balancing, but there is no need for that degree of precision. All that is required is a feeling of equilibrium on a page, not precise mathematical weighing.

Which elments need balancing? Any element on a page that has visual weight should be balanced. To determine which elements have visual weight one need only squint at a page and notice that much of the printed material disappears. What remains are pictures, headlines and black type rules of any kind. Although even body type has some weight, it isn't significant enough for consideration in visual weighing. The goal is to distribute prominently weighted objects pleasantly on the page.

Balance is most often done between top and bottom, rather between one side and another. The process is similar to balancing a heavy person with a light person on a seesaw. The heavy person must move close to the fulcrum, whereas the lighter person must move farther away on the opposite side of the fulcrum.

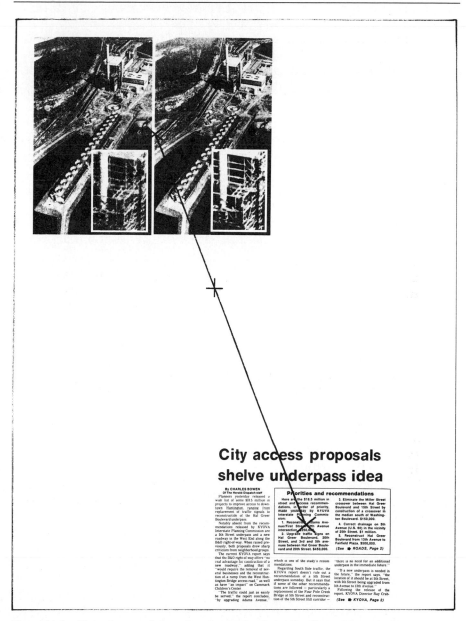

Figure 14-1.   Two elements balanced against each other. The illustration is the heavier of the two and therefore is closer to the optical center. Readers don't notice whether a page is balanced, but do know when a page is top- or bottom-heavy.

To implement the principle of balance, weigh the most outstanding elements, such as bold or large headlines, at the top of a page against similar headlines at the bottom. If the bottom of the page has no bold or large headline, the page is likely to be top-heavy. Plans should be made to include such headlines at the bottom. The same procedure should be followed with pictures. A headline or picture at the bottom need not be as large or bold as one at the top because it is farther away from the fulcrum.

Page balance may be formal or informal. Formal balance is achieved by placing headlines and pictures of the same size on either side of a page. It is sometimes called symmetrical balance because one side of the page tends to mirror the other. But symmetrical design may be unbalanced from top to bottom. Most newspapers employ an informal balance from top to bottom. The feeling of equilibrium is there even though it is not obvious.

CONTRAST

Contrast is the principle of using at least two or more elements on a page, each of which is dramatically different from the other. A light headline may contrast with a bold headline, a small picture with a larger one. Because one element is different from the other, the page is made to appear lively and interesting.

Contrast, therefore, is a means of preventing artistic pieces from becoming dull. Almost all art forms have some contrast—especially musical compositions, theatrical plays and printed material. A symphony, for example, contrasts a fast and loud first movement with a soft and slow second movement. A play has a relatively quiet scene contrasting with a lively scene. A book or magazine may have most pages printed in black and white contrasting with full-color illustrations.

In page layout and design, contrast prevents a page from appearing too gray, a problem that occurs when there is too much body copy and too many light headlines. Gray pages appear uninviting and forbidding (see Figure 14-2).

Sometimes when a page has been deliberately designed to feature balance, it may lack contrast and appear rather dull. The editor therefore may have to brighten that page by adding another picture and/or large, bolder headlines to bring about better contrast.

Indiscriminate use of contrast, however, is undesirable. If a page has too much contrast, it may overpower the reader because the contrasting elements call attention to themselves and not to the page as a whole. The goal is to provide pleasant, not overpowering, contrast. To achieve this goal the layout person will have to develop a sense of good taste.

Contrast may be achieved in four general ways: by shape, size, weight and direction. Shape contrast may consist of a story set flush on both sides in opposition to another story set flush left, ragged right. Or an outline picture may be used with a rectangular picture.

Size contrast may be achieved by using a large illustration on the same page as a smaller one, or large type with smaller type.

Weight contrast may employ a picture that appears very black with a lighter picture, or a story set in boldface type contrasted with one set in lighter typefaces.

Direction contrast could show vertically shaped stories contrasted with horizontally shaped stories.

These contrast alternatives are but a few of many that are possible on any given page. An objective of designing on page, however, is to achieve pleasant,

Figure 14-2.   This page lacks contrast. It is simply too light. Such pages tend to be boring.

rather than harsh or extreme, contrast. Too many contrasting elements on a single page may be artistically unsound and unattractive.

PROPORTION

Proportion is the principle of comparative relationships. In newspaper design, the length of one line may be compared with the length of another, the shape of one story with shapes of others or the width of a photograph with its depth. The goal of designers is to create pages in which the proportions of elements are pleasing to the eye. Certain proportions in this culture tend to look more pleasing than others. The Greeks worked out the proportions of many of their temples in classical dimensions. Artists and designers try to use pleasing proportions in their work because the public has come to appreciate such relationships. For example, artists rarely use a square shape because it appears uninteresting. More pleasing is a rectangle where one dimension is greater than the other (see Figure 14-3). Unequal proportions usually are more attractive than equal proportions. For that reason, newspapers, magazines and books have pages whose width is less than the depth.

Pleasing proportions should be considered in planning the sizes of pictures, headlines and even divisions of pages (see Figure 14-4). Unfortunately, the design of newspaper pages rarely reflects the principle of good proportion even though the size of paper pages does. The problem is that layout persons tend to think in terms of fitting news into columns, each of which is poorly proportioned. They can't be sure that the shape of the main story on a page is pleasantly related to other story shapes on that page. Persons using the total design concept are better able to control relationships and proportions than are makeup persons.

The beginner with little or no artistic training will have to develop a sense of proportion by following certain basic principles:

1. The best proportions are unequal and thus not obvious to the reader. Therefore, an element on a given page should not have square dimensions, whether it is a picture, story shape, box or division of a page.
2. Many pleasing proportions can be used, but one of the easiest and most pleasing is a 3:5 relationship. It is easy to remember and easy to use. To determine the shape of a story, for example, the layout person need only arbitrarily decide on one dimension (either the width or the length). Then that dimension can be multiplied (or divided) by 1.62,[1] to find the other dimension in the 3:5 proportion.

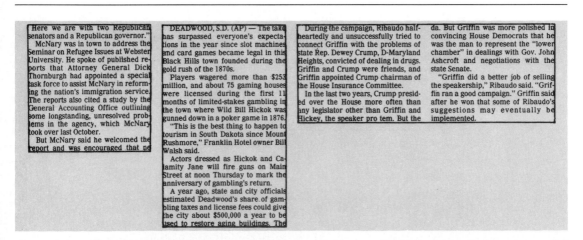

Figure 14-3. Which shapes are inherently more interesting: a square, a vertical rectangle or a horizontal rectangle? Research shows that the square is least interesting.

[1] 1.62 is a factor of a 3 to 4:85 relationship (most often called 3:5 for the sake of convenience). The 3 to 4:85 relationship is also sometimes called a golden oblong shape.

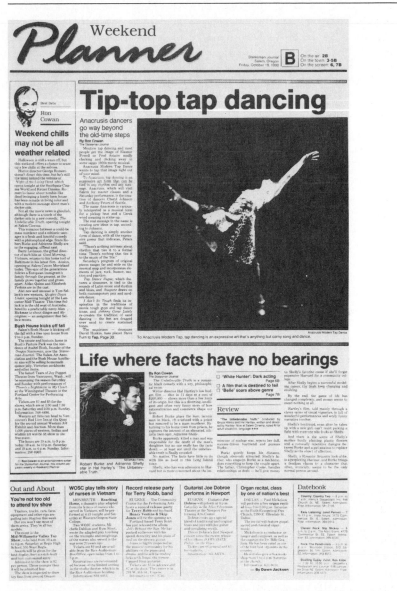

Figure 14-4.   A page showing contrast in size: a large and a smaller photograph. Photographs of equal size are not considered good art.

3.   While it is easy to calculate the unknown dimensions to arrive at 3:5 proportions, beginners may find it more convenient to guess at these proportions. Once one knows what the proportions look like, the slight errors that result from guessing will not distort the story or picture shape. It is impractical for picture editors to size every story or picture by mathematical calculations. In fact, mathematical precision is not even desirable in deciding on proportions because it limits artistic imagination.

Also, most persons cannot perceive precise mathematical proportions. But it should be obvious that a single-column story 11 picas wide and 64 picas long is not proportionately pleasing. For that reason, the page designer might divide that column into two equal-depth columns where the new dimensions would be 22.5 by 32 picas. If these dimensions were checked by the formula above, it would be found that the 32-pica dimension should really be 36.450 picas (22.5 $\times$ 1.62). But few persons will object to or complain about the difference.

4. In dividing a page, the editor should use some unequal proportions for determining the relationship of one area to another. For convenience a 3:5 relationship might again be used. But any obvious proportion should be avoided. Therefore, it would not do to divide a page in half either vertically or horizontally. The areas employed in the total design concept are those whose proportions are critical to the aesthetic appearance of the entire page.

In determining the relation of parts to wholes, the editor should avoid exaggerated proportions as well. That is why the 3:5 proportion is suitable for most page design problems. When pleasing proportions are used on a page, the result is not only interesting but attractive.

UNITY

The principle of unity creates a single impression, rather than multiple impressions, in a page design. Stories on a unified page each appear to contribute a significant share to the total page design. A page that does not have unity appears as a collection of stories, each fighting for the reader's attention to the detriment of a unified page appearance.

Lack of unity often results when stories are laid out from the top of the page downward. The layout editor is building a page piece by piece and cannot be sure how each story will contribute to the total page design until the layout is complete. At that point, however, the layout person may find that there is not enough time to shift stories around to achieve unity. The result is that readers may find it difficult to concentrate on any one part of a page because of too many centers of interest. A unified page, on the other hand, appears as if everything is in its correct position, and the page is therefore interesting.

One plans for a unified page by keeping the design of the entire page in mind at all times while working on any part of it. Each story, therefore, must be visually weighed against all other stories in terms of the probable appearance of the entire page. In page layouts, the editor may have to shift some stories around on the dummy* until a satisfactory arrangement has been found. As with the other principles of artistic design, layout editors must develop an appreciation of unity through a sensitivity to good design.

* See paragraph on the Mechanics of Preparing a Layout Dummy.

VISUALIZING THE
TOTAL PAGE STRUCTURE

Although the objectives of newspaper design may be clear enough, beginners may have difficulty implementing them because they cannot visualize the structure of a page before it has been completely dummied. Sometimes, even after a page has appeared in print, beginners may not be able to see the design easily. To overcome this difficulty, they should resort to the process of drawing heavy black lines around each story on a printed page. Now the design will emerge, and the editor can critically examine the total page design (see Figure 14-5).

If beginners study a page in this manner occasionally, they may be able to develop a feeling for page structure that should improve their ability to create effective page designs.

WHERE PAGE
LAYOUT BEGINS

Page layout is started at about the same time and place in the production of most newspapers: namely, after stories have been edited. But there are big differences from paper to paper in the way layout is done, especially if computers are available. If editing is done with word-processing equipment, the editor will have a list of stories available for the next edition, and the list can be seen on a video display screen.

On this list is the slug line which acts as an identification device for each story. Also shown may be the headlines, the length of the stories in inches (or picas) and perhaps the kind of headline that it will carry (such as a two- or three-line). At times, with sophisticated computing equipment, the editor may even have sized each story with a code indicating whether it is one, two or more columns in width, rather than simply indicating its length.

The editors may use this list when they meet to decide which story to feature. Other stories are then available for filling the spaces after the main stories are positioned on a page.

If computers are not used, then someone has to keep track of all stories and prepare a list similar to the one discussed above. This list eventually becomes the source of stories that are to be positioned on some page (see Figure 14-6). Usually stories are left over that are not used on any one day.

But the list of stories becomes the source for layouts.

Once a schedule of stories has been prepared, the editor is ready to lay out each page that has space remaining on it. In essence, an editor will position stories on each page dummy until most of the space has been filled. Some editors dummy only the most important stories and allow the printer (or

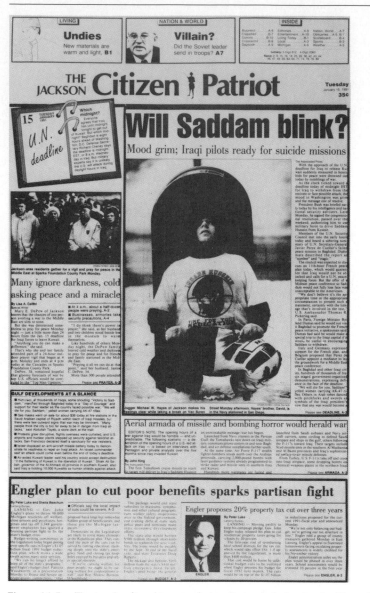

Figure 14-5.   Try to visualize this page design. It is relatively simple. If you have trouble, draw
lines around each story with a heavy felt tip pen and the design will become clear. Also note
proportions of stories.

pasteup person) to fill the remainder of the page. Others dummy the entire
page. A better-looking page can be achieved if 90 percent or more of a page
has been dummied, because there is better control over the entire page design
than in partial-page dummying.

```
WAR SCHEDULE for TUESDAY, FEB 5,        1991

Slug/source/size----  Synopsis-------------------------------- MW3-- 5Star Final
--------------------  -------------------------------------    -----  ----- -----
GULF                  B-52s bomb baghdad; iraq sez 9 planes  nu    ok
s. arabia atlas       downed; 2 GIs hurt in bus attack in
                      s.a.; USS Missouri fires 16-in guns
                      for 1st time since Korea
--------------------  -------------------------------------    -----  ----- -----
DIPLO        125-150  US cool to Iran offer to mediate war;  nu    ok
dc de lama            maybe harbinger of peace moves to come
--------------------  -------------------------------------    -----  ----- -----
SADKING          154  King Hussein depressed as Jordan's     nu    ok
amman crewdson        neutrality grows more tenuous
--------------------  -------------------------------------    -----  ----- -----
JORDAN            42  With Sadking. US tells Americans to    nu    ok
amman crewdson        leave jordan, cuts embassy staff
--------------------  -------------------------------------    -----  ----- -----
WARZONE               Notes col on life in the war zone      nu    ok
horrock
--------------------  -------------------------------------    -----  ----- -----
JAPAN             43  Kaifu tries to get parliament's OK     nu    ok
tokyo ap              for $9 billion for nonlethal war stuff
--------------------  -------------------------------------    -----  ----- -----
COPING           126  Soldiers turn to prayer and song to    nu    ok
saudi rowley          cope with stress
--------------------  -------------------------------------    -----  ----- -----
BOMBS                 4 pipe bombs found on methanol tanks   nu    ok
va newport news/tws   near Norfolk Naval Base
--------------------  -------------------------------------    -----  ----- -----
SECURE                SIDEBAR to bomb: Difficulty of preven- nu    ok
va newport news       ting terrorist acts
--------------------  -------------------------------------    -----  ----- -----
UN                60  Perez de Cuellar condemns allied bomb- nu    ok
n.y. ap               ing of Baghdad-jordan highway
--------------------  -------------------------------------    -----  ----- -----
                                                             nu    ok

--------------------  -------------------------------------    -----  ----- -----
                                                             nu    ok


--------------------  *** Gulf news in other sections ***     -----  ----- -----

POSTMAN               Postal worker at O'Hare protest delay  -----  (MET)
local rudd            in gulf-bound mail
--------------------  -------------------------------------    -----  (MET)----
RECRUIT               Recruiters get more inquiries but not         (MET)
local papajohn        necessarily more enlistees
--------------------  -------------------------------------    -----  (MET)----
PARTY                 Northbrook 1st grader celebrates              (MET)
local lucadamo        birthday with both parents in gulf war
--------------------  -------------------------------------    -----  ----- -----
                                                             nu    ok
```

Figure 14-6.   The *Chicago Tribune* schedule sheet. A design is composed of stories that have been previously chosen as part of a given page.

THE MECHANICS OF
PREPARING A LAYOUT DUMMY

A page dummy serves the same purpose as a blueprint—to tell the printer where to place each story, how long it will be and how it should be shaped (see Figures 14-7 and 14-8). A goal of the layout editor should be to make the dummy as clear, accurate and concise as possible. Many dum-

Figure 14-7.   A page dummy of the *Chicago Tribune*.

mies turn out to be a mass of scribbling rather than a neatly prepared blueprint that enables the printer to assemble type for a page with a minimum of confusion. The pressure of time is often blamed for hard-to-read dummies. But the consequence of poor preparation may mean time wasted in the composing room when the printer tries to decipher the dummy. Therefore, every effort should be taken to make the dummy neat, accurate and concise.

Some guidelines for preparing a dummy are as follows:

Figure 14-8.   The dummied page (14-7) in print.

1.   A front-page dummy is started by indicating the amount of space
     that the nameplate will take. (*Note:* a nameplate is the name of
     the newspaper, which appears somewhere at the top of the front
     page. It is sometimes called the masthead, but that is incorrect. It
     is also called "the flag" by others.) Some newspapers have specially
     prepared dummies with space already allocated for the nameplate.
     Where this is not available, a line should be drawn across the dummy
     indicating that the nameplate will occupy a certain depth.

2. Because most headlines have been assigned a number or some other designation in a headline schedule, this number and the slug for the story should be written wherever the story is to be placed on the dummy.

3. When a story with a one-column headline is noted on the dummy, the headline and slug word are indicated at the top of the story and a horizontal line is drawn across the column at the end. No arrows are needed to indicate that the story is to read in a downward direction. But when a story is continued to an adjacent column, arrows should be used to show where the story is continued. The arrows warn the printer that the story has not been completed in the column where the headline appeared. Whenever there is some doubt about where a story is continued, arrows should be used. But if they can be avoided they should be, because they tend to clutter the dummy.

4. Two-column lead paragraphs, cutlines and odd-measured stories (such as a $1\frac{1}{2}$-column width) should be indicated on the layout by wavy lines drawn the width of the type. Straight lines should not be drawn as they may be confused with finish or "30" lines.

5. Pictures or cartoons should be labeled appropriately with the slug word and an indication that it is either a picture or cartoon. Some newspapers use a large X drawn to the corners of the picture to make it clear that the space is to be used for a picture and not a story.

6. Boxes are indicated by a rectangle drawn to the dimensions required and labeled with the word *box*.

7. Jumps should be indicated by the word *jump* (or RO for runover) and the page number to which the story is to be continued.

8. If a story of two or more columns reads into a single column, then a cutoff rule may be used to separate the material that appears under the headline from nonrelated material. Also, an arrow should be drawn from the headline into the appropriate column where the story is to be continued. If a banner headline reads out into a deck, this too should be indicated by an arrow.

9. Any layout arrangement that is radically different from what has been used before should be indicated with notations if there is doubt that it will be clear to the printer. Sometimes only an arrow is needed; sometimes a few words will explain the situation.

Although dummying a page is important, and every editor should know how to do it, there are other more important layout concepts and practices. The following material discusses some of the concepts and practices that affect the attainment of objectives for good page design.

STEP-BY-STEP INSTRUCTIONS FOR LAYING OUT A PAGE

Before starting, it is assumed that a layout editor would have a good understanding of what it is that makes pages easy to read and look attractive.

PRELIMINARY STEPS

There are three prelimimary steps in laying out a page:

Preliminary Step 1.

Study a list of stories available for today's edition. Presumably the editor will discuss the selection of most important stories with other editors or those responsible for making such decisions. A limited number of stories then will be designated for featured treatment. These stories are placed on the dummy first.

Preliminary Step 2.

Decide precisely how these important stories will be given prominence and on which pages.

Here are some options for featuring these stories:

1. Placing the first and second most important stories in either the top left or right corners.
2. Boxing one large story on the front page, then placing it at either the top or bottom of the page; or perhaps placing it above the nameplate.
3. Using a large picture with a story and positioning it all across the page horizontally (either at the top or bottom).
4. Using any of a number of other available options.

Preliminary Step 3

Decide which photos (or other kinds of art) are to be used and whether each is to be featured alone or with a story. Should the picture be boxed? Should it run in color? What kind of cutline and/or overline should it have?

MAIN STEPS

Once the preliminaries are complete, the editor can turn to the four main steps of the layout process:

Step 1

Place the art first on the page by drawing its position on the page dummy. If there are other "standing columns," place them at the same time (see Figure 14-9).

Step 2

Now place the most important stories in positions discussed above (see Figures 14-10 and 14-11).

Step 3

Stop at this point and survey the stories and art that have already been placed. Answer this question: "How can I build an attractive page design *around* the art

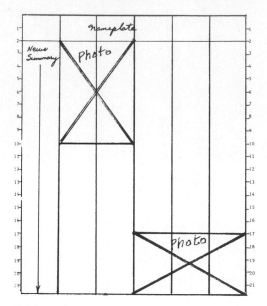

Figure 14-9. (How to lay out a page): Step 1—Place the art. In this illustration two photographs are positioned on the dummy and will affect the entire page's appearance.

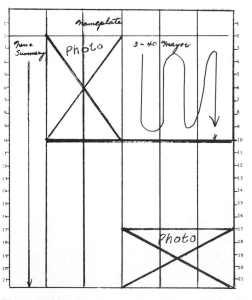

Figure 14-10. Step 2—Position the most important story.

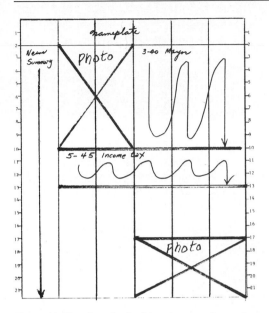

Figure 14-11. Step 3—Position the second most important story. At this point, the layout person must try to visualize the remainder of the page. There are alternative designs that could be used.

Figure 14-12. Step 4—Draw lines to show where stories go and fill page. Layout persons should make judgments about how attractive and readable the page design is at this point.

and stories already placed?" Answer the question by dividing the remainder of the page into attractive sections, and then find stories to fill in these spaces (see Figure 14-12).

Step 4

The result of step 3 will be a tentative page arrangement that may need to be revised a bit through trial and error until the right combination of stories and art end in an attractive and readable page.

Now the layout person can be assured that the most important stories are properly featured, and the remainder of the page is attractive.

IMPORTANT CONSIDERATIONS IN PAGE LAYOUT

The following pages cover some important, specific considerations that affect the layout of a page. They fall under the heading of the mechanics of page layout.

VERTICAL AND HORIZONTAL DESIGNS

A major consideration in layouts is the appearance of story shapes. In past years, story shapes have not been a major consideration of layout editors. But in recent years, as editors have sought ways of making pages more attractive, story shapes have become important. The selection of the most appropriate shapes involves a number of considerations. The first has to do with preventing a page from becoming one-directional. If there are too many vertically shaped stories all leading the reader's eyes downward, the page looks old-fashioned and unattractive. Newspapers circa 1850 were all vertical, and vertical makeup is distinctly old-fashioned.

A horizontal layout is preferable. Such a layout is distinguished by horizontally shaped stories that are continued into three or more adjacent columns. Although a story may be continued into the adjacent column, this does not necessarily produce horizontal layout if the shape of the story is vertical. Another distinguishing feature of horizontal layout is that stories are squared off at the bottom. This means that the depth of each column where the story is continued is the same (Figure 14-13). However, a page using horizontally shaped stories exclusively may be as monotonous as one with all vertically shaped stories. The best-looking pages have a mixture of shapes. (Figure 14-14).

AVOIDING ODDLY SHAPED STORIES

A second consideration in layout should be to avoid oddly shaped stories. In traditional layout many stories are not squared off and take odd shapes. One

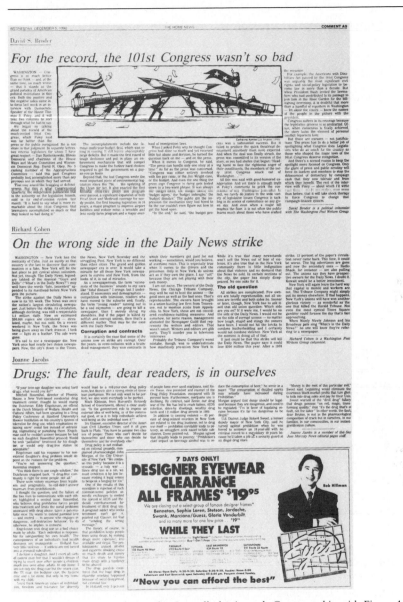

Figure 14-13.   A page design that is totally horizontal. Compare this with Figure 14-14.

such shape looks like an inverted L (Figure 14-15). It is caused by using a two- or three-column headline over a one-column story. This may also be called an "uneven wrap" (see following section on wraps).

When more than one uneven wrap occurs on a page, it tends to destroy the simplicity of the design. When an uneven wrap is used at the upper right side and another one in the upper left side, the design becomes complex. Other

Figure 14-14.   A vertically designed page. Compare this with Figure 14-13.

stories and pictures must fit around these shapes, and it is not an easy task. For example, the space underneath an unevenly wrapped story in the right-hand column usually requires a picture to fill the space underneath the headline. If another headline is placed underneath the upper headline, the result may be unattractive. To avoid unevenly wrapped stories, the layout editor should either use a single-column headline over a one-column story or wrap a story to the number of columns that the headline covers. A three-column headline

Negro Clergyman Defeated

Council of Churches Picks Woman Leader

From Our Wire Services

DETROIT, Dec. 4. — Dr. Cynthia Wedel, an Episcopalian and ardent advocate of women's rights, won overwhelmingly over a Negro clergyman Thursday to become the first woman president of the National Council of Churches.

Mrs. Wedel, of Washington, defeated the Rev. Albert B. Cleage Jr. of Detroit 387-93 in secret balloting at the NCC's triennial general assembly.

When the vote was announced, Mr. Cleage, the first Negro candidate for the presi-

*Profile and Picture
On Page 3*

dency, went to a microphone on the assembly floor and castigated what he called the "White racist establishment of the NCC."

"This organization is anti-Christ and until young people or oppressed people take over, you'll remain anti-Christ" Mr. Cleage declared. "Time is

Korean Report Raps Operation of Center By Buck Foundation

By EDWARD N. EISEN
Of The Inquirer Staff

The State Commission on Charitable Organizations made the Pearl S. Buck Foundation produce a letter Thursday from Korea's embassy highly critical of the foundation's work in that country.

The letter, by Sung Kwoo Kim, counsel and consul general at the embassy in Washington, said a 10-day inspection in August at the foundation's Sosa Opportunities Center, west of Seoul, showed unsanitary conditions, overcrowding, misuse of funds and other shortcomings.

REASONS DIVULGED

The letter was produced at a commission hearing on the foundation's appeal for a license to solicit funds in Pennsylvania. The foundation was to have presented new evidence, as demanded by Joseph J. Kelley Jr., Secretary of the Commonwealth.

Figure 14-15.   L-shaped stories. Stories wrapped to the left and right.

then would have a story wrapped underneath for three columns, presumably, and squared off.

Another kind of odd shape occurs when a story is continued to adjacent columns but each column depth containing the story is of a different length (Figure 14-16). Such shapes also tend to make the page look unattractive.

SAIGON (AP) — Gen. William C. Westmoreland, departing after four years in command of U.S. forces in Vietnam, said today American strength was greater than ever "but it is unrealistic to expect a quick and easy defeat of the Hanoi-led enemy."

"If he feels time is on his side, he can go on a long time," Westmoreland said of the enemy in a farewell news conference on the eve of his departure to become Army chief of staff in Washington.

He added that he could not predict what would happen at the peace talks in Paris, but from his view the enemy still appeared to be in search of major military victory.

"Price Can Be Raised"

Westmoreland said he felt that a classical military victory was not possible in South Vietnam in view of U.S. policy decisions not to escalate the war or to enlarge the geographic boundaries.

He added: "But the enemy can be attrited, the price can be raised. It is being raised to the point that it could be intolerable for the enemy. It may reach the point of the question of the destruction of his country, and jeopardizing the future of his country, if he continues to pay

the price he is now paying and destined to pay in the future."

Westmoreland said the enemy had lost 113,000 men since the first of the year and added "he doesn't have the manpower or resources to take these losses in stride."

Sees Net Reduction

Westmoreland said that although infiltration continued at a serious pace down the Ho Chi Minh trail through Laos, the Hanoi government was not able to make up its manpower losses in the South and that since mid-summer last year enemy strength had shown a net reduction.

He said Hanoi's strategy appeared to be to continue pressure against Saigon and its political structure and to seek some major victory on the battlefield.

Westmoreland departs tomorrow and will turn over the Saigon command to his deputy for the past year, Gen. Creighton Abrams Jr.

"At this time our military posture is at its height since our commitment," he said. "We are now capable of bringing major military pressure on the enemy.

"This we are doing, and the enemy is beginning to show the effect. The Vietnamese armed forces are growing stronger in size and effectiveness."

Headquarters Farewell

Earlier today, Westmoreland said goodbye with a "good luck and bless you all" to the officers and men of his headquarters.

"Please accept my very best wishes for continued success," Westmoreland told his staff,

"and my fervent hope that peace and security for the long suffering and freedom loving people of Vietnam will soon reward your efforts."

In his swing north yesterday, Westmoreland visited the headquarters of the South Vietnamese Army's 1st Military Corps in Da Nang, took a helicopter to Provisional Corps headquarters at Phu Bai 35 miles away, and visited the headquarters of the 3rd U.S. Marine Amphibious Force.

He wound up his tour with a flight to the nuclear carrier Enterprise in the Gulf of Tonkin to bid farewell to the U.S. 7th Fleet.

Figure 14-16.   An oddly shaped story whose purpose is to allow two one-column stories underneath without tombstoning heads. (See definition of tombstoning.)

Bethlehem directors OK drydock work

The Bethlehem Steel Corp. board of directors officially plunged the company into the Pleasure Island drydock project by stamping its approval on the months of work by company officials.

Richard E. Blackinton, general manager of operations and facilities for Bethlehem Steel, said the operating agreement between Bethlehem and the Port of Port Arthur "still contains some details that have to be worked out, but things are proceeding on schedule."

He anticipates the drydock will be working by the end of March.

Plans call for transporting the drydock from Pearl Harbor, assembling it on Pleasure Island, and relocating and rebuilding about a mile of Texas 82.

Blackinton said the Army Corps of Engineers received four objections to the drydock project but that he didn't expect them to delay corps approval of the dredging and operating permits.

Blackinton said one response came from the Environmental Protection Agency — which had questions not objections — and that Bethlehem was preparing an answer.

Karen Brown, a public information assistant with the Environmental Protection Agency in Dallas, said the agency questioned a private firm using a designated corps spoils area for disposing of dredge materials. Other questions by EPA involve whether Bethlehem considered other ways to dispose the dredge material, if a sediment analysis of the dredge material was conducted and if the drydock would cause adverse impact on area water quality.

Figure 14–17.   Wrap underneath a headline. This is also called a "squared-off story."

WRAPS

A major consideration in layout is the problem of what to do with stories that must be continued into adjacent columns because they will not fit in the space dummied. Should they be jumped or wrapped into the next right-hand column? Jumps are undesirable for reasons given earlier. The best procedure is to wrap (or turn[2]) a story underneath a headline or a two-column lead paragraph. If the wrap is under a headline as shown in Figure 14–17, it should be very clear to the reader where the second column has been continued.

Some editors, however, prefer to start a story with a two-column lead paragraph and wrap the second column under the lead. In such situations, two variations are commonly used: (1) wrapping the second column with a cutoff rule to separate the wrap from the lead or (2) wrapping the second column without a cutoff rule as shown in Figure 14–18. The first technique is preferred. It is unfortunate that many editors have abandoned both these techniques in the interest of saving production time. However, the benefits in

[2] A turn is another name for a wrap.

Lorelei McDonald bride of Jeffrey Earl Hammer

The wedding of Lorelei Shavonne McDonald, daughter of Mr. and Mrs. Lewis S. McDonald, 4313 Defiance Pike, Wayne, and Jeffrey Earl Hammer, son of Mr. and Mrs. Raymond Hammer, Gibsonburg, was solemnized Friday in St. Michael's Church. The Rev. Ray C. Przybyla officiated. The bride was given away by her father.

Altar decorations were two vases of yellow gladioli, ice blue carnations and white pompons with brown fall leaves.

With her lace-trimmed white wedding gown she wore a veil gathered to a lace bandeau and carried an old fashioned round bouquet of stephanotis, yellow silk rosebuds with baby's breath and ivy.

Her attendants were Mrs. Darlene Lentz of Bradner, matron of honor; and bridesmaids Mrs. Gary (Elaine) Lentz, Mrs. Alan (Patty) Adams and Ann Lentz, all of Bradner, and the bride's cousin, Mrs. Fred (Pam) Berno of Arcadia. Their colonial bouquets were light blue cosmos, white pompons and yellow silk rosebuds with baby's breath and ivy. The flower girl was the bride's niece, Michelle Cron of Portage.

The couple are at home at 110 County Road 26, Gibsonburg.

The bride, an Elmwood High School graduate, is employed at Fremont Memorial Hospital. The groom, who graduated from Gibsonburg High School, is employed by G.M. Sader Construction Co. of Bowling Green.

Figure 14-18.   An L-shaped story with a wrap underneath a two-column lead paragraph.

graphic design outweigh the benefits in production time, and the practice of using two-column leads is a good one.

When a story is wrapped underneath a picture, there is little danger of confusing the reader, so a cutoff rule is usually unnecessary (see Figure 14-19).

When a story is wrapped into an adjacent column at the top of a page without a covering headline it is called a raw wrap. In many instances raw wraps are undesirable; they are forbidden at all times by some newspapers. The makeup editor faced with a raw wrap should ask that a headline be written to cover the wrap and make it clear that the wrap belongs to the headline above it. But occasionally it is permissible to use a raw wrap at the top of an advertisement where there is no doubt in the reader's mind that the wrap belongs to the headline on the left (Figure 14-20).

When there is not enough time to reset a headline to a wider column measure, another layout procedure is to avoid raw wraps by filling the remaining space with shorter stories. Or perhaps one can use a long story and shorten it to fit the space by cutting story from the bottom.

In dummying a page, the layout editor should avoid the kind of wrap shown in Figure 14-21 where the reader is asked to jump from the bottom of a page to the very top above the ad. The size of the ad makes it appear as if

Killer storm cuffs Rockies, Midwest

Associated Press

A winter storm already blamed for 11 deaths stretched from the southern Rockies to the upper Midwest today after burying parts of Arizona and Colorado under 20 inches of snow, unleashing tornadoes in Texas and downing ice-laden power lines in Kansas.

Six inches of new snow were already on the ground today in Kansas and Nebraska, and forecasters said more was on the way.

Raging thunderstorms spun off at least two tornadoes that damaged more than 100 homes and businesses in Texas yesterday and motorists in the western part of the state were warned that snow and freezing rain today would make driving hazardous.

In the Pacific Northwest, meanwhile, travelers' advisories were posted for the Cascade Mountains of Washington and Oregon as a new storm gathered strength in the Gulf of Alaska.

The mercury tumbled to 15 degrees below zero overnight in West Yellowstone, Mont., but in the East more than a dozen cities reported record high temperatures yesterday.

The storm that dumped up to 20 inches of snow over the southern Rockies yesterday, closing schools in parts of Colorado and Arizona and surprising residents as far south as Tucson, brought more snow but lesser accumulations to New Mexico and northeast Arizona.

"It's all going to slowly push east, but its hard to say how quickly," Steve Corfidi of the National Severe Storms Forecast Center in Kansas City, Mo., said today. "It's a more pronounced pattern than you normally expect . . . an interesting pattern. It keeps us busy."

Since Tuesday, the weather has been blamed for the deaths of seven motorists in Colorado, two in a 23-car pileup during a blinding dust storm yesterday about 70 miles southeast of Los Angeles, two in Oklahoma on slick roads and three in a fog bank in southeast Georgia.

Up to a foot of snow fell last night at Hawley Lake in Arizona's White Mountains, and 10 inches fell at Flagstaff in northern Arizona.

Thunderstorms raked north-central Texas yesterday, spawning tornadoes that damaged more than 100 homes

Crow.

In Kansas, Wichita authorities said 15,000 homes and businesses temporarily lost electricity last night, as freezing rain snapped power lines. Service was restored within a few hours to about 12,000 residences, but Kansas Gas and Electric Co. officials said the rest were expected to go

Associated Press

A tornado yesterday in Mesquite, Texas, damaged more than a dozen houses and business-

es. It first touched down in Ferris, a community 25 miles southeast of Dallas.

Figure 14–19. A wrap underneath a photograph.

the story has ended at the bottom. The makeup person should either cut the story and end it at the bottom (placing a new story above the ad) or find a shorter story to place at the left of the ad.

FILLING REMAINING SPACE

When most of the page has been dummied, the layout procedure is complete. Small spaces may remain because not all stories fit precisely. The remaining

Figure 14–20. A naked or raw wrap.

Weekend garden show attracts 500 visitors

Figure 14-21.   A wrap that makes reader's eye jump from very bottom to top.

space may be filled in two ways: (1) If the space is large enough, fillers may be used. Editors assign someone the responsibility of providing a sufficient number of fillers each day. (2) If the space is relatively small, it is filled by leading. Leading is added between paragraphs until the column is filled.

FLEXIBILITY IN LAYOUT

In planning the layout of large newspapers, the editor should give some attention to flexibility of design to accommodate late-breaking news. There are two considerations in planning for a flexible design. The first is a mechanical consideration. Can one or two stories be replaced without too much effort? The task of remaking a page should be accomplished in the shortest amount of time to meet a press deadline. It may be necessary to rejustify as many as six columns of news in order to accommodate a late story. When the story to be replaced is oddly shaped, involving complex wraps, it will take more time to remake than it might if it were simply shaped. The new story may not be as long as the one it replaces, or it may be longer. Therefore, the design must be simple and flexible enough for any contingency.

A second consideration is the effect that a major story change will have on total page design. Although it is impossible to know how a late-breaking story will be shaped, it may be possible to anticipate how stories of various shapes will affect the design. If the original design is simple, chances are that any changes can be adapted easily to the old design without destroying the original appearance.

ADDITIONAL LAYOUT CONSIDERATIONS

POSITIONING OF NAMEPLATES

The nameplate of a newspaper (often incorrectly called the masthead) is the name usually appearing at the top of Page One. Editors sometimes want to move the nameplate to other positions on the page because they assume that readers know the name of the newspaper they are reading and the space occupied by the nameplate might be better used for other purposes. Once a decision has been made to move the nameplate, a question arises: Where on the page would the nameplate be most appropriate? Editors sometimes want to move it indiscriminately, considering the significance of news the most important criterion for positioning stories. Such editors feel that the nameplate is much less significant and therefore may be moved anywhere at almost any time. At other times, the nameplate seems to be moved around on Page One without any apparent reason.

On the one hand, it seems reasonable to move the nameplate from day to day. After all, most readers know the name of the newspaper without looking at the nameplate. But on the other hand, there are a number of reasons for keeping it in the top position most of the time. In debating the reasonableness of moving it around on the front page, one must consider all the purposes a nameplate serves.

Besides simply identifying the newspaper, a nameplate communicates the philosophical position of the publisher. The typefaces chosen for nameplates usually look distinguished and have strong connotations. The best position for communicating these connotations is at the top of the page because the top position itself communicates a feeling of authority. Any object standing foremost among other objects is judged to be more significant. When an object is buried, its importance is diminished.

But another consideration has to do with the importance of top position in serving as a device that provides readers with a feeling of stability as they read the paper. The nameplate usually represents the starting point for examining the contents of Page One. If it is not in its traditional position, readers may sometimes have a sense of uneasiness and a slight loss of familiarity with the paper. But if the readers know that, while the news may change, the nameplate position will not, the page gains a sense of stability that tends to make reading comfortable.

Furthermore, postal regulations require that a newspaper indicate that it is second-class material somewhere within the first five pages of the paper. In the past, this material might be placed in the editorial page masthead, or it might be buried in a box on Page 2. But it is also placed in small type near the nameplate, perhaps within the dateline rules that appear underneath it. If the nameplate serves this purpose, it should remain at the top.

A final reason for keeping the nameplate at the top relates to its function in the total page design. A nameplate floated down in the page becomes a component of the page's design and thereby complicates the process of layout and design. It is usually easier to lay out a front page when the nameplate is at the top, with some exceptions of course.

Yet there is some logic in moving the masthead if the move is not radical and if it is not done often. There are times when a six-column, horizontally arranged story might well be placed above the nameplate. This story may be of such significance that the editors want to be sure that everyone sees it. The very top position should provide such assurance. But if this practice becomes regular, the importance of the nameplate is diminished.

There is also some logic to the idea that a nameplate may be moved from side to side, but must always remain at the top of the page. Among the most unsightly makeup devices of newspapers are the ears. Ears are pieces of news placed at either or both sides of a nameplate. The editors may eliminate them by moving the nameplate to either side of the page and moving a one- or two-column story to the top. Another reason for moving the nameplate to the side may be to make room for more news than would be possible otherwise. Perhaps the editors who are most likely to experiment with moving the nameplate are those involved with publishing college newspapers. Their decisions to move it is sometimes based on the need to be creative. What is creative, however, may not be easy to read.

There are other uses for nameplates throughout the newspaper, but these do not involve moving the front-page nameplate. For example, some newspapers have identical nameplates on the first and third pages. The effect of this arrangement is to present a second front page to readers so that different kinds of news may be featured on each. Although national news might be used exclusively on Page One, local news might be featured on Page 3.

Finally, modified nameplates may be used in various sections of the newspaper. Family, sports or financial pages also might have special name-

Pachyderms perform as the GOP does Dallas

DALLAS (AP)—Elephants wearing red-white-and-blue dresses.

Elephants playing the harmonica.

Elephants waving American flags with their trunks.

A 700-pound elephant sculpted from Buick and Mercury bumpers.

The Republican National Convention, to get under way Aug. 20 here, is creating a virtual run on pachyderms.

Take 6-year-old "Kenya" of Africa, for instance. She's all booked up from Aug. 16 to Aug. 24.

Kenya will appear under the patriotic stage name of Betsy at the trendy Galleria shopping center wearing red, white and blue.

"She plays a harmonica," animal talent agency owner Chere Hickock told the Dallas Times Herald.

Unfortunately, the national anthem isn't in Kenya's — er, Betsy's — repertoire, Hickock said.

"She doesn't do any songs," Hickock explained.

Kenya-Betsy is also planning on a few parties, Hickock said. "We'll go to a party for a couple of hours and charge $400."

Fashionable Neiman Marcus is not about to be outdone. Neiman spokeswoman Carolyn Cobb said there will be an elephant at a party at the downtown store on Aug. 19, the day before the convention begins.

After the party, the elephant will grace the store's display windows, Cobb added.

"Abu" is another Dallas-area elephant who will be donning his party duds next month.

Abu — who stands 7 feet tall, weighs 7,000 pounds and needs an 18-wheel rig to get around town — has the Dallas Welcoming Committee reception downtown on Thanksgiving Square tentatively penciled in on his social calendar.

Even Republican delegates who eschew the parties, shopping extravaganzas and receptions will be seeing elephants before it's all over.

Oscar "Pumpin, a self-described "heavy-metal" sculptor, has fashioned

80 scrap Buick and Mercury bumpers into a welded elephant that will stand outside the Dallas Convention Center.

Sen. John Tower, the Texas Republican who'll retire soon, will accept the statue on behalf of the GOP at a champagne-and-peanuts ceremony on Aug. 12.

The bumper beast, which was commissioned by a Dallas developer, is the largest Pumpin has ever made. Pumpin said he plans move it from his New York studio to Dallas — a 1,660-mile drive — this weekend.

Pumpin apparently has yet to meet Kenya, Dallas' harmonica-playing pachyderm. Pumpin said he gave his elephant a "normal elephant expression. Bland and bored."

Figure 14-22.   Headline at left side of story.

plates. In reality, however, these are standing headlines rather than nameplates, and although they are designed to resemble the front-page nameplate, their function is to introduce special sections of the newspaper.

CONTEMPORARY HEADLINE PLACEMENT

The traditional-minded layout editor thinks of headlines in terms of large display typefaces placed at the top of stories. This treatment is logical for pages designed to be strongly vertical in appearance. But when makeup is conceived of as horizontal through the use of rectangularly shaped stories, headlines may be set in many different ways. These varied headlines not only summarize the news but make the page appear modern.

When horizontally shaped stories are used on a page, the headline may be placed in at least three places, and possibly a fourth. It may be placed at the left or right side, in the center, or at the bottom of the story. The last-named position is not as desirable as the others (Figures 14-22, 14-23 and 14-24).

If the headline is placed at the side of a story, it looks best if it aligns with the top line of body type. But the headline may be set flush left or flush right, both being contemporary treatments. The best position is at the left side of

By Tillman Durdin

HONG KONG—China-watchers are inclined to believe the Mao Tse-Tung-inspired Great Proletarian Cultural Revolution on the Communist mainland is at long last becoming a spent force.

Recent developments represent a decided gain for right-wing forces and a sharp setback for the radical aims and the most ardent partisans of the revolution as it was originally conceived.

Directives from Peking in the last two months widen still further the authority and the latitude of the military of conservative, bureaucratic elements allied to the military in a common desire to bring order and stability out of the chaos generated by the revolution.

The Red Guards and other "rebel" revolutionaries have been the instrument and power base of the so-called Cultural Revolution group in Peking, a directorate headed by Chen Po-Tan, an intimate of Communist party Chairman Mao Tse-Tung, with Mao's wife, Chiang Ching, its deputy director.

In late 1966 and early 1967 the Red Guards and other radicals were on effective force.

They rampaged about the country spreading and mercilessly enforcing the tenets of the new Maoism, disrupting the

China-watchers see shift from Mao revolution

old power structure at all levels, "dragging out" the old power-holders for denunciation and dismissal, staging massive demonstrations and fomenting a profound revolutionary climate.

Early in the game, however, these vanguard elements revealed what eventually became their greatest weakness and the cause of their downfall. They developed factions that began to fight each other in struggles and disputes over what was and who genuinely represented the Cultural Revolution and the Maoist philosophy.

In many cases officials threatened by the Cultural Revolution formed protective Red Guards of their own. These were set against guard groups seeking their ouster.

Since all groups, as well as the officials backing them, professed boundless

loyalty to the revolution and Mao, it became difficult, indeed, often impossible, for officials and army men not directly involved to tell if any one Red Guard group was more genuinely Maoist than another and which to favor.

The faction fighting added chaos to turmoil.

Last fall the Peking leadership, under pressure from the army and moderates, authorized the military to move in and restore order. There was relative stability over the winter, but the Cultural Revolution's left-wing reasserted itself again this summer and the predictable faction-fighting flared up again on a national scale.

The regime now has authorized another crackdown, once more presumably because of arguments from military lead-

ers and the Maoist right wing that to let the mounting strife go on would risk national disintegration.

This time the measures taken to subordinate the Red Guards and other revolutionaries of the left may mean the coup de grace for this sector of the Cultural Revolution.

Even Mao-Tse-Tung, whose concept of the revolution is "leftist and radical," has had to admit disillusionment with the Red Guards. Reliable Peking sources report here that he broke down and wept in a session with five Red Guard leaders in Peking in late July during which he bitterly condemned them for their disunity and failure to carry through effectively revolutionary objectives.

Mao has, reluctantly, it can be assumed, given his signature to directives which have authorized military units to suppress faction-fighting with arms, if necessary, normalize railway traffic, particularly along the Vietnam supply route through Kwangsi, and push through the formation of new power organs, or revolutionary committees, in provinces where they had not been organized at the end of July.

Closely related to these measures was a directive from Mao which proclaimed workers and peasants, backed by the army, as the leading force in the Cultural Revolution. Student Red Guards along with older intellectuals have been told they must integrate with the workers and peasants in a subordinate status.

Figure 14-23.   A headline buried inside the story.

by
dennis
wheeler

With Thanksgiving approaching, it is that time again to pause and consider the historical background for one of our most beloved holidays.

The Thanksgiving story, known to most of us from our earliest grade school days, is one of bravery in the face of giant adversity; one of achievement in the hour of supreme testing. It inspires reverence and hope in all of us. It is one of the true roots of our well-known American stick-to-itness.

You all remember, of course, how it happened back there in 1621. The Pilgrims had arrived at Plymouth Rock and had established their tiny foothold on the wild North American continent. Their lives beset by disease and tribulation, they managed to survive for some months. And then came winter, and near starvation. And the first Thanksgiving, at which the noble Pilgrims raised their eyes heavenward to thank the Almighty for providing them with enough food to make it through the long night of winter.

THOSE, OF COURSE, are the bare facts of the Thanksgiving tale. But people sometimes lose sight of how the Plymouth Rock adventure fit into the larger fabric of history. They overlook what was going on in the rest of the world: they forget against what historical backdrop the Pilgrim landscape was painted.

Well, I can help. A history buff of sorts, I can supply some of this additional information, the better to illuminate our heritage.

First of all, remember that the Pilgrims landed in North America at about the same time that old Will Shakespeare was writing his stuff back in England. In fact, some historians surmise that when Shakespeare wrote the famous line "Out, out, brief candle'" in MacBeth, he was referring to Candle Mather, the famous Bible-thumping leader of the Pilgrims, who was expelled from England by the King for complicity in burning Joan of Arc at the stake.

IT IS ALSO noteworthy that the landing of the Pilgrims took place shortly after the English defeated the Spanish in the famous sea battle of 1588, that's the one in which Sir Francis Tarkenton defeated the Spanish Armadillo mainly because the captains of the Armadillo's ships lost the toss and had to fight into the wind.

That's important because if the Armadillo had won, we might all be speaking Spanish today instead of English. But then on the other hand it is questionable whether the Spanish could have colonized North America as successfully as the English did. The Spanish are, after all, warm weather people, so they probably would have taken one look at cold Plymouth Rock and said, "No way, senors."

Besides, everybody knows you can't raise tacos in New England.

And don't forget the French.

AT THIS TIME, the French, led by Father University of Marquette and Louis XVI Joliet were selling booze to the Indians and canoeing down the Cal-Sag canal. One wonders what would have happened if communications in those days had been what they are today. If they were, the French would have heard on the 6 o'clock news that the Pilgrims had landed in Massachusetts, and knowing them they would have built the Erie canal across the Appalachian mountains and invaded Massachusetts from the west. Who knows? The battle of Bunker Hill could have happened 150 years early. I ask you: if that had occurred, where would Boston be today? In Montreal, that's where.

Not only that, we'd be speaking French today instead of English. Which means the entertainment center of New Orleans would be called the German Quarter.

Why the German Quarter? Well, it's obvious. Because at about the same time the Pilgrims landed, the 73rd battle of Alsace-Lorraine was being waged between the French and the Germans in the Black Forest. The Germans won that one, and in the subsequent Peace of Westphalia, Adolph Hitler was able to wrest huge territorial concessions from the losing Frenchmen. And among these would have been a piece of New Orleans, which had just been explored by University of Marquette and Louis XIV Joliet and claimed for France.

AND IT would have stuck, because you can grow saurkraut in a bayou.

But let's not jump so lightly over the Indians in this analysis. Remember, the Indians were here first, before any of these other guys, unless you want to count the Vikings, who under the leadership of Eric the Weird invaded the continent in the 11th Century, tried unsuccessfully to turn New York harbor into a fiord, and left in disgust two days later.

Most historians agree the Indians could have easily held on to North America against all European intruders if they had done just three things.

Dumped the tea into Boston harbor themselves instead of letting revolutionaires dressed up as Indians do it. Everybody knows the economy of the colonies would have buckled under without tea.

— LISTENED, WHEN Sitting Bull solemnly warned, "You can't trust no white men" instead of retorting, "Sitting, that's a lot of Bull."

— Let Custer go instead of massacring him. Custer was such a lousy general he would have lost the West without any help from anybody.

But no. The Indians chose instead to attack trains and observe treaties. It was the latter act, of course, that spelled their downfall.

But what does all this have to do with Thanksgiving?

Well, it's simple. It all shows how differently the loose end of the sweater of history might have unraveled. It shows that almost any combination of events, had they occurred even a little differently, could have resulted in there being no Thanksgiving at all.

AND THAT would have been a terrible shame.

Because one thing is crystal clear: you can readily grow thankfulness for our many blessings anywhere in the North American continent.

... *Thanksgiving's Place in History?*

Figure 14-24.   Headline at the bottom.

the story because readers proceed from the left to the right. Occasionally, the headline may look attractive when placed at the right.

When a long story is given horizontal treatment, the headline may be embedded in the center with type on all sides. There is some danger that readers could be confused by this arrangement if they start reading directly underneath the headline instead of starting at the top of the left column. To avoid that, the layout person must not start a sentence directly under the headline. This arrangement also requires the typesetter to plan typesetting around the headline. Because such treatment takes extra time, it is used primarily for feature stories.

Finally, a headline may be placed at the bottom of a story that is clearly set off from the remainder of the page, as in a large box. When the headline is at the bottom of the box, it will be apparent that it belongs to the story above. If it is not set inside a box, the readers may assume it belongs to some other story.

TREATMENT OF LEAD PARAGRAPHS

The lead paragraphs of most stories are placed at the top of a story, set in type sizes that are larger than body type and sometimes leaded. The widths of most lead paragraphs are the same as body type, although occasionally they are set one or even two columns wider than the body type. Lead paragraphs are often made to stand out not only from the headlines above them but from the body type below.

In contemporary newspaper design, however, some lead paragraphs are often given more prominence than they would receive in traditional design. The feeling is that because lead paragraphs have replaced the old headline decks, they deserve more prominence. Decks were formerly used to summarize a story, each deck featuring one outstanding aspect. The lead paragraph, by employing more words set in smaller type than decks, did a better job of summarizing the essential details. But as lead paragraphs came into common use, they were often accorded no better treatment than body type. In contemporary design, some have been made more dramatic in appearance and placed in more obvious positions relative to the remainder of the story.

When headlines are moved to the sides, center or bottom of a story, the lead paragraphs may be placed underneath the headline. However, in such cases, they should be set in a typeface and a size that clearly contrast with the remainder of the body type. Because the goal is to give them display treatment, lead paragraphs should appear markedly different from the body of the story. (Figure 14-25). The typeface should be one or two points larger than body type, set in sans serif, boldface or italic. Leading is necessary to make the lead paragraph stand out and yet be readable. One final treatment may be to set the lead flush left with ragged right, a distinctly contemporary appearance.

NEW APPROACHES TO CUTLINES, OVERLINES AND UNDERLINES

The traditional way of identifying photographs is to place cutlines underneath them. Overlines and underlines may be used alone or with cutlines. If the photograph is less than three columns wide, the cutlines are set full width, but if the photograph is wider, the cutlines may be wrapped in two or more columns underneath. When overlines and underlines are used, they are usually centered.

In contemporary layout, cutlines may be set flush left with ragged right or flush right with ragged left (Figure 14-26). When it is necessary to wrap cutlines into two adjacent columns, the flush-left or flush-right approach does not look pleasing. If, however, two pictures of the same size are placed next to each other (because they are related), it may be possible to set the left cutlines flush left and the right cutlines flush right.

Earthwatch

Looking for something a little different to do on your vacation this year? Earthwatch can find you some work to do, helping scientists with menial — but worthwhile — tasks all over the world. How about counting ants? Or recording the habits of the spotted hyena?

By Daniel Q. Haney

BELMONT, Mass. (AP) — For $1,000 or so, people buy the opportunity to lie on their bellies in 150-degree heat and count ants. Or, if it seems more attractive, they find out whether they can fool wild llamas by lugging their dung heaps back and forth.

his wife, Eleanor, consider themselves to be conservationists, so they picked a bird banding trip to Panama last year.

"We wanted something where we could actually participate actively ourselves," says Karl. "It was the most unpleasant one we could find, because it was in the wet season in the jungles of Panama with no housing or toilet facilities. But if we are really as ardent as we think we are, this would be the proof."

Before sunup each morning, Karl and his companions groped into the jungle ravines by flashlight to hang up 15-foot-long mesh nets. Then, once an hour, they ventured back out into the torrential rains to identify, weigh, band and then free the captured birds.

"IT WAS very hard, but

(See Earthwatch, Page 2C)

Figure 14-25.   A display paragraph underneath a headline.

Close call

Rescuers from Frenchtown Township near Monroe extend a ladder to help a man reach shore after he and four others got trapped on an ice floe on Lake Erie. The men were returning to Lake Sterling State Park after three hours of ice fishing when they realized they were on the chunk of floating ice. All were rescued and no one was injured.

Figure 14-26.   Cutlines justified on both sides.

A particularly modern style of cutline treatment, borrowed from magazine design, is to place them at the lower side of photographs. In such positions, they may be set in very narrow measures (from 6 to 9 picas in width), flush on both sides. But they also may be given the flush-left or flush-right treatment. The cutlines are set differently, depending on which treatment is used. When placed on the right side, they should be flush left, and when placed on the left side, they should be flush right (Figures 14-27 and 14-28) because the type nearest the photograph is aligned and looks more attractive.

U.S. Sen. Paul Simon is on the Senate Judiciary, Foreign Relations and Labor and Human Resources Committees, and his contributors reflect those assignments.

Figure 14-27.   Cutlines set flush left, ragged right.

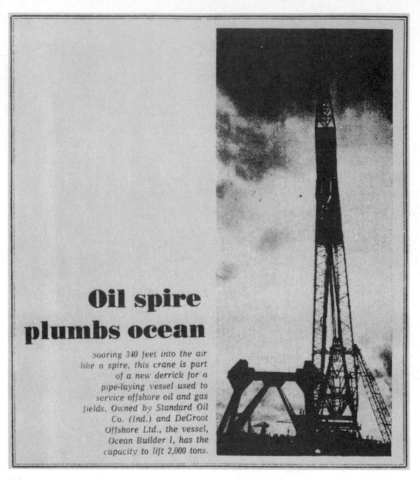

Oil spire plumbs ocean

Soaring 340 feet into the air like a spire, this crane is part of a new derrick for a pipe-laying vessel used to service offshore oil and gas fields. Owned by Standard Oil Co. (Ind.) and DeGroot Offshore Ltd., the vessel, Ocean Builder I, has the capacity to lift 2,000 tons.

Figure 14-28.   Cutlines set flush right, ragged left.

Overlines may be repositioned above cutlines placed at the sides of cuts. They, too, may receive the same flush-left or flush-right treatment as the cutlines. When they are positioned that way, there probably will be a large amount of white space above the overline (or above the cutlines when there is no overline). But this white space will enhance the appearance of the treatment and should not be considered wasted space.

INSERTS AND PAGE DESIGN

Inserts are additions to the story sometimes placed within the story body type. The ostensible purpose of breaking into a story was to provide information that would help the reader better understand the news. In traditional layout practices, editors often inserted freaks, refers or other material into the main body of a story. A *freak* is any material placed in a story that is set differently from the main story. A *refer* is something that refers to a related story. But no matter what the purpose was, the effect of any break in the news was a break in the reader's concentration.

What are the most likely alternative actions readers may take when confronted by an insert? They may notice the insert, ignore it temporarily and, upon finishing the article, return and read it. They may ignore it entirely. Or they may stop to read it and then try to pick up the thread of thought in the remainder. But no matter which option they choose, the insert may break the flow of reading, if only for an instant, and is therefore undesirable (see Figure 14-29).

Inserts may also be undesirable because they interrupt the rhythm of reading. Even if readers stop to read the insert, they may not read much more of the story.

Editors often tend to make inserts a continuing practice, including perhaps at least one in every edition. Too many inserts on one day make the page appear to be full of spots that are unattractive and uninviting. Even one insert stands out as a spot on the page. In such situations, the layout editor interrupts the reader with rules and even a small headline within the insert. That one spot, then, may hamper the efforts of the editor to design a pleasing page because inserts tend to call attention to themselves.

But what should be done with the material that may have been used in inserts? One answer might to be place that material at either the beginning, the end or the top center of a story (see Figures 14-30, 14-31, 14-32). Perhaps it can be incorporated into the body of the story and not be obtrusive. Finally, by careful analysis of the news the editor may treat additional editorial material as another story and place it adjacent to the story in question. If there is reference to a picture, then this may be set in lightface italics and incorporated into the story.

Abortion: Schoemehl Stirs Divided Response

By Pamela Schaeffer
Post-Dispatch Religion Writer

WHEN MAYOR Vincent C. Schoemehl Jr. announced on Tuesday a shift in his position on abortion, reactions from Catholic leaders were swift — and diverse.

Schoemehl earned disfavor from Archbishop John L. May, who didn't like what he heard: that Schoemehl, once a staunch foe of legalized abortion, now opposed further restrictions on the practice in Missouri.

Schoemehl's statement prompted a six-page rebuttal on Friday from The Pro-Life Committee of the Archdiocese of St. Louis.

But Schoemehl earned praise from the Rev. Kevin O'Rourke, a moral theologian, who asserted that Schoemehl's position was a prudent moral and political stand.

The controversy here reflects a storm in the Catholic Church nationally over the issue — a controversy in which bishops and politicians are increasingly pitted against one another, with moral theologians steering a path between.

Featured prominently is Gov. Mario Cuomo of New York, who says he is personally opposed to abortion but strongly supports its legal status.

Cuomo has been rebuked by many Catholics — even liberal Catholics — who contend that he has evaded responsibility with that stand, particularly because, in their view, he has done little by other means to prevent abortions.

At the far right of the Cuomo standoff is Bishop Austin Vaughan, auxiliary bishop of New York, who has warned that Cuomo is "in serious risk of going to hell" because of his support for legalized abortion.

While many Catholic leaders would like to see Cuomo do more, few are as strident as Vaughan.

The ongoing debate reflects a broad spectrum of views over how a basic moral principle — that abortion is evil — should be reflected in public policy.

Morality is one thing, many Catholic leaders say, but political strategy in a pluralistic society is another.

And O'Rourke, who helped Schoemehl arrive at his position, argues that in the realm of strategy, Schoemehl is way ahead. His position represents a leap forward for Catholic politicians nationally, O'Rourke asserts. What's more, he

See ABORTION, Page 5

> **Let us end the debate on restrictions [and rather work toward] a comprehensive program [encompassing both education and] health and family support services.**
>
> MAYOR VINCENT C. SCHOEMEHL JR.

Figure 14-29.   Insert placed at bottom-center of story. This is a comparatively new style.

Farmers in Midwest affected most by delay of CRP checks

By Alissa Rubin

Eagle Washington bureau

WASHINGTON — Nearly $1.6 billion in payments to farmers with land under contract to the government will be delayed at least one month because of the government's failure to pass spending bills for 1991, Agriculture Department officials said Thursday.

The land is under contract through the conservation reserve program, which pays farmers to take land out of production for 10 years to protect erodible or fragile land.

The delay hits hardest farmers in Midwest and Plains states, where thousands of farmers were scheduled to receive nearly $1 billion in early October. The states with the most land in the program are Kansas, Texas and Iowa where farmers are due $154 million, $156 million and $148 million, respectively.

"We do not have any appropriated funds so we cannot send out any checks," said Keith Bjerke, chief of the Agricultural Stabilization and Conservation Service, which administers

> **"We do not have any appropriated funds so we cannot send out any checks."**
> *Keith Bjerke, ASCS*

most of the farm program.

Congress has delayed passage of spending bills, under which payments are released from the Treasury, because legislators have been unable to agree how to cut the federal budget deficit.

"As soon as somebody tells us how much money we've got to spend, then we know who the people are who are due the checks and what they've got coming," said Bjerke.

None of this is much comfort to farmers, many of whom rely on checks to make loan payments on land and farm machinery.

"Their cash flows are such that they are expecting that check the first week of October — and the machinery dealer, banker, the seed dealer, the fertilizer dealer, they have to be paid. They have to hope their bankers will bridge them," Knight said.

The only good news is that, contrary to earlier reports, farmers will be paid — albeit a little late — the full amount even if automatic budget cuts go into effect, Bjerke said.

Figure 14–30.   Insert in the middle of a story (top to bottom and side to side). This insert does not interrupt the flow of reading.

BOXED STORIES

The use of boxed stories in contemporary modular layout is radically different from that in traditional layout. In traditional layout, a short human-interest story or an insert might have been placed in a box. Rarely was a long story boxed.

Contemporary layout seeks to dramatize a story or the design on a given page, often through the use of large boxed stories. There is, of course, a danger in using too many such stories on a page. But if only one is used per page, it may liven that page considerably.

An editor boxes a story because he or she considers it significant. Perhaps it is not as significant as the top two stories on the page, but it is still of major importance. The procedure, then, is to place the entire story in a boxed rule. The story must, of course, be squared off so that it fits neatly into the box. A photograph may accompany the story. But the keys to making this box look attractive are the use of type rules and more than an ordinary amount

LOS ANGELES TIMES

COLUMN LEFT/
GEORGE BLACK

A Hellish Life in 'Democratic' Guatemala

■ In this version of a capitalistic economy, the army always wins—whoever is elected.

There is some irony in the fact that, at a time of declining public faith in U.S. electoral democracy, one of our growth industries should be the monitoring of democratic procedures in other countries. There's always a team somewhere, it seems: one day Bulgaria, the next Pakistan. This week it's Guatemala, which is holding a presidential election today.

Two basic yardsticks are commonly employed to judge the propriety of elections in a place like Guatemala. The first, often used by the State Department, stresses that this is the first orderly transfer of the presidency in years, without a coup d'etat or other messy interruption.

The second, more the preserve of the semiofficial election monitors, is concerned with the niceties of the vote. Americans are especially given to this kind of quantifiable research—whether pinkies or thumbs are dipped in the proper indelible ink, whether penalties exist to deter multiple voting and fraudulent registrations. After decades of watching soldiers load ballot boxes onto the backs of unmarked pickup trucks and computers that mysteriously go down halfway through the count, these are understandable correctives.

In Guatemala, however, neither set of criteria is of much use. Election monitoring there is rather like conducting an autopsy and declaring the corpse to be healthy because you find no cavities in its teeth.

After today's election, votes will be tabulated and a winner declared. Perhaps it will be Jorge Carpio Nicolle, a mediocre right-wing newspaper magnate who ran a distant second in 1985. Carpio was an early leader in the opinion polls after the enforced withdrawal of retired Gen. Efrain Rios Montt, Guatemala's dictator in 1982-83, who was barred from running under a constitutional clause that prohibits the candidacy of anyone who has ever seized power violently.

But whoever is elected, the army gets in. Something Americans are slow to understand about Third World political elites is that they are excellent mimics. Even the Somozas and the Marcoses, in their own crude way, knew how to parrot the sweet language of democracy. The Guatemalan officer corps has learned that having the president wear a uniform may not be the best way of securing its long-term interests. Since the early 1980s it has come to see that the election of an ineffectual civilian in a clean vote, far from being a hindrance, may actually be a better cover than money could ever buy.

Still, it's too easy to blame all Guatema-

'The latest pastime of the Guatemala City police is killing [homeless] kids—perhaps in the name of some deranged conception of law and order; perhaps just for kicks.'

---

la's horrors on evil generals and naive or venal Americans. Outgoing President Vinicio Cerezo Arévalo is also responsible. A single adjective crops up constantly in discussions of the Cerezo presidency: "frivolous." It's an odd word to use about someone who survived three assassination attempts as a young Christian Democrat. But what Cerezo seems to have liked best about elective office was its perks—the cars, the country-house parties, the women. Recently he bought himself a little island in the Caribbean; Guatemala City gossip says he beat out pop singer Julio Iglesias in the bidding.

For other Guatemalans, the usual routines apply. Thanks to the economic austerity policies of the 1980s, thousands of children now live on the streets, the product of escalating misery. The latest pastime of the Guatemala City police is killing these kids—perhaps in the name of some deranged conception of law and order, perhaps just for kicks.

On Sept. 11 the anthropologist Myrna Mack was stabbed to death outside her office. She was the founder of the Guatemalan Assn. for the Advancement of the Social Sciences, which to the Guatemalan army is a little like saying you belong to the Society for the Spread of International Communism. Then on Oct. 25, gunmen opened fire on the journalist Byron Barrera, gravely wounding him and killing his wife. His newspaper, La Epoca, was firebombed into submission in 1988.

I mention these two cases not because they are especially unusual (there were 136 extrajudicial executions in September, an average sort of month), or even because I happened to know both Mack and Barrera professionally. I cite them because they show—to borrow some terminology from Eastern Europe—a state bent on extinguishing the breath of civil society.

This has been a year of celebrating the failure of communism and the spread of capitalist democracy to the entire world. But global systems deserve to be judged by their failures as well as their successes. For those who live in Guatemala's version of a market economy, life is hell—whoever is president, and no matter how many voters dip their thumbs in the ink today.

George Black is foreign editor of the Nation magazine.

Figure 14-31. Insert in middle of a long column of type. Such an insert may stop the reader.

'Many who attend law school will never hang out a shingle. Legal training will be used in another area — it will always stand them in good stead.'

Good lawyers are his goal

By Maureen Milford

Staff writer

J. Kirkland Grant admits there's a national glut of lawyers, but that's not going to stop him from cranking out hundreds — maybe thousands — of attorneys from the Delaware Law School of Widener University.

The new dean of Delaware's only law school believes quality, not quantity, is the real issue.

"It all depends on what kind of lawyers you're training. Lawyers who are morally and ethically upright, as well as competent, will always have enough work. The competition will be rough, but there's always room at the top," said Grant, who took over as dean in July.

The lawyer-professor said he hopes to get the Delaware legal community to rally around the law school. His figures show that 20 percent of the lawyers in the state are Delaware Law School graduates.

"It behooves the lawyers in the state to be very interested in the law school. After all, it is the only law school in a corporate state," Grant said.

Grant, who at age 37 is one of the youngest law school deans in the country, has his work cut out for him. Many people in Delaware's legal community are shaking their heads at the number of people coming out of law school every year. As one lawyer put it, "People are going to law school the way they used to go into real estate." Another attorney expressed concern that lawyers will take cases that have little or no merit on a contingency basis simply to have work.

The new dean is aware of these concerns, but he says the Delaware Law School graduates have proven themselves top notch in the First State. "The greatest strengths of the law school are its students and graduates," Grant said.

Delaware Law School was a familiar name to Grant when he was offered the job as dean. In 1978 he served on the American Bar Association inspection team for accreditation of the school.

See **DEAN — B2**, col. 5

J. Kirkland Grant

Staff photo by Pat Crowe

Figure 14–32.   Insert above the main headline.

of white space inside the box. The only function of the type rule is to set the story apart from all other stories on the page. It usually will not look good if very heavy rules are used. And a fancy border of any kind will call attention to itself, not to the contents of the box. The white spaces, especially between the rules and the body type, are the framing devices that, with the hairline rules, call attention to the story and make it easy to read. Headlines within a box also may be set smaller and in lighter-faced types than those normally used because the rules and white space framing the box make a larger type unnecessary. There is little competition from headlines outside the box.

Boxes, therefore, should be no less than two columns wide, and preferably larger, so that they may have dramatic impact. Some editors place at least one such box on every page where possible as a means of adding dramatic impact. The position of such boxes depends on the sizes and weights of other elements on the page. When other headlines are large and bold, a boxed story should be placed at the opposite side to balance the page. Often they look well at the bottom of the page. In some cases, they might well be used in place of the number-one story (upper-right side), as in Figure 14–30.

POLICY FOR DESIGN OF JUMP HEADS

Enough evidence is available through research studies to prove that stories that have been jumped or continued to other pages lose a great deal of readership (see Chapter 2). Nevertheless, the practice of jumping stories cannot always be avoided. Consequently, there should be a policy regarding the design of such heads.

Two related problems arise in the design of jump heads: (1) how to make them easy to find on a page and (2) how to keep their design consistent with both the page and overall newspaper design. It may seem easy to resolve the first problem by setting the headlines in larger and bolder typefaces than other headlines. But if the type is too large or bold, it will call attention to itself and tend to make the page look unattractive. If it is too light, readers may not be able to find the heads. Both problems may be resolved if the following guidelines are observed.

1. It is important to have a jump head consist of at least one word from the original head to make the transition easier (see Figure 14-33).
2. The typefaces and style of arrangement should be consistent with the headline schedule used for other headlines.
3. The number of lines and sizes of type used for jump heads should be the same as if the jumped portion were a separate story. The length and importance of the story should be considered in making this determination.
4. A contrasting typeface may be used to help the head stand out. If Tempo has been used for most other headlines, a Bodoni Bold italic may provide the necessary contrast.
5. Stars, bullets or asterisks, if they are not too obtrusive, may precede the first letter of the jump head to serve as attention-getting devices.
6. Ben Day screens may be used in the background for such heads.

Galileo didn't recognize Neptune

By Warren E. Leary
Associated Press

WASHINGTON — The famous astronomer Galileo apparently did not recognize a major planet when he saw it and thus missed out on adding the discovery to his list of credits.

The 17th century genius, using one of his early telescopes, saw the planet Neptune without knowing what it was. This left actual discovery to scientists hundreds of years later, an astronomer said yesterday.

Charles T. Kowal of the California Institute of Technology said he re-examined records of Galileo's observations and calculated that the Italian physicist saw the planet at least two times while working in Florence.

Galileo saw Neptune on Dec. 28, 1612, and Jan. 28, 1613, but erroneously thought it was a "fixed star,"

'When he saw Neptune, he was looking for satellites of Jupiter.'

even though he noted that it moved in relation to another star, Kowal reported to the National Science Foundation, which finances part of his work. Galileo's observations were 234 years before the distant planet formally was discovered.

Galileo, the first to put the telescope to practical use, discovered that the moon was marked by valleys and mountains, and reflected light instead of generating its own. He also discovered the four major moons of Jupiter and noted the peculiar form of Saturn, which was later recognized as being caused by its rings.

"When he saw Neptune, he actually was looking for satellites of Jupiter," Kowal said in a telephone interview. "It's also somewhat surprising that there are only two observations. Neptune should have been seen for the entire month of January."

Neptune, second only to Pluto as the solar system's most distant discovered planet, is 15 times more massive than the Earth. Very little is known about this cold, gaseous planet because of its distance from the sun — 2.8 billion miles — and the fact that no spacecraft has ever visited it.

Neptune was discovered on Sept. 23, 1846, by a young German astronomer, Johann Galle. Other scientists, notably John Couch Adams of Britain and Urbain Leverrier of France, calculated that an unknown planet had to be in a certain position because something was disturbing the motion of the planet Uranus.

Galle looked at that calculated position and found Neptune with ease.

Kowal said he is looking for early observations of Neptune because its orbit around the sun still is not well defined. The planet takes 165 years to circle the sun and has not yet completed one full revolution since its discovery in 1846, he noted.

Figure 14-33.   Insert at the top of columns two and three.

This is easy for a newspaper printed by the offset technique. Where letterpress is being used, perhaps the page number from which the story originally started may be placed in a screened background. If several page numbers could be screened and kept in logo form, they could be inserted easily under jump heads.

TOMBSTONING IN CONTEMPORARY DESIGN

Almost every editor, from the largest metropolitan newspaper or from the smallest high school paper, knows that tombstoning should be avoided. *Tombstoning* (also called *butting heads*) is a practice of placing two headlines next to each other in adjacent columns, both of which are set in the same type size, weight and style. They also have the same number of lines. But tombstoning was considered a poor layout practice in an age where only 6-point hairline rules were used between columns. Because some newspapers have used hairline rules of even less than 6 points (2- and 3-point rules), there was more danger that a reader might read across the column into the adjacent headline and be confused (Figure 14-34).

But in contemporary design, where the space between columns is at least 9 points and as much as 2 picas, tombstoning may not be objectionable. There may be so much white space between the columns that the reader can't be confused into reading a headline in the adjacent column. Then the only objection to tombstoning may be that there is not enough variety shown when two headlines of the same size, weight and number of lines are placed next to each other. This is a design consideration, and one of the heads may be changed to provide more type variety on the page.

Fired Perkins offers no excuses
Ex-coach believes his plan would have paid off for Tampa Bay

By FRED GOODALL
AP sports writer

TAMPA, Fla. — Ray Perkins said yesterday he's confident his efforts to build the Tampa Bay Buccaneers into a winner would have paid off if he had been allowed to complete his five-year contract.

The fired coach declined to discuss specifics about his inability to produce a winning record in four seasons, but did accept responsibility for the failure of his program.

"I'm very disappointed that we have not accomplished some of the things that I felt strongly that we could and that I felt strongly that we would," said Perkins, who was dismissed Monday and replaced by Richard Williamson.

"Being the head coach, being the guy that makes all the decisions, I have let our football players down. I have let our owner down. Needless to say, I understand the workings of the National Football League. I understand those things that go on behind closed doors, and I understand if you don't win that you get fired as a head coach."

The Bucs were 19-41 under Perkins, who sensed last week that he was finished as Bucs coach, regardless of whether the team pulled out of a tailspin that saw Tampa Bay lose seven of eight games.

He said he had no quarrel with the timing of owner Hugh Culverhouse's decision — one day after a victory over Atlanta stopped a six-game losing streak — because the decision already had been made not to bring him back in 1991.

"That's not what Mr. C said yesterday, but that's the fact," Perkins said, disputing the owner's contention he didn't decide to fire the coach until Monday afternoon.

"I felt very strongly on Friday that the decision had already been made. That was my gut feeling," Perkins said. "I had no basis for that except 49 years of 100 percent being right gut feelings."

Perkins, 49, left Alabama in December 1986 to take over a team that lost 28 of 32 games under Leeman Bennett. Using his unchallenged authority as vice president-football operations, he overhauled the team and began this season with 42 players who were not on Tampa Bay's roster when he arrived.

He feels he's leaving behind a good nucleus of talent, including his four No. 1 draft picks — Vinny Testaverde, Paul Gruber, Broderick Thomas and Keith McCants.

"I would like to stay throughout the remainder of my contract to show that it would work, because I still believe my plan will work," Perkins said. "But we'll never know.

"I have no excuses, no alibis," he added. "There are always a lot of reasons for failure ... There are a lot of reasons for us to start out strong and then go into a six-game losing streak. I won't go into them, but I won't deny that I'm part of those reasons. I was, and I am."

Perkins made a seven-minute statement and accepted no questions during a farewell news conference at the Bucs' training complex. He later met with a small group of reporters and said he hopes to coach again, probably on the college level.

"I'm sure I'll have opportunities, and I'm not sure I could do without football," said Perkins, adding he would not accept an offer from Culverhouse to remain with the Bucs organization during the final year of a contract that pays him about $800,000 annually.

"I've got a deep burning desire to be in football, but be in a position where I can make a difference. I don't just want to coach football. I want to just draw Xs and Os. I want to be in a position to contribute more to somebody else's life than just being a coach. That could be with or without football."

Early speculation about a possible successor centers around several big names, including former San Francisco 49ers coach Bill Walsh and current NFL coaches Joe Gibbs, Buddy Ryan, Sam Wyche and Lindy Infante.

San Francisco offensive coordinator Mike Holmgren, Giants defensive coordinator Bill Belichick and Dolphins quarterback coach Gary Stevens are pro assistants considered possibilities. And from the college ranks, the names of Louisville's Howard Schnellenberger and Notre Dame's Lou Holtz have surfaced.

Baseball salaries average $597,537

By RONALD BLUM
AP sports writer

NEW YORK — The average baseball salary rose by a record $100,000 in 1990 to $597,537, according to final figures issued yesterday by the Major League Baseball Players Association.

The dollar increase was the largest in baseball history and the 20.2 percent increase was the steepest single-season rise since the 1982 season.

Although they failed to repeat as World Series champions, the Oakland Athletics finished first in the payroll race with a team average of $804,643. They were followed by Boston ($777,683), the New York Mets ($758,575) and the New York Yankees ($725,872).

The Baltimore Orioles were the poorest-paid team at $279,326. The Seattle Mariners ($388,649) were the only other team below $400,000.

The union's survey was presented to its executive board last night by its staff. The executive board began a four-day meeting in Orlando, Fla., and details of the report were made available to The Associated Press.

EDDIE MURRAY
... highest at first

25 to 40.

The biggest jump of any team was the Milwaukee Brewers, who rose from 20th place in 1989 ($363,517) to 10th place in 1990 ($678,581). New multimillion-dollar contracts to Robin Yount and Paul Molitor contributed heavily to that

Figure 14-34.   Example of tombstoning.

BANNER HEADLINES

The use of daily across-the-page *banners* has been abandoned by many modern newspapers and often replaced by *spread heads* without readouts. A banner is a large-type headline that runs the full width of a page. A spread headline is a smaller head running more than two columns and less than full width. But when a story is assigned a banner headline, it is assumed that the body copy will be placed in the extreme right-hand column. Even though the first, or left-hand, column is the most important position on the page, the right-hand column enables the reader to continue reading the story without returning to the left side of the page. In contemporary design, a number of questions arise affecting the reader's ability to continue reading the story smoothly. The answers to these questions lead to principles of handling banner headlines and readouts.

Can the story be continued in any other column to provide a change of pace and variety in makeup? There are few occasions when the story can be continued elsewhere. Least effective is to continue the story to an inside column. Indeed, it should not be placed anywhere but in the extreme right-hand column (with exceptions that will be noted) because otherwise the reader would have to search for it. Although one may argue that the reader will not have to search very long, any time—even a fraction of a second—is too long. That fraction of a second may be just the time necessary for the reader to switch to some more interesting story. After all, the reader may already know the material in the banner headline and perhaps isn't interested enough to continue when there are any impediments to reading. This is the problem of all layout devices. None should slow the reader more than a fraction of a second. Considered individually, each layout device may seem to be effective. But when there are many such devices on a page, the even rhythm of reading may be broken and reading becomes a troublesome rather than a pleasant experience.

When stories are continued from a banner headline to any column other than the extreme right, the cutoff rule is used to separate the banner from unrelated stories. The assumption is that the only column not carrying a cutoff rule must be the one where the story is continued, and it will be obvious at a glance. Indeed, it is obvious at the right-hand side, less obvious when placed at the left-hand side (first column) and almost obscure when placed inside. Cutoff rules help, but not much. It is difficult to find the column where the story is continued.

Another question arises when using a banner headline. Can more than one story relating to the banner headline be arranged so that the banner reads into each story successfully? This might work in a situation when, say, an election story breaks and one political party wins both gubernatorial and mayoral races. The banner headline may therefore refer to both stories. When the readout headlines are only one column wide, they are often hard to find. But when they are two or more columns wide, they are relatively easy to find.

A final question concerns whether a banner headline should lead into a multiple- or single-column headline? One of the older layout rules was that when a large type was used in a top headline, the reader's eyes would have difficulty adjusting to smaller types in the decks or lead paragraphs. Therefore, the reduction in size was supposed to be at least 50 percent. If a 120-point headline was used for the banner, it should read into a headline of no less than 60-point type. The 60-point type would then read into a 30-point deck, which in turn might read into an 18-point deck and from there into a 10-point lead paragraph. There was never any valid evidence that readers had difficulty adjusting their eyes to the changes in type sizes. Therefore, the only reason for reading from a banner into a multiple-column headline is simply to provide more details in the headline than could have been included in the banner. The only trouble with multiple-column headlines is that they usually lead into a single-column story, leaving the space underneath to be filled in the best way possible. If a headline for an unrelated story is placed underneath a multiple-column headline, the effect might be to confuse the reader. At times a picture is placed underneath. But neither of these solutions looks attractive.

In contemporary layout, banner headlines often lead into a single-column headline, a simple device. Or, if a banner is used, it may lead into a three-column headline, and a story may be wrapped for three columns underneath by squaring off the bottom. A final alternative is to limit the use of banner headlines to rare occasions. When used with multiple-column readouts, they won't look awkward because the news is so sensational. Too many multiple-column headlines, however, make the page spotty because they appear dark (being set in bold typefaces and relatively large types). They become centers of interest because of their weight and may be difficult to balance.

HEADLINE DECKS, AN OLD IDEA FOR MODERN PAPERS

One technique of headline treatment that was used in the early 1900s and fell out of favor has been rediscovered. It is the headline *deck.* A deck is a small headline placed underneath a main headline to provide more information than the typical top headline provides. Because top headlines usually are set in relatively large type, they can use only a limited number of words to communicate the full impact of a story. But a deck is usually set in type that is about 50 percent smaller than the main head. Therefore, a headline using 48-point typeface may require a 24-point deck, and a 24-point top head may require a 12- or 14-point deck. The additional words found in a deck may be just what are needed to tell readers what they want to know about a story and help them decide whether to read or not (see Figure 14-35).

Decks also add white space around headlines, much as in magazines. They can therefore help make the total page design more attractive as long as they are neither overused nor too dominating. Most often decks are set in light- to medium-weight typefaces.

Most decks are used on special pages such as the front page, sports or business.

Measure 5 may force 2 sessions
Marion leaders urge early adjournment

SUPER BOWL
Players say focus is divided between war and big game

Figure 14-35.   Example of decks.

THE USE OF DESKTOP COMPUTERS IN PAGE LAYOUT

UNCLUTTERING PAGES

Desktop computers through programs like PageMaker or Quark Express have had a major effect on page layout. Most noticeably, they have helped layout editors produce cleaner, less cluttered pages. That is possible because the computer lends itself to the production of squared-off rectangular modules that lend an aura of keen organization to a page. Perhaps the most outstanding characteristic of contemporary layout is the use of various types of rectangular modules, both small and quite large, arranged both vertically and horizontally. All these variations are necessary to enliven the page.

Although the layout person need not necessarily be restricted to rectangles, he or she will most likely take advantage of the opportunities that modules (and the computer) provide.

Please note, however, that a modular page is not necessarily easier to read. It *is* easier to look at because of its orderliness. This orderliness also makes it relatively easy for readers to find stories they might miss on "busy" pages with a complex structure.

Desktop layout therefore provides great opportunities for achieving page simplicity, one of the main objectives of good newspaper layout.

SEEING AN ENTIRE PAGE
WHILE PLANNING THE LAYOUT

Desktop computers also allow the layout person to see how each element will look on the page. Such a bird's eye view is usually helpful because the planner can see relationships that might otherwise have gone unrecognized.

Laying out pages on a tiny screen may be difficult for some people, whereas a larger screen may provide a more realistic view. However, the small screen usually is an advantage rather than a hindrance. Even smaller are the thumbnail sketches of pages that some computer programs offer. By seeing thumbnail sketches of all pages at one time, the layout person can check the style for an entire newspaper section at one viewing.

COMPUTERS OFFER MANY
LAYOUT ALTERNATIVES

Another advantage is that many desktop programs allow a variety of useful layout alternatives. Among these are the ability to incorporate illustrations into the text, to set type by following picture contours, to turn type lines to an angular position and to add stylistic page devices such as type rules or type boxes.

The computer allows the user to move slowly or quickly, but the tendency is to move quickly.

COMPUTER PROGRAMS BRING
A NEW LANGUAGE TO PAGE LAYOUT

Unfortunately, some of the programs for page layout have created a new language for the layout person to learn. Type boxes, for example, do not mean the same thing they do in the printing industry. Some program designers call them *frames*. When new layout editors get on the job, they may find that the terminology is not exactly the same as they learned in school.

With desktop computers, layout editors can design pages quickly. It does not take long to decide where to place stories on a page. Many alternative designs can be explored until one looks right.

CHAPTER 15

AN INTRODUCTION TO CONTEMPORARY LAYOUT

AMERICAN NEWSPAPER LAYOUTS

The layouts of many American newspapers look very much alike. Although papers have always copied from one another to a certain extent, there is less variety than previously. Many look like *USA Today*, the most noticeable element being the abundant use of color splashed about in a seemingly indiscriminate manner on the front page. Weather maps and stories embedded in gray or colored tint boxes also make these papers look very much like *USA Today*. Presumably, one of the major purposes of adding so much color to these newspapers is to make them more noticeable. (Figure 15-1).

Other similarities among American newspapers did not come from *USA Today*. There is, for example, widespread use of gray or colored tint blocks printed under selected long and short short stories. Large section heads like "Local," "Sports," or "Business" are often styled in a remarkably similar manner from paper to paper. Smaller standing heads often are printed over a gray or colored screen. Some heads are set in reverse type or placed under or over a 12-point solid rule (which in turn is often printed in color). At the top of front pages one tends to see boxed inserts, usually in color, that call attention to a few stories that the editor would like to emphasize. News placement too is similar from newspaper to newspaper.

Of course, no law forbids newspapers to copy a good idea. But the similarities among American newspapers are so pronounced that one wonders why there is so little local innovation. Do layout editors believe that one certain layout style or design is universally better than any others?

READERSHIP AND CONTEMPORARY NEWSPAPER DESIGN

In this environment, publishers are facing a dilemma that may be directly related to newspaper design and layout: namely, the phenomenon of declining readership. Publishers all over the country are trying to deal with a continuing

Figure 15-1.   A newspaper that uses much color throughout the paper.

decline in newspaper readership that started some years ago and seems to be continuing. Although the U.S. population keeps growing every year, newspaper readership does not keep up with the rate of growth. Professor Robert L. Stevenson of the University of South Carolina Journalism School, who from 1979 to 1985 studied readership data produced by the National Research Center at the University of Chicago, said, "The ominous trend is that every age group is reading less now than 10 years ago. Each new generation does increase readership as it ages but reads less than the generation it replaces."[1]

There is no question that television and other media have become more attractive news sources than newspapers. Perhaps the American people have made certain lifestyle changes that predispose them to spend less time reading their newspapers than their parents and grandparents spent.

The big question that has been asked many times is, What can we do to reverse the situation and increase readership? And, even more significantly, What can contemporary newspaper designers do to help prevent a further decline?

This is no simple subject that can be fully answered in an editing text. It is a much larger sociological problem. But there are some clear-cut implications for those who work in newspaper layout and design.

The sameness of newspaper design and the copying of *USA Today*'s styling suggest that layout personnel may not see this problem as theirs. Readership may be perceived as belonging to the circulation department or someone else.

On the other hand, *USA Today* may have been copied because some editors believe that there is magic in that design. Precisely what can be achieved by using that design, however, has not been measured, at least for public consumption. But it is important to understand that what was good for *USA Today* may not be good for other newspapers. The marketing problem facing *USA Today* was so different from that of other papers that it may not have been appropriate for others. The extreme use of color found in many newspapers today may not have the same effect as it had in *USA Today* because (1) it tends to give a newspaper a circus atmosphere that is inconsistent with the nature of front-page news today; (2) those selecting color have shown that they do not necessarily understand how to use it; (3) there is no valid evidence that the use of color in newspaper design can build readership or circulation. In a paper previously titled "The Disappearing Newspaper Reader," Professor Robert L. Stevenson noted:

> Despite the efforts of newspapers to copy *USA Today* by reshaping the editorial package to the supposed interest of young readers, penetration continued to sink in the 1980s . . . .
>
> Apparently the slick graphics, color maps, and dummied-down content didn't help. The best that could be said is that they may have acted as a slight brake on the decline in readership.[2]

Stevenson also raised a question about readership in the future when he said:

> The question for the next century is at what point the downward trend line will finally level off, or whether newspapers, as we know them, will become museum artifacts like illuminated manuscripts and handset type.[3]

[1] M. L. Stein, "Target the Educated," *Editor and Publisher,* August 25, 1990, p. 18.
[2] Ibid.
[3] Ibid.

Figure 15-2.   A newspaper front page with no color.

The Newspaper Advertising Bureau has reported that between 1967 and 1988 the percentage of adults who read a newspaper every day dropped from 73 to 54 percent. Frank Capertown, writing in the *American Society of Newspaper Editors' Bulletin,* noted that one of the leading causes of this situation was "time pressure" that resulted in lost readers. In other words people are too busy doing other things to read.[4]

[4] Caperton, Frank, "It's Time to Get Organized," in the *ASNE Bulletin,* October, 1989, p. 5.

So it seems that a *full* solution to the readership problem cannot come from newspaper design alone. The role of design is still clear and important. But not much is known about the precise effects of design on readership. That answer will have to come from research on the subject. Relatively little research has been done in this area, so much of what we know about it is conjecture. In the case of people who are too busy to read because they don't have time, the potential for solutions is partially in the hands of layout editors, and the other part may be beyond that editor's reach.

The implications for contemporary newspaper design, then, may be as follows:

1. Contemporary newspaper design is not necessarily best represented by *USA Today,* although this paper seems to have caught the attention of many Americans. That does not mean it is the best layout for every newspaper in the country. Presumably, it has been effective for *USA Today,* but that paper has radically different needs from other papers in the country.

2. Newspaper editors who copied *USA Today*'s design did not achieve the identical results. In fact, had they tried, the copiers may have been able to achieve better results with other kinds of innovative designs created by themselves or with expert advice.

3. Contemporary newspaper design seems to have had done little or nothing to increase newspaper readership in an era dominated by television. Contemporary Americans do not have exactly the same reading lifestyles as their parents and grandparents, and those latter days may never return. Layout therefore may have to change as times change.

4. Contemporary design should reflect local community lifestyles. The fact that so many newspapers have become increasingly colorful without any necessary improvement in content suggests that the whole concept of color use is inadequately understood.

5. Today's adults tend to live very active lifestyles and have allotted little of their time to reading newspapers. Newspapers do not presently provide enough motivation to change those lifestyles. Therefore, the better strategy is to find ways to create layout that reduces the amount of time given to reading a paper or to help a reader read more in a shorter period of time. Innovative layouts may be able to help here.

CONTEMPORARY LAYOUT CONCEPTS

American editors began to make radical changes in newspaper design about 1970, when many switched from eight- to six-column papers. It was also about that time that publishers were changing from editing by hand to editing by computers and video display equipment. They were also changing from letterpress to offset printing equipment. It seemed to be the right time for newspaper design to have a new appearance.

What is contemporary layout or design? The following list summarizes the main features that almost anyone can discern. Contemporary layouts are

1. Cleaner looking than traditional designs (which tended to be cluttered).
2. Simpler in structure. One of the ways in which traditional design has been converted to contemporary is by squaring off most stories. In traditional layouts, a two-column story usually had one column longer than the other. When many such stories appeared on one page, the page tended to appear complex.
3. Designed with the total page in mind. Therefore the entire page is interesting. In bygone days, only the top was interesting.
4. Noted for the use of larger photographs on the front and feature pages than have ever been used before.
5. Usually six columns to the page, whereas older papers had eight.
6. Using much more color than ever before.
7. Noted for using larger, more dramatic boxes.
8. Noted for using more graphics (charts, maps, tables, etc.).

Contemporary design consists of three new design ideas that helped achieve a new "look": modular, grid and total design. These three ideas are part of what is called the contemporary design concept. Individually, however, they are expressed in different manners from newspaper to newspaper throughout the country.

MODULAR LAYOUT

Contemporary layouts are often composed of modules. A *module* consists of one or more stories grouped together, usually in a rectangular format. The columns in a module are squared off. If there are two or more columns to a story, each column ends in the same place as the others. Therefore, one sees modules as rectangles rather than as the oddly shaped stories that once were widely used in newspaper layout. These rectangles are either horizontal or vertical, and it is a mixture of these shapes that keeps a page from becoming boring. Modules also can be enclosed in boxes.

There are three major reasons for using modules in design. First, they enable the layout person clearly to separate one story from another. There is no intertwining with oddly shaped stories as there used to be. The consequence of separating stories is to make them easy to find and read. Story shapes are simple, not complex.

Second, modules make it easy to accommodate late-breaking stories. The layout person simply removes one rectangular module and replaces it with another. Time and effort are saved: a worthwhile goal.

Third, and perhaps most important, modules enable a layout person to create cleaner and simpler page structures, which are not only attractive but very readable.

The modular concept is relatively easy to implement because it fits any type of layout style. It even can be used with traditional layouts. It may be used without any rules around it (Figure 15-3) or inside boxed rules (Figure 15-4).

The most distinguishing feature of modules is that they are squared-off stories. As such, they exist simply as rectangles that are relatively easy to replace if necessary. They need not be placed in boxes and can be positioned

Figure 15-3   Each story is a module.

THE DAILY HERALD   Friday, August 17, 1984   Section 2—5

Car flop shattered fast rise

Nightmare may finally be ending for wife Cristina

Calm judge ruled trial

Jurors bear long trial

Verdict ends long string

Lawyer open to the press

Tapes not enough to convince jurors

ONE OF THE FBI video tapes used as evidence against John De Lorean in his trial shows the auto-maker on Oct. 19, 1982, toasting with champagne a suitcase full of cocaine he declared "better than gold." De Lorean was arrested by FBI agents immediately afterward.

Informant's past gave jury doubts

Figure 15-4   Modules of different sizes.

almost anywhere on a page. When they are not boxed, they can be set apart from other stories by generous amounts of white space above and below them.

When an entire page is designed in modular form, either type rules or white space may be used to separate stories. Column rules, coupled with cutoff rules or boxed rules, can be the separating devices (Figure 15-5). If a newspaper does not use column rules, white space in columns and above and below stories may be used to separate stories.

Figure 15-5.   Uneven wraps.

THE GRID CONCEPT

The grid concept carries the modular idea one step further. Although the modular concept is flexible and can be used with almost any kind of layout, the grid concept has to stand alone as a single unit. A grid consists of an entire page of various–sized modules designed in a distinctly contemporary style. The concept gets its name from the meaning of the term *grid*, a pattern of intersecting lines forming rectangles of various sizes and shapes. From this definition one can understand why a football field is often called a gridiron. In newspaper design, the grid lines are usually column spaces and/or spaces separating stories.

The intersecting lines of grid layout are not accidentally designed; in fact, they are highly structured. They are carefully placed to divide a newspaper page into very clean-cut and simple-appearing modules whose whole total effect is contemporary. Stories are usually squared off and designed into either vertical or horizontal shapes. Furthermore, the division of space on a page is usually unequal—never mathematically equal (Figure 15-6). One cannot

Figure 15-6.   Page division with two columns on the left and four on the right.

conceive of a grid layout with three-column stories on the left and three-column stories on the right of a page. A 3:3 division of space is not as attractive as an unequal division of space. It tends to call attention to itself and not the stories. Nevertheless, one sees 3:3 page divisions occasionally.

It is also important to realize that grid *as defined in this text is not the same term as some graphic designers use. They tend to define a grid as a fixed layout format into which stories are placed. Here it should more properly be called a "variable grid," meaning that there are different grids for different purposes. But most important, the grid is not created until after the photos and main stories have been positioned. Then a grid design is formed on the basis of the most important news of the day.*

A grid may feature either vertical or horizontal styling. In Figure 15-6 the grid design features a 4:2 division of space *vertically.* But in Figure 15-7 the grid is *horizontal.*

The objective of a grid is to give a page the kind of contemporary styling found in magazines, books and other reading materials. It makes a page look interesting. Furthermore, the layout personnel have complete control of page design. Pages don't look as if they had been designed accidentally. The page is never top-heavy as it may be in traditional design. But story placement is still based on the importance of each story: More important stories still get featured treatment. The main difference, however, between grid and traditional layout is that all stories have an opportunity of being seen in grid layout, something that may or may not be true in traditional layout.

An obvious limitation of the grid concept and contemporary layout is that readers could tire of rectangular stories. Although many alternative grid designs could be used, there may be a tendency to overuse a few designs.

THE TOTAL DESIGN CONCEPT

The total design concept is simply an extension of modular and grid concepts wherein the entire page is made interesting, not just the top. One can lay out a modular or grid design and have it appear boring and even confusing. But a page that uses total design principles should be ultrasimple and yet dramatic.

What makes a modular or grid design dramatic? The answer: Careful planning of a page to maximize dramatic possibilities. Large pictures, large boxes, the use of color and dramatic headlines will not of themselves make a page dramatic. But their positioning on a page may do so. That is what takes planning.

The following ideas are guidelines to total design:

1. Careful space division on a page is the one important key to this concept. No page should be divided into halves either vertically or horizontally. In other words, page balance will always be informal. This practice tends to create interesting pages.
2. The entire page is important—not just the top. The objective is to encourage readers to read everything on a page. Traditional page designers did not care much about the bottoms of pages.

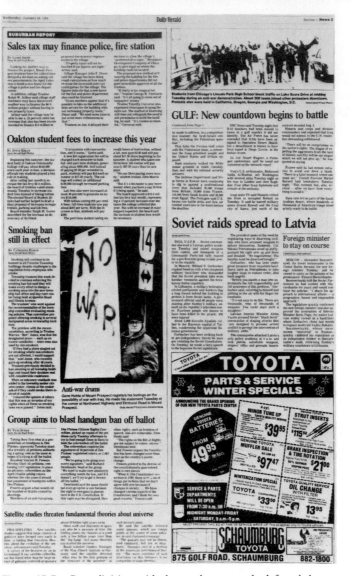

Figure 15-7.   Page division with three columns on the left and three on the right. The box on the left is a technique used to divert attention from the evenly split page.

3.   As always, however, the most important stories must be positioned to achieve "maximum readership." Because this will be at or near the top in many instances, the page will be laid out around the main stories and pictures. Once these key stories and photos have been placed, the remainder of a page is dummied in a dramatic style.

4.   Page layout persons should have in the backs of their minds ideas on how to design the remainder of a page *around* the important stories/photos.

5. Pages will have almost all stories squared off. Therefore a page will consist of various kinds of rectangles that look attractive relative to one another.

6. Usually there will be no less than five stories and no more than about 12 stories to a front page. Exceptions, of course, will occur. News summaries can take up the slack of the many stories that once appeared on the front page.

7. A generous amount of white space should appear between columns, such as no less than 1 pica of space. Also, the space between one story above and the next one below should be no less than 1 pica.

8. The test of whether the total design has been attained is when the entire page is not only interesting but inviting to readers.

SPECIAL CONSIDERATIONS IN CONTEMPORARY DESIGN

TOP-HEAVY PAGE DESIGNS

The subject of top-heavy page designs was first presented in Chapter 14 under the subject of "balance." Top-heavy pages are created by layout personnel who place all important stories at the top. Since this chapter covers contemporary layout, it is important to discuss the subject again because it has both good and bad layout implications.

It is reasonable for layout editors to place all important stories at the top because it is a way to tell readers where to find them.

Specifics of Traditional and Contemporary Layout

Some newspaper editors in this country still lay out their newspapers in a traditional manner, with many characteristics identified with the past. Although there was no single traditional layout, it is important to know in what ways most traditional layouts differ from contemporary layouts. The table below shows the main differences:

TRADITIONAL LAYOUT	CONTEMPORARY LAYOUT
a. Nameplates were almost always at the top of a page.	a. Nameplates may be moved around near the top.
b. All important stories were placed at the top of a page.	b. Important stories may appear anywhere on the page, though many appear at the top.
c. Large headlines appeared at the top.	c. Large headlines may appear anywhere on a page.
d. Front-page datelines had rules above and below them.	d. Many datelines have only one rule, either above or below them.

e. Stories were wrapped unevenly from one column to the next.

e. Stories are squared off at bottom in adjacent columns.

f. Many photographs were small and usually appeared at the top of a page.

f. Photgraphs tend to be larger and more dramatic. They may be placed anywhere on a page.

g. Almost all headlines had many decks.

g. Stories have only one deck, occasionally two.

h. Front pages usually had more than 10 stories on them. Some had 20.

h. Front pages have longer and fewer stories. Some have only five or six stories.

i. Many type rules were used. There were cutoff rules, finish dashes, jim dashes, etc.

i. Most type rules have been eliminated. Cutoff rules are used occasionally.

j. The bottoms of pages tended to be gray and dull.

j. The bottoms of pages are often as interesting as the tops.

k. Pages looked dark and tight because columns were very close together, often only 3 points apart.

k. Pages look open and light because columns are at least a pica apart.

That is why the practice has been continued for so many years. But it also has negative consequences.

This practice tends to "condition" readers to look mostly at the top of a page because they assume that there is little of importance at the bottom. "Conditioned response" is a term used by behavioral psychologists to mean the fixed habit that develops when a certain behavior is repeated often enough. The evidence for such conditioning comes from a great deal of newspaper readership research, which shows that the tops of pages received much larger percentages of readership than did the bottoms. The *Continuing Studies of Newspaper Readership,* made in the 1950s, clearly showed the power of the tops of pages versus the bottoms.

The problem is that readers often don't have time to read the bottom, and thereby miss some stories. There also isn't enough space at the top for all important stories. Some will have to be placed lower on the page. It would be detrimental to readers for them to miss a story simply because it had been placed at or near the bottom.

The solution to the problem is to get into the habit of placing some important stories at different places on a page. How will readers recognize important stories that are not placed at the top? Simply by their design treatment. Large or boldface headlines or boxed stories both help.

THE KEY GRID LINES

One of the most important artistic keys to contemporary design is the use of a column of white space to divide a page vertically into two uneven divisions such as two columns on the left and four on the right. The same idea can be used to divide a page horizontally through the use of bands of white space that cut across the page (see Figures 15-6 and 15-7).

These spaces work because each space clearly divides a page. The vertical division may run from the nameplate to the bottom, and the horizontal may run all the way across a page. These space divisions tend to simplify page structure.

In newspaper layout of a bygone age, the practice of dividing pages in this manner was frowned upon because it was feared that such divisions would cut a page into two distinct segments. But layout persons then did not realize that readers tend to perceive such page divisions not as two separate segments, but as one. That is because the human mind has a strong tendency to pull together the elements of objects seen at the same time. Of course, in the days of an 8-column newspaper such a division may indeed have been pronounced enough to affect page structure.

So these columns of space help implement the design. They not only simplify design, but they bring order to a page that tends to become complex because it contains stories and photographs of many different shapes. Of course, pages can be designed without these spaces, but they are rarely as simple or orderly as those using key grid lines.

OTHER CONTEMPORARY FEATURES

Other practices differentiate the traditional from the contemporary newspaper layout. Some are the result of major editorial policy and can be changed only by those in top authority, such as a publisher or an editor. Others, however, are within the province of the layout editor, who daily has the option of using traditional or contemporary treatments of editorial material.

ELIMINATION OF COLUMN RULES

One distinguishing feature of contemporary design is the elimination of column rules from the newspaper. The purpose is to bring more light (or white space) into the page and to make the page cleaner looking. Column rules simply add blackness to the page even though they separate the columns. But the additional white space not only separates the columns but makes the page more inviting to the reader because it appears less black.

In eliminating column rules, editors did not simply replace a 6-point hairline rule with 6 points of white space. They added more white space so that the columns were more clearly separated. The minimum amount of white space between columns seems to be 9 points, but more is preferred. The better-designed newspapers use no less than 12 points of white space and many use more.

Recently there has been a modest trend to using more column rules. If it continues, it will tend to add weight and clutter to a page.

Figure 15-8.   Use of many type rules on one page. Are there too many rules?

FEWER COLUMNS TO A PAGE

To gain more white space, editors who use contemporary layout have reduced the number of columns to a page from eight to as few as four (see Figure 15-5), which releases more space to be used between columns than was formerly possible. In contemporary layout it is not unusual to find some pages with 14 to 18 points of space between columns.

Another benefit of reducing the number of columns to the page is that the body type is made more readable because the line widths are increased. From a standard 11-pica width, some newspapers have increased the column widths to more than 14 picas. SAU widths are now $12\frac{1}{4}$ picas. An SAU is a standard advertising unit used for selling newspaper advertising. There are 36 different sized units for selling ads in a broadsheet newspaper.

On the inside pages, the reduced number of columns has proved to be harder to work with because advertising often is sold on the basis of a narrower column width. Some newspapers use the wider column widths for news and narrower column widths for advertisements. The layout of such pages may be difficult because of the differences in measures.

LIMITED USE OF CUTOFF RULES

The cutoff rule is used sparingly in contemporary layout. Wherever possible, white space should be substituted for a cutoff rule. When this is done, a bit more space is used so that the reader will clearly understand that two stories near each other are not related in any way. But there are certain times, especially when the page is crowded, that a cutoff rule is necessary. In such a case, the layout editor should not hesitate to use it. To clarify pages, some editors are using more cutoff rules more than they formerly did.

HEADLINE STYLES IN CONTEMPORARY LAYOUT

The flush-left headline is used almost exclusively in contemporary makeup. Droplines, inverted pyramids, centered heads and hanging indentions are styles of the past. Flush left is preferred because it is free-form in appearance, a distinctly modern style, and because it is so easy to set on the phototypesetting machines. On the other hand, each of the *other* three styles of headlines mentioned look old-fashioned and tend to call attention to themselves because of their unusual shapes.

Three other headline styles are sometimes considered contemporary. Each may serve a special purpose, so they are rarely used extensively. They are kickers, hammerheads and wickets.

A *kicker* is a line of type placed immediately above a main headline (see Figure 15-9). The purpose is to provide a quick summary of some outstanding

2 buildings confiscated
West Side drug ring broken up

Figure 15-9.   A kicker headline, underscored. Note that the kicker is set in roman type, but the line underneath is in italic.

'Miss' or 'Mrs.' preferred

Poll suggests majority of women want traditional designation, not 'Ms.'

Figure 15-10.   A reverse kicker, sometimes called a wicket.

feature of the story below, in addition to the summary provided by the main head. Kickers should be one-half the point size of the headline below. A 48-point headline should have a 24-point kicker. Also, the kicker line should be at least half the width of the line below. If it is too short, it will create an ugly gap of white space at the right side of the headline. If it is too long, it will detract from the headline.

A *hammerhead* is a one- or two-word kicker that is set in very large type to attract attention to the story (see Figure 15-10). Hammerheads stand out easily on a page. Hammerheads are sometimes called wickets. A *wicket* (sometimes called a reverse kicker) is a kicker that is set larger than the line below it (see Figure 15-11). Hammerheads usually are set in very large type.

The disadvantages of using a kicker, hammerhead or wicket may outweigh the advantages. The danger is that these devices may call too much attention to themselves. If more than one of these are used on a page, the effect may be a series of white holes that tend to destroy the page unity. As an alternative to these headline treatments, makeup persons could use a boxed story or have headlines set to the right or in the center of a story. These are contemporary treatments that accomplish the same task but do not call too much attention to themselves.

23-19
Bears amaze fans, 'Skins

Figure 15-11.   The words "23-19" are a hammerhead.

BODY COPY SET FLUSH LEFT, RAGGED RIGHT

One of the most dramatic design treatments is a column of body type set flush left, ragged right (Figure 15-12). Like the flush left headline, its free-form structure gives a page the kind of contemporary appearance found in modern furniture, swimming pools and architecture. The use of one such column to a page also provides pleasant contrast to the remainder of the type,

Figure 15-12. Flush left type in outer columns, and justified both sides in inner columns. Note the generous use of white space between columns. It helps make the page readable.

which is justified on both sides. Finally, such type allows more white space into the page than the flush left and flush right columns and this results in a cleaner-looking page. However, the layout person should take care not to overdo the use of the flush-left, ragged-right style of column. When the entire page is set this way, the charm and elegance of the style may be lost because there is too much of it. It is also useful to know that more leading may be required to make the lines easier to read. When they are set solid, they seem to be crowded. With the addition of even a 1-point lead per line, they appear to be easier to read.

SUBHEADS IN LAYOUTS

In traditional forms of layout, long gray columns were often broken by the use of boldface paragraphs. Perhaps every fourth or fifth paragraph might be set boldface and indented one en on each side to minimize the effect of the boldness. It is true that such pages never became masses of dull grayness. On the other hand, they did become full of spots that distracted the reader somewhat and also made the page look too bold.

The contemporary practice is to use subheads to replace boldface paragraphs. A subhead is usually a three- or four-word summary of an important fact in a paragraph immediately below it. About every fourth or fifth paragraph after the lead should have a subhead. However, there is no rule requiring them to be at any precise places in a story. They should be placed wherever they look best in breaking up a long gray mass of reading matter (see Figure 15-13).

The best way to use subheads is to set them flush left, keeping them consistent with the main headline styles. Then, too, they should be set in boldface italic, boldface sans serif, or any distinctly contrasting typeface. Because these lines will be so short and appear so infrequently, they will not glare at the reader as the boldface does. In some newspapers, editors have set subheads flush right rather than flush left with apparent success. Centered subheads tend to look old-fashioned, however.

Another acceptable form of subhead is a boldface read-in of the first two or three words in selected paragraphs. This form of head looks fairly attractive, but not so attractive as a free-standing head that might require 2 points of space above and below it.

Some editors have tried using various-sized dots or bullets at the beginning of a paragraph to break up large gray masses of type. Instead of allowing the usual 1-em paragraph indention, the editor places a dot in the indented space. The effect, however, is to call attention to the dot. In fact, dots are sometimes used to help the reader find paragraphs that are more significant than others. So the makeup editor might place a dot before key paragraphs. But neither technique is as adequate as the use of subheads (Figure 15-14).

WHAT TO DO WITH EARS

In the earlier discussion of nameplates, it was suggested that the ears be eliminated by moving the nameplate either to the left or right side of the page and

With the fall of the Berlin Wall, le Carre spies come in from cold

The Los Angeles Times

LOS ANGELES — How a mellow-voiced officer in the British Foreign Office named David Cornwell became John le Carre he says he no longer remembers at all. It is French for "the square," as in the village square, which is no help at all, except that it does have a slightly exotic Continental ring.

The thing was that Foreign Office staff were not allowed to publish under their own names and that Cornwell had begun to write fiction in his spare time. A publisher had accepted his first novel, *Call for the Dead*, and, by inspirations lost to history, John le Carre became the author, or vice versa.

The novel introduced, in a fairly minor capacity, an FO investigator named George Smiley, whom the author characterized as a "breathtakingly ordinary" man, but who has become perhaps the best-known spy in modern times in books and television series, among them *Tinker, Tailor, Soldier, Spy* and *Smiley's People.*

Then, as in most of the books that followed, Cornwell's theme was Cold War espionage, and the author revealed a knowledge of spycraft that could in some part, at least, have come only from firsthand knowledge. In Los Angeles recently for the premiere of *The Russia House,* adapted by Tom Stoppard from the le Carre novel, Cornwell admitted that in his time he had been "a minor spook," which is about as much as he has ever said on the subject.

"As the Cold War was ending, the critics were keen to say that it would be the end of all of us who wrote about the Cold War. The truth is it came as a blessed relief. The Cold War and I were sick of each other. The change came into my life at a perfect time," Cornwell says.

(It seems peculiar to write Cornwell. But, unlike film stars who bury their old names when they take on the new, the author continues to answer more readily to "David" than to "John.")

He had sensed the changes that were coming and was impatient to regard the later world. He had also, from the beginning, been less interested in the ideological conflict as such than in the private lives of the spies of any persuasion, and most especially in the impact of their livelihoods on the personalities.

Le Carre's newest book, *The Secret Pilgrim,* due later this month, is a kind of farewell tour by George Smiley, now retired but fetched back to the British equivalent of CIA headquarters in Langley, Va., to pass along his wisdom to a new generation of spies in training. He has been in-

Author John le Carre's real name is David Cornwell.

vited by the book's narrator, Ned, who also figured in *The Russia House* (played by James Fox in the film).

The novel is a kind of spiritual autobiography of Ned, "disturbing and almost poetic," as Cornwell says. Ned has put together fragments of love, brief affairs, in lieu of the great love he had forgotten how to give, or receive. Facing retirement himself, Ned will have to relearn how to live.

Smiley's reminiscences and observations trigger memories in Ned of past capers and the novel becomes a linked series of stories, almost novella length. Cornwell says some of the stories are whole-cloth fabrications, others adapted from realities he knew or heard about. An ironic and moving story centering on a pair of cuff links and an uncommon kindness by a senior spook, he says, did take place in the life of a late head of MI6. A source who had observed the Khmer Rouge at close hand gave Cornwell the material for the longest of the stories. The book is having a first printing of 350,000 copies.

Cornwell did his first writing at dawn before the day's work, during lunches taken at his desk, on his lap while commuting. The huge success of his third novel, *The Spy Who Came in From the Cold,* enabled him to take the plunge and go to writing full-time.

"*Spy* was written in real anger, in outrage." He was in Berlin as the Wall went up, and it symbolized for him the way the world "was locked into something obscene and degenerate."

In *The Secret Pilgrim,* Ned comments on his first visit to Berlin since The Wall came down, and remembers a small memorial the East Germans had built on their side to remember those killed trying to get over the Wall to the West.

"When the Wall came down —

hacked to pieces, sold," Ned says, "the memorial came down with it, which strikes me as an appropriate comment on the fickleness of human constancy."

It was six months before Cornwell realized what a life-changing success *The Spy Who Came in From the Cold* would be. When it was abundantly clear, he and his family lived on Crete for a year, and then in Vienna, where they leased Herbert von Karajan's house. His success has built upon success. *The Russia House* sold 550,000 copies in hard cover, remarkable for a suspenseful but essentially quiet and ambiguous study set in the first thawing days of glasnost.

"*The Russia House* is already a historical movie," Cornwell says. "It proves that you can't second-guess history. This is the decade of answered prayers. The balance of terror we all lived under for so long will never come back."

Cornwell was writing the novel in 1987 — "writing in the death throes of that age. When you think of it, we'd all been living for 30 years under the threat of mutual extinction. Now there's hardly been time for a sigh of relief."

He is immeasurably pleased with the Fred Schepisi-Tom Stoppard film of *Russia House.* Two of Stoppard's plays, Cornwell notes wryly, were parodies of the George Smiley series, notably "Hapgood," with its dizzy convolutions and it's "Who's-on-our-side?" betrayals and counter-betrayals.

For years Cornwell could not get a visa to enter Russia. Suddenly he was not only there to watch the shooting of the movie, he is also being published there — a first printing of *Russia House* of 400,000. "They wanted to do 600,000 but they couldn't get enough paper."

Cornwell's own favorite among his books is *The Perfect Spy,* with its extraordinary portrayal of the spy's con-man-politician father, Rick. Rick was inspired by Cornwell's own father, Ronnie, who was in and out of prison for various confidence tricks. But he was a charmer, perfectly enacted by the late Irish actor Ray McAnally on British television.

Cornwell insists that he is a terrible actor. He had one disastrous experience doing a bit in one of his films (innumerable takes doing what was presumably one of his own lines) and he swore off it forever.

Yet he has read frequently on the BBC, and his readings of his own work on audio cassettes are superb — better than the work of most professionals. It is un-

"As the Cold War was ending, the critics were keen to say that it would be the end of all of us who wrote about the Cold War. The truth is it came as a blessed relief. The Cold War and I were sick of each other. The change came into my life at a perfect time."

— John le Carre
About his novels

doubtedly a legacy from his grandparents. Previously he has read only abridgements of his work. But now he has recorded *The Secret Pilgrim* in its entirety. It will be released as four sets of cassettes, the first called *A Fledgling Spy* and doubtless containing the delicious story of the shoplifting royal visitor.

His second novel, *A Murder of Quality,* is being filmed by Thames Television, with Denholm Elliott playing a younger George Smiley and Glenda Jackson and Billie Whitelaw as ladies involved. It may be shown on television here and may also be released theatrically.

(*The Secret Pilgrim,* incidentally, is dedicated to the first and unforgettable Smiley, Alec Guinness.)

Cornwell is presently working on a book with a Swiss officer who spent 18 years in prison for spying for Russia. He is now free, and Cornwell has been interviewing him.

The thawing of the Cold War has clearly not deprived John le Carre-David Cornwell of material. "We've been defining ourselves as anti-Communists for all these years," Cornwell says. "Defined ourselves in terms of what we weren't. Now we're going to have to reconstruct ourselves. And we're going to have to deal with real enemies much less inviting and heroic. Ecological, sociological, the misery of two-thirds of the world's population. What did someone say? Having addressed ourselves to communism for a half-century, now we have to address capitalism."

But if some of Cornwell's spies, like Ned, have along the way surrendered some if not all of their capacities to savor love and living, Cornwell has not. He continues to work hard and to celebrate life. "If you can't enjoy this, now, what can you enjoy?"

Figure 15-13. A long story that could use subheads. The insert does not provide the needed space for readers to pause a bit while reading.

my may have felt bad about what he did, but Frances was the innocent victim.

Barry case prime example
    Perhaps saddest of all is Effi Barry's response to her husband's widely reported affairs.

January and it airs late at night on WMAQ-Ch. 5.
    ● "Call Me Anna," ABC's TV movie version of Patty Duke's best-selling autobiography, has been set for a mid-July production start—more than two years after

ance will be in Sydney on Oct. 2 in *Les Huguenots*,'
    ■ Singer **Anita Baker** and her husband are asking $950,000 for a historic house in Detroit that they bought for $575,000 and had once planned to de-

one of the two Republicans seeking the GOP nomination. "If they aren't afraid of the governor, they can give $51."
                          ■ ■ ■
    The Senate Democratic Alumni organization met last weekend at the Boise home of Bethine Church, and everyone involved

Figure 15-14.   Various ways to give the reader a pause or to call attention to a paragraph.

bringing a column of news up to the top. But when the newspaper's policy is to keep the nameplate in the center, ears probably will be used to fill the gaps of white space on either side.

In contemporary design, ears have been eliminated because they have become distracting devices that call attention to themselves rather than to the news columns. Most often ears are set within a boxed rule of some kind, and no matter how light these rules, they set the ears off from everything else on the page. They distract the reader not only from the news but from the nameplate itself. Therefore, white space is preferable to ears. Only when the rules have been eliminated and the typeface used is unobtrusive (small and lightface types) should ears be used. In such cases the ears will not tend to distract.

PICTURE SIZE AND PLACEMENT

In the scheme of contemporary layout, pictures are given dramatic treatment. They are sized larger, but that is not the main consideration. Now they are sized to be strongly vertical or strongly horizontal. The effect of such boldly shaped pictures is a dramatic change in page appearance, a change that makes a page look exciting. The reader can't help but look at the main picture and notice the difference in the entire page. Not every picture lends itself to such treatment, but when a significant one is available, it should be handled in a contemporary manner. The editor must have the imagination to look at a smaller picture and be able to visualize it in a larger size (Figures 15-15 and 15-16).

Such boldly shaped pictures require an increased amount of white space in the total page design. Otherwise the picture alone may be too strong for all other material on the page, and readers may have difficulty reading the news. White space should be increased between columns, headlines and stories as a compensatory device.

At times, questions arise about whether pictures should be used in outside columns and what directions individuals should be facing. The answer to the first question is that pictures may be used anywhere, even in outside columns, if the page is designed with adequate white space between columns. When the page appears tight because of 2- or 3-point column rules used throughout the paper, a picture in an outside column may not look attractive. In answer to the second question, it has been traditional practice to have individuals looking into the paper rather than out of it. The assumption is that when a person shown in the picture is looking away from the page, the reader, too, will tend to look in the same direction and perhaps turn to some other page. Research is not available to prove this assumption, and it is doubtful that it is true. But occasionally a reader may find it distracting and for that reason pictures ought to face inward. Most readers have been brought up on pages designed with pictures facing into a page.

Sometimes editors will flop a negative in order to have a person look in a different direction. In other words, by printing a negative on its reverse side the editor can bring about a change in direction. This may not look attractive, however, when a person's hair is parted on the wrong side due to the flopping of a negative.

Finally, there is a question about the traditional layout practice of not placing pictures on the folds. Contemporary layout ignores this practice because it started in the days when newspapers were sold folded, primarily from newsstands. Readers might make a decision to buy or not buy a newspaper on the basis of which newspaper looked best. Because only the top half of the paper was visible on the stand, it was prepared in such a way as to make it attractive. Any picture printed across the fold could not be seen in its entirety. Perhaps a sale might have been lost if only half a picture were seen. Therefore, pictures were never positioned across the folds. Now the practice seems unreasonable. Although papers are still delivered folded, they are read unfolded and the entire picture is thereby visible. The only drawback is pos-

Figure 15-15.   Strong vertically shaped photographs tend to make the page look exciting.

sible damage to a picture caused by printing on cheap newsprint. The picture may be unsightly because it is on the fold.

Another objection to placing pictures on the fold was that because the picture was a piece of art it should not be ruined by the fold. Here the reasoning is questionable. Readers seldom perceive pictures as art forms and are not upset because they appear on the fold. If the details of a picture should be obliterated because of a fold, there might be some objection to the practice. But this rarely, if ever, happens. The main and only placement consideration

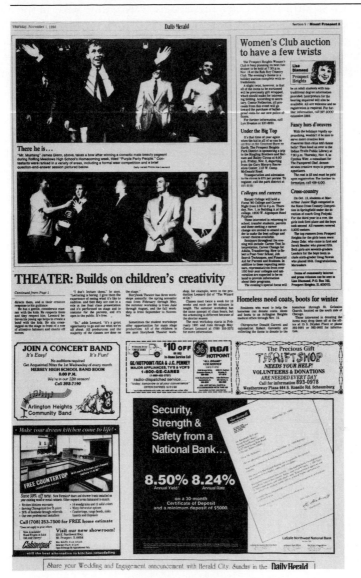

Figure 15-16.   Strong horizontally shaped photographs also help dramatize a page layout.

should be to find the position where the picture best harmonizes with every other element on the page.

ELIMINATION OF OTHER RULES

Contemporary design is recognized easily because it is so simple. One way that layout editors have simplified pages is by removing as many type rules from the page as possible. Column rules were the first to be eliminated, and the effect was attractive. Once these rules were eliminated, more white space appeared on the page and it became easier to read.

Next to go were jim dashes and finish dashes. Jim dashes were used to separate decks of a headline or to separate headlines from body type. But they were not needed. Finish or 30 dashes are still used in some newspapers, but they too have been eliminated by many other editors.

The white space at the end of the story did not confuse the reader as had been feared. In fact, the white space made the page easy to read because it eliminated one more of the black lines that cluttered the page.

Now two more rules should be eliminated if possible. The first is the cutoff rule, which should be used sparingly. White space, too, should be substituted wherever possible. Finally, the dateline rules at the top of Page One and inside pages should be removed. These also add to the clutter.

THE END PRODUCT OF CONTEMPORARY LAYOUT

The preceding discussion concerned major elements of contemporary layout practices. If all were used, and with discretion, the results would be a newspaper that looked as follows:

It would be simply designed. It would be functional. It would be dramatic and exciting. It would be clean-looking. It would be slower-paced than traditionally designed papers. Older designs often looked hectic and bewildering. Newer designs would show the effect of planning and sophistication. Thus a modern newspaper would be inviting and easy to read.

PROBLEMS IN ACHIEVING CONTEMPORARY DESIGN

The authors have examined, personally, hundreds of newspaper pages submitted to the Inland Daily Press Association Makeup and Design Contests over a period of 20 years and found the following significant problem areas in achieving contemporary layout.

1. *Cluttered pages.* Clutter means that the arrangement of stories on pages looks unplanned. Why would an editor deliberately make up a page without planning? The answer is that the editor probably did not intend for it to appear that way—but it did. Clutter is found when part of a page is overcrowded with stories and pictures and the other part is clean. Clutter also is found when an important story is buried among a group of unimportant stories. Finally clutter is found when a page has too many centers of interest so that a reader cannot easily focus on any one story because of the competition of other stories.

2. *Jigsaw puzzle design.* When stories are wrapped to nearby columns and are of varying column lengths, the page tends to look like

a jigsaw puzzle. Not only is it difficult for a layout person to plan such a page, but it is sometimes difficult for a reader to find the continuation of stories in adjacent columns. Such pages are confusing and unattractive to readers.

3. *Pages that are too dark.* Sometimes a page will appear dark and foreboding to the reader. This may happen because all the elements of a page are heavy in appearance. If a large, bold headline is used along with dark illustrations and headline typefaces that are too large for the body copy, the entire page may appear much too dark. Obviously such a page will be uninviting to some readers. No page should ever appear like that.

4. *Pages that are too gray.* Occasionally, the opposite occurs; a page is gray and consequently dull. Headline typefaces are medium to light. Pictures are small and not dark. There may not be much white space between columns or stories. Such pages are also uninviting to many readers.

5. *A device that calls too much attention to itself.* One of the most unattractive page styles is one in which a single element calls too much attention to itself. This element may be a nameplate that is too bold. Or it may be a cartoon, a four-color picture, a single story with too much emphasis on it or too much white space in only one section of the paper.

6. *Top-heavy pages.* Top-heavy pages tend to call too much attention to the upper stories, suggesting that those at the bottom are unimportant. (See Chapter 16 for a further discussion of this subject.)

7. *Pictures that are too small.* Small pictures tend to look like spots on a page rather than important visual communication. They detract from rather than enhance a page.

8. *Pictures that are square rather than horizontal or vertical.* Square pictures tend to be uninteresting, while a mixture of horizontal and vertical pictures tends to bring about pleasant space contrast.

9. *Two or more pictures that are about the same size.* When two or more pictures are about the same size, they tend to look unattractive. One of these pictures should dominate, while the others should be subordinate. Such contrast-sized pictures help make the entire page interesting.

10. *White space that is unevenly distributed.* When one part of a page has much white space and other parts do not, the imbalance calls attention to itself and the entire page looks unattractive.

If the principles of contemporary layout are practiced, as explained in this chapter, all these problems can be solved. The solutions are relatively simple. But they do require a sensitivity to the layout of the entire page. Practice in designing pages with an interesting and readable total layout is an important learning experience for any editor.

CHAPTER 16

SPECIAL DESIGNS FOR SPECIAL PAGES

While the design of a typical newspaper page is relatively simple and poses no difficult layout problems, it is generally conceded that unique designs are required for special pages such as the front page and the sports, business, and editorial pages. The extreme difference in subject matter is what makes these pages require special designs. Each has a distinct personality and presumably a unique page design as well. In fact, a special page design usually may not be used anywhere else in the paper.

Special pages pose two main problems: (1) how to create a unique design and (2) how to keep that design from losing its relationship with the remainder of the newspaper. If readers forget that they are reading the same newspaper, there is a loss of "newspaper image."

The concept of newspaper image comes from marketing, where a brand image consists of the feelings that consumers have about a brand. Every newspaper has such an image that is a constellation of its readers' opinions, knowledge and feelings about it. Editors work for years to build a consistent, likable image for a newspaper. When readers don't care which newspaper they are reading, there has to be a loss of loyalty to the paper. The reason that readers might not care about the image is that special page designs may be too different from designs of other pages in the same issue. Some editors seemingly don't care about the second half of this concept, but most do.

Some newspapers also have a *unique selling proposition,* in which a special design helps call attention to the news. Of course, design doesn't sell alone, but it certainly can make any particular page stand out from other pages. Special pages tend to stand out.

THE CONCEPT OF DESIGN DOMINANCE

Many newspaper layout people never heard of the concept of "design dominance," yet they practice it in their layouts inadvertently. It is the idea that some elements on special pages need to stand out more than others. Why? Because a newspaper often has so many stories on a page that all of them are competing for readers' attention to some degree. As a consequence, perhaps, no one story has enough pulling power to be considered much more important than any other. Yet one story should dominate. It is not possible for the design of all pages to have a dominant element. Pages with large amounts of advertising are limited to whatever is left over for news. When this space is small or irregular, news has to be laid out in an orderly manner. But there is little or no opportunity for dominant elements to be used on these pages. On a page with generous amounts of news space, the opportunity for dominance exists.

On a page where no dominance exists, readers may wander about trying to decide which stories to read. Perhaps that process ends with the reader reading little, because nothing stands out. When important news appears on a page, readers know which is the dominant story because a layout editor gave it some kind of feature treatment. Maitland Graves, a graphic designer, called attention to this problem long ago when he wrote, "Equality of opposing forces produces incoherence . . . . Without dominance, design disintegrates."[1] In other words, when too many stories appear to have equal importance on a page, the design loses its unity.

Some special pages have dominant elements of design. Sports pages, for example, invariably have something in their design that dominates, as do front pages. But other pages may or may not have dominant elements. If it is a special page, something ought to dominate.

The following material covers ideas for designing special pages. Discussed are techniques and practices that explain and/or show how to capture the special page concept of contemporary design.

THE SHOWCASE CONCEPT

One carryover from the older layout textbooks still makes sense, namely that the front page ought to be a showcase of the newspaper. Because the front page does not carry advertising, its design is free from restrictions, so that it may reflect whatever the editor wishes. Although editors agree on the showcase concept, however, they have not agreed on what should be displayed in the showcase. If one looks at the layout of most front pages in this country, one will not find anything particularly exciting, not even the news. When the news on a front page happens *not* to be particularly important, which happens on many days, it may be more difficult to create a showcase effect.

Nevertheless, editors ought to try to bring attractive design to the front page as a means of showing concern for readers. They can do this by designing a page that is not dull, one that is inviting at first glance. An inviting page seems to be saying: "Read me!"

DARK OR LIGHT PAGES DO NOT FIT THE SHOWCASE CONCEPT

Front pages that appear either too dark or too light may not be appreciated. Dark pages tend to repel readers because they *look* hard to read, and light pages tend to appear so placid that readers think they contain little important news. However, lighter ones may be the slightly better of the two.

[1] Maitland Graves, *The Art of Color and Design* (New York: McGraw-Hill, 1941), pp. 53–54.

Dark pages ususally are the result of a poor spacing policy on the paper. This means that there is not much white space anywhere to allow light into the page. There may not be enough space between headlines and body copy; not enough space between columns; not enough space anywhere, thereby bringing about a dark appearance. Headline typefaces may also be too bold and too tightly placed. (See Figure 16-1) Neither reflects the showcase concept.

THE PRINCIPLES OF FRONT-PAGE LAYOUT

Underlying the showcase concept, therefore, should be the following principles of front-page layout:

1. The layout should reflect the editor's concern for the reader so that the page is not only easy to read but attractive and inviting. *The front page should be easier to read than any other page in the newspaper.* Any device that impedes reading should be eliminated or replaced, no matter how important it may be for editorial purposes. Freaks, refers, inserts and kickers have worthwhile editorial purposes, but they often mar the page design.
2. The front page should also reflect the contemporary scene more than any other page in the newspaper. There is more opportunity on the front page than any other page to achieve this goal. It is not reasonable to place news in an old-fashioned setting, and the front page should not look like front pages of bygone days.
3. The front page should be orderly. But this does not mean that the page should be graded from the most important stories at the top to less important stories at the bottom. Other kinds of order can accomplish the same goal.
4. The front page should be distinctive, with a personality of its own. Although it should set the tone of the entire paper, the front-page personality should be one that readers like and respect because the news on that page is the most significant in the paper.
5. Readers should be offered alternative designs rather than one that is used every day with little change. Although it is true that readers may learn to like a format with no changes from day to day, such formats are not reasonable because the news changes and designs should reflect these changes. The design itself, therefore, as well as the words, helps to communicate.

THE STRUCTURE OF THE FRONT PAGE

One of the most important ways of achieving a well-designed front page is to use the principle of artistic dominance. Front pages are often busy and cluttered because there are too many stories competing for the readers' attention. As a result, readers may not know where to look, directing their attention to somewhere at the top because the largest and blackest headlines are located

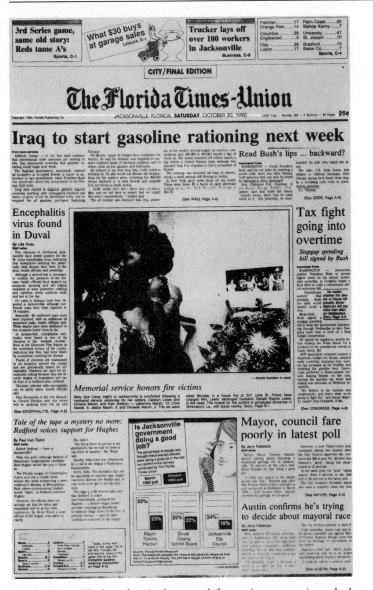

Figure 16-1. The large box in the upper left contains two stories and a large picture that dominates the page.

there. Even when a few strong headlines are located elsewhere on the page, readers can't focus their attention easily without some distraction from other headlines. In other words, the competition for attention is often too great. Another problem with front-page structure is that the shape of the main story, aside from its headline, is often not dominant. A single- or double-column story, no matter how long, does not necessarily dominate a page. As a result, many front pages lack unity.

The problem may be stated in another way. What should a front page look like? Should it look like *USA Today*? Should it have the cluttered look that many newspapers have had in the past? Should it look like the "modular" formats, with their tendency toward dullness? That's precisely the problem. Modular and grid designs can be attractive and they can be deadly dull.

To overcome the pull of competing stories and headlines and photos that lack strong visual power, editors should employ the dominance principle. To do this, they first select the story (or stories) with greatest news significance. This may include photographs and artwork of various kinds. They then combine all these elements (assuming that they are related) into a layout element that will be given feature treatment. A large box? Large type headlines? Top or bottom of the page position? Use of different style of typefaces? Even the box may require different handling. Perhaps a 2-point rule or parallel rule should be used? Spacing inside the box between type and border may be increased from 6 to 12 points. All these techniques may help. For some samples of page dominance as typically used in American newspapers, see Figures 16-2, 16-3 and 16-4. These tend to be underplayed rather than dramatized.

When one element dominates a page, all other elements will clearly be subordinate. But this relationship is very subtle. An element may overdominate a page to such an extent that the reader has trouble reading shorter stories. On the other hand, an element may not be dominating enough to keep it from competing with secondary elements. Here, the layout person simply has to develop a sense of good design. The situation demands sensitivity to the strength or weakness of an element.

Furthermore, the main element should be pleasing in shape as well as dominating. The layout person will have to use a sense of pleasing proportions to determine the shapes that add the most to page structure. Odd shapes such as uneven wraps are poorest.

Finally, the placement of the dominating element is related to its size. When a story with a bold headline is crammed into a small corner of the page, the remainder of the page may be hard to lay out in a pleasing arrangement. The dominating element, therefore, should be relatively large and placed close to the optical center of the page. To have stories long enough to be a center of dominant interest, the editor may have to create a policy that makes longer stories possible. Many newspapers have no such policy, and as a result it is hard to create front-page dominance.

NEW ORDERING ON THE FRONT PAGE

In traditional layout of the front page, the most important story was always placed in the upper-right corner. Other important stories may have been placed in the upper left and less important stories underneath. This is a logical way of ordering stories, but it isn't the only way. In fact, it isn't suited to contemporary design because it tends to produce top-heavy pages that never seem to vary in appearance.

A new ordering is based on the rotation of reading from the largest story to the smallest, where the largest story is the most dominant. But now the

Figure 16-2.   Fewer stories on the front page makes a dramatic design possible.

most dominant story may be placed anywhere on the page, and because it is so dominant, it will be read first (assuming that the reader is interested in the news content). Readers easily see where the most dominant story is located and proceed from there to less dominant stories until they have finished reading the page. Because the dominant story may be moved from day to day, there should be no fixed pattern of front-page layout that becomes prosaic. Each day should bring about an exciting design showing that the layout editor is placing the news of the day in a format unique for that day.

Figure 16-3.   A tightly spaced front page usually has very little light in its interior and tends to be somewhat difficult to read.

When reading a particular story, the reader proceeds from the top down. When the story is continued to adjacent columns, however, the order is back up again to the top of the next column in which the story is continued. The best way to inform the reader where the story is continued is to wrap it at the top of the next column, underneath a headline. The squared–off design should immediately tell the reader the order of procedure without the loss of even a second.

Figure 16-4.   A more loosely spaced page tends to have more light in it and may be easier to read. Pastel colors for tints at the top and bottom help make the page appear lighter.

PROMOTIONAL BOXES ON FRONT PAGE

In recent years, many large city newspapers have begun to use boxes at the top of the front page to promote news on the inside. These boxes fill the full six-column width and usually are printed in colors. The motivation for using these boxes has been to encourage the reading of inside news stories and features. They are supposed to accomplish this by calling such articles to the readers' attention before they start reading the main news.

Whether these boxes do what they are supposed to do has not been measured through any controlled research. Nevertheless, many editors use them because they feel that the boxes may work. However, many others use them because the competition does. These boxes take many shapes and sizes (see Figure 16-5).

THE ADVANTAGES AND DISADVANTAGES OF PROMOTIONAL BOXES

Since promotional boxes are an important part of front-page design, the user should be familiar with their advantages and disadvantages. Following is a list of each.

Advantages of promotional boxes:

1. They add color to a page. In many newspapers where layout budgets are tightly controlled, it is not easy to add more color.

Figure 16-5 Promotional techniques on the front page should be attractive and consistent with the remainder of the page design.

Yet papers with contemporary design are using more color than ever. It is expensive to add full-color halftones in order to brighten a page. But it is relatively inexpensive to add colorful boxes to meet a popular design trend.

2. They may do what they were created for: lead readers inside the newspaper. Advertisers, especially, will appreciate this because they increase the likelihood that their ads will be seen.

3. They brighten the top half of a page. When newspapers are sold through street-vending machines, the colorful promotional boxes will stand out and perhaps sell the newspaper to potential readers.

Disadvantages of promotional boxes:

1. They make the front page top-heavy. They are often so bright and powerful that they pull readers' eyes away from stories below. Even when people are reading at the bottom of a page, their peripheral vision can see the bright colors at the top. If the story being read is strong enough, the reader will probably stay with it. But if the reader is only halfhearted, the boxes will be a distraction.

2. They do not easily blend in with the remainder of front-page design. There is assumed to be such a thing as "good design" in newspaper layouts. But these boxes make it difficult to achieve.

3. They add confusion to the front page. When the front page has many stories, brightly colored boxes only make the page more complex. One of the features of contemporary design has been the trend toward simplicity, which in turn makes pages more inviting to the reader. Complexity tends to repel readers rather than invite them. The use of promotional boxes in their present form tends to make the front-page design complex.

COMPENSATING FOR THE POWER OF PROMOTIONAL BOXES

Since the use of promotional boxes is almost always a management decision, the layout personnel will have to compensate for them in some way. If they fail to do so, these boxes will distract the reader from more important news lower on the page. There are a number of methods for compensating:

1. Use bolder, larger headlines throughout the front page. This provides some balance to the page.

2. Use some larger boxes with heavier rules on the page. Such boxes may help bring about centers of attention that could compete with the promotional boxes.

3. Use more colored tint blocks underneath black type to counterbalance the color at the top.

4. Use larger and/or more photographs lower on the page.

SPECIAL PROBLEMS TO AVOID
IN FRONT-PAGE LAYOUT

Listed below are some recurring problems contributing to poor design on the front page. If the reader's best interest serves as the underlying basis for design, these problems will not occur. But because they have occurred so often, they are mentioned here. See checklist on page 357.

1. Use of a daily banner headline. Readers either resent newspapers that use a large banner headline daily or they learn to discount the effect of large type used in such headlines. They assume that what is printed is not necessarily most important. In some newspaper offices, banners are used each day because it has become traditional since the days when newspapers were sold on newsstands. Editorial policy should be changed so that banners are used only when the news warrants them. If not, the entire page is forced into a structure where the readout almost always occurs at the top right or perhaps somewhere at the top. It is difficult to create a contemporary design when a banner headline is used each day.

2. Breaking a page into two noticeable sections. When layout editors attempt to follow the principle of dominance in contemporary design, they may divide the page into two equal parts. This, in effect, asks the reader to read either one or the other part but not both. One part may not naturally lead into the other. Therefore, attempts should be made to prevent such a dichotomy from occurring.

    Whenever a page is divided into two equal parts, it tends to be noticeable. For example, a six-column page divided into three columns on the left and three on the right is very noticeable. On the other hand, a page divided into four on the left and two on the right would attract no special attention. The same principle applies to horizontal page divisions. It is imperative to avoid page divisions of 50 percent each (see Figure 16-7).

3. Alignment of elements. Layout editors sometimes have trouble noticing the effect of too many different alignments on a contemporary front page. Alignment occurs when elements on a page form an imaginary straight line. In traditional layout, alignment was easy because every story had to fit into a column structure, and columns were straight. In contemporary layout, stories and pictures may have different widths and be positioned differently. If they do not align, at least to some extent, the reader is faced with a ragged, unattractive appearance. Too many things seem to be vying for attention because there are too many different starting places. The goal, therefore, is to deliberately bring about more alignment without having all elements align. A little off-center placement adds a dash of interest and excitement to the page. A lot of the same thing becomes unattractive.

Most alignment should take place on the left side so that the reader's eyes always return to the same position. For example, it may not be as easy to read a column of type set flush left, ragged right as it is one set flush on both sides. The perfect alignment of the type set flush on both sides brings about an orderly arrangement of lines, and readers know from experience where to find the next line. But flush left, ragged right is much easier to read than both sides set ragged, as is sometimes done in advertisements. The design of type set with varying alignments presents an obstacle to reading. Lack of alignment on a page is something to be avoided.

4. Probably nothing affects the appearance of a front page more than pictures. When small pictures are used, the page tends to appear spotty and unattractive, no matter how important the news is. On the other hand, one or more large pictures tend to dramatize the appearance of the front page. If a large picture is sized to be strongly vertical or horizontal, then the page may appear even more dramatic and interesting. So one problem to avoid is the use of small pictures that add clutter to a page.

CHECKLIST OF TEN WAYS
TO IMPROVE FRONT PAGE LAYOUT

The following list summarizes techniques discussed in this and previous chapters on making the front page more readable and, at the same time, more attractive and exciting.

1. Create "open" as opposed to "tight" pages. This means adding more space between stories, pictures, and other page elements.
2. Use a large box on the page, with at least 12 points of white space between inside border and body type.
3. Use large vertical and/or horizontal pictures.
4. Mix direction of story shapes in uneven proportions: example: $1/3$ vertical and $2/3$ horizontal layout, or vice versa.
5. Use a news summary rather than many short stories on the page.
6. Make the bottom of the page as interesting as the top by use of large pictures, boxed stories or strong horizontal story shapes.
7. Avoid "holes" in the page caused by flush-left headlines that are too short or kickers set in large type.
8. Have one story dominate the page, rather than two or three that are about the same length and/or size.
9. Divide the page into dramatic divisions such as 2:4, or nonprecise divisions.
10. Avoid too many boxes, rules, or other attention–getting devices that pull readers' eyes from stories.

Along the same lines, it is important not to use two pictures of about the same size on the front page. One should be considerably larger than the other. This practice brings contrast to a page, which usually means that the page will be interesting and appealing to the reader.

Finally, it is important to break the habit of arranging front-page pictures in the same manner day after day. It is often difficult to dramatize story shapes or positioning because the news on any particular day may not lend itself to such techniques. Pictures, however, can be used in so many different ways and in so many different placements that they offer the editor the most opportunity for transforming an ordinary looking page into something exciting. It does take some imagination to use pictures in an interesting manner. For example, the occasional use of outline halftones offers readers a change of pace. Such pictures can be overused, but once a month should be about right.

INSIDE-PAGE LAYOUT

Almost any page on which advertisements have been placed presents layout problems. The only space for news is whatever remains after the advertisements have been dummied. Often the person who dummies advertisements does not consider the problems of the news layout editor. At other times, the advertising person simply cannot find enough pages on which to place advertising without increasing the total number of pages in the newspaper. This person may cram the advertisements into most of the available space, leaving the news layout editor with design problems. Modern techniques of contemporary layout, therefore, are hard to apply on inside pages.

Some tabloid newspaper editors partially solve the problem by keeping the first few inside pages free of advertising. This practice gives the layout editor more opportunities to create attractive and readable inside pages. But larger newspapers may not have the space to free such pages for news alone. To do so might cause other pages to be filled with so much advertising that neither the advertisements nor the news can be read easily. If, however, the management feels that it can spare the space, a policy can be made that keeps advertising from the first few pages.

PICTURE PLACEMENT

As previously discussed, pictures should not be placed in corners of a page. More important editorial material belongs in corners, and readers will find pictures no matter where they are placed on a page. A more reasonable approach, and one that will not affect page stability, is to place these pictures as low as possible on any given page unless they are of such an unusual shape that they could only be placed at the top (see Figure 16-6). They will get high readership no matter where they are placed. Therefore, the most important positions (corners) should not be used for photographs. Some kind of headline belongs in the corners: presumably a headline and story of significance if possible. The objective is to get the story read. If the story is buried underneath the picture it may not be read because it is in a less attractive position.

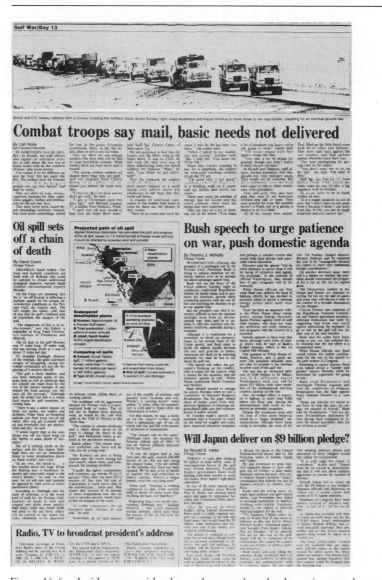

Figure 16-6.   Inside pages with a large photograph make the entire page layout interesting. The fact that photos are strongly horizontal or vertical helps the page design.

By giving a story an outstanding position, the editor may help the reader learn something significant. Meanwhile, the buried picture will brighten any position on the page (Figure 16-7). The bottoms of pages, where there is a combination of advertisements and editorial materials, need considerable brightening. Any effort to make this position more attractive benefits not only the reader, who finds the page better balanced, but the advertiser as well, because the reader will look at both the bottom and the top of inside pages.

Figure 16-7.   Moving photos down from the top brings the reader's attention down with it.

ADVERTISING PLACEMENT

The layout editor has little control over the placement of advertisements. But it may be wise to consult the advertising department about the possibility of placing advertisements in positions that enhance the design of inside pages for the benefit of both readers and advertisers. Traditionally, ads have been pyramided diagonally from the lower left of a page to the upper right (Figure 16-8). The left side of the newspaper, therefore, received most of the editorial material. This is a reasonable approach to advertising placement in relation to editorial matter because it always frees the left side of the page for news. Because reading takes place from left to right, it was assumed that all news material should align on the left as a means of making the page easy to read. Left- and right-hand pages were dummied in the same manner so that the pyramid faced the same direction on all pages.

It is just as reasonable, however, to believe that the present system of dummying advertisements is not always logical. Many readers do not see only one page at a time. Instead, they open the paper so that both the left- and right-hand sides are visible at once. Obviously readers cannot read two pages at one time but may see the total design of two facing pages in their peripheral vision (Figure 16-9). Therefore, the layout of a single page carrying advertisements should never be considered alone. The opposite page is also part of the total page design. Layout editors traditionally have not conceived of two facing pages as a single entity because they dummy only one page at a time. But it is reasonable to consider the combined effect of the two facing pages. In such a situation, the advertisements on the left side of the paper ought to be on the opposite side of the advertisements on the right-hand pages. This means that the advertisements on the left side of the page are dummied with the diagonal running from the top left to the lower right. The right-hand page is dummied in the opposite direction. Makeup procedure will concentrate all the news in the center between the two facing pages in a concave shape.

When pages are tightly dummied so that there is little room for news, the arrangement just described will not work very well. In that case, perhaps

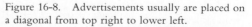

Figure 16-8.   Advertisements usually are placed on a diagonal from top right to lower left.

Figure 16-9. These two facing pages are each dummied toward the lower center. The left side is dummied the opposite of the right side. The net effect is to have all the news on both pages concentrated in one large area of space.

both pages should be dummied the traditional way; the layout editor will have to live with the fact that little can be done to make such a page attractive.

If there are at least two quarter-pages of space available on each of two facing pages, the editor should ask the advertising department whether the pyramid on the left-hand page can be reversed so that both left- and right-side pyramids decline toward the center fold. It is that simple. Where one page has about one-quarter of the space for news and the other has much more or less, the editor should ask that an advertisement be shifted to another page so that as many facing-page units as possible can be made up in an attractive design.

"OPEN" INSIDE PAGES

At times it is impossible to change the pyramid direction of advertisements, either because of the advertising department's policy or because there is little time left. Yet there is another approach to improving inside-page design provided space is available for news. Perhaps there may be as much as one-third or more of the space on a page for news. When that much space is available, the page may be considered "open." At that time a layout procedure may be used that completely fills the space immediately adjacent to advertisements so that the top of the news aligns across the page with the top of the highest advertisement. What remains, then, is a rectangle of white space that is also available for news. A rectangular space is relatively easy to use in creating an attractive page design. If the page were filled in the traditional manner, then the oddly shaped space may or may not provide the means of creating an attractive page. The rectangular approach may be used only when the pyramid advertisements do not extend much above the fold.

"TIGHT" INSIDE PAGES

Many times the layout editor is faced with so many advertisements on a page, or a few large advertisements, that there is little space for news. Either constitutes a *tight* page. In this situation, it is better to dummy a single long story in the remaining space than to use a number of short stories on the page. The long story may be wrapped from column to column until the space is filled. The reader should have no difficulty reading that story. On the other hand, where many short stories are dummied on a tight page, wraps are necessary and may be confusing because a headline may not cover each of them. There may not be enough time to reset a one-column headline in a two-column width, or there may not be enough multiple-column heads to cover all raw wraps. Furthermore, when many short stories are used on a tight page, it may be difficult to avoid tombstones. If no long stories are available and shorter ones must be used on tight pages, more than one headline may have to be positioned across the top of the page, usually an unsightly layout procedure. If the placement of headlines in such positions cannot be avoided, then they should be alternated at the top to avoid tombstones. Perhaps a two-column headline can be alternated with a single-column head, or perhaps a headline set in a roman type can be alternated with one set in italics. Least effective from a layout point of view is the use of headlines positioned next to each other at the top where two-line heads are alternated with three-line heads, especially when both are set in the same size and typeface. Alternation should provide more contrast.

Figure 16-10.   A very large picture box that helps bring drama to a page. Note, however, that the box floats in the large space. In other words, there is generous space surrounding the box.

BOXED STORIES
BRIGHTEN INSIDE PAGES

Pictures invariably brighten inside pages, but they may not be available or they may be too large for the space. Another means of brightening inside pages is boxing one story on a page or placing a boxed rule around a photograph (Figure 16-11). Only those stories whose contents are significant should be boxed. Assuming that there usually will be at least one such story per page, it should be boxed with a 2-point rule. The size of the box should be at least two columns but preferably three columns wide. The reason is that only a box of sufficient size to be noticed can create a dominant appearance. The effect of boxing a story is to enhance the appearance of the news portion of the page.

Another popular replacement for a boxed story is the use of a rectangular colored-tint background underneath (Figure 16-12).

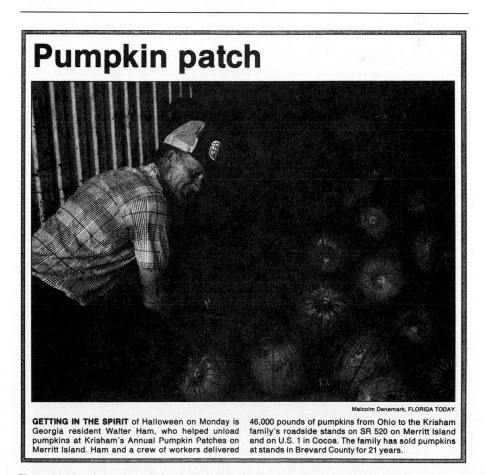

Pumpkin patch

Malcolm Denemark, FLORIDA TODAY

GETTING IN THE SPIRIT of Halloween on Monday is Georgia resident Walter Ham, who helped unload pumpkins at Krisham's Annual Pumpkin Patches on Merritt Island. Ham and a crew of workers delivered 46,000 pounds of pumpkins from Ohio to the Krisham family's roadside stands on SR 520 on Merritt Island and on U.S. 1 in Cocoa. The family has sold pumpkins at stands in Brevard County for 21 years.

Figure 16-11.   A 6-point rule border helps this box. It is in deep blue color.

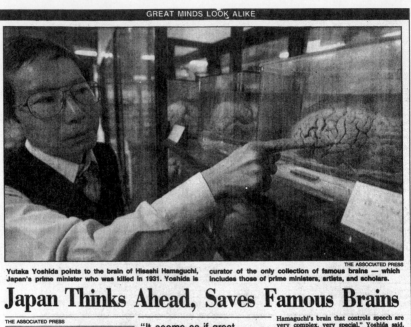

GREAT MINDS LOOK ALIKE

THE ASSOCIATED PRESS

Yutaka Yoshida points to the brain of Hisashi Hamaguchi, Japan's prime minister who was killed in 1931. Yoshida is curator of the only collection of famous brains — which includes those of prime ministers, artists, and scholars.

Japan Thinks Ahead, Saves Famous Brains

THE ASSOCIATED PRESS

TOKYO — The 120 brains of prime ministers, novelists, artists and scholars are each preserved in their own container in the University of Tokyo's medical department. It is the world's only collection of famous brains.

"We'd like to get many more," said Yutaka Yoshida, curator of the collection. "I'd especially like to get brains from mathematicians, musicians and singers."

The collection was begun in 1913, when the family of Taro Katsura, a three-time prime minister, asked that his brain be preserved for study after his death. The newest acquisition is the brain of former Prime Minister Takeo Miki, who died in 1988.

So far, the deep-rooted reluctance among Japanese to tamper with the dead has ensured that the museum's resources far outweigh its ability to use them.

"We try, as far as possible, not to cut them," Yoshida said.

University researchers have cross-sectioned several brains to allow some visual and microscopic comparisons. Most are undisturbed, however, immersed in amber formal-

"It seems as if great thinkers may indeed have heavier brains. But then, so do many criminals, I hear. Maybe they have a different sort of intelligence."

— Yutaka Yoshida, brain collector

dehyde, gleaming palely behind small handwritten cards giving the names and special qualities of their original owners.

The brain of Hisashi Hamaguchi, an eloquent prime minister assassinated in 1931, looks about the same as that of Natsume Soseki, a famous novelist who died in 1916, or of Yasuko Miyake, a writer who provided the only female brain in the collection.

"Researchers say the fibers in the part of

Hamaguchi's brain that controls speech are very complex, very special," Yoshida said, referring to a part of the left hemisphere that regulates speech and other motor functions in right-handed people.

"You can't do much research, just looking at the outside of the brains," Yoshida said. "We're obviously going to have to start doing histological (microscopic tissue) studies in the future."

The Tokyo collection resulted from a preoccupation with the differences between Asians and Caucasians, men and women, geniuses and average people, that emerged during the Meiji Era (1868-1912), when Japan began in earnest to study Western science and technology.

Japan's heaviest brain of record is that of Torasaburo Araki, a politician and doctor who left 57.4 ounces of gray matter behind when he died in 1942. Prime Minister Katsura's brain weighs in at second at 56 ounces. The average Japanese brain is said to weigh 45.5 ounces.

"It seems as if great thinkers may indeed have heavier brains," says Yoshida. "But then, so do many criminals, I hear. Maybe they have a different sort of intelligence."

Figure 16-12.   A light tan tint underneath this story serves in lieu of a box.

If there is any objection to the boxing process, it is usually that too much production time is taken. The type to be boxed may have to be reset to a narrower measure or a column of news may have to be eliminated to provide the space taken by the box, which is larger than regular-column width. When a column of news is eliminated as described previously, the remaining columns will have to be reset to odd-column measures, a procedure that usually is not appreciated because it takes so much time.

Yet the layout person will have to determine which is more important: improving the appearance of inside pages or keeping production costs down. If production cost is more important, the editor simply forces news into vacant holes on inside pages regardless of the appearance. As a result, many inside pages of newspapers are unsightly and difficult to read.

EDITORIAL PAGES

The editorial page is sometimes better designed than any other page in a newspaper. A better design can be achieved by following these guidelines:

1. Set editorials in larger type than ordinary body type used for news. If body type is 9-point, then editorials may be set in either 11- or 12-point type.
2. Set editorials in wider column widths. Although a paper may use a six-column format for news, the editorial page may be reduced to five columns, each wider than a typical news column (Figure 16-13).
3. Box editorials or stories. In order to make editorials (or stories) stand out from other material on a page, they may be boxed in either a 2-point rule or perhaps a tone-border rule.
4. Bring more white space into the page. Additional white space may be added to an editorial page by allowing twice as much space between editorials and stories than is used on news pages. For example, if the space between one story and another immediately underneath is normally 2 picas, then $3\frac{1}{2}$ or 4 picas are used to separate stories on the editorial page.
5. Place cartoons on the center or lower part of the page rather than at the top. The cartoon will get attention no matter where it is placed on this page. Therefore, it should not occupy a position of major importance. Editorials should occupy this position (Figure 16-14).
6. Place masthead (which formerly often occupied a position at the upper-left part of the page) on the lower right where it does not compete for attention with editorials. There is no value in placing the masthead in such a dominating position as the upper left.
7. Use photographs to enhance the appearance of editorial pages. This, however, is rarely done. The limited use of photographs is probably more a matter of tradition than anything else. A few papers have started to use photographs on this page, and others are beginning to copy the practice.
8. Use more horizontal layout on the editorial page. Some editors have changed their designs to totally horizontal pages. Others have simply added more horizontal styling than before (Figure 16-15).
9. Use a strong stylistic device such as flush left, ragged right body copy on the editorial page may also provide a distinctive appearance.

THE STRUCTURE OF THE EDITORIAL PAGE

Despite all these techniques of improving the appearance of editorial pages, some of them are still unattractive. There are a number of reasons why this is so. Probably the foremost reason is that the *page structure* is unattractive. White space may help a page, but that isn't all that is needed. A grid page is better than older styled layouts for editorial pages, because the grid simplifies

Figure 16-13.   An editorial page split with 50% on each side of the middle. (See Figure 15-8 for similar style page.)

and organizes materials on a page. Editorial pages usually include much more than editorials, and there is a need to organize these diverse elements. Such pages contain various articles by columnists, letters to the editor, historical notes and other miscellaneous material. A grid design will usually help make editorial pages more readable.

Figure 16-14.   A well-designed layout for an editorial page. There is no 50-50% division of space here.

Another structural problem concerns the sameness of page design that occurs over a long period of time. It tends to be boring. Some editors use an editorial page layout that never varies from day to day. The main advantage of a non–varying design is that it provides the reader with a familiar page. But that page can often appear boring, especially if the editorials are not especially noteworthy. It is therefore reasonable to vary editorial page makeup. Perhaps three or four alternative designs should be prepared beforehand and alternated

Figure 16-15.   Another well-designed editorial page.

from time to time. On the other hand, too much variety would have no particular advantages.

But the concept of editorial page layout should be based on the desirability of utilizing full layout control, coupled with a desire to personalize the page better than any other page. Editors have complete control over the contents of the editorial page, something they may not have in the layout of front pages. Front-page layout is often affected by the nature of the news, which results in designs that are a compromise between what is desired and what is most practical. But the editor does not have this problem on the editorial page. Furthermore, the nature of editorial material is personal. Editorials are personal messages in which the editor expresses the opinions of the newspaper the reader. Guest columnists tend to be personal in their approach to opinion or interpretation, and letters to the editor reflect readers' personal opinions. The concept of editorial page layout, therefore, should be based on a more personalized design than that used for any other page in the newspaper. A personalized style is warm, appealing and simple. Such design makes the page inviting. A complex and cold-looking page tends to make readers hesitate to read it. Because research has shown that readership traffic of editorial pages is often 50 percent less than on front pages, there is an urgent need to make the page more readable and increase traffic there. Presumably the editors have something to say, and readers need help to read what has been written. Some newspapers have done remarkably well in executing this concept; many have not.

OTHER LAYOUT TECHNIQUES
FOR EDITORIAL PAGES

The masthead is often placed at the top of editorial columns, apparently to relate the name of the newspaper and its staff with the opinions shown below. Sometimes when the editorial page is placed within the first five pages of an issue, it serves as the source of necessary postal information for second-class matter. There is, however, a good reason for not placing the masthead at the top of editorial columns.

Editorials usually are found near the front of the newspaper, in the left-hand column of a left-hand page. The upper-left corner of the page, therefore, is assumed to be the most important position on the page, perhaps the most important position in the entire issue. It should be devoted to the most significant piece of information on the page, which is not the masthead. Editorials are much more significant and demand top position. There is little justification for wasting a key position. If the masthead is attractively designed, as many are, it will not matter where it is placed on the page. The best placement, therefore, is in the lower-right corner because in that position it can achieve readership without distracting the reader from any other feature on the page.

Another editorial page feature that could well be buried is the editorial cartoon. As research has indicated, a cartoon will achieve readership no matter where it is located on a page. That being the case, why take one of the most crucial positions (top center) and place the cartoon there? If the position of the cartoon is fixed because of tradition, little can be done. But attempts should be made to move it to the bottom, where it will still achieve readership and yet free the top position for more significant editorial material.

Although larger type, wider columns, more white space between the columns and a cleaner page are the result, the editorial page often lacks drama because there is too much type on the page and relatively few illustrations. Occasionally a small portrait of a columnist may appear, but that plus the cartoon is the extent of decorative material. One key editorial or an important column may be boxed each day as a means of dominating the page. Sometimes editorials, although important, are not long enough to receive dramatic treatment. But often a columnist's material is. Even then, the same individual may not have an exciting column each day. But some other columnist may have material worthy of being boxed. The layout editor might select some story, editorial or column to be given dramatic treatment each day.

Finally, large initial letters are sometimes used for the first letter of each editorial as a means of making the page look more attractive. Their use is debatable. On the one hand, they sometimes look attractive if not too many of them are placed on the page. They are decorative devices. But they pose problems for the composing room. They take careful preparation in typesetting and may look unattractive if poorly done. Perhaps the most significant factor in their use should be whether they enhance or detract from the editorials. When they are too bold or too large, they may detract. If there is not enough space around them, they may not look attractive. Therefore, the use of large initial letters as a makeup device must be considered of undetermined value (Figure 16-16).

SPORTS PAGES

The most exciting pages in a newspaper ought to be the sports pages because almost all the pictures show people in action. Unfortunately, such is not often the case. Sports page layout has seldom shown much imagination or drama even though it is easier to bring about such results there than anywhere else in the newspaper.

First, sports pages need good organization. Nothing destroys the design of a page more than a number of interesting sports stories thrown about carelessly on a page. Modular grid design provides a simple solution to the problem, if properly used. Every story on that page has an opportunity to be read. Yet every story is drama-packed not only because of the headlines and pictures, but because of the page design.

Second, sports pages need powerful pictures, and these are usually available. Note the difference between Figure 16-16 and Figure 16-17. Some will need enlarging and others sharp cropping. But such pictures should not be small or cluttered on a page. Figure 16-17 is an example of a page that shows the power of large, dramatically sized pictures. The picture editor has to be aware of the opportunities afforded by such pictures, and the layout editor has to incorporate them into an interesting design on a sports page.

Finally, although large pictures help make a sports page exciting, they are not enough. The entire page needs to be considered. Often, only the top of such pages is interesting, while the bottom fades out. However, Figure 16-18 and 16-19 show that both the top and bottom of a sports page can be interesting. A large boxed story placed at the bottom may help make the entire page interesting.

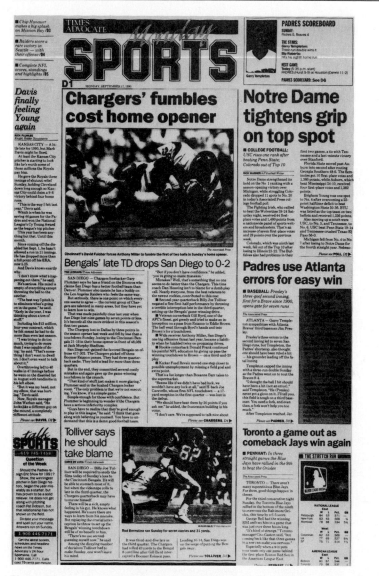

Figure 16-16.   A sports page with relatively small illustrations. Larger photographs are often used on sports pages.

Figure 16-17.   An extraordinary sports photograph. But is this photo too large?

Figure 16-18. A large and smaller photograph provide interest at both top and bottom of the page.

Figure 16-19.   Two sports photos, but of contrasting sizes.

THE LIFESTYLE PAGE

The proper concept of lifestyle pages generally has been unclear. The basic idea has been to present news and features of interest to women in a distinctly feminine style. To implement that idea, a style of layout was devised that used lighter typefaces for headlines and body copy and perhaps a bit more space between the columns. Column rules were sometimes eliminated on these pages to help lighten the page. This concept, however, was really inadequate to fulfill the need for feminine design; the only change from the layout of other pages in the same issue was the lightness of the pages. But lightness is hardly the most significant dimension needed for communicating with women, who are often sensitive to good design. Women's facial makeup, hair, clothes, homes and gardens all express sensitivity to some or large proportions of contemporary design. In other words, lifestyle's page layout must still be radically changed to be more in line with the contemporary frame of reference in which women tend to think. Of course many women object to the whole concept of writing pages devoted exclusively to women's interests, preferring a nonsexist approach.

The use of lightface types for headlines often results in rather ugly pages. Simply because a typeface is light rather than bold does not make it feminine. Furthermore, the widespread use of italic, script or cursive typefaces on lifestyle pages is intended to bring about a feminine appearance. But some of these typefaces are so grotesque they defeat the goal. For example, Lydian Cursive, Brush Script, Coronet or Mandate are types that, although different from roman faces, are not necessarily attractive on lifestyle pages. They are too ornate and are more suited for advertising. Ultra Bodoni Italic, Bodoni Book Italic, Cheltenham Light or Medium Italic and Century Italic also are not feminine. Garamond or Caslon Italic may be appropriate, but they lack charm in bolder versions and neither is a contemporary type style. Contemporary styles are noted for their extended appearance and their use of ultrafine serifs coupled with contrasting heavier elements (see Figure 16-20). Although headline types can help achieve a feminine styling, more than typeface selection is needed.

A number of newspapers, mostly the larger ones, have felt the need for change and have designed lifestyle pages that make them radically different from what they were before. They have adopted a newer concept, which is to make the page appear charming and dramatic rather than feminine. A page may appear feminine and yet may be in poor taste or lack charm. The newer concept has been implemented with bold and imaginative planning.

The most important means of implementing this new concept is to design, rather than make up, pages. In other words, pages are not dummied as they have been traditionally—they are designed with the total page concept in mind. Because much of the material appearing on lifestyle pages is advance or time copy that can be set before the current news, there is usually time to design a page rather than build it piece by piece. But the design task is of such major importance that sometimes newspapers hire persons with strong commercial art backgrounds to create the lead lifestyle page. Unless the layout editor is capable of creating a dramatic, imaginative design, it should be left to experts. Young persons who are now becoming layout editors may have the kind of sensitivity and ability to design such pages.

Rather than using a total page design concept of dramatic appearance, some papers use four-color printing to further enhance the page. But color added to unimaginative design does not achieve the goal of the newer concept. In fact, it calls the inadequacy of design to the attention of readers.

It is important to note that lifestyle pages in smaller circulation newspapers have a somewhat different editorial concept that affects page design. In larger newspapers, such pages tend to be devoted to more feature articles

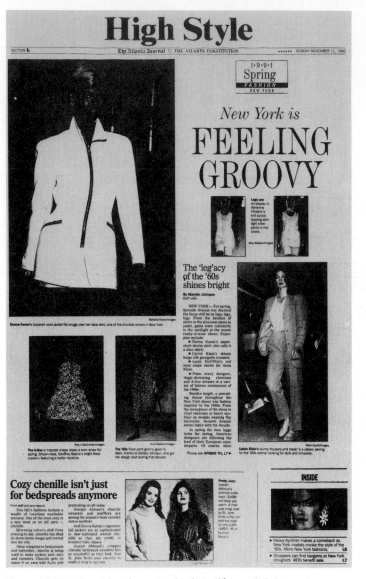

Figure 16-20.   Special style section lends itself to stylish layout.

dealing with homes, family and living. These articles are relatively long and are given adequate space on a page to make them look attractive. In smaller newspapers, a lifestyle page is more an omnibus of news *and* features of interest mostly to women. Smaller newspapers tend to devote more space to engagements and wedding announcements, with appropriate photographs. Such pages pose problems to the layout person.

Generally, the principles of good contemporary design apply to lifestyle pages as well as to any other page. This includes the use of large boxes, large photographs and modular design among others.

OTHER SPECIAL PAGES

Other special pages ought to achieve a distinctive layout that relates to the stories they carry. If a special page carries a story of great significance, a dominating illustration may be used as the basis for the design. This is shown in Figure 16–21. The story is about a man who has not been identified despite many articles written about him. Thus the main design element is the

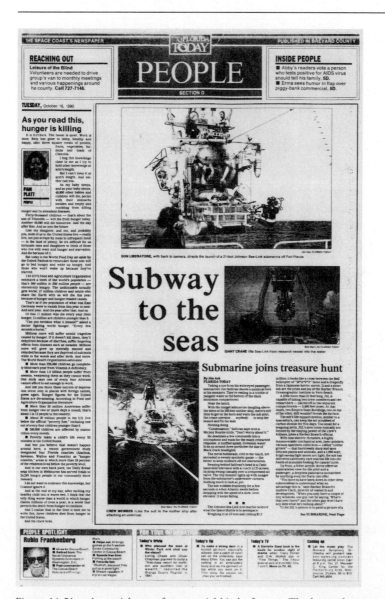

Figure 16–21.   A special page for a special kind of news. The large photograph is a major part of the effect sought by the layout person.

photograph that gives readers an opportunity to get involved in solving the mystery. Whether the photograph accomplishes that function alone or in conjunction with the accompanying story is debatable.

Drama on special pages is important. The design concept of Figures 16-22 and 16-23 is based on human interest stories that are given feature treatments. They take up much space, and they are given generous amounts of white space for the stories to stand out. Large illustrations help bring the story subjects into clearer focus for readers.

Figure 16-22.   A large feature story dominates a special page.

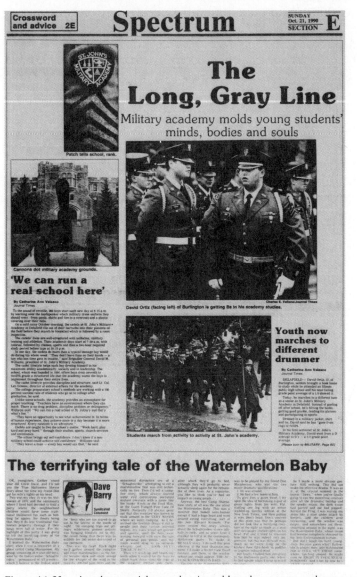

Figure 16-23.   Another special page dominated by a large story and accompanying photographs.

BOTTOMS OF SPECIAL PAGES
NEED BRIGHTENING

Because the bottoms of inside pages lack news space, the layout editor tends to allow them to disintegrate. To whatever extent the bottoms of pages can be brightened, they should be. Pictures, horizontally made-up stories and boxes can help accomplish the job if the space is there. Even when the only editorial space available is a "well" between two ads, the editor can use a one-column picture at the bottom to help brighten the page.

BOXES OR PICTURES
WITH ROUNDED CORNERS

Occasionally, to offer the reader a change of pace in design, the editor will round off the corners of pictures or boxes. The effect is novel and interesting if not overdone. When used occasionally, it tends to brighten the page. When overused, it loses whatever novelty it has and may be ignored by readers.

POSITIONING OF
COLUMNISTS' ARTICLES

Traditionally, columnists' articles are positioned in the same section of the newspaper every day so that readers will know where to find them. But they need not be placed in or near major sections. If the columnist has a loyal following, chances are that readers will search for the column no matter where it appears. The main sports column is often placed in the most favorable position. It robs the more exciting sports stories because they must be placed in less conspicuous positions. The main columnist should be given a less favorable position to prevent this from happening. Readers will not avoid reading the column.

DATELINES AND FOLIOS

One way to help modernize inside pages is to eliminate datelines, folios and accompanying rules that traditionally have appeared at the tops of inside pages. They not only waste space, but they look old-fashioned. If the space occupied by the dateline (including the rule and some white space underneath) is 2 picas, as it often is, then multiplying that by 6 (for the six-column page) equals 12 picas of wasted space per page. If that same issue has 84 pages in it, then it wastes 1008 picas (12 × 84) or 168 inches (about a full page) each day.)

Datelines cannot be eliminated entirely from pages where advertisements appear because they must be included in the tearsheets sent to the advertisers as proof of publication. But datelines can be shortened to one- or two-column widths and condensed into not more than three lines. The top line may carry the page number; the second line, the newspaper's name; and the last line, the date. These three lines may be placed in the first column on left-hand pages and in the last column on right-hand pages. If there is no first or last column, either because this is a full-page advertisement or because an eight-column banner headline is used, then the three lines may be placed at the bottom of the page or run sideways, but both set in the margin.

In some newspapers, the datelines are buried anywhere near the top of the newspaper in the most convenient place possible. After all, they can be circled when they appear on tearsheets. If the newspaper has an index, the page number may be of considerable importance in helping readers find a page. In such cases, plans can be made to position the page numbers as close to the outside as possible.

TYPE RULES USED AS STYLISTIC DEVICES

Laying out a page should consist of more than writing headlines or placing stories on a page. Even though the design that has been created through such practices may look attractive, it often could look more attractive if only some stylistic devices were added to the design.

One of the most common stylistic devices in contemporary design is the use of type rules of various weights to add charm to a page.

So popular have these type rules become that they are used in many different ways. Essentially all such rules separate stories on a page. But that is not all. They can add artistic charm to the layout. Whether they do or not depends on how well they are used. The following list provides some useful suggestions:

1. A few rules on a page may be very attractive, but when many of them are used, layout may be overdone. In other words, there is a point of diminishing returns in using rules for style only.
2. Heavy rules, such as 12 or 14 points, can look attractive, but their saturation point (where they begin to make the page look unattractive) comes quickly. It takes fewer of them to make a page look bad than it does of 4-, 6- or 8-point rules.
3. When boxed rules are used, they should be relatively light, such as 1-, 2- or 3-point weights. It should be obvious that many vertical and horizontal rules tend to become garish.
4. Rules may be used between stories, to underline headlines (both standing and regular heads), and between columns. When used between columns, however, even hairline rules tend to add unnecessary weight to the page.
5. Generous spacing around rules helps them appear more attractive than when they are used on tightly spaced pages.
6. They may be used around standing headlines such as those found in compartmentalized news (local, regional or national).

The objective of using these rules is for styling, primarily. Good taste in using them is a prerequisite for success.

SOME CONCLUDING THOUGHTS ABOUT NEWSPAPER LAYOUT AND DESIGN

Students who want to appreciate the subject of newspaper layout and design should remember that readers *spend very little time* thinking about or reacting to it. They write very few letters or make very few telephone calls to editors to complain about it. Some editors may get about one complaint a year, and often it will be from an elderly reader saying "your newspaper is too hard to read because the letters are so small."

On the other hand, the sensitive layout person and/or managing personnel may spend a great deal of time thinking about it. Graphic design consultants are often hired to recommend changes in design, and it is easily possible
for recommendations to become iron-clad rules that are never to be violated.
Most consultants do not say "never do that again." Most often say: "I think
this design looks better than that." That is, however, their perception. Even
the recommendations in this book ought to be approached as suggestions
in an artistic environment and can be violated if there is a good reason for
doing so. Some decisions, however, may even be the subject of controversy
between the layout personnel and management and discussions may become
quite heated.

Young persons beginning their careers on a newspaper staff should realize that layout and design is not a matter of life or death. It is simply a way to
help readers read. What is always appreciated is a rule or reason for or against
using any layout idea. The better the reasoning, the more likely others will
approve of it.

PART V

EDITING FOR
OTHER MEDIA

CHAPTER 17

MAGAZINE EDITING

THE SUNDAY SPECIAL

For six days a week the staff of a metropolitan daily writes, edits, assembles and produces the daily paper. Then on Sunday emerges the giant, the marvel of American journalism. This mighty tome is crammed with news and news summaries, interpretives and features, sports, business and finance, real estate, comics, classified and display advertising, advertising supplements and magazines.

Advertising probably claims at least 60 percent of the Sunday paper's space. News and editorials, including interpretives and columns, may take roughly one-fourth of the remaining space and magazine supplements almost one-half.

Unlike its daily counterpart, the Sunday edition has been days or weeks in the making. A closing deadline of four weeks before publication is not unusual for a four-color rotogravure magazine. Other supplements may have a closing deadline of about a week before publication.

Supplement sections have to be printed before the final run of the spot news, sports and markets. At one time some metropolitan dailies predated the Sunday edition. That is, they printed the entire Sunday paper in the middle of the week for delivery to outlying areas on Saturday or Sunday. Today, most run-of-press supplements have a one-week deadline. They are printed on the Friday before delivery.

Even with automation and high-speed presses, the production of the big Sunday edition is a week-long process involving the early closing of as many pages as possible.

LOCALLY EDITED MAGAZINES

Among the gems of the Sunday paper are the locally edited magazines, especially those printed by rotogravure. These magazines differ from the old-time Sunday supplements, started shortly after the Civil War, in that they no longer aim to startle and titillate or concern themselves with the famous and the infamous. Instead, today's magazines seek to educate as well as entertain and to portray real people close to the readers.

Although this weekly supplement is an integral part of the newspaper, it is distinctly a magazine. It is built like a magazine and printed like a magazine. It may be identified with its parent newspaper, but it has a style and personality of its own.

The Sunday magazine is more carefully designed and edited than the hastily prepared news sections. And because readers tend to judge it as a magazine and not as just another section of the newspaper, the magazine editor is compelled to follow exacting standards of magazine presentation.

Although some newspaper magazines are provincial in both content and presentation, more are demonstrating that readers in all regions have common interests in topics such as medicine, science, psychiatry, economics, ecology and religion. Almost any topic may be associated in some manner with a particular area.

For example, why would the *Denver Post's Empire Magazine,* which bills itself as the voice of the Rocky Mountain Empire, feature a story on oil in Alaska? Because the oil rush there had some elements in common with the gold rush, a part of the heritage of the mountain states. Also, many of these states, especially Colorado, Wyoming and Utah with their oil shale deposits, are engaged in oil exploration and production. But this particular story happened by chance. A free-lance photographer had brought in striking photos he had taken on a trip to the frozen North Slope of Alaska. But without an accompanying story the editor could not use the pictures. Then a professional writer offered a story based on material he had collected in the same area. The result was a well-written and well-illustrated piece for *Empire* readers.

Writing that goes beyond the reach of the routine feature writer and pictures that surpass those shot by a harried news photographer have made the newspaper magazine a favorite with readers. One survey has shown that 59 percent of female readers and 48 percent of male readers read the average inside page of a local magazine section, even topping the readership for a nationally syndicated supplement distributed with the same papers.

MAGAZINE CHARACTERISTICS

A magazine format does not necessarily make a magazine. Some newspaper executives who take over the job of editing a Sunday magazine or an independent magazine fail to produce a good magazine because newspaper techniques differ from magazine techniques. Even display advertising may not be the same in newspapers as it is in magazines.

A magazine differs from a newspaper in many ways, including:

1. Magazines use a better grade of paper, or stock. The cover paper may be heavier than the paper for inside pages. Different grades and weights of paper may be used for inside pages.
2. Magazines use more color, not only in illustrations but in type and decoration as well.

Elegance

Set in French Script
with Clearcut initial.

DIGNITY

Set in Forum type.

Antiquity

Satanick

UNUSUALNESS

Newfangle

Fluency

Mandate

Distinctiveness

Civilite

CIRCUS

Playbill

Figure 17-1.   Mood typefaces.

3.   Illustrations often are more dominant in a magazine than in a newspaper. The illustrations may run (or bleed) off the page or extend into the fold.

4.   Magazines breathe; they use air or white space to emphasize text and illustrations much more often than newspapers.

5.   Magazines vary typefaces to help depict the mood, tone or pace of the story (Figure 17-1). They use initial capital letters to help readers turn to the message or to break up columns of type (Figure 17-2). They wrap type around illustrations (Figure 17-3).

6.   Magazines may use reverse plates (white on black) or use display type over the illustration (overprinting) for display heading or even text.

7.   Magazines may vary the placement as well as the design of the headline (Figure 17-4).

A WILD Alaskan wolf yawns broadly ɛ
he lolls in the warm sun of the arcti
spring. Trumpeter swans dabble in a smɛ

There aren't any weekend beer par
pus. No pep rallies. No homecomin
dormitories and no football team.

Figure 17-2.   (Top) Two-line sunken initial cap. (Bottom) Upright initial cap.

The path of time that
will lead us from today
through the 21st cen-
tury will be lined with
many new mechanical
and electronic marvels,
better energy sources, and
new construction materials and
methods.

Figure 17-3.   Wraparound type.

"The first and singularly most difficult fact for many newspaper editors to grasp about a Sunday newspaper magazine is that it is not a newspaper," writes Henry Barker, special projects editor for the *Fort Myers* (Fla.) *News-Press*. He adds:

A true Sunday magazine never will carry material that could have run practically anywhere in the paper but just happened to wind up in the magazine.

A [cover story] should be able to pass three tests:

1. Does it feel big? Does it have relevance to the lives of many people, ask a question many people ask, deal with some area of common human experience?

2. Does it feel necessary? Can readers be told why they should care about it right now? What's so important about it today?

3. Does it feel whole? Does it have a quality of compactness and unity; is it a single, solid thing, not a diffuse cloud?

This third test is largely a problem of focus, the key element to every successful magazine story. Any story that lacks sharp focus on a theme, an individual or an event will never hold a reader.

Each issue would carry . . . articles of 1,000 to 2,500 words—a cover story and secondary stories. With occasional exceptions the cover story would be the strongest, most important of the [stories]—a story with a loud ring of urgency about it for everyone in the state.

Figure 17-4.   Headline Designs.

A secondary story could be of less vital interest and contain more of a [regional] slant.

Subject matter could be anything clean enough to have lying around the family living room—profiles, perspectives on a big news story, surveys of what's new in a field, trend stories, narratives, first-person or as-told-to stories, humor, travel, fashion—so long as it passed those three tests, could be narrowed to a sharp focus and dealt with [area] people, places and things.[1]

THE EDITING PROCESS

An editor who does not understand art cannot hope to produce a superior publication. Magazine editing is essentially a joint endeavor; the editor provides editorial excellence, and the artist creates the visual image.

Front pages of daily newspapers often look alike. But the magazine comes in a distinctive wrapper or cover that reflects the nature of the publication, stresses a seasonal activity or merely directs readers to the "goodies" inside the magazine.

News, as we have seen, may be presented in many styles, but the inverted pyramid usually prevails. In a magazine the space is likewise limited, but the writing style is more relaxed, more narrative and more personal. The pace of the magazine piece may be slower—but certainly no less dramatic—than that of the news story. Here is the beginning of a magazine feature:

In Chicago some middle-aged businessmen plan a skiing trip to Colorado. In Miami a middle-aged woman with high blood pressure seeks medical advice before leaving for Denver to visit her daughter. In Baltimore a family is cautioned against vacationing in Colorado because one of the children has a lung ailment.

All three of these examples involve a change from low to high altitude, and owing to air travel, making the change in a relatively short period.

Coupled with exertion, cold temperatures and high altitude, won't the businessmen who have been sedentary for months be risking heart attacks? Won't the visiting mother experience even higher blood pressure? And won't high altitude aggravate the child's illness?

Not until later in the story does the angle that normally would be in the lead of a news story appear:

Contrary to the popular belief that reduced oxygen pressure at high altitude has an adverse effect on the coronary artery system, research indicates high altitude may be beneficial and even afford a degree of protection against coronary artery disease.[2]

---

[1] "Magazine Not Just an Extension," *Gannetteer,* March 1976 (p. 1 of "Editorially Speaking" section).

[2] Gerry Himes, "High Altitude Can Be Good," *Denver Post Empire,* March 28 1976, p. 10.

So rigid are the style requirements of some magazine editors that they lean heavily on staff writers, use staff writers to reshape free-lance material or buy only from free-lancers who demonstrate they are acquainted with the magazine's requirements. Still, Sunday magazines may get more than half their material from free-lancers, a greater volume than is procured by the news sections.

Free-lance photographers likewise seek out the Sunday magazine market. One magazine editor remarked, "An exciting roto works like a magnet, drawing in talented free-lance contributors you never realized existed."

ARTICLE HEADINGS

Typically, a newspaper uses illustrations to focus the readers' attention to a page. It relies on the headline to lure readers into the story. But in a magazine the whole page—headline, pictures, placement—is designed to stop the readers in their tracks. They may get part of the story from a big dramatic picture before they ever see the head. This combination of elements must make readers say to themselves, "I wonder what this is all about."

The magazine editor is not confined to a few standardized typefaces for headings. Instead, the editor may select a face that will help depict the mood of the story. Nor is the editor required to put the heading over the story. It may be placed in the middle, at the bottom or on one side of the page.

The heading may occupy the whole page or only part of a page. It may be accented in a reverse plate or in some other manner. It may be overprinted on the illustration. More often it will be below the illustration rather than above it. Almost invariably it is short, not more than one line. Frequently it is a mere tag or teaser. A subtitle, then, gives the details:

Oil from the Heart Tree
An exotic plant from Old China produces
a cash crop for the South

I Can HEAR Again!
This was the moment of joy, the rediscovering
of sound: Whispers . . . rustle of a sheet . . .
ticking of a clock

The Pleasure of Milking a Cow
Coming to grips with the task at hand
can be a rewarding experience,
especially on cold mornings

Industry is finding
that it pays to rely on
Models of Efficiency

MAGAZINE LAYOUTS

Type and illustrations, or gray and black blocks, are the dominant elements in newspaper page layout. In magazine layout a third block—white—is used more frequently. To the magazine art editor, white space is not wasted space but rather a means of emphasizing other elements.

The editor may use space generously around headings, between text and illustrations and around illustrations. The editor deliberately plans to get white space on the outside of the pages. To gain extra space, illustrations may bleed off the page.

Some stories are told effectively in text alone; others are told dramatically in pictures. The ideal is a combination of text and pictures, and the emphasis depends on the quality of the illustrations or the significance of the text. A picture's value, says one editor, is best exploited when it sweeps the reader rhythmically into the text. Too often, the story is adequate but good pictures are lacking, thus robbing the story of its dramatic appeal and producing a dull page of straight text.

A magazine page usually has these elements: (1) at least one dominant picture; (2) a title, preferably with a subtitle; and (3) a block of text, usually beginning with a typographical device that will compel the reader's attention to the opening of the story. The device may be a dingbat such as a black square followed by a few words in all-capital letters. Or it may be an initial capital letter, either an inset initial (its top lined up with the top of the indented small letter) or an upright or stick-up initial (the bottom of the initial lined up with the bottom of the other letters in the line) (see Figure 17-2).

Simplicity is the keynote in effective page layout. An easy, modular arrangement is more likely to attract readers than a tricky makeup with oddly shaped art and a variety of typefaces. Illustrations need not be in the same dimensions, but they should be in pleasing geometric proportions. Margins should be uniform or at least give the effect of uniformity. Usually the widest margin is at the bottom of the page, the next widest at the side, the third at the top and the narrowest at the inside or gutter. The content of the page is thus shoved slightly upward, emphasizing the eye level or optical center of a rectangle. The outside margin is larger than the gutter because the latter, in effect, is a double margin.

Kenneth B. Butler, author of a series of practical handbooks (published by Butler Typo-Design Research Center in Mendota, Ill.) treating the creative phases of magazine typography and layout, advises layout editors to touch each margin at least once, regardless of whether illustrations are used. He contends that the eye is so accustomed to the regular margin that even when the margin is touched only once, an imaginary margin is defined clearly in the reader's mind. If the illustration bleeds off the page, the margin on the bleed side may be widened to give more impact to the bleed device.

The art director must know the position of the page—whether left, right or double spread—and whether the page contains advertising. It also would help if the art director knew the content and appearance of the advertising on the page to avoid embarrassing juxtaposition. If the art director is working on a one-page layout, he or she should know the content and appearance of the facing page.

The artist tries to visualize what the page is supposed to say. From experience the artist has developed a feel for the magazine page and knows how it will look on the finished page. The beginner may have to use trial and error to find an appropriate design. He or she may, for example, cut out pieces from construction paper to represent the black blocks, then juggle these blocks until they form a usable design.

Layout is a means rather than an end. If the reader becomes aware of the layout, the layout is probably bad.

One danger most art directors seek to avoid is cluttering. This occurs when too many illustrations are placed on the same page, when the pages are crowded because of lack of spacing or uneven spacing or when too many elements—dingbats, subtitles, boldface type—make the page appear busy. The primary goals of a layout are to catch and direct the reader's attention and to make the pages easy to read.

COPY FITTING

Widths of magazine columns may vary with the number, shape and size of the ads or the size and shape of the illustrations. It is not unusual for a magazine story to be strung over four pages in four different widths. The editor must be able to estimate whether the story will fit the space allocated. Computer terminals have simplified this process because they allow exact copy fitting even before the story is typeset. If terminals are not available for copy fitting, the process is more difficult.

The most accurate manual method of determining copy length is by counting characters in the manuscript. These steps are used:

1. Count the number of typewritten characters, including spaces between words and for indentations, in an average line of the manuscript. An average line can be determined visually or it can be measured by placing a ruler over most of the line endings and drawing a line down these endings.
2. Multiply the number of lines of copy by the number of characters to the average typewritten line. A line extending half the width of the line is counted as a full line.
3. Consult a type book to determine the CPP, characters per pica, for the body size and typeface. For example, 10-point Bodoni Book measures an average of 2.75 characters per pica. If the type line is to be 20 picas wide, 55 typewritten characters will fill one line of type.
4. Divide the number of lines of type by the number of typeset lines per column inch. If the type is in 10-point with 2-point spacing, the number of type lines per column inch is determined by dividing 72 (the number of points in an inch) by 12. The result will be the number of column inches the manuscript will occupy.

The same figure can be obtained by multiplying the number of typeset lines by the point size (including leading space or spacing between lines) of the typeface, then dividing the total points by 72 to find column inches. To convert into pica depth, divide the point total by 12 (points per pica) rather than by 72.

For fitting copy into a specified space, the method can be used in reverse. Suppose the space to be filled is 6 inches deep and 24 picas wide. The type is to be 12-point. The type chart shows 2.45 characters per pica or 59 characters to the 24-picas line. Twelve-point type set 6 inches deep requires 36 type lines. Multiplying 59 by 36 gives 2,124 characters. If the manuscript lines average 65 characters, 32 lines of the manuscript will be needed.

A simpler method can be used. Set the typewriter stops at 59 characters and retype 36 lines of the manuscript. Some editors use ruled sheets so that for a given typeface, size and measure, the copy can be sent to the printer typed with the proper number of characters to the line. The typeset copy will correspond almost line for line with the copy.

PLACEMENT OF ADVERTISING

The usual newspaper practice is to pyramid the ads on the right of the page. In a magazine the ads generally go to the outside of the pages or may appear on both outside and inside, leaving the *well* for editorial copy. The ads need not restrict editorial display, especially if the well is on a double spread.

At magazines where the advertising manager determines ad placement, there is a give and take between ad manager and editor. The editor may want to start a story in a certain part of the magazine, but there is a two-column ad on the most likely page. The editor then asks the ad manager if the ad can be moved to another page. Unless the ad was sold with position guaranteed, the ad manager usually is able to comply.

SCHEDULING AND DUMMYING

No story, heading or picture will leave the editor's desk until it has been properly slugged and scheduled. Sluglines relay information such as name of publication, the date the story is to be used, story identification and the number of the page on which the story is to appear. Other instructions placed on the copy may include the set (width of type line in picas), body type size and typographic indicators such as initial capitals or italics.

The headline copy likewise carries all the information needed for the desired style, size and set and a line to match the headline with the story.

Illustrations contain special instructions for the roto camera operator for effects such as cropping or mortising. Usually the photos are numbered consecutively through a story and carry the number of the page on which they are to appear.

EMPIRE MAGAZINE   ISSUE *July 27*   PAGES _____

FORM	PAGE	SLUG	TO ROTO	TIME
	1	COVER	7-3	
	2	POST TIME - LETTERS		
	3	FRITO PG 4/C	✕	✕
	4	CAROUSEL	7-7	3⁰⁰
	5	MAY CO.	✕	✕
	6	TOSHI	7-7	2⁰⁰
	7	"	7-7	2⁰⁰
	8	GHOST	7-8	9⁰⁰
	9		7-8	9⁰⁰
	10	MAGEE PG 4/C	✕	✕
	11	MAGEE PG 4/C	✕	✕
	12	GHOST	7-8	9⁰⁰
	13	SLEEP PG 4/C	✕	✕
	14	LOMBARDI "	7-7	2⁰⁰
	15	HOMESTEAD PG 4/C	✕	✕
32	16	DIGEST	7-7	3⁰⁰
33	17		7-7	3⁰⁰
34	18		7-7	3⁰⁰
35	19		7-7	3⁰⁰
36	20	DENVER DRY 20-32	✕	✕
37	21			
38	22		7-8	8⁰⁰
39	23		7-8	8⁰⁰
40	24	HOUSE DOC	7-3	2³⁰
41	25	"	7-7	2⁰⁰
42	26	LIBRARY	7-7	2⁰⁰
43	27	"	7-7	2⁰⁰
44	28	FOOD	7-3	2⁰⁰
45	29	FOOD	7-3	2⁰⁰
46	30	JOHN	7-11	9⁰⁰
47	31		✕	✕
48	32		✕	✕
49	33	DIGEST	7-8	2⁰⁰
50	34	MOUSE	7-8	2⁰⁰
51	35	"	7-8	2⁰⁰
52	36	MAY CO PG 4/C	✕	✕
53	37	MAY CO PG 4/C	✕	✕
54	38	DANCERS	7-8	2⁰⁰
55	39	"	7-8	2⁰⁰
56	40			
57	41			
58	42			
59	43			
60	44			
61	45			
62	46			
63	47			
64	48			

Figure 17-5.   A Sunday magazine schedule.

The schedule is simply a record to remind the editor of the copy that has been edited and sent on for processing. An important item in the schedule is a line showing the date and time the material was delivered to roto (Figure 17-5).

At the start of the planning stage of each edition, the editor first obtains a schedule for the issue, showing the pages on which ads have been dummied and indicating whether the ads are in monotone, duotone or full-color. This schedule then tells the editor how much space is available and the likely color positions.

Closing deadlines regulate the priority of editing. A story may start toward the end of a run of monotone but spill over to a four-color page. This means the story will have to make the earlier deadline of the four-color pages rather than the later deadline of the monotone pages (Figure 17-6).

COLOR COPY SCHEDULE

DATE OF ISSUE ..... JULY 27 ....

Page No.	Subject	Date Received	Signature
28/44	1 KODA Kord	7-1	
1	COVER	7-1	
8	1 KODA	7-2	
12	1 KODA	7-2	
2	KODAS	7-3	

Figure 17-6.   A color schedule for a Sunday magazine.

IMPOSITION

This deadline problem would suggest that the editor should know something about *imposition*, or the arrangement of pages for binding. Imposition refers to the way the pages are positioned on the reproduction proof and not the way they will appear on the printed sheet. The printer can give the editor the imposition pattern, or the editor can diagram the imposition if the editor knows whether pages in the form are upright or oblong.

For a 16-page form, the editor makes three right-angle folds and numbers the pages. This will show Page One opposite Page 8, 16 opposite 9, 13 opposite 12, 4 opposite 5. The remaining eight pages will be in this order—7 and 2, 10 and 15, 11 and 14, 6 and 3. For an oblong form, printed work and turn, the pattern is 1 and 16, 4 and 13, 5 and 12, 8 and 9, 15 and 2, 14 and 3, 11 and 6, 10 and 7. Again, the editor may determine the pattern by making three parallel or accordion folds and one right-angle fold. Or the editor may use the following formula: the size of the book plus one page. Thus, in a 32-page section, Page 4 is opposite 29 (33 − 4) (Figure 17-7).

Figure 17-7.   Imposition pattern for a 32-page section in four-page forms. The pattern is obtained by gathering four quarter-sheets and making two right-angle folds. The facing pages total 33 (pages in the section plus one).

For a spread story, the editor tries to get the pages on the fewest forms possible to avoid tying up too many forms with one story. Understanding imposition also can serve as a guide in using color. If one page in a four-page form is in full color, four forms will be needed, one each for red, yellow, blue and black. The other three pages on the same form can accommodate color with little added expense.

Page layout usually starts with the preparation of a thumbnail or miniature dummy. The rough sketch shows pages blocked off in rectangles of facing pages (Figure 17-8).

The thumbnail dummy serves as the artist's working plan. It gives the first image of the total publication. Using the thumbnail as a guide, the artist is ready to sketch the layout on full-sized sheets (Figures 17-9a, 17-9b, 17-9c).

First the artist receives photocopy proofs for copy checking and correction. These are returned to the composing room for changes. Then the artist receives corrected proofs, which are used for the pasteup, on slick paper. All the elements in the pasteup are arranged precisely as they will appear in print. In a sense, the artist assumes the function of makeup editor, and in arranging the proofed material on the page makes sure that flaws in magazine makeup are avoided. Among such flaws are leaving a widow or lone word at the top of the column, placing subheads near the feet of the columns or in parallel positions in accent columns, or having the last line on the right-hand page of a continued story end with a period.

The completed pasteup goes to the makeup department, where a negative of the page materials is stripped in. Generally the art director insists on inspecting page proofs to be sure the makeup pattern has been followed.

At some magazines the editors receive duplicate sets of corrected proofs. One set is used to check further for errors; the other is used in a pasteup. Galley proofs used for this pasteup bear numbers on each paragraph corresponding to the galley number. This helps the makeup worker in the printing department locate the proper galley.

MAGAZINE PRODUCTION

A magazine editor relies on an artist to help achieve editorial excellence. By the same token the artist relies on a production expert, usually a printer, to help produce the best possible publication within the budget.

The editor is responsible for providing the printer with complete specifications of the magazine, not only the size of the publication, the number of pages and the press run but the use and placement of color, the number and size of the illustrations, the type area, size of type and any items that will require special handling.

The editor can save money, and make the printer happy, by giving clear and adequate instructions, presenting clean copy, editing the copy thoroughly rather than making changes in proofs, promptly reading and returning all proofs, meeting copy deadlines and giving the printer time to do top-quality work.

Figure 17-8. A sample of the thumbnail dummy roughing out the first pages of a 48-page magazine (see Page 399).

Figure 17-9a. Completed pasteup is ready for the roto camera operator. Note the instructions for flashing-in unattached photographs and for line and tone work, created for double-exposing the negative or positive.

Figure 17-9b.   Flash Tones.

STOCK

An editor should have some acquaintance with the elementary principles of production. In addition to imposition, there are two other key elements—stock and composition—with which the editor must be familiar.

Paper comes in various sizes, weights and textures. Use of the stock and its appearance determine the class of paper used. One grade may be used for the cover, another for inside pages. One grade may be preferred for color, another if the pages are in black and white. In offset printing, the grade must be designed to accommodate moisture and other problems peculiar to offset printing. In roto printing, the selection is determined by the paper's ability to absorb the large amount of ink required in that process.

The magazine editor is concerned with only three of the many classifications of stock—newsprint, book and cover. Newsprint does not necessarily mean cheap paper. A good grade of offset newsprint takes halftones with 100-line screens. Rotogravure, by comparison, frequently allows the use of 150-line screens.

The surface smoothness of book paper is determined by the degree of calendering or smoothing during the paper-making process. Antique or eggshell has a minimum of calendering, hence its resemblance to paper used in the early days of printing. More extensive calendering is used on machine finish, giving a smoother surface. English finish, next in the degree of calendering, was used primarily in letterpress. Super-calendered paper has the slickest surface of the uncoated book stocks.

Coating is a supplementary process giving the paper a surface suitable for fine-screened halftones. Coated finishes range from dull-coated, which is smooth but not glossy, to grades of glossy-coated, usually called enamel finish.

world

pleasure of it when I'm on the ground. And there is a cute little farm set, complete with the farmhouse, barn and outbuildings, a mirror for a pond and a nice assortment of animals. There's the farmer's truck and tractor, and look, he drives a school bus, too. He has plowed his fields, and the pasture land is starting to green up. The ground shows through in spots, like a carpet that is wearing out.

Here comes a train winding through the hills of a toy display in a department store. Will that little car on the road around the bend stop in time? Yes, the crossing gate is going down. At a little country airport a wee plane, like ours, is landing, and there's another one approaching in back of him—much too close. That second plane should have waited just a little longer, but it's all right now; they've both landed safely.

There's so much to oversee from up here. I just can't do everything at once. Now look at that factory belching reddish-brown smoke into the air. The sky ahead is completely filled with this ominous cloud. We'll have to do something about that. That has no place in this sparkling world of mine.

A lovely lake is nestled in the hills with some sailboats skimming over it, their wakes trailing through the water like knives cutting through the frosting on a cake. And back in that sheltered inlet is a fisherman, perhaps with a load of microscopic fish. Where have I seen that campground before, with the tents scattered through the woods where the little creek tumbles into the lake? Why, I know, that's the model Indian village we made for a display in grade school.

This miniature world of mine has everything you could possibly want. Wouldn't it be a delight to go down there and live? Back on earth again, the vantage point will be lower, but may I keep these pictures in my mind, and may I keep this joy in my heart.

There's really no place in my personal kingdom for an ominous cloud. But that'll change soon.

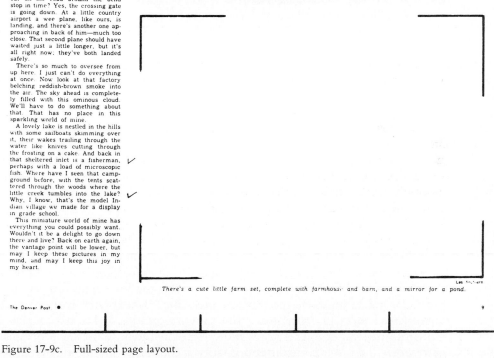

There's a cute little farm set, complete with farmhouse and barn, and a mirror for a pond.

Figure 17-9c.   Full-sized page layout.

Paper weight is calculated on the basis[3] size of a ream (500 sheets) of a particular paper. For book paper the basis size is 25 × 38 inches. Fifty-pound book paper is the weight of a ream of book paper in a sheet of 25 × 38 inches. Sheet stock can be ordered in many sizes other than 25 × 38 inches. For web presses, stock is ordered by the roll. However the paper is packaged, the basis weight prevails.

For example: a booklet is 6 × 9 inches, 48 pages of 40-pound paper and a run of 25,000 copies: $\frac{25 \times 38}{6 \times 9}$ = 16 × 2 (both sides of sheet) = 32 × 500 = 16,000 pages in one ream. That makes 48 × 25,000 = $\frac{240,000}{16,000}$ = 75 reams; 75 × 40 = 3,000 pounds of paper.

The basis size of newsprint is 24 × 36. Most newsprint is 28- or 30-pounds basis weight. Some magazines use the same weight of paper on the cover as on inside pages. Heavier cover stock may call for a different basis size, usually 20 × 26 inches.

The different weights of basic sheet sizes may cause confusion. The basic sheet size for bond paper, for instance, is 17 × 22 inches. But 20-pound bond is not the equivalent of 20-pound book paper. Each sheet of 20-pound bond would be the equivalent of approximately 50-pound book because of the differences in the basic sheet sizes.

An editor who intends to bleed pages of a magazine may run into a higher paper cost because trimming is needed on pages with bleeds.

COMPOSITION

The editor need not know the cost basis of composition (the setting of type). The editor should realize, however, that straight matter can be composed more quickly and more economically than lines of small capitals, numbered lines, various indentations (see Figure 17-3) and initial capital letters. Complicated work takes more time and thus increases labor costs.

OTHER COST ITEMS

Press-run costs reflect the time required to print the job. Here the printing process can determine the speed of the press run. Rotogravure is the fastest, then offset and finally letterpress. But gravure printing is limited to plants with roto presses and generally is more expensive than the other processes. Letterpress and offset costs differ primarily according to the number of illustrations used. Offset is cheaper when the ratio of illustrations to type is high and when the press run is higher.

The cost of ink depends on the amount needed, which varies with the grade of paper, the printing process and other factors. Tint blocks and zinc

[3] This term generally is used in describing paper sizes and weights. The word may be interchanged with *basic.*

etchings, for example, require extra ink. The cost of using color includes, in addition to the ink itself, the cost of washing up rollers and fountains on the press. If color is applied by sizing or by metallic powders, printers may charge the equivalent of two extra colors.

Printing in color entails the separation of the colors as well as plates or negatives for each color and an additional expense in makeup and press work.

CHAPTER 18

BROADCAST
NEWS EDITING

Most of the techniques suggested for the presentation of news in newspapers apply as well to news on radio and television. Those responsible for news copy for any medium must have good news judgment, a feeling for an audience and the ability to handle the language.

Broadcast news differs from other types of news in two major respects. Both radio and television news programs must aim at the majority audience and cannot, as newspapers can, serve the interests of the minority. And because the broadcast newscaster must pack enough items into the newscast to give listeners and viewers the feeling they are getting a summary of the big and significant news of the moment, condensation is required. (Figure 18-1 shows a typical network-affiliated newsroom.)

A newspaper often offers its readers a 1,000-word story and lets them decide how much, if any, they want to read. The broadcast audience has no

Figure 18-1.   Control room of a network-affiliated television station. [Photo by Scott Serio]

such choice. If the newscaster gives too much time to items in which listeners and viewers have only a mild interest, they can turn the dial.

Here are two wire service accounts of the same story, one intended for the newspaper members, the other for radio and television stations:

MASSENA, N.Y. (AP)—Unarmed Canadian police scuffled with some 100 Mohawk Indians today and broke an Indian blockade of the international bridge that goes through Mohawk territory in linking the United States and Canada.

The Indians put up the human and automobile blockade after Canadian government officials refused to stop levying customs duties on Indians—duties the Indians say are illegal under the Jay Treaty of 1794.

The Indians had brought 25 automobiles into line at the center of the bridge linking the United States and Canada, and Indian women had thrown themselves in front of police tow trucks to hinder the clearing of the roadway.

There were no reports of serious injury. Forty-eight Indians were arrested—including most leaders of the protest—and taken into Canadian custody by police on Cornwall Island.

A spokesman for the Indians called for the other five nations of the Iroquois Confederacy to join the protest Thursday.

The Indians began the blockade after the Canadian government refused Tuesday to stop customs duties on Indians who live on the St. Regis Reservation, part of which is in the United States and part in Canada.

Scattered fighting and shoving broke out among the Mohawks and police when officers tried to move in to clear away the automobile blockade. One automobile and two school buses were allowed over the international span around noon.

A newspaper copy editor might trim as many as 50 words from that lengthy story to make it tighter and to eliminate repetition. The story was pared to about 70 words for the broadcast wire round-up item:

(MASSENA, NEW YORK)—UNARMED CANADIAN POLICE HAVE ARRESTED 48 MOHAWK INDIANS. THE INDIANS HAD FORMED A HUMAN WALL AND BLOCKED THE INTERNATIONAL BRIDGE LINKING CANADA AND THE UNITED STATES NEAR MASSENA, NEW YORK, TODAY.

THE MOHAWKS ARE UP IN ARMS ABOUT CANADA'S INSISTENCE ON COLLECTING CUSTOMS DUTIES FROM INDIANS TRAVELING TO AND FROM THEIR RESERVATION ON THE BRIDGE. THEY SAY IT'S A VIOLATION OF THE 1794 JAY TREATY.

As an item in the broadcast news summary, it was cut even more:

FORTY-EIGHT INDIANS HAVE BEEN ARRESTED BY CANADIAN POLICE NEAR THE NEW YORK STATE BORDER. THE INDIANS BLOCKED THE BRIDGE, WHICH LINKS THE U-S AND CANADA. THEY CLAIM VIOLATION OF A 1794 TREATY. THE MOHAWKS SAY THEY PLAN NO BLOCKADE TOMORROW.

(Although AP style still uses the term *Indians,* the term *Native Americans* is preferred by many as less offensive.)

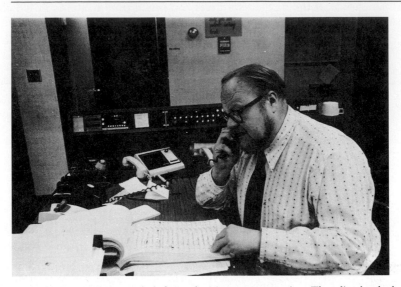

Figure 18-2.   Assignment desk for a television news operation. The editor's telephone is a direct line to a radio station newsroom. Another telephone is used for emergency messages, and a third connects with the station's mobile units. The panel in the background monitors police and fire calls. [*Courtesy of KMGH-TV, Denver*]

News is written and edited so that readers will have no trouble reading and understanding it. Broadcasters must write news that they can read fluently and that sounds right to the listeners. Broadcast news style must be so simple that listeners can grasp its meaning immediately. The language must be so forceful that even casual listeners will feel compelled to give the story their full attention.

A reader's eyes may on occasion deceive but not to the extent that the listener's ears deceive. A reader who misses a point can go over the material again. A listener who misses a point likely has lost it completely. All radio-television news manuals caution against the use of clauses, especially those at the beginning of a sentence and those that separate subject and predicate. *The AP Radio-Television News Stylebook* uses this example: "American Legion Commander John Smith, son of Senator Tom Smith, died today." Many listeners may be left with the incorrect impression that Sen. Tom Smith died.

The broadcast message is warm and intimate, never flippant or crude. The tone is more personal than that of the newspaper story. It suggests, "Here, Mr. Doe, is an item that should interest you."

The refreshing, conversational style of broadcast news writing has many virtues that all news writers might study. Broadcast writing emphasizes plain talk. The newspaper reporter may want to echo a speaker's words, even in an indirect quote: "The city manager said his plan will effect a cost reduction at the local government level." Broadcast style calls for simple words: "The city manager said his plan will save money for the city."

The newspaper headline is intended to capture the attention and interest of news readers. The lead on the broadcast news story has the same function. First, a capsule of the news item, then the details:

> THE F-B-I SAYS THERE WAS AN OVER-ALL 19 PERCENT CRIME RATE INCREASE THE FIRST MONTHS OF THIS YEAR. AND THE CRIME THAT INCREASED THE MOST WAS PURSE-SNATCHING—UP 42 PERCENT....
>
> THE NEW YORK STOCK MARKET TOOK A SHARP LOSS AFTER BACKING AWAY FROM AN EARLY RISE. TRADING WAS ACTIVE. VOLUME WAS 15 (M) MILLION 950-THOUSAND SHARES COMPARED WITH 16 (M) MILLION 740-THOUSAND FRIDAY....

The newscast is arranged so that the items fall into a unified pattern. This may be accomplished by placing related items together or by using transitions that help listeners shift gears. Such transitions are made with ideas and skillful organization of facts and not with crutch words or phrases. Said one wire-service editor, "Perhaps the most overworked words in broadcast copy are MEANWHILE, MEANTIME and INCIDENTALLY. Forget them, especially 'incidentally.' If something is only 'incidental' it has no place in a tight newscast."

Broadcast copy talks. It uses contractions and, often, fragmentary sentences. It is rhythmic because speech is rhythmic. The best broadcast copy teems with simple active verbs that produce images for the listener.

The present tense, when appropriate, or the present perfect tense create immediacy and freshness in good broadcast copy and help eliminate repetition of "today." An example:

> AN AWESOME WINTER STORM HAS BLANKETED THE ATLANTIC SEABOARD—FROM VIRGINIA TO MAINE—WITH UP TO 20 INCHES OF SNOW. GALE-FORCE WINDS HAVE PILED UP SIX-FOOT DRIFTS IN VIRGINIA, BRINGING TRAFFIC THERE AND IN WEST VIRGINIA TO A VIRTUAL HALT. THE STORM HAS CLOSED SCHOOLS IN SIX STATES.
>
> TRAINS AND BUSES ARE RUNNING HOURS LATE. PENNSYLVANIA AND MASSACHUSETTS HAVE CALLED OUT HUGE SNOW-CLEARING FORCES.

COPY SOURCES

Copy for the broadcast newsroom comes from the wires of newsgathering associations and from local reporters. The news agencies deliver the news package in these forms:

1. *Spot summary,* a one-sentence item:

(DENVER)–F-B-I sharpshooters have shot and killed a gunman who killed two hostages aboard a private plane at Stapleton International Airport in Denver.

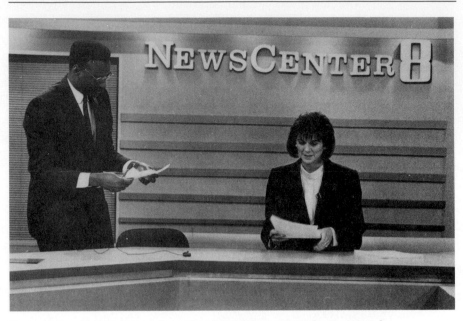

Figure 18-3.   Anchors prepare for a television newscast. [Photo by Scott Serio]

2.   *Five-minute summary:*

(DENVER)—F-B-I agents fatally shot a gunman early today as he boarded an airline jet in Denver, which he thought was to fly him to Mexico. The F-B-I said the gunman had his two hostages with him at the time of the shooting. He had held them on a small private plane for seven hours. Before he left the first plane, the gunman had told authorities over the radio, "I'll tell you what. I'm still gonna have this gun right up the back of his (the hostage's) head, and it's gonna be cocked, and if anybody even budges me, it's gonna go off, you know that."—DASH—

The chief of the Denver office of the F-B-I, Ted Rosack, said 31-year-old Roger Lyle Lentz was killed shortly after midnight, ending an episode that began in Grand Island, Nebraska, and included two separate flights over Colorado aboard the commandeered private plane. Neither hostage was injured.

3.   *Takeout.* This is a detailed, datelined dispatch concerning one subject or event.
4.   *Spotlights and vignettes.* Both are detailed accounts, the latter usually in the form of a feature.
5.   *Flash.* This is seldom used and is restricted to news of the utmost urgency. A flash has no dateline or logotype and is limited to one or two lines. It is intended to alert the editor and is not intended to be broadcast. The flash is followed immediately by a bulletin intended for airing.

6. *Bulletin.* Like the flash, it contains only one or two lines. A one-line bulletin is followed immediately by a standard bulletin giving details.

7. *Double-spacers.* This indicates a high-priority story not as urgent as a bulletin. The double-spacing makes the item stand out on the wire and calls the item to the attention of news editors:

HOSTAGES (TOPS)

(DENVER)—AN F-B-I SPOKESMAN SAYS A GUNMAN WAS SHOT

TO DEATH AFTER HE SEIZED A PRIVATE PLANE IN NEBRASKA, OR-

DERED THE PILOT TO FLY TO DENVER AND HELD TWO HOSTAGES

FOR SEVEN HOURS. F-B-I SPOKESMAN TED ROSACK SAYS THE

GUNMAN, 30-YEAR-OLD ROGER LENTZ OF GRAND ISLAND, NE-

BRASKA, WAS SHOT AND KILLED IN AN EXCHANGE OF GUNFIRE

WITH F-B-I AGENTS ABOARD A CONVAIR 990 AT STAPLETON IN-

TERNATIONAL AIRPORT.

ROSACK SAYS THE HOSTAGES WERE NOT HURT.

8. *Special slugs.* These include AVAILABLE IMMEDIATELY (corresponds to the budget on the news wire), NEW TOP, WITH (or SIDEBAR), SPORTS, WOMEN, FARM, WEATHER, BUSINESS, CHANGE OF PACE, PRONUNCIATION GUIDE, EDITORS NOTE, ADVANCE, KILL, CORRECTION, SUBS (OR SUBS PREVIOUS).

Some local stations broadcast the news in the form they receive it from the news agency. This may suggest that an announcer dashes into the news room, rips the latest summary off the machine and goes on the air with it. Although that may have been true in the early days and at the smaller stations, the practice is becoming increasingly rare because news has commercial as well as public service value. Furthermore, the many typographical errors in wire copy force the reporter to read it and edit for errors. Here is a fairly typical example:

A U-S DEPARTMENT OF AGRICULTURE OFFICIAL SAYS IN DENVER HE FEELS INSPECTION REPORTS OF COLORADO MEAT-PLANTING PACKS HAVE BEEN ACCURATE.

How about "packing plants"?

Most broadcast news today is handled by trained reporters who know how to tailor the news for a specific audience. This is done by combining items from several round-ups and double-spacers to create the desired format. Increasingly, almost all wire copy is rewritten before it is assembled for broadcast to give the listener some variety in items that may be repeated several times during the broadcast period.

Some radio and television stations subscribe to the national newswire of a wire service as well as to the broadcast newswire. That provides a greater number and variety of stories.

PREPARATION OF COPY

All copy should be triple-spaced. Copy should be easier to read in capital and lowercase than in all caps, but because reporters are used to reading all-cap wire copy, some prefer the all-cap script style. If a letter correction is to be made in a word, the word should be scratched out and the correct word substituted in printed letters. If word changes are made within sentences, the editor should read aloud the edited version to make sure the revised form sounds right. If the copy requires excessive editing, it should be retyped before it is submitted to an anchorperson.

Most television news anchors read stories on the air using a script projection system called a TelePrompTer. The TelePrompTer works by beaming a picture of the script to a monitor mounted on the studio camera. The script image reflects in a two-way mirror mounted over the camera lens, so the newscaster actually can read the script while appearing conversational and pleasant. There is no need to refer to notes.

To accommodate the TelePrompTer system, script copy should be typed with dark ink and at a specified width. Such copy averages only four words a line, so that the newscaster's eyes do not have to travel noticeable distances back and forth across the page.

All editing of broadcast copy is done with the newscaster in mind. If a sentence breaks over from one page to another, the newscaster will stumble. No hyphens should be used to break words from one line to the next.

News editors prefer to put each story on a separate sheet. That enables them to rearrange the items or to delete an item entirely if time runs short. A few briefs tacked near the end of the newscast help fill the allotted time.

Properly edited broadcast copy also should include pronunciation aids when necessary. The most common dilemma for newscasters concerns place names, many of which get different pronunciations in different regions. No newscaster should confuse the Palace of Versailles (vur-SIGH) in France with the town of Versailles (vur-SALES) in Missouri. The copy editor should add the phonetic spelling to the script, and the newscaster can underline the word on his copy as a reminder.

The wire services provide a pronunciation list of foreign words and names appearing in the day's report. The guide is given in phonetic spelling (Gabon—Gaboon') or by rhyme (Blough—rhymes with how; Like-like Highway—rhymes with leaky-leaky).

PHONETIC SPELLING SYSTEM USED BY WIRE SERVICES

A—like the "a" in cat	OW—like the "ow" in cow
AH—like the "a" in arm	U—like the "u" in put
AW—like the "a" in talk	UH—like the "u" in but
AY—like the "a" in ace	K—like the "c" in cat
EE—like the "ee" in feel	KH—gutteral
EH—like the "ai" in air	S—like the "c" in cease
EW—like the "ew" in few	Z—like the "s" in disease
IGH—like the "i" in tin	ZH—like the "g" in rouge
IH—like the "i" in time	J—like the "g" in George
OH—like the "o" in go	SH—like the "ch" in machine
OO—like the "oo" in pool	CH—like the "ch" in catch

BROADCAST STYLE

ABBREVIATIONS

No abbreviations should be used in radio-television news copy with these exceptions:

1. Common usage: Dr. Smith, Mrs. Jones, St. Paul.
2. Names or organizations widely known by their initials: U-N, F-B-I, G-O-P (but AFL-CIO).
3. Acronyms: NATO.
4. Time designations: A-M, P-M.
5. Academic degrees: P-H-D.

PUNCTUATION

To indicate a pause where the newscaster can catch a breath, the dash or a series of dots is preferable to a comma: THE HOUSE PLANS TO GIVE THE 11-BILLION-500-MILLION DOLLAR MEASURE A FINAL VOTE TUESDAY . . . AND THE SENATE IS EXPECTED TO FOLLOW SUIT— POSSIBLY ON THE SAME DAY.

The hyphen is used instead of the period in initials: F-B-I. The period is retained in initials in a name: J.D. Smith. All combined words should have the hyphen: co-ed, semi-annual. (Spelling should also use the form easiest to pronounce: employee.)

Contractions are more widely used in broadcast copy than in other news copy to provide a conversational tone. Common contractions—isn't, doesn't, it's, they're—may be used in both direct and indirect quotes:

MEMBERS OF THE TRANSPORT WORKERS UNION IN SAN FRAN- CISCO SAY IF THE MUNICIPAL STRIKE DOESN'T BEGIN LOOK- ING LIKE A GENERAL STRIKE BY THIS AFTERNOON, THEY'LL RE- CONSIDER THEIR SUPPORT OF THE WALK-OUT. THE REFUSAL BY

DRIVERS TO CROSS PICKET LINES SET UP BY STRIKING CRAFT UNIONS HAS SHUT DOWN MOST TRANSPORTATION IN THE CITY.

Good broadcast writers, however, avoid contractions when they want to stress verbs, especially the negative: "I do not choose to run" instead of "I don't choose to run."

Even in broadcast copy, contractions should not be overworked. Nor should the awkwardly contrived ones be attempted. The result would be something like this:

IT'S POSSIBLE THERE'S BEEN A MAJOR AIR DISASTER IN EUROPE.

A BRITISH AIRLINER WITH 83 PERSONS ABOARD DISAPPEARED DURING THE DAY AND IS CONSIDERED CERTAIN TO'VE CRASHED IN THE AUSTRIAN ALPS.

APPARENTLY NO SEARCH'LL BE LAUNCHED TONIGHT. THERE'S NO INDICATION OF WHERE THE AIRCRAFT MIGHT'VE GONE DOWN.

QUOTATION MARKS

The listener cannot see quotation marks. If the reporter tries to read them into the script—"quote" and "end of quote"—the sentence sounds trite and stilted. It is easier and more natural to indicate the speaker's words by phrases such as "and these are his words," "what he called,"' "he put it in these words," "the speaker said." Direct quotations are used sparingly in the newscast. If they are necessary, they should be introduced casually and the source should precede the quotation:

THE SOVIET NEWS AGENCY TASS SAID TODAY THAT SOVIET SCIENTISTS WERE AWARE OF AN IMPENDING EARTHQUAKE THIS MONTH IN CENTRAL ASIA FIVE DAYS BEFORE IT HAPPENED. . . .

THE NEWS AGENCY SAID, IN THESE WORDS, "AT THAT TIME, A CONNECTION WAS FIRST NOTICED BETWEEN THE GAS-CHEMICAL COMPOSITION OF ABYSSAL (DEEP) WATERS AND UNDERGROUND TREMORS."

Quotation marks are placed around some names that would otherwise confuse the reporter:

IN AN ANSWER TO AN S-O-S, THE U-S COAST GUARD CUTTER "COOS BAY" ALONG WITH OTHER VESSELS STEAMED TO THE AID OF THE STRICKEN FREIGHTER. THE NORWEGIAN VESSEL "FRUEN" PICKED UP NINE SEAMEN FROM THE "AMBASSADOR" IN A TRICKY TRANSFER OPERATION IN THE TEMPEST-TOSSED SEAS.

In this illustration the reporter is more likely to fumble "tempest-tossed seas" than the names of the vessels.

FIGURES

Numbers are tricky in broadcast copy. "A million" may sound like "eight million." No confusion results if "one million" is used.

In most copy, round numbers or approximations mean as much as specific figures. "Almost a mile" rather than "5,200 feet," "about half" rather than "48.2 percent," "just under two percent" rather than "1.9 percent."

An exception is vote results, especially where the margin is close. It should be "100-to-95 vote" rather than "100-95 vote." The writer or editor can help the listener follow statistics or vote tallies by inserting phrases such as "in the closest race" and "in a landslide victory."

Fractions and decimals should be spelled out: one and seven-eights (not 1⅞), five-tenths (not 0.5).

Numbers under 10 and over 999 are spelled out and hyphenated: one, two, two-thousand, 11-billion-500-million, 15-hundred (rather than one-thousand-500), one-and-a-half million dollars (never $1.5 million).

When two numbers occur together in a sentence, the smaller number should be spelled out: twelve 20-ton trucks.

Any figure beginning a sentence should be spelled out.

Figures are used for time of day (4:30 this afternoon), in all market stories and in sports scores and statistics (65-to-59, 5-foot-5). If results of horse races or track meets appear in the body of the story, the winning times should be spelled out: two minutes, nine and three-tenths seconds (rather than 2:9.3).

In dates and addresses the *-st, -rd, -th* and *-nd* are included. June 22nd, West 83rd Street. Figures are used for years: 1910.

On approximate figures, writers sometimes say, "Police are looking for a man 50 to 60 years of age." This sounds like "52" to the listener. It should read, "Police are looking for a man between 50 and 60 years old."

TITLES

The identification prepares the ear for the name. Therefore, the identification usually precedes the name: Secretary of State Brown. Some titles are impossible to place before the name: The vice president of the Society for the Preservation and Encouragement of Barbershop Quartet Singing, Joe Doe. Use "Vice president Joe Doe of the Society for the Preservation and Encouragement of Barbershop Quartet Singing." Use "Police Chief Don Vendel" rather than "Chief of Police Don Vendel."

Some radio and television newsrooms insist that the president should never be referred to by his last name alone. It would be President Bush, the president or Mr. Bush.

Broadcast copy seldom includes middle initials and ages of persons in the news. Of course, some initials are well-known parts of names and should be included: Richard M. Nixon.

Ages may be omitted unless the age is significant to the story: "A 12-year-old boy—Mitchell Smith—was crowned winner," and so on. Ages usually appear in local copy to aid in identification. Place the age close to the name. Do not say, "A 24-year-old university student died in a two-car collision today. He was John Doe." Use "A university student died.... He was 24-year-old John Doe."

Obscure names need not be used unless warranted by the story. In many cases the name of the office or title suffices: "Peoria's police chief said," and so on. The same applies to little-known place names or to obscure foreign place names. If the location is important, you may identify it by placing it in relation to a well-known place—"approximately one hundred miles south of Chicago." In local copy, most names and places are important to listeners and viewers.

Where several proper names appear in the same story, it is better to repeat the name than to rely on pronouns unless the antecedent is obvious. Also, repeat the names rather than use *the former, the latter* or *respectively*.

DATELINES

The site of the action should be included in broadcast copy. The dateline may be used as an introduction or a transition: "In Miami." Or the location may be noted elsewhere in the lead: "The Green Bay Packers and the Chicago Bears meet in Chicago tonight in the annual charity football game."

On the newspaper wire *here* refers to the place where the listener is. Because radio and television may cover a wide geographical area, such words as *here* or *local* should be avoided. Said a radio news editor, "If the listener is sitting in a friendly poker game in Ludowici, Georgia, and hears a radio report of mass gambling raids 'here,' he may leap from the window before realizing the announcer is broadcasting from Picayune, Mississippi."

TIME ANGLE

In the newspaper wire story nearly everything happens "today." Radio copy breaks up the day into its component parts: "this morning," "early tonight," "just a few hours ago," "at noon today." The technique gives the listener a feeling of urgency in the news. Specific time should be translated for the time zone of the station's location: "That will be 2:30 Mountain Time."

In television especially, use of the present and present perfect tenses helps downplay the time element:

SEARCHERS HAVE FOUND THE WRECKAGE OF A TWIN-ENGINE AIR FORCE PLANE IN PUERTO RICO AND CONTINUE TO LOOK FOR THE BODIES OF SIX OF THE AIRCRAFT'S EIGHT CREWMEN. AUTHORITIES CONFIRM THAT THE PLANE, MISSING SINCE SATURDAY, CRASHED ATOP A PEAK 23 MILES SOUTHEAST OF SAN JUAN.

TASTE

Broadcast news editors should be aware of all members of their audience—the young and the aged, the sensitive and the hardened. Accident stories can be reported without the sordid details of gore and horror. Borderline words that may appear innocent to the reader carry their full impact when given over the more intimate instruments of radio and television. If spicy items of divorce and suicide are tolerated by the station, at least they can be saved until the late-hour news show when the young are in bed.

The wire services protect the editor by prefacing the morbid or "gutsy" items with discretionary slugs:

(FOR USE AT YOUR DISCRETION)
   (RAPE)
   MIAMI, FLORIDA—POLICE IN MIAMI REPORT THEY SUSPECT JOHN DOE IN THE CRIMINAL ASSAULT (RAPE) OF AN 18-YEAR-OLD GIRL. DOE—27 YEARS OLD—WAS ARRESTED IN THE CITY MUSEUM AND CHARGED WITH STATUTORY ASSAULT (RAPE).
   (END DISCRETIONARY MATTER)

References to physical handicaps or deformities are avoided unless they are essential to the story. Never say "blind as a bat," "slow as a cripple" and the like. Similarly, unless they are essential, references to color, creed or race should not be used.

Wire services handle items involving pertinent profanity by bracketing the profanity:

"GODFREY SAID—IT HURTS (LIKE HELL)."

The practice of including a humorous item, usually near the end, in a newscast has produced some unfunny stories such as the one about a man breaking his neck by tripping over a book of safety hints. But a truly humorous item lightens the heavy news report. Invariably it needs no embellishment by the editor or reporter.

On many stations someone other than the news reporter gives the commercials. One reason for this practice is to disassociate the newsperson from the commercial plugger. Even so, the director or reporter should know the content of commercials sandwiched in news. If a news story concerns a car crash in which several are killed, the item would not be placed ahead of a commercial for an automobile dealer. Airlines generally insist that their commercials be canceled for 24 hours if the newscast contains a story of an airliner crash, a policy that is likewise applied to many metropolitan newspapers.

The sponsor does not control or censor the news. The story of a bank scandal should never be omitted from a news program sponsored by a bank. Nor should a sponsor ever expect sponsorship to earn news stories publicizing the business.

ATTRIBUTIONS

Attribution is an important aspect of all news writing. If an error is discovered, the writer has an "out" if the item has official attribution. Example: "The state patrol said Smith was killed when his car overturned in a ditch" rather than "Smith was killed when his car overturned in a ditch." Attribution can also be vital in the event of any court action over a story written and aired by the news staff.

Should identification of accident victims be made before relatives have been notified? Some stations insist on getting the coroner's approval before releasing names of victims. If the release is not available, the tag would be, "Police are withholding the name of the victim until relatives have been notified."

In stories containing condition reports on persons in hospitals, the report should not carry over the same condition from one newscast to another without checking with the hospital to find out whether there has been a change.

AUDIO TAPES

All news copy for radio and television should show the date, the time block, the story slug, the writer's name or initials, the story source and an indication whether the story has a companion tape cartridge or a video segment. If more than one tape accompanies a story, the slug would indicate the number of tapes. A tape cartridge is simply a tape recording or audio tape from a news source.

If a tape is used, a cue line is inserted for each tape. Many stations use a red ribbon to type the out-cues or place red quotation marks around the cue line. At the end of the tape, the radio newscaster should again identify the voice used on the tape.

If several tapes are used in one newscast, they should be spaced so that the same voices, or series of voices, are not concentrated in one part. The control room needs time to get the tapes ready for broadcast.

The out-cues of the tape should be noted in the *exact* words of the person interviewed. That will ensure that the engineer will not cut off the tape until the message is concluded. The producer should provide the engineer or board operator with a list of news cartridges to be used and the order in which the producer intends to use them.

The same would hold true of telephone interviews, either taped or live.

The broadcast reporter also may have access to audio news services provided by networks, group-owned facilities and the wire services. These feeds, provided to the station on audio tapes, may be voiced reports or recorded natural sound.

Listeners with news tips frequently call the station newsroom. Such tips often lead to scoops. Newsroom personnel receiving such calls should try to get as much information as possible, including the caller's name and telephone number. If a telephoned message is to be used on the air, the reporter should get the caller's permission to use the voiced interview.

If a tip sounds important, the reporter checks it out by telephone with the Police Department or sheriff's office before using it on the air. It is illegal to use information obtained from radio monitors. This prohibition, however, is flagrantly violated in times of emergency. During such times, police dispatchers are too busy to take calls from 15 or 20 broadcasting stations. A reporter would be derelict in not warning the listeners of an oncoming flood or tornado merely because a dispatcher couldn't be reached to confirm the police radio report.

TELEVISION NEWS

Newspapers communicate with printed words, radio with spoken words and television with spoken words and moving pictures. Editing a television news or special event show involves all three levels. As described by Chet Huntley, one-time National Broadcasting Co. news commentator, television news editing is the marriage of words to pictures, words to sound, pictures to sound and ideas to ideas.

Reuven Frank, former president of NBC News, contended that the highest power of television is to produce an experience. Television cannot disseminate as much information as newspapers, magazines or even radio. But in many instances it causes viewers to undergo an experience similar to what would happen if they were at the scene. One can feel sympathy when reading about napalmed civilians or the drowning of a child at a swimming pool. But watching the same thing on a television newscast is a wrenching personal experience that gets people worked up, even angry. Television is an instrument of power, not because of the facts it relates but because of the experience it conveys to viewers.

Words speak for themselves to the newspaper reader. In radio, a newscaster voices the words for the listener. In television, the newscaster is there, talking directly to the viewer about the news. The newscaster is the key actor, and many a station has fallen behind in ratings for its news shows, not because the station did not have good reporters and camera operators or lacked a well-paced news format, but because competing stations had better on-air talent.

In the early days of television, stations hired journalists to report and write the news, then handed over the polished manuscript to a good-looking announcer with mellifluous tones. Today more and more newscasters are men and women with journalistic backgrounds who may not sound like movie stars but who know what they are talking about (Figure 18-4).

News editing, the sorting or processing of the news, requires more time for television than for radio. Producers and writers must spend hours reviewing, sifting and editing all the material available for a single half-hour newscast.

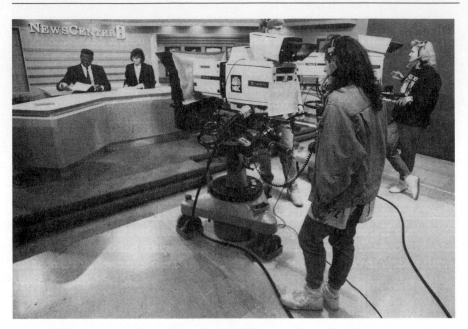

Figure 18-4.   News, weather, sports. These have become the traditional pattern in television news. In this modern studio, those on camera are supported by many behind the scenes. These include producer, director, assignment editor, reporters, photographers, video editors and others. [Photo by Scott Serio]

They use these criteria in selecting items: how significant the item is, whether it is interesting either factually or visually, how long it is and how well its content complements the rest of the program.

Before local videotape is edited, it must be examined to determine how much to cut. Sometimes a tape may have relatively little news value but is included because of its visual quality. A barn fire might not rate mention on a radio newscast but the video could be spectacular.

Network tapes also are examined. Later afternoon network news stories are reviewed to determine what can be lifted for the late-evening local news program. The networks provide their affiliates with an afternoon news feed for use as the affiliates see fit. This closed-circuit feed from New York consists of overset material not used on the network news. These feeds are recorded on videotape and usually include more than a dozen one- to two-minute video stories from the nation and the world. The producer has to monitor these feeds to decide which stories to use.

Chain-owned stations maintain a Washington or New York bureau that sends member stations daily video reports. These, too, must be reviewed.

In addition to editing these videotape reports, the producer must also go over the vast number of wire-service news and facsimile pictures, not to mention stories filed by station reporters. Having selected what to use, the producer's next job is to determine how and where it can be used within the few minutes allotted the news show.

Most American television stations today use portable electronic videotape equipment rather than film. These tape minicams, known as ENG (for electronic news gathering), shoot ¾-inch videotape, usually in 15-minute cassettes. The small recorder and battery pack give the ENG camera crew enough mobility to cover fast-paced news stories, and although the minicam rig is heavier than a film camera, the ENG photographer can see immediately the pictures shot instead of having to wait, often hours, for the film to be developed. That instant image-making, along with the high picture quality and increased editing advantages, make the ENG rig well worth the weight.

It is the ¾-inch videotape editing systems that have transformed television news production procedures most in recent years. The tape editor plays back on one recording machine the pictures shot in the field, selects the shots he or she wants, their length and order, and assembles the edited story by transfer-dubbing those shots to a second tape cassette in another recorder.

The editor also may add a reporter's narrative, natural sound recorded in the field, music and other audio components to the same edited cassette. In most situations, ENG editing is more precise, more versatile and quicker than film editing. Best of all, the editor finishes with a compact videocassette containing all the elements of the story. That simplifies production of the newscast.

In a typical newscast, the anchor newscasters, sitting in a brightly lighted studio set, read stories into studio cameras. The newscasters also introduce edited videotape stories, which beam onto the air when the newscast director instructs an engineer to start the playback machines. A studio camera also may shoot close-ups of still pictures in the studio to help illustrate stories.

The minicam's portability has added a new dimension to local television newscasts. Lightweight transmitters allow a reporter and engineer to beam live reports back from remote locations—even from an airborne helicopter—straight to the station and onto the air. Portable editing rigs mean the remote reports can include packaged pieces as well.

COPY FORMATS

There are almost as many copy formats and scripting styles as there are broadcast newsrooms. Terminology varies, as well. In one newsroom the script designation "voiceover" (or "VO") might mean that an anchorperson is reading over videotape; in another news room "voiceover" might mean that the reporter's recorded voice is running with video.

Figures 18-5 and 18-6 are typical scripts from KOMU-TV in Columbia, Mo. They are from a 6 o'clock newscast devoted to local news.

The robbery arrest story (Figure 18-5) calls for the anchor to read it all, but after a few lines the picture will change form the newscaster's face to videotape illustrating the story. The script instructions tell the director that the

```
NewsCenter 8  Slug arrest
Newscast  6   Date 9/1   Writer mm                           Length :28

moc:                    Columbia police have
                        charged a Moberly
                        man with last week's
                        robbery of the Boone
ENG :22                 County Bank.
----------------------------------------
ENG :00-:22             An eyewitness
Cassette E-100          identified 23-year old
Cut 1 Cued              Robert Wilson of
                        Moberly as the man
VOICEOVER               who took almost
                        10-thousand dollars
                        from the bank
Key: File Tape          Friday afternoon.
     (:05-:10.)         Acting on a tip,
                        police took Wilson
                        into custody this
                        morning in downtown
                        Columbia.
                               (more)


NewsCenter 8  Slug arrest ADD
Newscast  6   Date 9/1   Writer mm                           Length --

tape rolling for        Wilson denies
VOICEOVER:              committing the robbery,
                        but remains in jail
                        under 50-thousand
                        dollar bond.
                        These bank photographs
                        show the robber
                        escaping with the
                        money bag under
                        his arm.
----------------------------------------
back to moc:            Police say they
                        also want to question
                        Wilson about a series
                        of burglaries in the
                        county over the past
                        year.
```

Figure 18-5. Television script indicating use of voiceover. The anchor continues to read the script while videotape illustrates the story. [*Courtesy of KOMU-TV, Columbia, Mo.*]

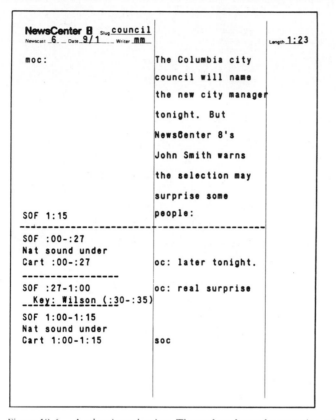

```
NewsCenter 8  Slug council
Newscast _6_ _ Date _9/1___ Writer _mm_                              Length _1:23_

moc:                          The Columbia city
                              council will name
                              the new city manager
                              tonight. But
                              NewsCenter 8's
                              John Smith warns
                              the selection may
                              surprise some
SOF  1:15                     people:
- - - - - - - - - - - - - -  - - - - - - - - - - - -
SOF :00-:27
Nat sound under
Cart :00-:27                  oc: later tonight.
- - - - - - - - - - - - -
SOF :27-1:00                  oc: real surprise
  Key: Wilson (:30-:35)
SOF 1:00-1:15
Nat sound under
Cart 1:00-1:15                soc
```

Figure 18-6.   Anchor introduction. The anchor shares the reporting with another reporter whose story is on film. [*Courtesy of KOMU-TV, Columbia, Mo.*]

video source is ENG videotape, to begin as the anchor says "an eyewitness" and to last for 22 seconds. Other designations show the number of the cassette, the location of the story of the cassette ("Cut 1 cued") and whatever written information ("key") will be superimposed on the screen and when.

Figure 18-6 shows the other common TV script, the anchor's introduction to a packaged report. In this story, the anchor shares the reading with the reporter. This example involves a filmed story, so the scripting differs from the previous example. The "soc" designation alerts the director that the reporter's narration ends with a standard outcue such as "John Smith, NewsCenter 8, Columbia."

A good television script should not compete with the pictures. It should prepare viewers for what they are about to see or specify what may be difficult to see, but it should avoid repeating what viewers can see or hear. If the mayor has criticized the city's water supply and his statement is on videotape, the script merely sets up the statement with a brief introduction. Good scripts also direct the viewer's attention to significant details in the video, but they should avoid phrases such as "we're now looking" or "this picture shows."

PART VI

A LOOK TO THE FUTURE

CHAPTER 19

NEWSPAPERS AND THE FUTURE

NEWSPAPERS' DILEMMA

In the competitive marketplace, the print media have a lot going against them. Consider these items:

- Newspapers depend on a steady and inexpensive supply of newsprint, yet costs continue to climb at a rate much higher than inflation.
- To be large enough to harvest for wood pulp, trees must grow for 10 or more years, which ties up increasingly valuable land and runs up costs.
- The cost of hauling newsprint from mills in Canada and the Southern United States, where most newsprint is made, is increasing rapidly.
- Newspapers must establish an extensive distribution network that is labor-intensive. Perhaps even worse, timely distribution is complicated by the ever-increasing traffic on busy city streets.
- Magazines have all those problems in addition to their almost total dependence on government mail rates.
- Both newspapers and magazines are under increasing attack for adding to environmental problems. Some estimate that as much as 10 percent of the volume of material going to landfills consists of newspapers and magazines.

Contrast these problems, particularly as they relate to production and distribution, to those of the broadcast industry. Once a broadcast station buys its transmitter and other production equipment, its distribution costs are almost non-existent. Furthermore, radio and television pose no threat to the environment. So, whereas newspapers and magazines are labor-intensive manufacturing entities with environmental problems, radio and television are environmentally sound, high-technology industries with no distribution problems. To media industry experts, the importance of those differences should not be underestimated.

Still, magazines are proliferating and newspapers remain one of the most profitable of all industries. In all likelihood, that is the result of the advantages the print media have over broadcasting—portability and permanence. Newspapers and magazines can be carried anywhere, while television cannot. And the print media can be read when the reader chooses; the radio listener and television viewer have no such luxury. The print media also excel in their ability to handle large volumes of information; it would be awful to be forced to listen to someone read the grocery or classified ads. Finally, newspapers and magazines do a far better job of analysis and offer a superior forum for the discussion of abstract ideas.

For all those reasons, the high-tech industries of radio and television have failed to replace the older manufacturing industries of newspapers and magazines. One should not assume, however, that this will always be the case.

As we learned in Chapter 2, Nicholas Negroponte and his team of experts at the Massachusetts Institute of Technology's Media Lab are intent on designing the ultimate information medium that would combine all the advantages of print and broadcast. Others are focused on the same objective. Their intent is to create an entirely new medium, which some have dubbed the *magic box,* that would provide these advantages to the user:

- The ability to receive news and information in the form desired—text, audio, video or any combination of the three.
- The ability to shop and bank at home and have items delivered.
- Improved video-screen technology that solves the problem of eyestrain. Current technology is inferior for prolonged periods of reading. High-definition television (HDTV), which the Japanese have embraced, may be an interim step toward that goal. Ultimately, holographic images may be projected.
- The ability to make a printout quickly and inexpensively to continue reading or to save a grocery coupon or refer to the help-wanted ads.
- The ability to choose the type of information, the time it is received and the medium—audio, video or text—through which it is consumed.

Those are the key elements of the magic box of our future. In this scenario, a consumer might sit down at the breakfast table and turn on the *Today* show, much as we do today. But, when intrigued by a news item, that consumer would have the option of calling up another network's account of the same thing, the National Public Radio in-depth account or even a *Wall Street Journal* article on the topic.

Those who ponder the implications of such a medium often come to the conclusion that newspapers have no future. Although it is true that the arrival of such a medium in affordable form would have far-reaching impact on the media industry as a whole, it is difficult to determine who will be the winners and losers. It is tough to image a world without at least some newspapers, although it is likely that such an era would see a dramatic reduction in the number of them. The ones that remained probably would be more and more expensive; newspapers might then become a medium for the elite.

But it also is difficult to see how radio and television would be big winners in such a scenario. At present, radio and television depend on analog technology, and it is clear that the medium of the future will be digitally based. As we enter the 1990s, newspapers are the clear leader in digital processing of information. Because of the nature of the new medium, it is likely that neither print nor broadcasting will emerge as a clear winner in the battle for consumers' attention. Instead, consortiums of print and broadcast companies are the most logical means of delivering such a medium to the public.

The student journalist preparing for a career in the evolving media industry would be wise to remember one thing: There will always be a demand, probably an ever-increasing demand, for those who can gather and process information. One who is well-versed in the basics of information gathering and dissemination and who is not wed to a particular medium will have an advantage in the future.

HINTS OF THE FUTURE

For a glimpse of our probable future, a good place to look is the computer industry. In a system such as the one we have described, massive amounts of information will have to be stored, probably on large mainframe computers. Sears and IBM Corp. have formed a company called Prodigy to deliver information into the home over telephone lines. The system uses color effectively to create computer screens that are pleasing to the eye. Combine a system like that with the power of older, text-based retrieval systems such as Dow Jones News Retrieval™, CompuServe™, VuText™and DataTimes™and one gets a glimpse of what the future could be like. Finally, add to the system moving pictures, improved screen technology and an inexpensive, high-quality printer. The result is just the type of system that Negroponte and others envision.

To observers of the computer industry, the pieces seem to be coming together. IBM and Apple Computer both have introduced machines capable of displaying full-motion video. HDTV and other screen technologies appear to offer potential solutions for the screen problem, and printer technology gets better by the month. Laser printers, which once were affordable only to large companies, are now commonly found in people's homes.

Clearly, all the key pieces of technology for the magic box already exist. Not yet clear, however, is the means of distribution. Broadcast technology as we know it is incapable of handling the large volumes of information that would be required in such a system. More likely delivery mechanisms are fiber-optic telephone or cable television lines. Only those have the potential to handle massive amounts of data with full-motion video. Again, the technology exists; the key is putting all the pieces together. When those pieces are put together, a new medium will begin to emerge.

INTERIM TECHNOLOGIES

Newspapers are well-positioned to take advantage of emerging technologies. They are accustomed to dealing with massive amounts of digital information, and they have the largest and most sophisticated news-gathering staffs of any medium. They also are innovative enough to have embraced technological advance more rapidly than other media.

One thinks of television as a high-tech medium, and it clearly is, but the industry has suffered because it has invested more heavily in equipment than in people. A major-market television station may have satellite uplink trucks, microwave-equipped news vans and the latest in video gadgetry. Yet the typical television news staff in a city will be a fraction of the size of the newspaper staff in that town. Interestingly, television lags far behind newspapers in computerizing newsrooms. It is not unusual, even today, to find television newsrooms with typewriters rather than computers. Computers are still rare in radio newsrooms, too.

If, as we expect, the future of news delivery is digital in nature and unsuited for broadcast transmission, newspapers have a clear lead in employing digital technology. That translates into more experience for newspaper managers and a technological advantage. On the other hand, it is clear that the new medium will go nowhere without full-motion video, and television has the advantage of experience there.

To bridge that knowledge gap, newspaper publishers have begun to experiment with alternative means of delivering information. Some newspapers have started doing television-like broadcasts from their newsrooms over cable television channels. Others have set up audiotext systems, which permit callers to dial a number and have the latest news read to them. Such systems increasingly store the recorded voice information in digital form. Still others have started facsimile newspapers.

Innovative approaches such as these are giving publishers and editors experience in alternative delivery systems. Some may have no long-term future, but in the process editors gain invaluable experience about what works and what doesn't.

THE ROLE OF GOVERNMENT

Seldom discussed as editors look to the future is the role that government will play. That subject should not be dismissed lightly. A dramatic reduction in the number of newspapers and magazines would mean that the impact of the last of the media free of government-imposed content rules and licensing would be diminished. Television and radio are subject to the Fairness Doctrine and equal time provisions and must have licenses—granted by the government—to operate. Cable television systems once were regulated by local government, and Congress is being pressed to reinstitute such controls. Telephone service also is subject to government regulation and licensing. Newspapers and magazines, like all institutions, must comply with laws, but they are not licensed, and they are not subject to content regulation similar to that imposed by the equal time provision. So if newspapers and magazines are less prevalent, government would have greater control of the media through its control of licensing and content. Richard Nixon, when president, tried to harass broadcasters by delaying FCC license renewals for stations that had reported unfavorably on his activities. The *Washington Post,* which was subject to no such regulation, exposed Nixon's involvement in the Watergate affair. Is it possible that with most media subject to government regulation even more serious abuses of authority could occur in the future? We have no way of knowing, but it is an ominous prospect for those who believe in press freedom and who view the press as a watchdog on government.

THE FUTURE OF JOURNALISTS

If the impact of newspapers diminishes in the future, it is reasonable to ask where that leaves those now training for careers as journalists. No futurist has yet seriously suggested that computers can be trained to gather the news, to take photographs or to edit. It seems clear that, while the tools of the journalist may change, the function of the journalist will not. There will continue to be a demand for competent reporters, photographers and editors for the foreseeable future.

NEWSPAPER STYLE

The stylebooks of The Associated Press and United Press International are reference books as well as stylebooks, and much useful information can be found in them. This appendix is a condensation of the key rules of usage found in those stylebooks. *Webster's New World Dictionary* is the primary source for references not found in the stylebooks. The information herein is used with permission.

CAPITALIZATION

In general, avoid unnecessary capitals. Use a capital letter only if you can justify it by one of the principles listed here:

PROPER NOUNS

Capitalize nouns that constitute the unique identification for a specific person, place or thing: *John, Mary, America, Boston, England.*

Some words, such as the examples just given, are always proper nouns. Some common nouns receive proper noun status when they are used as the name of a particular entity: *General Electric, Gulf Oil.*

PROPER NAMES

Capitalize common nouns such as *party, river, street* and *west* when they are an integral part of the full name for a person, place or thing: *Democratic Party, Mississippi River, Fleet Street, West Virginia.*

Lowercase these common nouns when they stand alone in subsequent references: *the party, the river, the street.*

Lowercase the common elements of names in all plural uses: *the Democratic and Republican parties, Main and State streets, lakes Erie and Ontario.*

POPULAR NAMES

Some places and events lack officially designated proper names but have popular names that are the effective equivalent: *the Combat Zone* (a section of downtown Boston), *the Main Line* (a group of Philadelphia suburbs), *the South Side* (of Chicago), *the Badlands* (of North Dakota), *the Street* (the financial community in the Wall Street area of New York).

The principle applies also to shortened versions of the proper names for one-of-a-kind events: *the Series* (for the World Series), *the Derby* (for the Kentucky Derby). This practice should not, however, be interpreted as a license to ignore the general practice of lowercasing the common noun elements of a name when they stand alone.

DERIVATIVES

Capitalize words that are derived from a proper noun and still depend on it for their meaning: *American, Christian, Christianity, English, French, Marxism, Shakespearean.*

Lowercase words that are derived from a proper noun but no longer depend on it for their meaning: *french fries, herculean, manhattan cocktail, malapropism, pasteurize, quixotic, venetian blind.*

Other key points of capitalization:

academic departments   Use lowercase except for words that are proper nouns or adjectives: *the department of history, the history department, the department of English, the English department.*

administration   Lowercase: *the administration, the president's administration, the governor's administration, the Bush administration.*

air force   Capitalize when referring to U.S. forces: *the U.S. Air Force, the Air Force, Air Force regulations.*

Use lowercase for the forces of other nations: *the Israeli air force.*

animals   Capitalize the name of a specific animal, and use Roman numerals to show sequence: *Bowser, Whirlaway II.*

For breed names, follow the spelling and capitalization in *Webster's New World Dictionary.* For breeds not listed in the dictionary, capitalize words derived from proper nouns, use lowercase elsewhere: *basset hound, Boston terrier.*

army   Capitalize when referring to U.S. forces: *the U.S. Army, the Army, Army regulations.*

Use lowercase for the forces of other nations: *the French army.*

Bible   Capitalize, without quotation marks, when referring to the Scriptures of the Old Testament or the New Testament. Capitalize also related terms such as *the Gospels, Gospel of St. Mark, the Scriptures, the Holy Scriptures.*

Lowercase *biblical* in all uses.

Lowercase *bible* as a nonreligious term: *My dictionary is my bible.*

brand names   When they are used, capitalize them.

Brand names normally should be used only if they are essential to a story.

Sometimes, however, the use of a brand name may not be essential but is acceptable because it lends an air of reality to a story: *He fished a Camel from his shirt pocket* may be preferable to the less specific *cigarette.*

building   Capitalize the proper names of buildings, including the word building if it is an integral part of the proper name: *the Empire State Building.*

bureau   Capitalize when part of the formal name for an organization or agency: *the Bureau of Labor Statistics, the Newspaper Advertising Bureau.*

Lowercase when used alone or to designate a corporate subdivision: *the Washington bureau of The Associated Press.*

cabinet   Capitalize references to a specific body of advisers heading executive departments for a president, king, governor, etc.: *The president-elect said he has not made his Cabinet selections.*

The capital letter distinguishes the word from the common noun meaning "cupboard," which is lowercase.

Cabinet titles   Capitalize the full title when used before a name, lowercase in other uses: *Secretary of State James A. Baker III,* but *Richard B. Cheney, secretary of defense.*

century   Lowercase, spelling out numbers less than 10: *the first century, the 20th century.*

For proper names, follow the organization's practice: *20th Century-Fox, Twentieth Century Fund, Twentieth Century Limited.*

chairman, chairwoman   Capitalize as a formal title before a name: *company Chairman Henry Ford, committee Chairwoman Margaret Chase Smith.*

Do not capitalize as a casual, temporary position: *meeting chairman Robert Jones.*

Do not use *chairperson* unless it is an organization's formal title for an office.

chief   Capitalize as a formal title before a name: He spoke to *Police Chief Michael Codd.* He spoke to *Chief Michael Codd of the New York police.*

Lowercase when it is not a formal title: *union chief Walter Reuther.*

church   Capitalize as part of the formal name of a building, a congregation or a denomination; lowercase in other uses: *St. Mary's Church, the Roman Catholic Church, the Catholic and Episcopal churches, a Roman Catholic church, a church.*

Lowercase in phrases where the church is used in an institutional sense: *He believes in separation of church and state. The pope said the church opposes abortion.*

city council   Capitalize when part of a proper noun: *the Boston City Council.*

Retain capitalization if the reference is to a specific council but the context does not require the city name:

BOSTON (AP)–The City Council . . .

Lowercase in other uses: *the council, the Boston and New York city councils, a city council.*

committee   Capitalize when part of a formal name: *the House Appropriations Committee.*

Do not capitalize committee in shortened versions of long committee names: *the Special Senate Select Committee to Investigate Improper Labor-Management Practices,* for example, became the *rackets committee.*

congress   Capitalize *U.S. Congress* and *Congress* when referring to the U.S. Senate and House of Representatives. Although Congress sometimes is used as a substitute for the House, it properly is reserved for reference to both the Senate and House.

constitution   Capitalize references to the U.S. Constitution, with or without the *U.S.* modifier: *The president said he supports the Constitution.*

When referring to constitutions of other nations or of states, capitalize only with the name of a nation or a state: *the French Constitution, the Massachusetts Constitution, the nation's constitution, the state constitution, the constitution.*

Lowercase in other uses: *the organization's constitution.*

Lowercase *constitutional* in all uses.

courthouse   Capitalize with the name of a jurisdiction: *the Cook County Courthouse, the U.S. Courthouse.* Lowercase in other uses: *the county courthouse, the courthouse, the federal courthouse.*

Court House   (two words) is used in the proper names of some communities: *Appomattox Court House, Va.*

court names   Capitalize the full proper names of courts at all levels.

Retain capitalization if U.S. or a state name is dropped: *the U.S. Supreme Court, the Supreme Court; the Massachusetts Superior Court, the state Superior Court, the Superior Court, Superior Court.*

For courts identified by a numeral: *3rd District Court, 8th U.S. Circuit Court of Appeals.*

directions and regions   In general, lowercase *north, south, northeast, northern,* etc., when they indicate compass direction; capitalize these words when they designate regions.

federal   Use a capital letter for the architectural style and for corporate or governmental bodies that use the word as part of their formal names: *Federal Express, the Federal Trade Commission*

Lowercase when used as an adjective to distinguish something from state, county, city, town or private entities: *federal assistance, federal court, the federal government, a federal judge.*

Also: *federal District Court* (but *U.S. District Court* is preferred) and *federal Judge John Sirica* (but *U.S. District Judge John Sirica* is preferred).

federal court   Always lowercase. The preferred form for first reference is to use the proper name of the court.

Do not create nonexistent entities such as *Manhattan Federal Court.* Instead, use *a federal court in Manhattan.*

food   Most food names are lowercase: *apples, cheese, peanut butter.*

Capitalize brand names and trademarks: *Roquefort cheese, Tabasco sauce.*

Most proper nouns or adjectives are capitalized when they occur in a food name: *Boston brown bread, Russian dressing, Swiss cheese, Waldorf salad.*

Lowercase is used, however, when the food does not depend on the proper noun or adjective for its meaning: *french fries, graham crackers, manhattan cocktail.*

former   Always lowercase. But retain capitalization for a formal title used immediately before a name: *former President Reagan.*

geographic names   Capitalize common nouns when they form an integral part of a proper name, but lowercase them when they stand alone: *Pennsylvania Avenue, the avenue; the Philippine Islands, the islands; the Mississippi River, the river.*

Lowercase common nouns that are not part of a specific proper name: *the Pacific islands, the Swiss mountains, Chekiang province.*

government   Always lowercase: *the federal government, the state government, the U.S. government.*

governmental bodies   Follow these guidelines:

FULL NAME: Capitalize the full proper names of governmental agencies, departments and offices: *the U.S. Department of State, the Georgia Department of Human Resources, the Boston City Council, the Chicago Fire Department.*

WITHOUT JURISDICTION: Retain capitalization in referring to a specific body if the dateline or context makes the name of the nation, state, county, city, etc., unnecessary: *the Department of State* (in a story from Washington), *the Department of Human Resources* or *the state Department of Human Resources* (in a story from Georgia), *the City Council* (in a story from Boston), *the Fire Department* or *the city Fire Department* (in a story from Chicago).

Lowercase further condensations of the name: *the department, the council,* etc.

FLIP-FLOPPED NAMES: Retain capital letters for the name of a governmental body if its formal name is flopped to delete the word *of*: *the State Department, the Human Resources Department.*

GENERIC EQUIVALENTS: If a generic term has become the equivalent of a proper name in popular use, treat it as a proper name: *Walpole State Prison,* for example, even though the proper name is *the Massachusetts Correctional Institution-Walpole.*

PLURALS, NONSPECIFIC REFERENCES: All words that are capitalized when part of a proper name should be lowercased when they are used in the plural or do not refer to a specific existing body. Some examples:

All states except Nebraska have a state senate. The town does not have a fire department. The bill requires city councils to provide matching funds. The president will address the lower houses of the New York and New Jersey legislatures.

heavenly bodies   Capitalize the proper names of planets, stars, constellations, etc.: *Mars, Arcturus, the Big Dipper, Aries.*

For comets, capitalize only the proper noun element of the name: *Halley's comet.*

Lowercase *sun* and *moon,* but if their Greek names are used, capitalize them: *Helios* and *Luna.*

historical periods and events   Capitalize the names of widely recognized epochs in anthropology, archaeology, geology and history: *the Bronze Age, the Dark Ages, the Middle Ages, the Pliocene Epoch.*

Capitalize also widely recognized popular names for periods and events: *the Atomic Age, the Boston Tea Party, the Civil War, the Exodus* (of the Israelites from Egypt), *the Great Depression, Prohibition.*

Lowercase *century: the 18th century.*

Capitalize only the proper nouns or adjectives in general descriptions of a period: *ancient Greece, classical Rome, the Victorian era, the fall of Rome.*

holidays and holy days   Capitalize them: *New Year's Eve, New Year's Day, Groundhog Day, Easter, Hanukkah,* etc.

house of representatives Capitalize when referring to a specific governmental body: *the U.S. House of Representatives, the Massachusetts House of Representatives.*

Capitalize shortened references that delete the words *of Representatives: the U.S. House, the Massachusetts House.*

Retain capitalization if *U.S.* or the name of a state is dropped but the reference is to a specific body:

BOSTON (AP)–The House has adjourned for the year.

Lowercase plural uses: *the Massachusetts and Rhode Island houses.*

Apply the same principles to similar legislative bodies such as *the Virginia House of Delegates.*

judge Capitalize before a name when it is the formal title for an individual who presides in a court of law. Do not continue to use the title in second reference.

Do not use *court* as part of the title unless confusion would result without it:

No *court* in the title: *U.S. District Judge John Sirica, District Judge John Sirica, federal Judge John Sirica, Judge John Sirica, U.S. Circuit Judge Homer Thornberry, appellate Judge John Blair.*

Court needed in the title: *Juvenile Court Judge Angela Jones, Criminal Court Judge John Jones, Superior Court Judge Robert Harrison, state Supreme Court Judge William Cushing.*

When the formal title *chief judge* is relevant, put the court name after the judge's name: *Chief Judge John Sirica of the U.S. District Court in Washington, D.C.; Chief Judge Clement F. Haynsworth Jr. of the 4th U.S. Circuit Court of Appeals.*

Do not pile up long court names before the name of a judge. Make it *Judge John Smith of Allegheny County Common Pleas Court.* Not: *Allegheny County Common Pleas Court Judge John Smith.*

Lowercase *judge* as an occupational designation in phrases such as *beauty contest judge Bert Parks.*

legislature Capitalize when preceded by the name of a state: *the Kansas Legislature.*

Retain capitalization when the state name is dropped but the reference is specifically to that state's legislature:

TOPEKA, Kan (AP)–Both houses of the Legislature adjourned today.

Capitalize *legislature* in subsequent specific references and in such constructions as: *the 100th Legislature, the state Legislature.*

Lowercase *legislature* when used generically: *No legislature has approved the amendment.*

Use *legislature* in lowercase for all plural references: *The Arkansas and Colorado legislatures are considering the amendment.*

magazine names Capitalize the name but do not place it in quotes. Lowercase *magazine* unless it is part of the publication's formal title: *Harper's Magazine, Newsweek magazine, Time magazine.*

Check the masthead if in doubt.

monuments Capitalize the popular names of monuments and similar public attractions: *Lincoln Memorial, Statue of Liberty, Washington Monument, Leaning Tower of Pisa,* etc.

mountains   Capitalize as part of a proper name: *Appalachian Mountains, Ozark Mountains, Rocky Mountains.*

Or simply: *the Appalachians, the Ozarks, the Rockies.*

nationalities and races   Capitalize the proper names of nationalities, peoples, races, tribes, etc.: *Arab, Arabic, African, Afro-American, American, Asian, Caucasian, Cherokee, Chinese* (both singular and plural), *Eskimo* (plural *Eskimos*), *French Canadian, Gypsy (Gypsies), Japanese* (singular and plural) *Jew, Jewish, Latin, Negro (Negroes), Nordic, Oriental, Sioux, Swede,* etc.

Lowercase *black* (noun or adjective), *white, red, mulatto,* etc.

Lowercase derogatory terms such as *honky* and *nigger.* Use them only in direct quotes when essential to the story.

navy   Capitalize when referring to U.S. forces: *the U.S. Navy, the Navy, Navy policy.*

Lowercase when referring to the naval forces of other nations: *the British navy.*

newspaper names   Capitalize *the* in a newspaper's name if that is the way the publication prefers to be known.

Lowercase *the* before newspaper names if a story mentions several papers, some of which use *the* as part of the name and some of which do not.

organizations and institutions   Capitalize the full names of organizations and institutions: *the American Medical Association; First Presbyterian Church; General Motors Corp.; Harvard University; Harvard University Medical School; the Procrastinators Club; the Society of Professional Journalists, Sigma Delta Chi.*

Retain capitalization if *Co., Corp.* or a similar word is deleted from the full proper name: *General Motors.*

FLIP-FLOPPED NAMES: Retain capital letters when commonly accepted practice flops a name to delete the word *of: College of the Holy Cross, Holy Cross College; Harvard School of Dental Medicine, Harvard Dental School.*

Do not, however, flop formal names that are known to the public with the word *of: Massachusetts Institute of Technology,* for example, not *Massachusetts Technology Institute.*

planets   Capitalize the proper names of planets: *Jupiter, Mars, Mercury, Neptune, Pluto, Saturn, Uranus, Venus.*

Capitalize *earth* when used as the proper name of our planet: *The astronauts returned to Earth.*

Lowercase nouns and adjectives derived from the proper names of planets and other heavenly bodies: *martian, jovian, lunar, solar, venusian.*

plants   In general, lowercase the names of plants, but capitalize proper nouns or adjectives that occur in a name.

Some examples: *tree, fir, white fir, Douglas fir, Dutch elm, Scotch pine, clover, white clover, white Dutch clover.*

police department   In communities where this is the formal name, capitalize *police department* with or without the name of the community: *the Los Angeles Police Department, the Police Department.*

If a police agency has some other formal name such as *Division of Police,* use that name if it is the way the department is known to the public. If the story uses *police department* as a generic term for such an agency, put *police department* in lowercase.

If a police agency with an unusual formal name is known to the public as a police department, treat *police department* as the name, capitalizing it with or without the name of the community. Use the formal name only if there is a special reason in the story.

If the proper name cannot be determined for some reason, such as the need to write about a police agency from a distance, treat *police department* as the proper name, capitalizing it with or without the name of the community.

Lowercase police department in plural uses: *the Los Angeles and San Francisco police departments.*

Lowercase *the department* whenever it stands alone.

political parties and philosophies   Capitalize both the name of the party and the word *party* if it is customarily used as part of the organization's proper name: *the Democratic Party, the Republican Party.*

Capitalize *Communist, Conservative, Democrat, Liberal, Republican, Socialist,* etc., when they refer to the activities of a specific party or to individuals who are members of it. Lowercase these words when they refer to political philosophy.

Lowercase the name of a philosophy in noun and adjective forms unless it is the derivative of a proper name: *communism, communist; fascism, fascist.* But: *Marxism, Marxist; Nazism, Nazi.*

pontiff   Not a formal title. Always lowercase.

pope   Capitalize when used as a formal title before a name; lowercase in all other uses: *Pope John Paul II spoke to the crowd. At the close of his address, the pope gave his blessing.*

presidency   Always lowercase.

president   Capitalize *president* only as a formal title before one or more names: *President Reagan, Presidents Carter and Reagan.*

Lowercase in all other uses: *The president said today. He is running for president. Lincoln was president during the Civil War.*

religious references   The basic guidelines:

DEITIES: Capitalize the proper names of monotheistic deities: *God, Allah, the Father, the Son, Jesus Christ, the Son of God, the Redeemer, the Holy Spirit,* etc.

Lowercase pronouns referring to the deity: *he, him, his, thee, thou, who, whose, thy,* etc.

Lowercase *gods* in referring to the deities of polytheistic religions.

Capitalize the proper names of pagan and mythological gods and goddesses: *Neptune, Thor, Venus,* etc.

Lowercase such words as *god-awful, goddamn, godlike, godliness, godsend.*

LIFE OF CHRIST: Capitalize the names of major events in the life of Jesus Christ in references that do not use his name: *The doctrines of the*

Last Supper, the Crucifixion, the Resurrection and *the Ascension* are central to Christian belief.

But use lowercase when the words are used with his name: *The ascension of Jesus into heaven took place 40 days after his resurrection from the dead.*

Apply the principle also to events in the life of his mother: *He cited the doctrine of the Immaculate Conception and the Assumption.* But: *She referred to the assumption of Mary into heaven.*

RITES: Capitalize proper names for rites that commemorate the Last Supper or signify a belief in Christ's presence: *the Lord's Supper, Holy Communion, Holy Eucharist.*

Lowercase the names of other sacraments.

Capitalize *Benediction* and the *Mass.* But: *a high Mass, a low Mass, a requiem Mass.*

OTHER WORDS: Lowercase *heaven, hell, devil, angel, cherub, an apostle, a priest,* etc.

Capitalize *Hades* and *Satan.*

seasons Lowercase *spring, summer, fall, winter* and derivatives such as *springtime* unless part of a formal name: *Dartmouth Winter Carnival, Winter Olympics, Summer Olympics.*

senate Capitalize all specific references to governmental legislative bodies, regardless of whether the name of the nation or state is used: *the U.S. Senate, the Senate; the Virginia Senate, the state Senate, the Senate.*

Lowercase plural uses: *the Virginia and North Carolina senates.*

The same principles apply to foreign bodies.

Lowercase references to nongovernmental bodies: *The student senate at Yale.*

sentences Capitalize the first word of every sentence, including quoted statements and direction questions:

Patrick Henry said, "I know not what course others may take, but as for me, give me liberty or give me death."

Capitalize the first word of a quoted statement if it constitutes a sentence, even if it was part of a larger sentence in the original: *Patrick Henry said, "Give me liberty or give me death."*

Capitalize the first word of every direct question, even if it falls within a sentence and is not enclosed in quotation marks: *The story answers the question, Where does true happiness really lie?*

Social Security Capitalize all references to the U.S. system.

Lowercase generic uses such as: *Is there a social security program in Sweden?*

state Lowercase in all *state of* constructions: *the state of Maine, the states of Maine and Vermont.*

Do not capitalize *state* when used simply as an adjective to specify a level of jurisdiction: *state Rep. William Smith, the state Transportation Department, state funds.*

Apply the same principle to phrases such as *the city of Chicago, the town of Auburn,* etc.

statehouse   Capitalize all references to a specific statehouse, with or without the name of the state: *The Massachusetts Statehouse is in Boston. The governor will visit the Statehouse today.*

Lowercase plural uses: *the Massachusetts and Rhode Island statehouses.*

subcommittee   Lowercase when used with the name of a legislative body's full committee: *a Ways and Means subcommittee.*

Capitalize when a subcommittee has a proper name of its own: *the Senate Permanent Subcommittee on Investigations.*

titles   In general, confine capitalization to formal titles used directly before an individual's name. Lowercase and spell out titles when they are not used with an individual's name: *The president issued a statement. The pope gave his blessing.*

Lowercase and spell out titles in constructions that set them off from a name by commas: *The vice president, Walter Mondale, declined to run again. John Paul II, the current pope, does not plan to retire.*

ABBREVIATED TITLES: The following formal titles are capitalized and abbreviated as shown when used before a name outside quotations: *Dr., Gov., Lt., Gov., Rep., Sen.* and certain military ranks. Spell out all except *Dr.* when they are used in quotations.

All other formal titles are spelled out in all uses.

ACADEMIC TITLES: Capitalize and spell out formal titles such as *professor, dean, president, chancellor, chairman,* etc., when they precede a name. Lowercase elsewhere.

Lowercase modifiers such as *history* in *history Professor Oscar Handlin* or *department* in *department Chairman Jerome Wiesner.*

FORMAL TITLES: Capitalize formal titles when they are used immediately before one or more names: *Pope John Paul II, President Washington, Vice Presidents John Jones and William Smith.*

LEGISLATIVE TITLES: Use *Rep., Reps., Sen.* and *Sens.* as formal titles before one or more names in regular text. Spell out and capitalize these titles before one or more names in a direct quotation. Spell out and lowercase *representative* and *senator* in other uses.

Spell out other legislative titles in all uses. Capitalize formal titles such as *assemblyman, assemblywoman, city councilor, delegate,* etc., when they are used before a name. Lowercase in other uses.

Add *U.S.* or *state* before a title only if necessary to avoid confusion: *U.S. Sen. Christopher Bond spoke with state Sen. Hugh Carter.*

First Reference Practice. The use of a title such as *Rep.* or *Sen.* in first reference is normal in most stories. It is not mandatory, however, provided an individual's title is given later in the story.

Deletion of the title on first reference is frequently appropriate, for example, when an individual has become well known: *Robert Dole endorsed President Bush's budget plan today. The Kansas senator said he believes the budget is sound.*

Second Reference. Do not use a legislative title before a name on second reference unless part of a direct quotation.

Congressman, Congresswoman. Rep. and *U.S. Rep.* are the pre-ferred first-reference forms when a formal title is used before the name of a U.S. House member. The words *congressman* or *congress-woman,* in lowercase, may be used in subsequent references that do not use an individual's name, just as *senator* is used in references to members of the Senate.

Congressman and Congresswoman should appear as capitalized formal titles before a name only in direct quotation.

Organizational Titles. Capitalize titles for formal, organiza-tional offices within a legislative body when they are used before a name: *Majority Leader Richard A. Gephardt, Chairman Les Aspin of the House Armed Services Committee.*

MILITARY TITLES: Capitalize a military rank when used as a formal title before an individual's name.

Spell out and lowercase a title when it is substituted for a name: *Gen. John J. Pershing arrived today. An aide said the general would review the troops.*

ROYAL TITLES: Capitalize *king, queen,* etc., when used directly before a name.

trademark A trademark is a brand, symbol, word, etc., used by a man-ufacturer or dealer and protected by law to prevent a competitor from using it: *AstroTurf,* for a type of artificial grass, for example.

In general, use a generic equivalent unless the trademark name is essential to the story.

When a trademark is used, capitalize it.

union names The formal names of unions may be condensed to conven-tionally accepted short forms that capitalize characteristic words from the full name followed by *union* in lowercase.

ABBREVIATIONS AND ACRONYMS

A few universally recognized abbreviations are required in some circum-stances. Some others are acceptable depending on the context. But in general, avoid alphabet soup.

The same principle applies to acronyms—pronounceable words formed from the initial letters in a series of words: *ALCOA, NATO, radar, scuba,* etc.

Guidance on how to use a particular abbreviation or acronym is provided in entries alphabetized according to the sequence of letters in the word or phrase.

Some general principles:

BEFORE A NAME

Abbreviate the following titles when used before a full name outside direct quotations: *Dr., Gov., Lt. Gov., Mr., Mrs., Ms., Rep., the Rev., Sen.* and certain military designations. Spell out all except *Dr.*, *Mr.*, *Mrs.* and *Ms.* when they are used before a name in direct quotations.

AFTER A NAME

Abbreviate *junior* or *senior* after an individual's name. Abbreviate *company, corporation, incorporated* and *limited* when used after the name of a corporate entity.

In some cases, an academic degree may be abbreviated after an individual's name.

WITH DATES OR NUMERALS

Use the abbreviations *A.D., B.C., a.m., p.m., No.,* and abbreviate certain months when used with the day of the month.

IN NUMBERED ADDRESSES

Abbreviate *avenue, boulevard* and *street* in numbered addresses: *He lives on Pennsylvania Avenue. He lives at 1600 Pennsylvania Ave.*

STATES AND NATIONS

The names of certain states, the United States and the Union of Soviet Socialist Republics (but not of other nations) are abbreviated with periods in some circumstances.

ACCEPTABLE BUT NOT REQUIRED

Some organizations and government agencies are widely recognized by their initials: *CIA, FBI, GOP.*

If the entry for such an organization notes that an abbreviation is acceptable in all references or on second reference, that does not mean that its use should be automatic. Let the context determine, for example, whether to use *Federal Bureau of Investigation* or *FBI.*

AVOID AWKWARD CONSTRUCTIONS

Do not follow an organization's full name with an abbreviation or acronym in parentheses or set off by dashes. If an abbreviation or acronym would not be clear on second reference without this arrangement, do not use it.

Names not commonly before the public should not be reduced to acronyms solely to save a few words.

An alphabetical listing of other key points involving abbreviations and acronyms:

academic degrees   If mention of degrees is necessary to establish someone's credentials, the preferred form is to avoid an abbreviation and use instead a phrase such as: *Alma Jones, who has a doctorate in psychology.*

Use an apostrophe in *bachelor's degree, a master's,* etc.

Use such abbreviations as *B.A., M.A., LL.D.* and *Ph.D.* only when the need to identify many individuals by degree on first reference would make the preferred form cumbersome. Use these abbreviations only after a full name, never after just a last name.

When used after a name, an academic abbreviation is set off by commas: *Daniel Moynihan, Ph.D., spoke.*

Do not precede a name with a courtesy title for an academic degree and follow it with the abbreviation for the degree in the same reference.

addresses   Use the abbreviations *Ave., Blvd.* and *St.* only with a numbered address: *1600 Pennsylvania Ave.* Spell them out and capitalize when part of a formal street name without a number: *Pennsylvania Avenue.* Lowercase and spell out when used alone or with more than one street name: *Massachusetts and Pennsylvania avenues.*

All similar words (*alley, drive, road, terrace,* etc.) always are spelled out. Capitalize them when part of a formal name without a number; lowercase when used alone or with two or more names.

Always use figures for an address number: *9 Morningside Circle.*

Spell out and capitalize *First* through *Ninth* when used as street names; use figures with two letters for *10th* and above: *7 Fifth Ave., 100 21st St.*

aircraft names   Use a hyphen when changing from letters to figures; no hyphen when adding a letter after figures.

AM   Acceptable in all references for the amplitude modulation system of radio transmission.

a.m., p.m.   Lowercase, with periods. Avoid the redundant *10 a.m. this morning.*

armed services   Do not use the abbreviations *U.S.A., USAF* and *USN.*

assistant   Do not abbreviate. Capitalize only when part of a formal title before a name: *Assistant Secretary of State George Ball.* Wherever practical, however, an appositional construction should be used: *George Ball, assistant secretary of state.*

association   Do not abbreviate. Capitalize as part of a proper name: *American Medical Association.*

attorney general, attorneys general   Never abbreviate. Capitalize only when used as a title before a name: *Attorney General Richard Thornburgh.*

Bible   Do not abbreviate individual books of the Bible.

Citations listing the number of chapter(s) and verse(s) use this form: *Matthew 3:16, Luke 21:1–13, 1 Peter 2:1.*

brothers   Abbreviate as *Bros.* in formal company names: *Warner Bros.*

For possessives: *Warner Bros.' profits.*

Christmas   Never abbreviate *Christmas* to *Xmas* or any other form.

CIA   Acceptable in all references for *Central Intelligence Agency.*

c.o.d.   Acceptable in all references for *cash on delivery* or *collect on delivery.* (The use of lowercase is an exception to the first listing in *Webster's New World*).

company, companies   Use *Co.* or *Cos.* when a business uses either word at the end of its proper name: *Ford Motor Co., American Broadcasting Cos.* But: *Aluminum Company of America.*

If *company* or *companies* appears alone in second reference, spell the word out.

The forms for possessives: *Ford Motor Co.'s profits, American Broadcasting Cos.' profits.*

corporation   Abbreviate as *Corp.* when a company or government agency uses the word at the end of its name: *Gulf Oil Corp., the Federal Deposit Insurance Corp.*

Spell out *corporation* when it occurs elsewhere in a name: *the Corporation for Public Broadcasting.*

Spell out and lowercase *corporation* whenever it stands alone.

The form for possessives: *Gulf Oil Corp.'s profits.*

courtesy titles   [NOTE: Many newspapers consider the AP style (UPI style varies) on this subject to be sexist and have chosen to treat all women as men are treated—by first and last name on first reference and last name only on second reference. For the same reason, other newspapers use courtesy titles for both men and women on second reference. Despite those increasingly common deviations, the AP policy is quoted here; it is still the predominant policy at U.S. newspapers.]

In general, do not use the courtesy titles *Miss, Mr., Mrs.* or *Ms.* of first and last names of the person: *Barbara Bush, Jimmy Carter.*

Do not use *Mr.* in any reference unless it is combined with *Mrs.; Mr. and Mrs. John Smith.*

On sports wires, do not use courtesy titles in any reference unless needed to distinguish among people of the same last name.

On news wires, use courtesy titles for women on second reference, following the woman's preference. If the woman says she does not want a courtesy title, refer to her on second reference by last name only. Some guidelines:

MARRIED WOMEN: The preferred form on first reference is to identify a woman by her own first name and her husband's last name: *Susan Smith.* Use *Mrs.* on the first reference only if a woman requests that her husband's first name be used or her own first cannot be determined: *Mrs. John Smith.*

On second reference, use *Mrs.* unless a woman initially identified by her own first name prefers *Ms.: Carla Hills, Mrs. Hills, Ms. Hills* or no title: *Carla Hills, Hills.*

If a married woman is known by her maiden last name, precede it by *Miss* on second reference unless she prefers *Ms.: Jane Fonda, Miss Fonda, Ms. Fonda* or no title: *Jane Fonda, Fonda.*

UNMARRIED WOMEN: For women who have never been married, use *Miss, Ms.* or no title on second reference according to the woman's preferences.

For divorced women and widows, the normal practice is to use *Mrs.* or no title, if she prefers, on second reference. But, if a woman returns to the use of her maiden name, use *Miss, Ms.* or no title if she prefers it.

MARITAL STATUS   If a woman prefers *Ms.* or no title, do not include her marital status in a story unless it is clearly pertinent.

detective   Do not abbreviate.

district attorney   Do not abbreviate.

doctor   Use *Dr.* in first reference as a formal title before the name of an individual who holds a doctor of medicine degree: *Dr. Jonas Salk.*

The form *Dr.,* or *Drs.* in a plural construction, applies to all first-reference uses before a name, including direct quotations.

If appropriate in the context, *Dr.* also may be used on first reference before the names of individuals who hold other types of doctoral degrees. However, because the public frequently identifies *Dr.* only with physicians, care should be taken to assure that the individual's specialty is stated in first or second reference. The only exception would be a story in which the context left no doubt that the person was a dentist, psychologist, chemist, historian, etc.

In some instances it also is necessary to specify that an individual identified as *Dr.* is a physician. One frequent case is a story reporting on joint research by physicians, biologists, etc.

Do not use *Dr.* before the names of individuals who hold only honorary doctorates.

Do not continue the use of *Dr.* in subsequent references.

ERA   Acceptable in all references to baseball's *earned run average.* Acceptable on second reference for *Equal Rights Amendment.*

FBI   Acceptable in all references for *Federal Bureau of Investigation.*

FM   Acceptable in all references for the frequency modulation system of radio transmission.

ICBM, ICBMs   Acceptable on first reference for intercontinental ballistic missile(s), but the term should be defined in the body of a story.

Avoid the redundant *ICBM missiles.*

incorporated   Abbreviate and capitalize as *Inc.* when used as part of a corporate name. It usually is not needed, but when it is used, do not set off with commas: *J.C. Penney Co. Inc. announced . . .*

IQ   Acceptable in all references for *intelligence quotient.*

junior, senior   Abbreviate as *Jr.* and *Sr.* only with full names of persons or animals. Do not precede by a comma: *Joseph P. Kennedy Jr.*

The notation *II* or *2nd* may be used if it is the individual's preference. Note, however, that *II* and *2nd* are not necessarily the equivalent of junior—either may be used by a grandson or nephew.

If necessary to distinguish between father and son in second reference, use *the elder Smith* or *the younger Smith.*

mount   Spell out in all uses, including the names of communities and of mountains: *Mount Clements, Mich.; Mount Everest.*

mph   Acceptable in all references for *miles per hour* or *miles an hour.*

No.   Use as the abbreviation for *number* in conjunction with a figure to indicate position or rank: *No. 1 man, No. 3 choice.*

Do not use in street addresses, with this exception: *No. 10 Downing St.,* the residence of Britain's prime minister.

Do not use in the names of schools: *Public School 19.*

point   Do not abbreviate. Capitalize as part of a proper name: *Point Pleasant.*

saint   Abbreviate as *St.* in the names of saints, cities and other places: *St. Jude; St. Paul, Minn.; St. John's, Newfoundland; St. Lawrence Seaway.*

state names   Follow these guidelines:

STANDING ALONE: Spell out the names of the 50 U.S. states when they stand alone in textual material. Any state name may be condensed, however, to fit typographical requirements for tabular material.

EIGHT NOT ABBREVIATED: The names of eight states are never abbreviated in datelines or text: *Alaska, Hawaii, Idaho, Iowa, Maine, Ohio, Texas* and *Utah.*

ABBREVIATIONS REQUIRED: Use the state abbreviations listed at the end of this section:

In conjunction with the name of a city, town, village or military base in most datelines.

In conjunction with the name of a city, county, town, village or military base in text. See examples in punctuation section below.

In short-form listings of party affiliation: D-Ala., R. Mont.

The abbreviations are:

Ala.	Kan.	Nev.	R.I.
Ariz.	Ky.	N.H.	S.C.
Ark.	La.	N.J.	S.D.
Calif.	Md.	N.M.	Tenn.
Colo.	Mass.	N.Y.	Vt.
Conn.	Mich.	N.C.	Va.
Del.	Minn.	N.D.	Wash.
Fla.	Miss.	Okla.	W. Va.
Ga.	Mo.	Ore.	Wis.
Ill.	Mont.	Pa.	Wyo.
Ind.	Neb.		

TV   Acceptable as an adjective or in such constructions as *cable TV.* But do not normally use as a noun unless part of a quotation.

UFO, UFOs   Acceptable in all references for *unidentified flying object(s).*

U.N.   Used as an adjective, but not as a noun, for *United Nations.*

U.S.   Used as an adjective, but not as a noun, for *United States.*

PUNCTUATION AND HYPHENATION

Think of punctuation and hyphenation as a courtesy to your readers, designed to help them understand a story.

Inevitably, a mandate of this scope involves gray areas. For this reason, the punctuation entries in the stylebooks refer to guidelines rather than rules. Guidelines should not be treated casually, however.

ampersand (&)   Use the ampersand when it is part of a company's formal name: *Baltimore & Ohio Railroad, Newport News Shipbuilding & Dry Dock Co.*

The ampersand should not otherwise be used in place of *and.*

all–   Use a hyphen.

  all-around (not all-round)   all-out
  all-clear   all-star

anti–   Hyphenate all except the following words, which have specific meanings of their own:

antibiotic	antiknock	antiphony
antibody	antimatter	antiseptic
anticlimax	antimony	antiserum
antidote	antiparticle★	antithesis
antifreeze	antipasto	antitrust
antigen	antiperspirant	antitoxin
antihistamine	antiphon	antitussive

★ And similar terms in physics such as antiproton.

This approach has been adopted in the interests of readability and easy remembered consistency.

apostrophe (')   Follow these guidelines:

  POSSESSIVES: See the possessives entry.

  OMITTED LETTERS: *I've, it's, don't, rock 'n' roll. 'Tis the season to be jolly. He is a ne'er-do-well.*

  OMITTED FIGURES: *The class of '62. The Spirit of '76. The '20s.*

  PLURALS OF A SINGLE LETTER: *Mind your p's and q's. He learned the three R's and brought home a report card with four A's and two B's. The Oakland A's won the pennant.*

  DO NOT USE: For plurals of numerals or multiple-letter combinations.

by   In general, no hyphen. Some examples:

  byline   byproduct
  bypass   bystreet

By-election is an exception

co–   Retain the hyphen when forming nouns, adjectives and verbs that indicate occupation or status:

co-author	co-owner	co-signer
co-chairman	co-partner	co-star
co-defendant	co-pilot	co-worker
co-host	co-respondent (in a divorce suit)	

  (Several are exceptions to *Webster's New World* in the interests of consistency.)

  Use no hyphen in other combinations:

coed	coexist	cooperative
coeducation	coexistence	coordinate
coequal	cooperate	coordination

Cooperate, coordinate and related words are exceptions to the rule that a hyphen is used if a prefix ends in a vowel and the word that follows begins with the same vowel.

colon   The most frequent use of a colon is at the end of a sentence to introduce lists, tabulations, texts, etc.

Capitalize the first word after a colon only if it is a proper noun or the start of a complete sentence: *He promised this: The company will make good all the losses.* But: *There were three considerations: expense, time and feasibility.*

INTRODUCING QUOTATIONS: Use a comma to introduce a direct quotation of one sentence that remains within a paragraph. Use a colon to introduce longer quotations within a paragraph and to end all paragraphs that introduce a paragraph of quoted material.

PLACEMENT WITH QUOTATION MARKS: Colons go outside quotation marks unless they are part of the quotation itself.

comma   The following guidelines treat some of the most frequent questions about the use of commas. Additional guidelines on specialized uses are provided in separate entries.

For more detailed guidance, consult, "The Comma" and "Misused and Unnecessary Commas" in the Guide to Punctuation section in the back of *Webster's New World Dictionary.*

IN A SERIES: Use commas to separate elements in a series, but do not put a comma before the conjunction in a simple series: *The flag is red, white and blue. She would nominate Tom, Dick or Jane.*

Put a comma before the concluding conjunction in a series, however, if an integral element of the series requires a conjunction: *I had orange juice, toast, and ham and eggs for breakfast.*

Use a comma also before the concluding conjunction in a complex series of phrases: *The main points to consider are whether the athletes are skillful enough to compete, whether they have the stamina to endure the training, and whether they have the proper mental attitude.*

WITH EQUAL ADJECTIVES: Use commas to separate a series of adjectives equal in rank. If the commas could be replaced by the word *and* without changing the sense, the adjectives are equal: *a thoughtful, precise manner; a dark, dangerous street.*

Use no comma when the last adjective before a noun outranks its predecessors because it is an integral element of a noun phrase, which is the equivalent of a single noun: *a cheap fur coat* (the noun phrase is a fur coat); *the old oaken bucket; a new, blue spring bonnet.*

WITH INTRODUCTORY CLAUSES AND PHRASES: An comma normally is used to separate an introductory clause or phrase from a main clause: *When he had tired of the mad pace of New York, he moved to Dubuque.*

The comma may be omitted after short introductory phrases if no ambiguity would result: *During the night he heard many noises.*

But use the comma if its omission would slow comprehension: *On the street below, the curious gathered.*

WITH CONJUNCTIONS: When a conjunction such as *and, but* or *for* links two clauses that could stand alone as separate sentences, use a comma before the conjunction in most cases: *She was glad she had looked, for a man was approaching the house.*

As a rule of thumb, use a comma if the subject of each clause is expressly stated: *We are visiting Washington, and we also plan a side trip to Williamsburg. We visited Washington, and our senator greeted us personally.* But no comma when the subject of the two clauses is the same and is not repeated in the second: *We are visiting Washington and plan to see the White House.*

The comma may be dropped if two clauses with expressly stated subjects are short. In general, however, favor use of a comma unless a particular literary effect is desired or it would distort the sense of a sentence.

INTRODUCING DIRECT QUOTES: Use a comma to introduce a complete, one-sentence quotation within a paragraph: *Wallace said, "She spent six months in Argentina and came back speaking English with a Spanish accent."* But use a colon to introduce quotations of more than one sentence.

Do not use a comma at the start of an indirect or partial quotation: *He said his victory put him "firmly on the road to a first-ballot nomination."*

BEFORE ATTRIBUTION: Use a comma instead of a period at the end of a quote that is followed by attribution: *"Rub my shoulder," Miss Cawley suggested.*

Do not use a comma, however, if the quoted statement ends with a question mark or exclamation point: *"Why should I?" he asked.*

WITH HOMETOWNS AND AGES: Use a comma to set off an individual's hometown when it is placed in apposition to a name: *Mary Richards, Minneapolis, and Maude Findlay, Tuckahoe, N.Y., were there.* However, the use of the word *of* without a comma between the individual's name and the city name generally is preferable: *Mary Richards of Minneapolis and Maude Findlay of Tuckahoe, N.Y., were there.*

If an individual's age is used, set it off by commas: *Maude Findlay, 48, Tuckahoe, N.Y., was present.* The use of the word *of* eliminates the need for a comma after the hometown if a state name is not needed: *Mary Richards, 36, of Minneapolis and Maude Findlay, 48, of Tuckahoe, N.Y., attended the party.*

IN LARGE FIGURES: Use a comma for most figures higher than 999. The major exceptions are: street addresses *(1234 Main St.)*, broadcast frequencies *(1460 kilohertz)*, room numbers, serial numbers, telephone numbers, and years *(1976)*.

PLACEMENT WITH QUOTES: Commas always go inside quotation marks.

dash   Follow these guidelines:

ABRUPT CHANGE: Use dashes to denote an abrupt change in thought in a sentence or an emphatic pause: *We will fly to Paris in June—if I get a raise. Smith offered a plan—it was unprecedented—to raise revenues.*

SERIES WITHIN A PHRASE: When a phrase that otherwise would be set off by commas contains a series of words that must be separated by commas, use dashes to set off the full phrase: *He listed the qualities— intelligence, charm, beauty, independence—that he liked in women.*

ATTRIBUTION: Use a dash before an author's or composer's name at the end of a quotation: *"Who steals my purse steals trash."—Shakespeare.*

IN DATELINES:
NEW YORK (AP)—The city is broke.

IN LISTS: Dashes should be used to introduce individual sections of a list. Capitalize the first word following the dash. Use periods, not semicolons, at the end of each section. Example:
Jones gave the following reasons:
—He never ordered the package.
—If he did, it didn't come.
—If it did, he sent it back.

WITH SPACES: Put a space on both sides of a dash in all uses except the start of a paragraph and sports agate summaries.

ellipsis (. . .)   In general, treat an ellipsis as a three-letter word, constructed with three periods and two spaces, as shown here.

Use an ellipsis to indicate the deletion of one or more words in condensing quotes, texts and documents. Be especially careful to avoid deletions that would distort the meaning.

ex-   Use no hyphen for words that use *ex-* in the sense of *out of:*
excommunicate   expropriate

Hyphenate when using *ex* in the sense of former:
ex-convict   ex-president

Do not capitalize *ex-* when attached to a formal title before a name: *ex-President Carter.* The prefix modifies the entire term: *ex-New Jersey Gov. Thomas Kean;* not *ex-Gov. Thomas Kean.*

Usually *former* is better.

exclamation point (!)   Follow these guidelines:

EMPHATIC EXPRESSIONS: Use the mark to express a high degree of surprise, incredulity or other strong emotion.

AVOID OVERUSE: Use a comma after mild interjections. End mildly exclamatory sentences with a period.

PLACEMENT WITH QUOTES: Place the mark inside quotation marks when it is part of the quoted material: *"How wonderful!" he exclaimed. "Never!" she shouted.*

Place the mark outside quotation marks when it is not part of the quoted material: *I hated reading Spenser's "Faerie Queene"!*

extra-   Do not use a hyphen when *extra-* means *outside of* unless the prefix is followed by a word beginning with *a* or a capitalized word:
extralegal   extraterrestrial
extramarital   extraterritorial
    But
extra-alimentary   extra-Britannic

Follow *extra-* with a hyphen when it is part of a compound modifier describing a condition beyond the usual size, extent or degree:
extra-base hit   extra-large book
extra-dry drink   extra-mild taste

fore-   In general, no hyphen. Some examples:
forebrain   foregoing
forefather   foretooth

There are three nautical exceptions, based on long-standing practice:

    fore-topgallant   fore-topsail
    fore-topmast

full- Hyphenate when used to form compound modifiers:

    full-dress   full-page
    full-fledged   full-scale
    full-length

great- Hyphenate *great-grandfather, great-great-grandmother,* etc.

    Use *great grandfather* only if the intended meaning is that the grandfather was a great man.

hyphen Hyphens are joiners. Use them to avoid ambiguity or to form a single idea from two or more words.

    Some guidelines:

AVOID AMBIGUITY: Use a hyphen whenever ambiguity would result if it were omitted: *The president will speak to small-business men.* (*Businessmen* normally is one word. But *The president will speak to small businessmen* is unclear.)

COMPOUND MODIFIERS: When a compound modifier—two or more words that express a single concept—precedes a noun, use hyphens to link all the words in the compound except the adverb *very* and all adverbs that end in *ly: a first-quarter touchdown, a bluish-green dress, a full-time job, a well-known man, a better-qualified woman, a know-it-all attitude, a very good time, an easily remembered rule.*

    Many combinations that are hyphenated before a noun are not hyphenated before a noun are not hyphenated when they occur after a noun: *The team scored in the first quarter. The dress, a bluish green, was attractive on her. She works full time. His attitude suggested that he knew it all.*

    But when a modifier that would be hyphenated before a noun occurs instead after a form of the verb *to be,* the hyphen usually must be retained to avoid confusion: *The man is well-known. The woman is quick-witted. The children are soft-spoken. The play is second-rate.*

    The principle of using a hyphen to avoid confusion explains why no hyphen is required with *very* and *ly* words. Readers can expect them to modify the word that follows. But if a combination such as *little-known man* were not hyphenated, the reader could logically be expecting *little* to be followed by a noun, as in *little man.* Instead, the reader encountering *little known* would have to back up mentally and make the compound connection on his own.

TWO-THOUGHT COMPOUNDS: *serio-comic, socio-economic.*

COMPOUND PROPER NOUNS AND ADJECTIVES: Use a hyphen to designate dual heritage: *Italian-American, Mexican-American.*

    No hyphen, however, for *French Canadian* or *Latin American.*

AVOID DUPLICATED VOWELS, TRIPLED CONSONANTS: Examples:

anti-intellectual

pre-empt

shell-like

WITH NUMERALS: Use a hyphen to separate figures in odds, ratios, scores, some fractions and some vote tabulations. See examples in entries under these headings.

When large numbers must be spelled out, use a hyphen to connect a word ending in *y* to another word: *twenty-one, fifty-five,* etc.

SUSPENSIVE HYPHENATION: The form: *He received a 10- to 20-year sentence in prison.*

in-   No hyphen when it means "not"

inaccurate   insufferable

Often solid in other cases:

inbound   infighting

indoor   inpatient (n., adj.)

infield

A few combinations take a hyphen, however:

in-depth   in-house

in-group   in-law

Follow *Webster's New World* when in doubt.

-in   Precede with a hyphen:

break-in   walk-in

cave-in   write-in

parentheses   In general, use parentheses around logos, as shown in the datelines entry, but otherwise be sparing with them.

Parentheses are jarring to the reader. Because they do not appear on some news service printers there is also the danger that material inside them may be misinterpreted.

The temptation to use parentheses is a clue that a sentence is becoming contorted. Try to write it another way. If a sentence must contain incidental material, then commas or two dashes are frequently more effective. Use these alternatives whenever possible.

There are occasions, however, when parentheses are the only effective means of inserting necessary background or reference information.

periods   Follow these guidelines:

END OF DECLARATIVE SENTENCE: *The stylebook is finished.*

END OF A MILDLY IMPERATIVE SENTENCE: *Shut the door.*

Use an exclamation point if greater emphasis is desired: *Be careful!*

END OF SOME RHETORICAL QUESTIONS: A period is preferable if a statement is more a suggestion than a question: *Why don't we go.*

END OF AN INDIRECT QUESTION: *He asked what the score was.*

INITIALS: *John F. Kennedy, T.S. Eliot.* (No space between T. and S., to prevent them from being placed on two lines in typesetting.)

Abbreviations using only the initials of a name do not take periods: *JFK, LBJ.*

ENUMERATIONS: After numbers or letters in enumerating elements of a summary: *1. Wash the car. 2. Clean the basement.* Or: *A. Punctuate properly. B. Write simply.*

possessives Follow these guidelines:

PLURAL NOUNS NOT ENDING IN S: Add *'s: the alumni's contributions, women's rights.*

PLURAL NOUNS ENDING IN S: Add only an apostrophe: *the churches' needs, the girls' toys, the horses' food, the ships' wake, states' rights, the VIPs' entrance.*

NOUNS PLURAL IN FORM, SINGULAR IN MEANING: Add only an apostrophe: *mathematics' rules, measles' effects.* (But see INANIMATE OBJECTS below.)

Apply the same principle when a plural word occurs in the formal name of a singular entity: *General Motors' profits, the United States' wealth.*

NOUNS THE SAME IN SINGULAR AND PLURAL: Treat them the same as plurals, even if the meaning is singular: *one corps' location, the two deer's tracks, the lone moose's antlers.*

SINGULAR NOUNS NOT ENDING IN S: Add *'s: the church's needs, the girl's toys, the horse's food, the ship's route, the VIP's seat.*

Some style guides say that singular nouns ending is *s* sounds such as *ce, x,* and *z* may take either the apostrophe alone or *'s.* See SPECIAL EXPRESSIONS below, but otherwise, for consistency and ease in remembering a rule, always use *'s* if the word does not end in the letter *s: Butz's policies, the fox's den, the justice's verdict, Marx's theories, the prince's life, Xerox's profits.*

SINGULAR PROPER NAMES ENDING IN S: Use only an apostrophe: *Achilles' heel, Agnes' book, Ceres' rites, Descartes' theories, Dickens' novels, Euripides' dramas, Hercules' labors, Jesus' life, Jules' seat, Kansas' schools, Moses' law, Socrates' life, Tennessee Williams' plays, Xerxes' armies.*

SPECIAL EXPRESSIONS: The following exceptions to the general rule for words not ending in *s* apply to words that end in an *s* sound and are followed by a word that begins with *s: for appearance's cost, my conscience's voice.*

PRONOUNS: Personal, interrogative and relative pronouns have separate forms for the possessive. None involves an apostrophe: *mine, ours, yours, his, hers, its, theirs, whose.*

Caution: If you are using an apostrophe with a pronoun, always double-check to be sure that the meaning calls for a contraction: *you're, it's, there's, who's.*

Follow the rules listed above in forming the possessives of other pronouns: *another's idea, other's plans, someone's guess.*

COMPOUND WORDS: Applying the rules above, add an apostrophe or *'s* to the word closest to the object possessed: *the major general's decision, the major generals' decisions, the attorney general's request, the attorneys generals' request.* See the plurals entry for guidelines on forming the plurals of these words.

Also: *anyone else's attitude, John Adams Jr.'s father, Benjamin Franklin of Pennsylvania's motion.* Whenever practical, however, recast the phrase to avoid ambiguity: *the motion by Benjamin Franklin of Pennsylvania.*

JOINT POSSESSION, INDIVIDUAL POSSESSION: Use a possessive form after only the last word if ownership is joint: *Fred and Sylvia's apartment, Fred and Sylvia's stocks.*

Use a possessive form after both words if the objects are individually owned: *Fred's and Sylvia's books.*

DESCRIPTIVE PHRASES: Do not add an apostrophe to a word ending in *s* when it is used primarily in a descriptive sense: *citizens band radio, a Cincinnati Reds infielder, a teachers college, a Teamsters request, a writers guide.*

Memory Aid: The apostrophe usually is not used if *for* or *by* rather than *of* would be appropriate in the longer form: *a radio band for citizens, a college for teachers, a guide for writers, a request by the Teamsters.*

An *'s* is required, however, when a term involves a plural word that does not end in *s: a children's hospital, a people's republic, the Young Women's Christian Association.*

DESCRIPTIVE NAMES: Some governmental, corporate and institutional organizations with a descriptive word in their names use an apostrophe; some do not. Follow the user's practice: *Actors Equity, Diners Club, the Ladies' Home Journal, the National Governors' Conference, the Veterans Administration.* See separate entries for these and similar names frequently in the news.

QUASI POSSESSIVES: Follow the rules above in composing the possessive form of words that occur in such phrases as *a day's pay, two weeks' vacation, three days' work, your money's worth.*

Frequently, however, a hyphenated form is clearer: *a two-week vacation, a three-day job.*

DOUBLE POSSESSIVE: Two conditions must apply for a double possessive—a phrase such as *a friend of John's*—to occur: 1. The word after *of* must refer to an animate object, and 2. The word before *of* must involve only a portion of the animate object's possessions.

Otherwise, do not use the possessive form on the word after *of: The friends of John Adams mourned his death.* (All the friends were involved.) *He is a friend of the college.* (Not *college's,* because *college* is inanimate).

Memory Aid: This construction occurs most often, and quite naturally, with the possessive forms of personal pronouns: *She is a friend of mine.*

INANIMATE OBJECTS: There is no blanket rule against creating a possessive form for an inanimate object, particularly if the object is treated in a personified sense. See some of the earlier examples, and note these: *death's call, the wind's murmur.*

In general, however, avoid excessive personalization of inanimate objects, and give preference to an *of* construction when it fits the makeup of the sentence. For example, the earlier references to mathematics' rules and measles' effects would better be phrased: *the rules of mathematics, the effects of measles.*

post- Follow *Webster's New World.* Hyphenate if not listed there. Some words without a hyphen:

postdate	postgraduate	postscript
postdoctoral	postnuptial	postwar
postelection	postoperative	

Some words that use a hyphen:

post-bellum   post-mortem

prefixes See separate listings for commonly used prefixes.

Three rules are constant, although they yield some exceptions to first-listed spellings in *Webster's New World Dictionary:*

Except for *cooperate* and *coordinate,* use a hyphen if the prefix ends in a vowel.

Use a hyphen if the word that follows is capitalized.

Use a hyphen to join doubled prefixes: *sub-subparagraph.*

pro- Use a hyphen when coining words that denote support for something. Some examples:

pro-business   pro-life
pro-labor   pro-war

No hyphen when *pro* is used in other senses:

produce   pronoun
profile

question mark Follow these guidelines:

END OF A DIRECT QUESTION: *Who started the riot?*

Did she ask who started the riot? (The sentence as a whole is a direct question despite the indirect question at the end.)

You started the riot? (A question in the form of a declarative statement.)

INTERPOLATED QUESTION: *You told me—Did I hear you correctly?—that you started the riot.*

MULTIPLE QUESTIONS: Use a single question mark at the end of the full sentence:

Did you hear him say, "What right have you to ask about the riot?"
Did he plan the riot, employ assistants, and give the signal to begin?

Or, to cause full stops and throw emphasis on each element, break into separate sentences: *Did he plan the riot? Employ assistants? Give the signal to begin?*

CAUTION: Do not use question marks to indicate the end of an indirect question:

She asked who started the riot. To ask why the riot started is unnecessary. I want to know what the cause of the riot was. How foolish it is to ask what caused the riot.

QUESTION AND ANSWER FORMAT: Do not use quotation marks. Paragraph each speaker's words:

Q. Where did you keep it?
A. In a little tin box.

PLACEMENT WITH QUOTATION MARKS: Inside or outside, depending on the meaning:

> *Who wrote "Gone With the Wind"?*
> *He asked, "How long will it take?"*

MISCELLANEOUS: The question mark supersedes the comma that normally is used when supplying attribution for a quotation: *"Who is there?" she asked.*

quotation marks   The basic guidelines for open-quote marks (") and close-quote marks ("):

FOR DIRECT QUOTATIONS: To surround the exact words of a speaker or writer when reported in a story:

> *"I have no intention of staying," she replied.*
> *"I do not object," he said, "to the tenor of the report."*
> *Franklin said, "A penny saved is a penny earned."*
> *A speaker said the practice is "too conservative for inflationary times."*

RUNNING QUOTATIONS: If a full paragraph of quoted material is followed by a paragraph that continues the quotation, do not put close-quote marks at the end of the first paragraph. Do, however, put open-quote marks at the start of the second paragraph. Continue in this fashion for any succeeding paragraphs, using close-quote marks only at the end of the quoted material.

If a paragraph does not start with quotation marks but ends with a quotation that is continued in the next paragraph, do not use close-quote marks at the end of the introductory paragraph if the quoted material constitutes a full sentence. Use close-quote marks, however, if the quoted material does not constitute a full sentence.

DIALOGUE OR CONVERSATION: Each person's words, no matter how brief, are placed in a separate paragraph, with quotation marks at the beginning and the end of each person's speech:

> *"Will you go?"*
> *"Yes."*
> *"When?"*
> *"Thursday."*

NOT IN Q/A: Quotation marks are not required in formats that identify questions and answers by Q. and A.

NOT IN TEXTS: Quotation marks are not required in full texts, condensed texts or textual excerpts.

IRONY: Put quotation marks around a word or words used in an ironic sense: *The "debate" turned into a free-for-all.*

UNFAMILIAR TERMS: A word or words being introduced to readers may be placed in quotation marks on first reference:

> *Broadcast frequencies are measured in "kilohertz."*

Do not put subsequent references to kilohertz in quotation marks.

AVOID UNNECESSARY FRAGMENTS: Do not use quotation marks to report a few ordinary words that a speaker or writer has used:

> Wrong: *The senator said he would "go home to Michigan" if he lost the election.*
>
> Right: *The senator said he would go home to Michigan if he lost the election.*

PARTIAL QUOTES: When a partial quote is used, do not put quotation marks around words that the speaker could not have used.

> Suppose the individual said, "I am horrified at your slovenly manners."
>
> Wrong: *She said she "was horrified at their slovenly manners."*
>
> Right: *She said she was horrified at their "slovenly manners."*
>
> Better when practical: Use the full quote.

QUOTES WITHIN QUOTES: Alternate between double quotation marks *("or")* and single marks *('or')*:

> *She said, "I quote from his letter, 'I agree with Kipling that "the female of the species is more deadly than the male," but the phenomenon is not an unchangeable law of nature,' a remark he did not explain."*
>
> Use three marks together if two quoted elements end at the same time: *She said, "He told me, 'I love you.'"*

PLACEMENT WITH OTHER PUNCTUATION: Follow these long-established printers' rules:

> The period and the comma always go within the quotation marks.
>
> The dash, the semicolon, the question mark and the exclamation point go within the quotation marks when they apply to the quoted matter only. They go outside when they apply to the whole sentence.

re-   The rules in prefixes apply. The following examples of exceptions to first-listed spellings in *Webster's New World* are based on the general rule that a hyphen is used if a prefix ends in a vowel and the word that follows begins with the same vowel:

re-elect	re-enact	re-entry
re-election	re-engage	re-equip
re-emerge	re-enlist	re-establish
re-employ	re-enter	re-examine

For many other words, the sense is the governing factor:

recover (regain)	resign (quit)	reform (improve)
re-cover (cover again)	re-sign (sign again)	re-form (form again)

Otherwise, follow *Webster's New World.* Use a hyphen for words not listed there unless the hyphen would distort the sense.

semicolon   In general, use the semicolon to indicate a greater separation of thought and information than a comma can convey but less than the separation that a period implies.

suffixes   See separate listings for commonly used suffixes.

> Follow *Webster's New World Dictionary* for words not in this book.
>
> If a word combination is not listed in *Webster's New World,* use two words for the verb form; hyphenate any noun or adjective forms.

suspensive hyphenation   The form: The 5- and 6-year-olds attend morning classes.

NUMERALS

A numeral is a figure, letter, word or group of words expressing a number.

Roman numerals use the letters *I, V, X, L, C, D* and *M.* Use Roman numerals for wars and to show personal sequence for animals and people: *World War II, Native Dancer II, King George VI, Pope John Paul II.*

Arabic numerals use the figures *1, 2, 3, 4, 5, 6, 7, 8, 9* and *0.* Use Arabic forms unless Roman numerals are specifically required.

The figures *1, 2, 10, 101,* etc., and the corresponding words—*one, two, ten, one hundred one,* etc.—are called cardinal numbers. The term ordinal number applies to *1st, 2nd, 10th, 101st, first, second, tenth, one hundred first,* etc.

Follow these guidelines in using numerals:

LARGE NUMBERS

When large numbers must be spelled out, use a hyphen to connect a word ending in *y* to another word; do not use commas between other separate words that are part of one number: *twenty; thirty; twenty-one; thirty-one; one hundred forty-three; one thousand one hundred fifty-five; one million two hundred seventy-six thousand five hundred eighty-seven.*

SENTENCE START

Spell out a numeral at the beginning of a sentence. If necessary, recast the sentence. There is one exception—a numeral that identifies a calendar year.

Wrong: *993 freshmen entered the college last year.*
Right: *Last year 993 freshmen entered the college.*
Right: *1976 was a very good year.*

CASUAL USES

Spell out casual expressions:

A thousand times no! Thanks a million. He walked a quarter of a mile.

PROPER NAMES

Use words or numerals according to an organization's practice:

20th Century-Fox, Twentieth Century Fund, Big Ten.

FIGURES OR WORDS

For ordinals:

Spell out first through ninth when they indicate sequence in time or location—*first base, the First Amendment, he was first in line.* Starting with *10th,* use figures.

Use *1st, 2nd, 3rd, 4th,* etc., when the sequence has been assigned in forming names. The principal examples are geographic, military and political designations such as *1st Ward, 7th Fleet* and *1st Sgt.*

OTHER USES

For uses not covered by these listings: Spell out whole numbers below 10, use figures for 10 and above. Typical examples: *The woman has three sons and two daughters. She has a fleet of 10 station wagons and two buses.*

IN A SERIES

Apply the appropriate guidelines: *They had 10 dogs, six cats and 97 hamsters. They had four four-room houses, 10 three-room houses and 12 10-room houses.*

What follows is an alphabetical listing of other key points of using numerals.

addresses Always use figures for an address number: *9 Morningside Circle.*

Spell out and capitalize *First* through *Ninth* when used as street names; use figures with two letters for *10th* and above: *7 Fifth Ave., 100 21st St.*

ages Always use figures. When the context does not require years or years old, the figure is presumed to be years.

aircraft names Use a hyphen when changing from letters to figures; no hyphen when adding a letter after figures.

Some examples for aircraft often in the news: *B-1, BAC-111, C-5A, DC-10, FH-227, F-14, Phantom II, F-86 Sabre, L-1011, Mig-21, TU-144, 727-100c, 747, 747B, VC-10.*

amendments to the Constitution Use *First Amendment, 10th Amendment,* etc.

Colloquial references to the Fifth Amendment's protection against self-incrimination are best avoided, but where appropriate: *He took the Fifth seven times.*

Arabic numerals The numerical figures *1, 2, 3, 4, 5, 6, 7, 8, 9, 10.* In general, use Arabic forms unless denoting the sequence of wars or establishing a personal sequence for people and animals.

betting odds Use figures and a hyphen: *The odds were 5-4. He won despite 3-2 odds against him.*

The word *to* seldom is necessary, but when it appears it should be hyphenated in all constructions: *3-to-2 odds, odds of 3-to-2, the odds were 3-to-2.*

Celsius Use this term rather than centigrade for the temperature scale that is part of the metric system.

When giving a Celsius temperature, use these forms: *40 degrees Celsius* or *40 C* (Note the space and no period after the capital C) if degrees and Celsius are clear from the context.

cents   Spell out the word *cents* and lowercase, using numerals for amounts less than a dollar: *5 cents, 12 cents.* Use the $ sign and decimal system for larger amounts: *$1.01, $2.50.*

Numerals alone, with or without a decimal point as appropriate, may be used in tabular matter.

congressional districts   Use figures and capitalize *district* when joined with a figure: *the 1st Congressional District, the 1st District.*

Lowercase *district* whenever it stands alone.

court decisions   Use figures and a hyphen: *The Supreme Court ruled 5-4, a 5-4 decision.* The word *to* is not needed, but use hyphens if it appears in quoted matter: *"the court ruled 5-to-4, the 5-to-4 decision."*

court names   For courts identified by a numeral: *2nd District Court, 8th U.S. Circuit Court of Appeals.*

dates   Always use Arabic figures, without *st, nd, rd* or *th.*

decades   Use Arabic figures to indicate decades of history. Use an apostrophe to indicate numerals that are left out; show plural by adding the letter *s: the 1890s, the '90s, the Gay '90s, the 1920s, the mid-1930s.*

decimal units   Use a period and numerals to indicate decimal amounts. Decimalization should not exceed two places in textual material unless there are special circumstances.

dimensions   Use figures and spell out inches, feet, yards, etc., to indicate depth, height, length and width. Hyphenate adjectival forms before nouns.

Use an apostrophe to indicate feet and quote marks to indicate inches *(5'6")* only in very technical contexts.

distances   Use figures for 10 and above, spell out one through nine: *He walked four miles.*

district   Use a figure and capitalize district when forming a proper name: *the 2nd District.*

dollars   Use figures and the $ sign in all except casual references or amounts without a figure: *The book cost $4. Dad, please give me a dollar. Dollars are flowing overseas.*

For specified amounts, the word takes a singular verb: *He said $500,000 is what they want.*

For amounts of more than $1 million, use the $ and numerals up to two decimal places. Do not link the numerals and the word by a hyphen: *She is worth $4.35 million. She is worth exactly $4,351,242. He proposed a $300 billion budget.*

The form for amounts less than $1 million: *$4, $25, $500, $1,000, $650,000.*

election returns   Use figures, with commas every three digits starting at the right and counting left. Use the word *to* (not a hyphen) in separating different totals listed together: *George Bush defeated Michael Dukakis 48,881,221 to 41,805,422 in 1988* (this is the actual final figure).

Use the word *votes* if there is any possibility that the figures could be confused with a ratio: *Bush defeated Dukakis 16 votes to 3 votes in Dixville Notch.*

Do not attempt to create adjectival forms such as *the 48,881,221-41,805,422 vote.*

fractions   Spell out amounts less than *1* in stories, using hyphens between the words: *two-thirds, four-fifths, seven-sixteenths,* etc.

Use figures for precise amounts larger than *1,* converting to decimals whenever practical.

Fractions are preferred, however, in stories about stocks.

When using fractional characters, remember that most newspaper type fonts can set only $\frac{1}{8}$, $\frac{1}{4}$, $\frac{3}{8}$, $\frac{1}{2}$, $\frac{5}{8}$, $\frac{3}{4}$, and $\frac{7}{8}$ as one unit; use $1\frac{1}{2}$, $2\frac{5}{8}$, etc. with no space between the figure and the fraction. Other fractions require a hyphen and individual figures, with a space between the whole number and the fraction: *1 3-16, 2 1-3, 5 9-10.*

highway designations   Use these forms, as appropriate in the context, for highways identified by number: *U.S. Highway 1, U.S. Route 1, U.S. 1, Route Q, Illinois 34, Illinois Route 34, state Route 34, Route 34, Interstate Highway 495.* On second reference only for Interstate: *I-495.*

mile   Use figures for amounts under 10 in dimensions, formulas and speeds: *The farm measures 5 miles by 4 miles. The car slowed to 7 mph. The new model gets 4 miles more per gallon.*

Spell out below 10 in distances: *He drove four miles.*

millions, billions   Use figures with million or billion in all except casual uses: *I'd like to make a billion dollars.* But: *The nation has 1 million citizens. I need $7 billion.*

Do not go beyond two decimals: *7.51 million persons, $2.56 billion, 7,542,500 persons, $2,565,750,000.* Decimals are preferred where practical: *1.5 million.* Not: *1½ million.*

Do not mix millions and billions in the same figure: *2.6 billion.* Not *2 billion, 600 million.*

Do not drop the word million or billion in the first figure of a range: *He is worth from $2 million to $4 million.* Not: *$2 to $4 million,* unless you really mean $2.

Note that a hyphen is not used to join the figures and the word million or billion, even in this type of phrase: *The president submitted a $3 billion budget.*

minus sign   Use a hyphen, not a dash, but use the word minus if there is any danger of confusion.

Use a word, not a minus sign, to indicate temperatures below zero: *minus 10* or *5 below zero.*

No.   Use as the abbreviation for number in conjunction with a figure to indicate position or rank: *No. 1 person, No. 3 choice.*

Do not use in street addresses, with this exception: *No. 10 Downing St.,* the residence of Britain's prime minister.

Do not use in the names of schools: *Public School 19.*

page numbers   Use figures and capitalize *page* when used with a figure. When a letter is appended to the figure, capitalize it but do not use a hyphen: *Page 2, Page 10, Page 20A.*

One exception: *It's a Page One story.*

percentages   Use figures: *1 percent, 2.5 percent* (use decimals not fractions), *10 percent.*

For amounts less than 1 percent, precede the decimal with a zero: *The cost of living rose 0.6 percent.*

Repeat percent with each individual figure: *He said 10 percent to 30 percent of the electorate may not vote.*

political divisions   Use Arabic figures and capitalize the accompanying word when used with the figure: *1st Ward, 10th Ward, 3rd Precinct, 22nd Precinct, the ward, the precinct.*

proportions   Always use figures: *2 parts powder to 6 parts water.*

ratios   Use figures and a hyphen: *the ratio was 2-to-1, a ratio of 2-to-1, a 2-1 ratio.* As illustrated, the word *to* should be omitted when the numbers precede the word *ratio.*

Always use the word *ratio* or a phrase such as *a 2-1 majority* to avoid confusion with actual figures.

scores   Use figures exclusively, placing a hyphen between the totals of the winning and losing teams: *The Reds defeated the Red Sox 4-3, the Giants scored a 12-6 football victory over the Cardinals, the golfer had a 5 on the first hole but finished with a 2-under-par score.*

Use a comma in this format: *Boston 6, Baltimore 5.*

sizes   Use figures: *a size 9 dress, size 40 long, 10½ B shoes, a 34½ sleeve.*

speeds   Use figures. *The car slowed to 7 mph, winds of 5 to 10 mph, winds of 7 to 9 knots, 10-knot winds.*

Avoid extensively hyphenated constructions such as *5-mile-per-hour winds.*

telephone numbers   Use figures. The forms: *(212) 262-4000, 262-4000.* If extension numbers are given: *Ext. 2, Ext. 364, Ext. 4071.*

temperatures   Use figures for all except zero. Use a word, not a minus sign, to indicate temperatures below zero.

times   Use figures except for noon and midnight. Use a colon to separate hours from minutes: *11 a.m., 1 p.m., 3:30 p.m.*

Avoid such redundancies as *10 a.m. this morning, 10 p.m. tonight* or *10 p.m. Monday night.* Use *10 a.m. today, 10 p.m. Monday,* etc., as required by the norms in time element.

The construction *4 o'clock* is acceptable, but time listings with *a.m.* or *p.m.* are preferred.

weights   Use figures: *The baby weighed 9 pounds, 7 ounces. She had a 9-pound, 7-ounce boy.*

years   Use figures, without commas: *1985.* Use an *s* without an apostrophe to indicate spans of decades or centuries: *the 1890s, the 1800s.*

Years are the lone exception to the general rule in numerals that a figure is not used to start a sentence: *1984 was a very good year.*

GRAMMAR, SPELLING AND WORD USAGE

This section lists common problems of grammatical usage, word selection and spelling.

a, an   Use the article *a* before consonant sounds: *a historic event, a one-year term* (sounds as if it begins with the letter *w*), *a united stand* (sounds like *you*.).

Use the article *an* before vowel sounds: *an energy crisis, an honorable man* (the *h* is silent), *an MBA record* (sounds as if it begins with the letter *e*), *an 1890s celebration.*

accept, except   *Accept* means to receive.

Except means to exclude.

adverse, averse   *Adverse* means unfavorable: *She predicted adverse weather.*

Averse means reluctant, opposed: *He is averse to change.*

affect, effect   *Affect,* as a verb, means to influence: *The game will affect the standings.*

Affect, as a noun, is best avoided. It occasionally is used in psychology to describe an emotion, but there is no need for it in everyday language.

Effect, as a verb, means to cause: *He will effect many changes in the company.*

Effect, as a noun, means result: *The effect was overwhelming. She miscalculated the effect of her actions. It was a law of little effect.*

aid, aide   Aid is assistance.

An *aide* is a person who serves as an assistant.

ain't   A dialectical or substandard contraction. Use it only in quoted matter or special contexts.

allude, refer   To *allude* to something is to speak of it without specifically mentioning it.

To *refer* is to mention it directly.

allusion, illusion   *Allusion* means an indirect reference: *The allusion was to his opponent's record.*

Illusion means an unreal or false impression: *The scenic director created the illusion of choppy seas.*

among, between   The maxim that *between* introduces two items and *among* introduces more than two covers most questions about how to use these words: *The funds were divided among Susan, Robert and William.*

However, *between* is the correct word when expressing the relationships of three or more items considered one pair at a time: *Negotiations on a debate format are under way between the network and the Jackson, Kennedy and Mondale committees.*

As with all prepositions, any pronouns that follow these words must be in the objective case: *among us, between him and her, between you and me.*

anticipate, expect   *Anticipate* means to expect and prepare for something; *expect* does not include the notion of preparation:

They expect a record crowd. They have anticipated it by adding more seats to the auditorium.

anybody, any body, anyone, any one   One word for an indefinite reference: *Anyone can do that.*

Two words when the emphasis is on singling out one element of a group: *Any one of them may speak up.*

apposition   A decision on whether to put commas around a word, phrase or clause used in apposition depends on whether it is essential to the meaning of the sentence (no commas) or not essential (use commas).

because, since   Use *because* to denote a specific cause-effect relationship: *He went because he was told.*

Since is acceptable in causal sense when the first event in a sequence led logically to the second but was not its direct cause: *He went to the game, since he had been given the tickets.*

blond, blonde   Use *blond* as a noun for males and as the adjective for all applications: *She has blond hair.*

Use *blonde* as a noun for females.

boy   Applicable until 18th birthday is reached. Use *man* or *young man* afterward.

brunet, brunette   Use *brunet* as a noun for males and as the adjective for both sexes.

Use *brunette* as a noun for females.

burglary, larceny, robbery, theft   Legal definitions of burglary vary, but in general a *burglary* involves entering a building (not necessarily by breaking in) and remaining unlawfully with the intention of committing a crime.

Larceny is the legal term for the wrongful taking of property. Its nonlegal equivalents are stealing or theft.

Robbery in the legal sense involves the use of violence or threat in committing larceny. In a wider sense it means to plunder or rifle, and may thus be used even if a person was not present: *Her house was robbed while she was away.*

Theft describes a larceny that did not involve threat, violence or plundering.

USAGE NOTE: You rob a person, bank, house, etc., but you steal the money or the jewels.

collective nouns   Nouns that denote a unit take singular verbs and pronouns: *class, committee, crowd, family group, herd, jury, orchestra, team.*

Some usage examples: *The committee is meeting to set its agenda. The jury reached its verdict. A herd of cattle was sold.*

PLURAL IN FORM: Some words that are plural in form become collective nouns and take singular verbs when the group or quantity is regarded as a unit.

Right: *A thousand bushels is a good yield.* (A unit.)

Right: *A thousand bushels were created.* (Individual items.)

Right: *The data is sound.* (A unit.)

Right: *The data have been carefully collected.* (Individual items.)

compose, comprise, constitute   *Compose* means to create or put together. It commonly is used in both the active and passive voices: *She composed a song. The United States is composed of 50 states. The zoo is composed of many animals.*

Comprise means to contain, to include all or embrace. It is best used only in the active voice, followed by a direct object: *The United States comprises 50 states. The jury comprises five men and seven women. The zoo comprises many animals.*

Constitute, in the sense of form or make up, may be the best word if neither *compose* nor *comprise* seems to fit: *Fifty states constitute the United*

States. Five men and seven women constitute the jury. A collection of animals can constitute a zoo.

Use *include* when what follows is only part of the total: *The price includes breakfast. The zoo includes lions and tigers.*

contractions   Contractions reflect informal speech and writing. *Webster's New World Dictionary* includes many entries for contractions: *aren't* for *are not,* for example.

Avoid excessive use of contractions. Contractions listed in the dictionary are acceptable, however, in informal contexts or circumstances where they reflect the way a phrase commonly appears in speech or writing.

contrasted to, contrasted with   Use *contrasted to* when the intent is to assert, without the need for elaboration, that two items have opposite characteristics: *He contrasted the appearance of the house today to its ramshackle look last year.*

Use *contrasted with* when juxtaposing two or more items to illustrate similarities and/or differences: *He contrasted the Republican platform with the Democratic platform.*

dangling modifiers   Avoid modifiers that do not refer clearly and logically to some word in the sentence.

Dangling: *Taking our seats, the game started.* (Taking does not refer to the subject, game, nor to any other word in the sentence.)

Correct: *Taking our seats, we watched the opening of the game.* (Taking refers to we, the subject of the sentence.)

either   Use it to mean *one or the other,* not *both.*

Right: *She said to use either door.*

Wrong: *There were lions on either side of the door.*

Right: *There were lions on each side of the door. There were lions on both sides of the door.*

either ... or, neither ... nor   The nouns that follow these words do not constitute a compound subject; they are alternate subjects and require a verb that agrees with the nearer subject: *Neither they nor he is going. Neither he nor they are going.*

essential clauses, nonessential clauses   These terms are used instead of restrictive clause and nonrestrictive clause to convey the distinction between the two in a more easily remembered manner.

Both types of clauses provide additional information about a word or phrase in the sentence.

The difference between them is that the essential clause cannot be eliminated without changing the meaning of the sentence—it so "restricts" the meaning of the word or phrase that its absence would lead to a substantially different interpretation of what the author meant.

The nonessential clause, however, can be eliminated without altering the basic meaning of the sentence—it does not "restrict" the meaning so significantly that its absence would radically alter the author's thought.

PUNCTUATION: An essential clause must not be set off from the rest of a sentence by commas. A nonessential clause must be set off by commas.

The presence or absence of commas provides the reader with critical information about the writer's intended meaning. Note the following examples:

Reporters who do not read the stylebook should not criticize their editors. (The writer is saying that only one class of reporters, those who do not read the stylebook, should not criticize their editors. If the *who . . . stylebook* phrase were deleted, the meaning of the sentence would be changed substantially.)

Reporters, who do not read the stylebook, should not criticize their editors. (The writer is saying that all reporters should not criticize their editors. If the *who . . . stylebook* phrase were deleted, this meaning would not be changed.)

USE OF WHO, THAT, WHICH: When an essential or nonessential clause refers to a human being or an animal with a name, it should be introduced by *who* or *whom*. (see the *Who, Whom* entry.) Do not use commas if the clause is essential to the meaning; use them if it is not.

That is the preferred pronoun to introduce essential clauses that refer to an inanimate object or an animal without a name. *Which* is the only acceptable pronoun to introduce a nonessential clause that refers to an inanimate object or an animal without a name.

The pronoun *which* occasionally may be substituted for *that* in the introduction of an essential clause that refers to an inanimate object or an animal without a name. In general, this use of *which* should appear only when *that* is used as a conjunction to introduce another clause in the same sentence: *He said Monday that the part of the army which suffered severe casualties needs reinforcement.*

essential phrases, nonessential phrases   These terms are used instead of restrictive phrase and nonrestrictive phrase to convey the distinction between the two in a more easily remembered manner.

The underlying concept is the one that also applies to clauses:

An *essential phrase* is a word or group of words critical to the reader's understanding of what the author had in mind.

A *nonessential phrase* provides more information about something. Although the information may be helpful to the reader's comprehension, the reader would not be misled if the information were not there.

PUNCTUATION: Do not set off an essential phrase from the rest of a sentence by commas:

We saw the award-winning movie "One Flew Over the Cuckoo's Nest." (No comma, because many movies have won awards, and without the name of the movie the reader would not know which movie was meant.)

They ate dinner with their daughter Julie. (Because they have more than one daughter, the inclusion of Julie's name is critical if the reader is to know which daughter is meant.)

Set off nonessential phrases by commas:

We saw the 1976 winner in the Academy Award competition for best movie, "One Flew Over the Cuckoo's Nest." (Only one movie won the award. The name is informative, but even without the name no other movie could be meant.)

> *They ate dinner with their daughter Julie and her husband, David.* (Julie has only one husband. If the phrase read *and her husband David*, it would suggest that she had more than one husband.)

> *The company chairman, Henry Ford II, spoke.* (In the context, only one person could be meant.)

> *Indian corn, or maize, was harvested.* (*Maize* provides the reader with the name of the corn, but its absence would not change the meaning of the sentence.)

DESCRIPTIVE WORDS: Do not confuse punctuation rules for nonessential clauses with the correct punctuation when a nonessential word is used as a descriptive adjective. The distinguishing clue often is the lack of an article or pronoun:

> Right: *Julie and husband David went shopping. Julie and her husband, David, went shopping.*

> Right: *Company Chairman Henry Ford II made the announcement. The company chairman, Henry Ford II, made the announcement.*

every one, everyone   Two words when it means each individual item: *Every one of the clues was worthless.*

> One word when used as a pronoun meaning all persons: *Everyone wants his life to be happy.* (Note that *everyone* takes singular verbs and pronouns.)

farther, further   *Farther* refers to physical distance: *He walked farther into the woods.*

> *Further* refers to an extension of time or degree: *She will look further into the mystery.*

fewer, less   In general, use *fewer* for individual items, *less* for bulk or quantity.

flaunt, flout   To *flaunt* is to make an ostentatious or defiant display: *She flaunted her beauty.*

> To *flout* is to show contempt for: *She flouts the law.*

flier, flyer   *Flier* is the preferred term for an aviator or a handbill.

> *Flyer* is the proper name of some trains and buses: *The Western Flyer.*

good, well   *Good* is an adjective that means something is as it should be or is better than average.

> When used as an adjective, *well* means suitable, proper, healthy. When used as an adverb, *well* means in a satisfactory manner or skillfully.

> *Good* should not be used as an adverb. It does not lose its status as an adjective in a sentence such as *I feel good.* Such a statement is the idiomatic equivalent of *I am in good health.* An alternative, *I feel well,* could be interpreted as meaning that your sense of touch was good.

hopefully   It means in a hopeful manner. Do not use it to mean *it is hoped, let us hope* or *we hope.*

> Right: *It is hoped that we will complete our work in June.*

> Right: *We hope that we will complete our work in June.*

> Wrong as a saying to express the thought in the previous two sentences: *Hopefully, we will complete our work in June.*

imply, infer   Writers or speakers *imply* in the words they use. A listener or reader *infers* something from the words.

in, into   *In* indicates location: *He was in the room.*

Into indicates motion: *She walked into the room.*

lay, lie   The action word is *lay*. It takes a direct object. *Laid* is the form for its past tense and its past participle. Its present participle is *laying*.

Lie indicates a state of reclining along a horizontal plane. It does not take a direct object. Its past tense is *lay*. Its past participle is *lain*. Its present participle is *lying*.

When *lie* means to make an untrue statement, the verb forms are *lie, lied, lying.*

like, as   Use *like* as a preposition to compare nouns and pronouns. It requires an object: *Jim blocks like a pro.*

The conjunction *as* is the correct word to introduce clauses: *Jim blocks the linebacker as he should.*

majority, plurality   *Majority* means more than half of an amount. *Plurality* means more than the next highest number.

marshall, marshaled, marshaling, Marshall   *Marshal* is the spelling for both the verb and the noun: *Marilyn will marshal her forces. Erwin Rommel was a field marshal.*

Marshall is used in proper names: *George C. Marshall, John Marshall, the Marshall Islands.*

obscenities, profanities, vulgarities   Do not use them in stories unless they are part of direct quotations and there is a compelling reason for them.

Confine the offending language, in quotation marks, to a separate paragraph that can be deleted easily.

In reporting profanity that normally would use the words *damn* or *god,* lowercase *god* and use the following forms: *damn, damn it, goddamn it.* Do not, however, change the offending words to euphemisms. Do not, for example, change *damn it* to *darn it.*

If a full quote that contains profanity, obscenity or vulgarity cannot be dropped but there is no compelling reason for the offensive language, replace letters of an offensive word with a hyphen. The word *damn,* for example, would become

d— or *—.*

off of   The *of* is unnecessary: *He fell off the bed.* Not: *He fell off of the bed.*

on   Do not use *on* before a date or day of the week when its absence would not lead to confusion: *The meeting will be held Monday. He will be inaugurated Jan. 20.*

Use *on* to avoid an awkward juxtaposition of a date and a proper name: *John met Mary on Monday. He told Reagan on Thursday that the bill was doomed.*

Use *on* also to avoid any suggestion that a date is the object of a transitive verb: *The House killed on Tuesday a bid to raise taxes. The Senate postponed on Wednesday its consideration of a bill to reduce import duties.*

over   It is interchangeable with *more than.*

Usually, however, *over* refers to spatial relationships: *The plane flew over the city. More than* is used with figures: *More than 40,000 fans were in the stadium.*

people, persons   Use *people* when speaking of a large or uncounted number of individuals: *Thousands of people attended the fair. Some rich people pay few taxes. What will people say?* Do not use *persons* in this sense.

    Persons usually is used when speaking of a relatively small number of people who can be counted, but people also may be used:

    Right: *There were 20 persons in the room.*

    Right: *There were 20 people in the room.*

    People is also a collective noun that takes a plural verb and is used to refer to a single race or nation: *The American people are united.* In this sense, the plural is *peoples: The peoples of Africa speak many languages.*

principal, principle   *Principal* is a noun and adjective meaning someone or something first in rank, authority, importance or degree: *She is the school principal. He was the principal player in the trade. Money is the principal problem.*

    Principle is a noun that means a fundamental truth, law, doctrine or motivating force: *They fought for the principle of self-determination.*

prior to   *Before* is less stilted for most uses. *Prior to* is appropriate, however, when a notion of requirement is involved: *The fee must be paid prior to the examination.*

reign, rein   The leather strap for a horse is a *rein,* hence figuratively: *seize the reins, give free rein to, put a check rein on.*

    Reign is the period a ruler is on the throne: *The king began his reign.*

should, would   Use *should* to express an obligation: *We should help the needy.*

    Use *would* to express a customary action: *In the summer we would spend hours by the seashore.*

    Use *would* also in constructing a conditional past tense, but be careful:

    Wrong: *If Soderholm would not have had an injured foot, Thompson would not have been in the lineup.*

    Right: *If Soderholm had not had an injured foot, Thompson would not have been in the lineup.*

spelling   The basic rule when in doubt is to consult the stylebooks followed by, if necessary, a dictionary.

    Memory Aid: Noah Webster developed the following rule of thumb for the frequently vexing question of whether to double a final consonant in forming the present participle and past tense of a verb:

    If the stress in pronunciation is on the first syllable, do not double the consonant: *cancel, cancelling, canceled.*

    If the stress in pronunciation is on the second syllable, double the consonant: *control, controlling, controlled; refer, referring, referred.*

    If the word is only one syllable, double a consonant unless confusion would result: *jut, jutted, jutting.* An exception, to avoid confusion with *buss,* is *bus, bused, busing.*

    Here is a list of commonly misspelled words:

accommodate	baby sitter	chauffeur
adviser	baby-sitting	cigarette
Asian flu	cannot	clue
ax	cave-in (v.)	commitment
baby-sit	cave-in (n., adj.)	consensus

consul	hanged	restaurateur
copter	harass	rock 'n' roll
council	hitchhiker	skillful
counsel	homemade	subpoena
drought	imposter	teen-age (adj.)
drunken	judgment	teen-ager (n.)
embarrass	kidnapping	under way
employee	likable	vacuum
eyewitness	machine gun	weird
firefighter	percent	whiskey
fulfill	percentage	X-ray (n.,
goodbye	restaurant	v. and adj.)

subjunctive mood   Use the subjunctive mood of a verb for contrary-to-fact conditions, and expressions of doubts, wishes or regrets:

If I were a rich man, I wouldn't have to work hard.

I doubt that more money would be the answer.

I wish it were possible to take back my words.

Sentences that express a contingency or hypothesis may use either the subjunctive or the indicative mood depending on the context. In general, use the subjunctive if there is little likelihood that a contingency might come true:

If I were to marry a millionaire, I wouldn't have to worry about money.

If the bill should overcome the opposition against it, it would provide extensive tax relief.

But:

If I marry a millionaire, I won't have to worry about money.

If the bill passes as expected, it will provide an immediate tax cut.

that (conjunction)   Use the conjunction *that* to introduce a dependent clause if the sentence sounds or looks awkward without it. There are no hard-and-fast rules, but in general:

That usually may be omitted when a dependent clause immediately follows a form of the verb to say: *The president said he had signed the bill.*

That should be used when a time element intervenes between the verb and the dependent clause: *The president said Monday that he had signed the bill.*

That usually is necessary after some verbs. They include: *advocate, assert, contend, declare, estimate, make clear, point out, propose* and *state.*

That is required before subordinate clauses beginning with conjunctions such as *after, although, because, before, in addition to, until* and *while: Haldeman said that after he learned of Nixon's intention to resign, he sought pardons for all connected with Watergate.*

When in doubt, include *that.* Omission can hurt. Inclusion never does.

that, which, who, whom (pronouns)   Use *who* and *whom* in referring to persons and to animals with a name: *John Jones is the man who helped me.* See the Who, Whom entry.

Use *that* and *which* in referring to inanimate objects and to animals without a name.

See the Essential clauses, Nonessential clauses entry for guidelines on using *that* and *which* to introduce phrases and clauses.

under way   Two words in virtually all uses: *The project is under way. The naval maneuvers are under way.*

One word only when used as adjective before a noun in a nautical sense: *an underway flotilla.*

verbs   In general, avoid awkward constructions that split infinitive forms of a verb (*to leave, to help,* etc.) or compound forms (*had left, are found out,* etc.).

Awkward: *She was ordered to immediately leave on an assignment.*

Preferred: *She was ordered to leave immediately on an assignment.*

Awkward: *There stood the wagon that we had early last autumn left by the barn.*

Preferred: *There stood the wagon that we had left by the barn early last autumn.*

Occasionally, however, a split is not awkward and is necessary to convey the meaning:

He wanted to really help his mother.

Those who lie are often found out.

How has your health been?

The budget was tentatively approved.

who, whom   Use *who* and *whom* for references to human beings and to animals with a name. Use *that* and *which* for inanimate objects and animals without a name.

Who is the word when someone is the subject of a sentence, clause or phrase: *The woman who rented the room left the window open. Whom do you wish to see?*

See the Essential clauses, Nonessential clauses entry for guidelines on how to punctuate clauses introduced by *who, whom, that* and *which.*

who's, whose   *Who's* is a contraction for *who is,* not a possessive: *Who's there?*

Whose is the possessive: *I do not know whose coat it is.*

widow, widower   In obituaries: A man is survived by his wife, or leaves his wife. A woman is survived by her husband, or leaves her husband.

Guard against the redundant *widow of the late.* Use *wife of the late* or *widow of.*

PROOFREADING

Proofs have several uses other than that of indicating typographical errors.

Copy editors, as we have seen in Chapter 9, use a galley proof or a photocopy proof as a marker to show where insertions and new leads go.

Copy editors also may be assigned the task of updating overset matter and stories that made the later editions but not the earlier ones. Before the pages are torn up at the end of the press run, an editor goes over the paper, circling items that should be retained for future use. Proofs of the circled stories go to the desk for updating. Proofs of overset material likewise go to the desk for updating.

At larger papers a dozen or so proofs may be made from each strip of type. A set goes to each department head, including the desk chief, and perhaps to the wire service of which the paper is a member or client.

Duplicate sets of revised proofs go to the layout editor on offset papers and to editors of out-of-office publications for paste-up dummies. When the dummies are returned, type is assembled in pages and page proofs go to the respective editors.

When the page has been assembled, a layout editor or some other executive should scan the page to note:

- Whether the date, the issue number and the page number in the folio are correct.
- Whether the headlines have been placed over the right stories.
- Whether the pictures are right side up.
- Whether the sluglines have been removed.
- Whether the jump-line information is accurate.
- Whether a layout change is properly noted in the index.

THE PROOFREADER

Thorough editing should be done on the paper copy or VDT before the story ever reaches the composing room. A proof is no place to make editing judgments. Misspelled words and names, factual errors, grammatical errors and libelous statements have to be changed even though the errors should have been caught in the editing. But minor or nit-picking errors usually are allowed to remain. The reason is a matter of cost. One change in a line of type may result in the resetting of a paragraph of type. Sometimes, where a word replacement is desired, a word of similar character length can be used, thus averting the resetting of more than one line.

One of the irritating flaws, and one that may or may not be corrected on proofs, is improper division of words at the end of the type line. Here are a few taken at random from several columns of type: "reci-pient" for *recip-ient,* "opera-te" for *oper-ate,* "pal-aver" for *pa-laver,* "ne-bula" for *neb-ula,* "reven-ue" for *reve-nue,* "obes-ity" for *obesi-ty,* "implac-able" for *implaca-ble,* "child-ren" for *chil-dren.*

Even in computerized typesetting, in which rules, rule exceptions and tables can be applied, word division accuracy can never be reliable because of ambiguities, dual meanings, different hyphenations for identically spelled words and different hyphenations in different usages.

In newspaper composition one hyphenation occurs in every seven lines of text, depending on the type size and line length. Roughly 10 percent of these hyphenations will be in error. Some newspapers manually reset the incorrect lines after the type has been set. Some do not, as already indicated in the examples given of words incorrectly divided.

If VDTs are used the editor has complete control of the typesetting. But if compositors must retype the copy, all that changes. Compositors are expected to follow copy. Some hew to this rule so closely that they faithfully reproduce misspelled words. Others take it upon themselves to make corrections. If the copy editor suspects that a compositor will try to second-guess, the editor indicates that the spelling as written is correct no matter what the compositor thinks. If the name is Billi, the copy editor or reporter marks *cq* or *ok* above the spelling so that it will not come out as Billie.

Compositors, like other humans, look at one word but see another. Errors that spell a word are harder to catch than a misspelling. So, costumer comes out as customer, miliary as military, eclectic as electric, exorcise as exercise, diary as dairy, collage as college, calvary as cavalry, model as motel, farce as force, defective as detective, morality as mortality, bottle as battle, conservation as conversation, winch as wench.

PROOFREADING METHODS

Two methods are used in marking proofs. One is the formal or book method in which two marks are used—one within the line, to indicate the offender, and the other in the margin, to indicate the correction. If only one error appears in the line, the correction is noted in the left margin. If more than one error occurs, the corrections are in the right margin, each correction being separated by a slash mark (Figure II-1).

The second method is the guideline system, probably used by the majority of newspapers. Here a line is drawn from the error within a line to the

Arlette Schmitt, a brown-eyed blonde from Nice, France, speaks four languages and can tell a housewife how to use each item in the store.

Arlette and store manager Bal Raj ~~DROGRA~~, OF New ~~De~~ *|DogRA|| DeLhi* India, agree on one point: The shoppers are mostly American — not foreign.

"A woman comes up to me and says, 'What's this stuff? ~~○~~ *| ↙ // ↖* Dogra relates. "I tell her it's Egyptian jam. She says, 'okay, I'll try it,' and dumps it in her cart. Next week she may buy three jars."

Two years ago, Dogra says, items were new to most customers. But now he says they've become picky, even over brand names.

Although he is MARRIED | Dogra, 29, came here seven years ago as a student. ~~Married~~ to an American girl, his food favorites still are Indian.

He's proud of an "instant curry dinner from Bombay. Just heat and serve it." There are packets of curry rice, herb rice and rice flamenco, too — *Add |* ~~and~~ water and boil.

Dogra says food is bought as soon as it's put on the shelves. "You can't believe how fast it goes. It's fantastic."

MORE MORE

Figure II-1.   Formal method of marking proofs.

nearest margin. If several errors appear within the same type line, the guidelines may be drawn to both margins. Care is taken not to obliterate the place in the type line where the error occurs (Figure II-2).

In neither system is the correction made inside the type line or between lines of type.

If more than one error appears in the same word, the word should be circled and the correct word printed in the margin. Also, it is usually safer to rewrite a figure in the margin than to indicate changes in the figure by proof symbols.

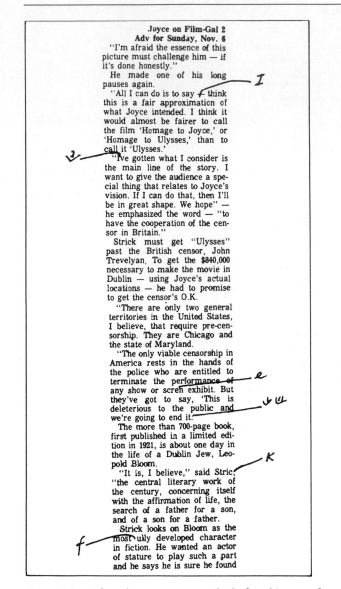

Figure II-2.   Informal or newspaper method of marking proofs.

USING PROOF SYMBOLS

If several lines have to be inserted, it is better to type the lines and show on the proof where they are to be inserted rather than to attempt to write the lines in longhand on the margin of the proof.

Proof symbols are used to indicate editorial changes (Figure II-3) and typographical changes (Figure II-4).

EDITORIAL CHANGES

e /	Common sense decres that every	*Add a letter*
ℛ	A common gripe against ~~the~~ young	*Delete or take out*
ℬ	N~~e~~ever forget that the period	*Delete and close up*
stet	Don't strain to be ~~witty or~~ funny	*Let all matter above dots stand*
i /	Never stop trying to fend	*Correct the word marked*
⊙ or ⊗	Insert period⊗	
⌃ or ,/	Insert comma⌄	
⌃ or :/	Insert colon⌄	
;/	Insert semicolon⌃	
⌄ or ʾ/	Put in apostrophe or ʾsingleʿ quote	
ʿʿ/ ʾʾ	Insert quotation marks	
!/	Insert exclamation point !	
=/ or -/	Insert hyphen —	
ⓈⓅ	Spell out	
⅟m or ⊢	Use one-em dash	
2em	Use two-em dash	
(/)	Insert (parentheses)	
[/]	Insert [brackets]	
¶	⌞Begin a paragraph	
no ¶	No paragraph.	
run in	Run in⌐ ~~or run on~~	

Figure II-3. Standard proofreading symbols.

TYPOGRAPHICAL CHANGES

wf	Wrong font
lc	Lower case letter
c	capitalize letter
sm. caps	Set in small capitals
rom.	Set in roman type
ital.	Set in italic type
lf.	Set in lightface type
bf	Set in boldface type
tr	Transpose letters
tr	Transpose words the in line
tr	Rearrange words of order number in
⌐	Move to right ⌐
[	Move to left
⌣	Lower letters or words
⌐	Raise letters or words
∥	Straighten line horizontally
∥	Align type vertically
◡	Close up
#	Leave some space
Eq #	Equalize space between words
□	Em quad space or indention
□ □ □	Indent number of em quads shown
ld.	Insert a lead between lines
l/s	L e t t e r - S p a c e
↓ *or* ⊥	Push down a space which prints as a mark
x or + or ⊗	Broken or imperfect type
⌢	Print AP as a ligature
ↄ	Turn a reverse letter

Figure II-4.   Standard proofreading symbols and how they are applied.

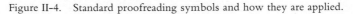

DATABASE SEARCHES

Each day thousands of news stories and magazine articles are written, and many of them contain material that can be invaluable to reporters researching stories. Those articles also can be invaluable for copy editors who need to check facts.

Until recently, it was impractical for copy editors to consult such resources if they were not located in the newspaper library. Going to the public library to check a fact was out of the question because of the time involved. Now, however, many newspapers have installed computer terminals that provide access to literally thousands of databases with material on almost every conceivable subject.

Among the most useful databases to journalists are the comprehensive files of Dialog, a Palo Alto, Calif., company that has files on everything from national statistics (American Statistics Index) to magazine article listings (Magazine Index). Unfortunately, many of Dialog's services still require the researcher to go to the original document for the complete text. Only a synopsis of the article is provided.

Of greater value to the fast-paced world of daily journalism may be services such as that provided by Dow Jones News Retrieval. These full-text services allow the user to read a story exactly as it was published in *The Wall Street Journal*. Let's say you are searching for an offbeat story you remember reading in the *Journal* about a haunted house in Louisiana. You go to your computer terminal and sign on to the Dow Jones News Retrieval free-text search service. The service asks you to describe key words that might help locate the article. You enter *Louisiana* and find that the service has 441 listings, or articles, containing that word. That won't do. It would take far too long to search all those articles for the one in question, and you are being charged for each minute connected to the service. You must narrow the search, so you decide to ask the computer for the number of stories that contain the words Louisiana and ghosts. There are two stories that fit the description. You give the computer a simple command to display the first of the two stories on the screen. The result is shown in Figure III-1.

That's it. The search has turned up the story you remembered. But the search words you used were unique, and the computer indicated there were two stories that matched the description. Is it possible there was a followup you missed? To determine that, you decide to look at the other story. (see Figure III-2).

```
                DOCUMENT=        1 OF        2    PAGE =      1 OF      16
AN              841031-0161.
HL              As Spooky Places Go,
                An Inn in the Bayous
                Goes a Bit Too Far

                ---
                'Most Haunted House' Teems
                With Spirits, Legend Says;
                How Our Man Faces Them
                ---
                By Bryan Burrough
                                    - MORE -



                DOCUMENT=        1 OF        2    PAGE =      2 OF      16
                Staff Reporter of The Wall Street Journal
DD              10/31/84
SO              WALL STREET JOURNAL (J)
TX                 ST. FRANCISVILLE, La. -- They never extinguish all the
                lights at the Myrtles, a 188-year-old mansion outside this
                sleepy bayou town. Total darkness, legend says, brings out
                ghoulish things that go bump in the night.
                   At first glance, the house doesn't look haunted. Huge oaks
                dripping Spanish moss cover the plantation, and out back a
                gazebo sits on an island in a tiny pond. The white two-story
                                    - MORE -



                DOCUMENT=        1 OF        2    PAGE =      3 OF      16
                mansion is attractively encircled by a veranda lined with
                colonial-blue wrought iron.
                   But those who know about the Myrtles whisper stories of
                phantoms and voodoo curses, of two long-dead girls who peer
                into the mansion's windows at night, of picture frames that
                fly from the wall and of a ghostly one-eared slave woman who
                glides by the canopied beds at night, chilling the bones of
                those she encounters.
                   Unexplained sights and sounds have been observed by
                everyone from psychics to local officials, and since the
                                    - MORE -



                DOCUMENT=        1 OF        2    PAGE =      4 OF      16
                Myrtles was converted into a six-bedroom inn four years ago,
                the owner says, many tourists have been so spooked in the
                night that they have vowed never to return. As for me, in the
                words of the "Ghostbusters" movie theme song, "I ain't 'fraid
                of no ghosts." I agree to spend a weekend there, in the
                building that the book "Houses of Horror" by Richard Winer
                calls America's most haunted house. . . .
```

Figure III-1.

It's obvious why our search revealed *Louisiana* for this story, but it isn't about a haunted house. The last paragraph, however, reveals why our search gave us two choices (see Figure III-3).

The writer merely happened to write a story from Louisiana that included the word *ghosts*. The two stories found in this search indicate not only how useful such databases can be but also the limitations of search techniques.

```
            DOCUMENT=      2 OF      2    PAGE =    1 OF    16
AN       840614-0143.
HL           LEISURE & ARTS:
             Mississippi Mermaids: World's Fair Takes a Dive
             ---
             By Manuela Hoelterhoff
DD       06/14/84
SO       WALL STREET JOURNAL (J)
TX           New Orleans -- The last time the Crescent City had a huge
         exposition was 100 years ago, and the event is not happily
         remembered. The director absconded with part of the state
                     MORE



            DOCUMENT=      2 OF      2    PAGE -    2 OF    16
         treasury, attendance was lower than projected and reviews
         were mixed, despite such unusual exhibitions as 200,000
         insect species from Maryland and a reception hosted by
         costumed pigs.
             Maybe a combo of smart porkers playing jazz would help out
         the current World's Fair, which opened on May 12 for a
         six-month run. Despite a decade of planning and a cost of
         $350 million, America, never mind the world, hasn't been
         rushing down to this 84-acre extravaganza deposited along the
         Mississippi River. Attendance figures have been well below
                     - MORE -
```

Figure III-2.

On one hand, you found the article you sought, but you wasted time looking at one that produced nothing of use.

Such limitations apply to card catalog searchings of libraries, too. While database search techniques may not be perfect, the results give the copy editor far more flexibility in checking facts than ever was possible before. Thus, the ability of the editor to check facts is vastly expanded. Widespread use of database searches at newspapers and broadcast stations should make the news reports of the future more accurate than ever.

```
    DOCUMENT=      2 OF      2    PAGE =    15 OF    16
    After Nov. 11, this show will be returning to Paris via a
stop in Washington, and the expo site will be redeveloped
into yet another waterside shrine of gentrification via Rouse
Co. and a second investment group. Mr. Gehry's striking
theater will come down, and at most a small chunk of
Wonderwall will be preserved. I cannot think of a city less
in need of additional ethnic harbor-view food shops than New
Orleans, which overflows with gumbo and already has a market
by the river. Still, I guess even this dull prospect will be
better than what happened to the fairgrounds in Knoxville --
                - MORE -



    DOCUMENT=      2 OF      2    PAGE =    16 OF    16
decrepit and abandoned, frequented only by joggers and
ghosts.
```

Figure III-3.

Here are some of the major data bases of interest to journalists. There are thousands, and this is merely a sample:

BRS/After Dark
1200 Route 7
Latham, N.Y. 12110
(518) 783-1161

CompuServe
P.O. Box 20212
5000 Arlington Centre Blvd.
Columbus, Ohio 43220
(800) 848-8199

Dialog
3460 Hillview Ave., Dept. 79
Palo Alto, Calif. 94304
(800) 227-1927

Dow Jones News Retrieval
P.O. Box 300
Princeton, N.J. 08540
(800)345-8500

Prodigy Services
445 Hamilton Ave.
White Plains, N.Y. 10601
(914) 962-0310

Vu/Text Information Services
325 Chestnut St.
Philadelphia, Pa. 19106
(800) 258-8080

GLOSSARY

Accordion folds   parallel folds used to determine an imposition pattern on sheet of paper.

Ad   short for advertisement.

Ad alley   section in mechanical department where ads are assembled.

Add   material to be added to news story, usually with a number and slug: *add 1 fire*.

Add end   addendum to a story after it has been apparently closed.

Ad lib   unscripted comment made before a microphone.

Ad-side   advertising department as distinguished from editorial department.

ADV   abbreviation for advance. A story intended for later use.

Advance   story sent out in advance of the scheduled publication date.

Agate   name of a type size, e.g., agate type, or type that is $5^1/_2$ points high. Advertising is also sold on the basis of agate lines, or 14 agate lines to an inch.

Air   white space.

Align   to place adjacent to an even baseline on a horizontal plane.

Alley   portion in composing room devoted to special sections, such as ad alley.

Alphanumeric   pertaining to a character set that contains letters, numerals and usually other characters.

A.M.   morning edition.

Analog   data in the form of varying physical characteristics such as voltage, pressure, speed, etc. A computer term.

Angle   special aspect of a story; a slant.

Antique   rough-surfaced paper resembling old handmade papers.

AP   short for The Associated Press, a major news agency.

Art   newspaper or magazine illustrations excluding photos.

Attribution   source of the material in a story.

Audio tape   tape on which sound has been transcribed.

Audiotext   delivery of news verbally over telephone lines, a process increasingly being automated with digital technology.

Autofunctions   copy symbols or commands placed on copy. Used to instruct the computer on type sizes, column widths, etc.

Auxiliary storage   any peripheral devices (tape, disk, etc.) upon which computer data may be stored.

Back timing   timing of a script so that it ends at the proper time.

Back up   printing the reverse side of a sheet.

Bad break   bad phrasing of a headline; bad wrapping of headline type; bad arrangement of type in columns that gives the reader the impression a paragraph ending is the end of the story.

Bagasse   residue of sugar cane stalks used experimentally as a substitute for wood pulp in making newsprint.

Bank   the lower portion of a headline (deck).

Banner   usually a headline stretching across all columns of a newspaper.

Barker   reversed kicker in which the kicker is in larger type than the lines below it. Also called a *hammer*.

Bastard type   type that varies from the standard column width.

Baud   speed rate of transmission. News personnel speak in terms of 66 or 1,200 words a minute. Computer personnel talk of 1,200 bits (or 150 characters) a second.

Binary   a base 2 numbering system using the digits 0 and 1. Widely used in computer systems whose binary code may represent numbers, letters, and punctuation marks. Performs "in" and "out" or "on" and "off" function.

Binder   inside page streamer; head that binds together two or more related stories.

Bit   one eighth of a byte in computer terminology. Combinations of eight basic bits yield up to 256 characters.

Black and white   reproduction in one color (black).

Black Letter   text or Old English style of type.

Blanket head   headline over several columns of type or over type and illustration.

Bleed   running an illustration off the page.

Blooper   any embarrassing error in print or broadcast.

Body   main story or text; body type is the size of type used for the contents.

Boil   to trim or reduce wordage of a story.

Boiler plate   syndicated material.

Boldface   type that is blacker than normal typeface; also *black face*. Abbreviated *bf*.

Book   sheet of paper on which a story is written. A basic category of printing paper.

Book number   number assigned to each item in a wire service report.

Box   unit of type enclosed by a border.

Brace   type of makeup, usually with a banner headline and the story in the right-hand column. A bracket.

Break   point at which a story turns from one column to another. Also, an exclusive story.

Break over   story that jumps from one page to another.

Brightener   short, amusing item.

Broadsheet   term used to describe a full-size newspaper page as opposed to tabloid.

Broadside   large sheet printed on only one side.

Broken heads   headlines with lines of different widths.

Budget (or BJT, called "News Digest" by AP)   listing of the major stories expected to be delivered by the wire service.

Bug   type ornament; a logotype; a star or other element that designates makeovers.

Bulldog   an early edition of a newspaper.

Bulletin   last-minute story of significance; a wire service designation of a story of major importance, usually followed by bulletin matter. Abbreviated *bun*.

Bullets   large periods used for decoration, usually at the beginning of paragraphs.

Bumper   two elements placed side by side or one immediately beneath the other. A bumped headline is also called a *tombstone*.

Bureau code letters   each wire service uses its own code letters to designate a bureau. UPI uses WA for Washington, the AP uses WX.

Byline   credit given to the author.

Byte   in computer terms, one alphanumeric character.

Canned copy   copy released by press agents or syndicates.

Canopy head   streamer headline from which two or more readout heads drop.

Caps   short for capital or uppercase letters.

Caption   display line over a picture or over the cutline. Also used as a synonym for a *cutline*.

Cartridge   holder for audio tapes. Also a *staccato lead*.

Centered   type placed in the middle of a line.

Center spread   two facing pages made up as one in the center of a newspaper section; also called *double truck*.

Character   an alphanumeric or special symbol.

Character generator   a cathode ray tube or laser used to display characters in high-speed phototypesetters.

Chase   metal frame in which forms are locked before printing or stereotyping in the old hot-type process.

Chaser   fast, urgent replate.

Cheesecake   slang for photographs emphasizing women's legs. Good newspapers don't use such pictures.

Circuits   refers to wire services used. The A wire is the main trunk news circuit. Regional news trunk systems carry letter designations such as B, G and E wires. High-speed circuits have replaced many of these.

Circumlocution   wordy, roundabout expressions. Also *redundancy*.

Circus makeup   flamboyant makeup featuring a variety of typefaces and sizes.

City room   main newsroom of a newspaper. The city editor presides over the city desk.

Clean copy   copy with a minimum of typographical or editing corrections. Clean proof is proof that requires few corrections.

Clips   short for clippings of newspaper stories.

Closeup   photo showing head or head and shoulders or an object seen at close range.

Closing   time at which pages are closed. Also *ending*.

Cloze   method of testing readability. Respondents are asked to fill in words in blank spaces.

Col.   abbreviation for column.

Cold type   reproduction of characters composed photographically.

Color page   page on which color is used.

Column inch   unit of space measurement; one column wide and one inch deep.

Column rule   printing units that create vertical lines of separation on a page.

Combination cut illustration that includes both halftone and line work.

Combo short for combination, pictures of the same subject used as a single unit.

Compose type is set or composed in a composing room by a compositor.

Composition all typesetting.

Computer a device capable of accepting information, applying prescribed processes to the information, and supplying the results of these processes; a computer system usually consists of input and output devices, storage, arithmetic and logical units and a control unit. Various types of computers are calculators, digital computers and analog computers.

Computer program a set of stored instructions that controls all hardware.

Constant element used regularly without change. Also called *standing* or *stet* material.

Copy words typewritten by reporters or editors from which type is set.

Copy fitting editing copy to fit a required space.

Copyreader antiquated term for *copy editor,* one who edits copy and writes headlines.

Core the main memory of a computer in which data may be stored. Also called *core memory*.

CPU an abbreviation for central processing unit. That portion of the computer that handles input, output and memory.

CQ abbreviation for correct.

CQN abbreviation for correction.

Credit line line indicating source of a story.

Crop to eliminate unwanted portions of a photograph. Marks used to show the elimination are called *crop marks*.

Crossline headline composed of a single line.

Cue signal given to announcer; a line in a script indicating a change.

Cursor a mobile block of light the size of a single character on the computer screen indicating the position at which an editing change is to be made.

Cut illustration or engraving. Or a direction to trim or shorten a story.

Cut-in may refer to an *initial letter* beginning a paragraph or to a side head that is set into the opening lines of a paragraph.

Cutline explanatory material, usually placed beneath a picture. Also called *underline, legend* and *caption*.

Cutoff hairline that marks the point where the story moves from one column to another or to separate boxes and cuts from text material or to separate a headline from other elements.

Cx   short for correction. Indicates that corrections are to be made in type. Also called *fix*.

Cycle   complete news report for either morning or afternoon newspapers.

Cycle time   the length of time used by a computer for one operation, usually measured in microseconds (millionths) or nanoseconds (billionths).

Dangler   short for *dangling participle* or similar grammatical error.

Dash   short line separating parts of headlines or headline and story.

Data   any kind of information that can be processed by a computer.

Dateline   opening phrase of story showing origin, source and sometimes date of story.

Dead   newspaper copy or type that is no longer usable.

Deadline   the shutoff time for copy for an edition.

Debug   eliminating problems in a new or revised computer program or system.

Deck   section of a headline.

Delete   take out. The proofreader uses a symbol for a delete mark.

Desk   standing alone, usually the copy desk. Also *city desk, sports desk,* etc.

Digit   in computers, a character used to represent one of the non-negative integers smaller than the radix, e.g., in decimal notation, one of the characters 0 to 9.

Digital   in computers, pertaining to data in the form of digits, in contrast with *analog*.

Dingbat   typographic decoration.

Disk drive   a unit somewhat like a record turntable that contains a computer storage disk pack and rotates it at high speed.

Disk pack   a set of magnetic disks used by computers for storing data or text. Also called disk cartridge.

Disk storage   a means of storing data on a magnetic disk, a technique similar to magnetic tape or record, so that data can be read into the computer, changed by the computer or erased.

Display   term given to a type of advertising that distinguishes it from classified advertising. Display lines are those set in larger sizes than regular body type.

Dissolve   in broadcasting, a smooth transition from one image to another.

Dog watch   late shift of an afternoon paper or early shift of a morning paper. Also *lobster trick*.

Double-spacer   term used on broadcast news wire to designate a story of unusual significance. Extra space is used between copy lines to alert the editor to the story.

Double truck   two pages at the center of a section made up as a single unit.

Downstyle   headline style using a minimum of capital letters.

Dropout   a subsidiary headline. Also called *deck*.

Dub   transfer of film or tape.

Dummy   diagram outlining the makeup scheme. A rough dummy has little detail; a pasteup dummy is created by pasting page elements on a sheet of paper the actual size of the page.

Dump   a routine that causes the computer to dump data from storage to another unit.

Dupe   short for *duplicate* or *carbon copy*.

Dutch wrap   breaking body type from one column to another not covered by the display line. Also called *dutch turn* or *raw wrap.*

Ears   small box on one or both sides of the nameplate carrying brief announcements of weather, circulation, edition and the like.

EBCDIC   Extended Binary Coded Decimal Interchange Code. An eight-bit computer code that can represent 256 characters.

Edition   one of several press runs such as *city edition* and *home edition.*

Em   measurement of type that is as wide as it is high. A *pica em* is 12 points wide. Some printers still refer to all picas as *ems.*

En   one-half em. Mostly used to express space. If the type measures 10 points, an indentation of an en would equal 5 points.

Endmark   symbol (such as # or 30) to indicate the close of the story. An *end dash* (sometimes called a *30 dash*) is used at the end of the story in type.

Etching   process of removing non-printing areas from a relief plate by acid.

Extra   now rare, a special edition published to carry an important news break.

Eyebrow   another name for a *kicker* head.

Face   style or cut of type; the printing surface of type or of a plate.

Family   as applied to type, all the type in any one design. Usually designated by a trade name.

Fat head   headline too large for the space allowed for it.

Fax   short for facsimile or transmission by wire of a picture.

Fax newspaper   a brief news update transmitted to clients by facsimile machine.

Feature to give special prominence to a story or illustration. A story that stresses a human-interest angle.

Feed story or program electronically transmitted to other stations or broadcast to the public.

Filler short items, usually set in type in advance and used to fill out space in a column of type. Also called *briefs* or *shorts*.

Fingernails parentheses.

Fix to correct or a correction.

Flag title of paper appearing on Page One. Also *nameplate*.

Flash rare announcement by a wire service of extremely urgent news. Usually followed by a *bulletin*.

Float ruled sidebar that may go anywhere in a story. To center an element in space that is not large enough to fill.

Flop illustration reversed in engraving.

Flush even with the column margin. Type aligned on one side. Alignment may be on either left or right side.

Folio lines showing the newspaper name, date and page number.

Follow related matter that follows main story. Abbreviated *folo*.

Follow copy set the story as set; disregard seeming errors. Abbreviated *fc*.

Followup second-day story.

Format physical form of a publication. Also, a series of alphas and/or numerics that cause a computer to function in certain special ways.

Frame makeup vertical makeup.

Freaks devices that depart from normal indented body and headline type, etc.

Futures file record kept by the city desk of future events.

FYI for your information.

Gain sound level.

Galley metal tray used to hold hot type.

Galley proof print of the assembled type, used in proofreading.

Gatekeeper one who decides whether to pass a news story along. The account of an event goes through many gatekeepers before it reaches the reader.

Glossy photograph with a hard, shiny finish.

Gobbledygook editor's slang for material characterized by jargon and circumlocution.

Gothic   sans serif type. Also called *block letter*.

Graf   short for paragraph.

Gravure   process of photomechanical printing. Also *rotogravure* or *intaglio* (printing ink is transferred to paper from areas sunk below the surface) printing.

Grease pencil   type of pencil used to make crop marks on pictures.

Guideline   instructions on copy to direct a printer. Usually includes slug, edition, section, etc.

Gutter   vertical space that separates one page from another on two facing pages. Also, long, unbroken space between two columns of type.

Hairline   finest line available in printing. Often used for rules between columns.

Halftone   photoengraving. A dot pattern gives the illusion of tones.

Hammer   see *barker*.

Handout   release from a public relations agency.

Hanger   headline that descends from a banner. Also called *readout* or *deck*.

Hanging indent   headline style in which the top line is set full measure and succeeding lines are indented from the left.

Hard copy   original copy, distinguishing it from monitor copy or carbon copy. Also a glossy photographic print as contrasted to facsimile.

Hard news   spot news or news or record as contrasted to features and background material.

Hardware   the physical equipment that is part of the overall production system. (Computers, phototypesetting machines, etc.)

Hard-wired   electronically connected, as in the case of one or more pieces of hardware connected to others.

Head count   number of letters and spaces available for a headline.

Headlinese   overworked short words in a headline, such as *cop, nab, hit, set.*

Head shot   photo of person's head or head and shoulders. Also called *face shots* and *mug shots.*

HFR   hold for release.

Highlight   white or light portions of a photograph. Also the high point of a story.

Hold for release   copy that is not to be used until a specified time.

Holdout   portion held out of a story and placed in the overset.

Hot type   linecaster slugs as opposed to cold type or type set photographically.

HTK   headline to come. Also HTC.

Hugger mugger   newspaper lead crammed with details.

Hyphenless justification   a system of justifying lines by interword and interletter spaces, without breaking any words at the end of lines. Usually accomplished by computers.

Imposition   process of placing type and illustrations in pages.

Impression   any printing of ink on paper. Also appearance of the printed page. Also the number of times a press has completed a printing cycle.

Index   newspaper's table of contents, usually found on Page One.

Infomedium   a term sometimes used to describe a new medium of the future that would incorporate both text and moving pictures.

Information Age   sociologists and others often describe the current era this way because computers have made available a vast amount of information.

Information graphics   illustrations, charts, tables or maps used to convey information graphically.

Initial (Initial cap)   first letter in a paragraph set in type larger than the body type.

Input   bringing data or text from external sources (typewriters, paper tape, through interfaces, etc.) into computer storage.

Insert   addition to a story placed within the story.

Interface   a device through which one piece of computer hardware or equipment communicates with another. The translation of output to input.

Intro   short for introduction. Opening copy to film or tape. Also, wire-service term for lead of story.

Inverted pyramid   news story structure in which the parts are placed in a descending order of their importance. Also a headline in inverted pyramid shape.

Issue   all copies produced by a newspaper in a day.

Italics   slanted letter form. Shortened form is *itals.*

Jargon   language of a profession, trade or group. Newspaper jargon.

Jump   to continue a story from one page to another.

Jump head   headline over the continued portion of a story.

Jump lines   continuation lines: *continued on Page X.*

Justify   spacing out a line of type to fill the column; spacing elements in a form so form can be locked up.

K   thousands of units of core or computer storage referring to storage for bytes, usually in multiples of 4.

Kenaf field crop used experimentally as a substitute for wood pulp in making newsprint.

Kicker overline over a headline. Also *eyebrow*.

Kill to discard copy, type, mats and so on.

Label head dull, lifeless headline. Sometimes a standing head such as **News of the World.**

Layout pattern of typographic arrangement. Similar to dummy.

Lead beginning of a story or the most important story of the day (pronounced "leed").

Lead piece of metal or spacing increment varying from $1/2$ to 3 points placed between lines of type for spacing purposes (pronounced "led").

Leaders line of dots.

Leading the space between lines of type.

Lead out to justify a line of type.

Legend information under an illustration. Also *cutline*.

Letterpress technique of printing from raised letters. Ink is applied to the letters, paper is placed over the type and impression implied to the paper, resulting in printing on paper.

Library newspaper's collection of books, files and so on. Also called *morgue*.

Ligature two or more letters run together for superior typesetting—*fi, ffi*.

Linecaster any keyboarded machine that casts lines of type.

Line cut illustration without tones. Used for maps, charts and so on.

Line gauge pica rule or a ruler marked off in pica segments.

Logotype single matrix of type containing two or more letters commonly used together: AP, UPI. Also a combination of the nameplate and other matter to identify a section. Also an advertising signature. Commonly abbreviated *logo*.

Lowercase small letter as distinguished from a capital letter. Abbreviated *lc*.

Machine language a language used directly by a computer; a set of instructions a computer can recognize and execute.

Macro instruction a single instruction that is expanded to a predetermined sequence of instructions during the assembly of a computer program.

Magnetic storage any device using magnetic materials as a medium for computer storage of data: magnetic disk, film, tape, drum, core, etc.

Makeover to change page content or layout.

Makeready   process of aligning elements on the page to ensure a uniform impression.

Makeup   design of a newspaper page. Assembling elements in a page.

Marker   proof or tearsheet used to show where inserts are to go after story has been sent to the composing room or other instructions for guidance of printers and makeup editors.

Masthead   informational material about a newspaper, usually placed on the editorial page.

Mat   short for matrix or mold for making a stereotype plate in letterpress printing. The mat of a page is made of papier-mâché. In typesetting machines, the matrix is made of brass.

Measure   length of a line of type.

Modem   a piece of hardware that facilitates interfacing between two other pieces of hardware in a system.

Monitor copy   tearsheet copy or copy produced electronically. A monitor is also a television or radio receiver. To monitor is to watch or time a radio or television program.

Montage   succession of pictures assembled to create an overall effect. Usually a single photograph using several negatives. This technique is usually discouraged.

Morgue   newspaper reference library or repository for clippings.

Mortise   cutaway section of a photo into which type is inserted. Usually considered bad practice.

Mug shot   same as *photo closeup* or *face shot.*

Multiplexor (MUX)   a device that allows the computer to handle input or output simultaneously from several different devices connected to it.

Must   matter that someone in authority has ordered published.

Nameplate   name of newspaper displayed on Page One. Also called *flag, title* or *line.*

News hole   space left for news and editorial matter after ads have been placed on pages.

Newsprint   low-quality paper used to print newspapers.

NL   slug on copy and notation on a marker indicating new lead. Also wire service designation for *night lead.*

Obit   abbreviation for obituary.

OCR   optical character reader, or "scanner," which converts typewritten material to electronic impulses for processing within a computer system. The process itself also is known as OCR, optical character recognition. Employs technology now considered outdated.

Offset method of printing differing from letterpress. A photograph is taken after the page has been assembled. The negatives are placed over a light-sensitive printing plate and light is exposed through the open spaces of the negative. The result is that the letters are hardened and the non-printing surface is washed away. This method of printing involves inking the printed plate with a water solution and then with ink. The water resides only on the non-printing surface, whereas the ink resides on the printing surface. The inked letters are then printed on a rubber blanket, which in turn prints (or offsets) on paper.

On-line a unit "on-line" is interaced in the computer system as opposed to units operating independently of the system.

Op. ed. page opposite the editorial page.

Optional matter that may be used without regard to the time element. Also called *time copy, grape* and *AOT* (any old time).

Outcue cue telling a news director or engineer that a film or tape is near the end.

Outlined cut halftone with background cut out. Also *silhouette*.

Output data coming from the computer system, in either printed, typeset or paper tape form.

Overset type in excess of amount needed.

Pad to make a story longer with excess words.

Page proof proof of an entire page.

Pagination makeup of a newspaper page on a computer to allow output of the composed page. Also the organization of pages within the newspaper.

Parameter symbol in computer programming indicating a constant such as a figure.

Parens short for parentheses.

Photocomposition type composed photographically.

Photolithography printing process such as offset where the impression is transferred from a plate to a rubber roller and to paper.

Pica linear measure in 12 points. A *pica em* is a standard measure, but only 12-point type can be a *pica em*.

Pickup material in type that is to be used with new material such as a new lead.

Pix short for pictures. The singular may be *pic* or *pix*.

Pixel small picture element to denote gray or color values for computer storage.

Plate stereotyped or lithographic page ready for the press.

Play prominence given a story, its display. Also the principal story.

Point   unit of printing measurement, approximately $^1/_{72}$ inch. Actually 0.01384 inches. Also any punctuation mark.

Pos.   positive film image.

Precede   material such as a bulletin or an editor's note appearing at the top of a story.

Predate   edition delivered before its announced date. Usually a Sunday edition delivered to outlying areas.

Printer   machine that produces copy by telegraphic impulses. A Teletype machine. Also a person who prepares composition for imprinting operations.

Printout   visual copy produced by a computer, usually for proofreading. Same as *master copy* or *tear sheet.*

Process color   method of printing that duplicates a full-color original copy.

Proof   print of type used for proofreading.

Proofreader   one who corrects proofs.

Prop   an object used during a newscast to give credence to an item.

Pullout   a special section within a paper, designed to be removed from the main portion.

Purge   a method by which data or text is removed from computer storage by erasure from the disk.

Put to bed   to lock up forms for an edition.

Pyramid   arrangement of ads in half-pyramid form from top right to lower left.

Quad   short for quadrant, a blank printing unit for spacing.

Quadrant   layout pattern in which the page is divided into fourths.

Query   brief message outlining a story. Also a question put to a news source.

Queue   directing a story file to another operation, such as a line printer or photocomposition machine. The electronic equivalent of an in-basket or holding area.

Quotes   short for quotation marks.

Race   classification of type, such as *roman, text, script.*

Railroad   to rush copy to the printer before it is edited; to rush type to press without proofreading. Also a term for a headline type.

Read in   secondary head leading in to the main head.

Readout   secondary head accompanying a main head.

Rear projection   projection of a film, photo, map or graph placed on a screen behind the newscaster.

Regional split   interruption in the wire to permit the transmission of regional news.

Register   alignment of printing plates to get true color reproduction.

Release copy   copy to be held until a specified release time. Same as advance copy.

Repeat   a rerun of a story for a wire service member or client.

Replate   to make a page over after an edition has gone to press.

Retouch   to alter a photograph by painting or airbrushing.

Reverse plate   reversing the color values so that white letters are on a black background.

Revised proof   second proof after corrections have been made.

Ribbon   another name for a *banner* or *streamer* headline.

Rim   outer edge of a copy desk. Copy editors once were known as *rimmen* or *rim women.*

Rip and read   derogatory expression applied to radio newspersons who simply read the latest summary from the radio wire without careful editing.

Rising initial   initial capital letter that aligns with the body type at the baseline.

Rivers   streaks of white space within typeset columns caused by excessive word spacing or letterspacing.

ROP   run of the paper. Stories or art that do not demand upfront position. Ads that may appear anywhere in the paper. Color printed in a newspaper without the use of special presses.

Rotogravure   means of printing from recessed letters. One of the major printing techniques (along with letterpress and offset). Used mostly in catalogs, magazines and fine color work.

Rough   may be applied to a dummy that gives little or no detail or to an uncorrected, unjustified proof.

Roundup   compilation of stories.

Rules   any line that is printed. Lines are cast in type metal form. Hairline rules are often used in newspaper work. The underscore of the preceding is a type rule.

Run   reporter's beat.

Runaround   method of setting type around a picture.

Run-in   to incorporate sentences or lists into one paragraph.

Running story   story handled in takes or small segments. Each take is sent to the composing room as soon as it is edited.

Runover portion of a story that continues from page to the next. Also a *jump story*.

Sans serif typeface without serifs.

Sc proofreader's mark meaning *see copy*.

Schedule list of available stories and pictures; desk's record of stories edited.

Scoop to get an exclusive story. Also a *beat*.

Screen to view film or videotape.

Script in broadcast news, the arrangement of news, together with an opening and closing and leads to commercials.

Scroll a means of moving story text forward or backward so it can be displayed on a computer screen.

Second front page first page of the second section. Also called a *split page*.

Section page first page of a pullout section.

Serifs the fine cross strokes at the top and bottom of most styles of letters.

Set solid lines of type without extra spacing between lines.

Shirt tail slang for follow story.

Short brief item of filler.

Sidebar brief story with a special angle that goes with the main story.

Signature group of pages on one sheet. Also an advertiser's name displayed in an ad.

Silhouette form of halftone with the background removed. Same as *outline cut*.

Skyline headline across top of page over nameplate.

Slant angle of a story. A story written a certain way.

Slug label identifying a story. Same as *guideline* or *catchline*. Also a piece of metal used for spacing. Also used to designate linecaster slugs.

Software the programs that make computer hardware work.

Sound-on-film film carrying its own sound track. Abbreviated *SOF.*

Sound under audio level where background sounds may be heard.

Space out direction to the printer to add space between lines until the story fills the space allotted for it.

Split term used to designate a break in a wire-service circuit to permit the filing of other material, such as regional news.

Split page first page of the second section of a newspaper.

Split run making a change in part of a press run of the same edition.

Spot news   news obtained firsthand; fresh news.

Spread   story prominently displayed, often over several columns and with art.

Squib   short news item or filler.

Standalone   a picture without an accompanying story.

Standing box   type box kept on hand for repeated use. Likewise with standing head.

Standing type   similar to standing boxes and head; type kept standing for future use.

Standupper   television report at the scene with the camera on the reporter.

Step lines   headline with top line flush left, second line centered and third line flush right.

Stereotype   process of casting a plate from a papier-mâché mold.

Stet   let it stand. Disregard correction.

Stinger   another term for *kicker* or *eyebrow*.

Stock   paper used for any printing job.

Straight matter   copy set in one size of type for the main reading matter of a page. Also called body type.

Streamer   another name for a *banner* or a *ribbon* headline.

String   clippings of stories, usually from a correspondent.

Stringer   correspondent paid on space rate. In television news, a freelance camera operator.

Strip-in   to insert one illustrative element into another.

Sub   short for substitute. *Sub bomber* means a new story for a story slugged *bomber.*

Subhead   one- or two-line head used within the body of a story in type.

Summary   may be a news index or a news roundup. A summary lead gives the gist of the facts in the story.

Supplemental service   syndicated service in addition to major wire service.

System   a combination of computer programs and hardware designed to perform specific tasks.

TAB   indicates tabular matter in wire service copy.

Tabloid   newspaper format, usually four or five columns wide and approximately 14 inches deep.

Take   small part of a running story. Also the part of a story given to a compositor.

Tear sheet   sheet or part of a sheet used for corrections. Also copy produced by a computerized copy follower.

Tease   news announcement before the station break with details to follow the break.

Telephoto   UPI system of transmitting pictures by wire.

Teletext   home information retrieval system using television signal for transmission of data.

Teletype   automatic printer used to send and receive wire copy.

Terminal   a point in a system or communication network at which data can either enter or leave.

Thirty dash   end mark.

Thumbnail   half-column portrait.

Tie-back   part of a story providing background material.

Tight paper   paper containing so much advertising there is limited space for news.

Time copy   copy that may be used anytime. Also called *grape, plug copy* and so on.

Tombstone   to place headlines of the same type side by side. Such adjacent heads are called *bumped heads*.

Turn story   same as jump story (continues from last column on one page to first column on the next page).

Typo   short for typographical error.

Undated   story without a dateline (but usually a credit line) summarizing related events from different origins.

Underline   same as cutline.

Update   to bring a story up to date or to give it a timely angle.

UPI   short for United Press International, a major news agency.

Upstyle   headline style in which each word is capitalized.

VDT   an acronym for video display terminal, a device that looks like a typewriter with a small television set attached. Stories may be composed or corrected on these minicomputer-based units, which increasingly are being replaced by networked personal computers.

Videotape   tape that projects pictures.

Videotex   home information retrieval systems using television-type displays.

Viewdata   home information retrieval system using direct link to computer through telephone or cable television lines.

Vignette   halftone with a fading background. Also a feature story or sketch.

Visible   tape perforations arranged so that they spell words or symbols.

VTR   short for videotape recording.

wf   short for wrong font or type of a different size or style from that used in text.

Wicket   kicker-like element placed to one side of a headline.

Widow   one or two words appearing at the end of a paragraph and on the last line. It is unsightly because of the excessive white space appearing after the widow, particularly at the top of a column.

Wirephoto   AP system of transmitting pictures by wire.

Wooden head   one that is dull and lifeless.

Wrap around   ending the top line of a headline with a preposition, conjunction or the like, or splitting words that are properly a unit. Also, setting type to wrap around a picture.

Wrapup   complete story. Wire services use a wrapup to contain in one story all elements of the same story sent previously.

INDEX

M